The Paths of History

Tracing an outline of historical processes from palaeolithic times to the present day, *The Paths of History* provides a unique, concise and readable overview of the entire history of humanity and the laws governing it. This is a broad and ambitious study which takes as its point of departure Marx's theory of social evolution. Professor Diakonoff, however, has expanded Marx's five stages of development to eight. In addition, and in contrast to Marx, Professor Diakonoff denies that our transition from one stage to the next is marked by social conflict and revolution and demonstrates that these transitions are sometimes achieved peacefully and gracefully. Professor Diakonoff's focus is not limited solely to the economic and socio-economic aspects of our development, rather he examines in detail the ethnic, cultural, religious and military-techno-logical factors which have been brought to bear over the centuries. Professor Diakonoff also denies that social evolution necessarily implies progress and shows how 'each progress is simultaneously a regress'. Finally the book concludes with a prognosis for the future of humanity, leaving the reader to draw their own conclusion about what the future holds. As the book moves through the various chronological stages, the reader is drawn into a remarkable and thought-provoking study of the process of the history of the human race which promises to be the most important work of intellectual world history since Toynbee.

IGOR M. DIAKONOFF is Emeritus Professor at the Institute of Oriental Studies, University of St Petersburg. He is the author of many scholarly publications including the three-volume *History of the Ancient World* (1989), of which he was principal editor, and *Archaic Myths of Orient and Occident* (1993).

The Paths of History

IGOR M. DIAKONOFF

CAMBRIDGE
UNIVERSITY PRESS

PUBLISHED BY THE PRESS SYNDICATE OF THE UNIVERSITY OF CAMBRIDGE
The Pitt Building, Trumpington Street, Cambridge CB2 1RP, United Kingdom

CAMBRIDGE UNIVERSITY PRESS
The Edinburgh Building, Cambridge, CB2 2RU, UK   http://www.cup.cam.ac.uk
40 West 20th Street, New York, NY 10011–4211, USA   http://www.cup.org
10 Stamford Road, Oakleigh, Melbourne 3166, Australia

Originally published in Russian as *Puti Istorii. Ot drevneishego chelovek do nashikh dnei*
by Vostochnaia Uteratwa 1994 and © Igor M. Diakonoff
First published in English by Cambridge University Press as *The Paths of History*
English edition © Igor M. Diakonoff 1999

First published 1999

Printed in the United Kingdom at the University Press, Cambridge

Typeface Lexicon A (*The Enschedé Type Foundry*) 9/12.5pt   *System* QuarkXPress   [SE]

A catalogue record for this book is available from the British Library

ISBN 0 521 64348 1 hardback
ISBN 0 521 64398 8 paperback

Contents

Foreword by Geoffrey Hosking

The collapse of the Soviet Union and the ending of the Marxist monopoly on intellectual life freed Russian social scientists and historians to deploy a broader range of theoretical approaches to the history of their own country and the world. When one couples this renewed freedom with the very distinctive personal experience of those who have lived through the Soviet experiment, the results are sometimes remarkable. *The Paths of History* is one of the most intriguing and innovative fruits of this intellectual and spiritual milieu.

Its author, Igor Mikhailovich Diakonoff, was born on 12 January 1915 in Petrograd, the son of a bank employee. His father had enough experience of finance and banking to be sent as an employee to the Commercial Department of the Soviet embassy in Christiana (Oslo). Thus Igor received his primary education at a Norwegian school, and learned to speak Norwegian fluently, the first of the many languages which he displayed a remarkable ability and desire to learn in later life. (At the age of seventy-three he confessed to a colleague who was learning modern Greek: 'I'm always jealous of someone who knows a language I don't!') His highly unusual linguistic range has enabled him to penetrate the mentality of many different cultures, and this undoubtedly underlies the wide sweep of human sympathy evident in *The Paths of History*. One of his acquisitions was English, which he knows so well that he has translated some of the works of Keats and Tennyson, and was able to prepare this translation of *The Paths of History* largely himself.

After returning to the Soviet Union and matriculating in 1930 from a secondary school in Leningrad, he studied in the Assyriological Section of the History Faculty in the Leningrad Institute of Linguistics and History, mastering Akkadian, Sumerian, Hebrew, Aramaic and Arabic. Following graduation, he worked in the Hermitage Museum, with its unique collection of Oriental and Middle Eastern artefacts.

He married in 1936, but the following year both his father and his wife's father were arrested. After 'learning the art of standing in prison queues', Igor was informed that his own father had been 'sentenced to ten years' imprisonment without right of correspondence' – a sentence which he rightly interpreted as execution by firing squad.

When the war came, his wife Nina, who was pregnant, was evacuated from Leningrad to Tashkent, while Igor was mobilised into military intelligence. He worked in Karelia, preparing propaganda material for distribution among the enemy. Then, in 1944, he was sent to Kirkenes, in Finnmark, at the northern extremity of Norway, which was temporarily occupied by the Red Army as the Germans retreated. Speaking fluent Norwegian, he was made deputy commandant of the occupied zone. He admired Norwegian democracy and loved the Norwegian people, and so became an invaluable mediator between the occupiers and the population. He was so much valued by them that in 1994 he and Nina were invited to Oslo to a fiftieth anniversary celebration of the liberation from the Germans, was formally presented with the thanks of the Norwegian people and was received by the King as a guest of honour.

Demobilised in 1946, he returned to the Hermitage and later worked at the Oriental Institute of the Academy of Sciences for most of the rest of his professional life. There were very few oriental specialists in the Soviet Union when he started work there, and he played a major role in building up the Institute. However, he also managed to publish a major series of scholarly works on the languages, cultures, socio-economic systems and histories of, among others, Assyria, the Hittite kingdom, Babylon, Parthia and Armenia. The climax of his scholarly career was the publication in 1989 of a three-volume *History of the Ancient World*, of which he was the principal editor.

Having brought out this *magnum opus* in his mid-seventies, Diakonoff might have been expected to relax from his lifelong endeavours. On the contrary, he resolved on the opposite course – to embark on his most ambitious project yet, an outline of world mythology. It so happened that a team which he and several colleagues had assembled to compile a comparative dictionary of Afro-Asian languages fell apart, undoing several years' work. In a recent letter to me, Diakonov wrote that 'For a long while I was deeply frustrated by this. But the large amount of material collected by our group led me to some inferences on the mentality of ancient man, who expressed his understanding of the world and his feelings toward it in the only way available to him, namely in myths.'

The outcome of these reflections was his *Archaic Myths of Orient and Occident* (Göteborg, 1993). This work in its turn stimulated him to attempt something even more wide-ranging, a universal history in which socio-psychological factors would occupy a far more dominant position than was normal in Marxist and even post-Marxist accounts. As early as 1983 he had delivered a theoretical paper to the Oriental Institute on the importance of socio-psychological factors in history, tacitly casting doubt on the primary role which Marxists attribute to material factors. Having learnt in his earlier work to give close attention to myth, religion, science and philosophy, he believed he observed certain regularities at work in the spiritual as well as material evolution of the world's earliest civilisations, those of the Middle East. He set out to discover if similar regularities could be discerned in others parts of the world and at other times. He came to the conclusion that they could.

The result is the present book. Diakonoff's point of departure is the theory of social evolution as elaborated by Marx and Engels. However, he has introduced some changes of cardinal importance, which impart to the theory both greater flexibility and greater explanatory power. In the first place, he has expanded Marx's five stages of social evolution (primitive; slave-owning; feudal; bourgeois capitalist; socialist) to eight (Primitive; Primitive-Communal; Early or Communal Antiquity; Late or Imperial Antiquity; Middle Ages; Absolutist Post-Middle Ages; Capitalism; Post-Capitalism). He denies that the transition from one stage to another is necessarily marked by heightened social conflict and revolution: on the contrary, he asserts, it is sometimes accomplished peacefully and gradually. The conflict which does take place is not only between the forces of production and the social relationships surrounding them, but much more broadly between religious, ethnic and other socio-psychological formations. (Though, it should be noted, Diakonoff denies the overriding importance which the late-twentieth-century Russian theorist Lev Gumilev ascribes to ethnic factors.)

Altogether Diakonoff is much more interested in ethnic, cultural and religious factors than Marx was, and also in military technology. He ascribes to them not just the residual significance of an airy and derivative superstructure over a substantial and primary base, but sees them as independent and powerful influences in themselves.

He denies that social evolution necessarily implies progress, other than in the narrowly technological sense. Rather, he sees humanity as developing simultaneously in two contradictory directions: 'each progress is simultaneously a regress'. On the one hand humans attain greater technological mastery, mounting prosperity and mutual tolerance and they move towards the gradual elimination of war through the mediation of international institutions; but at the same time they also generate unrestrained population growth, ethnic cleansing, exhaustion of resources and gross degradation of the environment, while those wars which do occur are unprecedentedly destructive. Diakonoff declines to say which tendency he thinks is likely to take the upper hand, but in his exposition the idea of the 'end of history' has a very different ring from the one evoked by Francis Fukuyama in his book *The End of History and the Last Man*.

What makes Diakonoff's book so remarkable is both the wide sweep of its learning and the humanity of its insights. Few if any theorists of world history before him have been experts on ancient Asian and Middle Eastern societies, so that his chapters on Primitive Society, Antiquity and the Middle Ages are written with a penetration, sympathy and awareness of diverse possibilities which none of his rivals can match. At the same time his personal experience of war and political terror, but also of the attempts since World War II to create greater confidence and better relations between nations, have deepened his insights, instilling in them both a profound concern about the fate of humanity and also an ambivalent attitude towards its future.

There have of course been other post-Marxist theorists of world history, such as Perry Anderson[1] and Immanel Wallerstein,[2] but none of them has Diakonoff's depth of personal insight, nor have they emancipated themselves so fully from Marx. As for the non-Marxist theorists, they do not usually offer such a detailed and elaborate periodisation of social evolution as Diakonoff. Ernest Gellner,[3] for example, whose work has similar range and penetration, operates with a relatively simple scheme of 'agrarian', 'industrial' and 'post-industrial' societies. Michael Mann[4] ascribes as much importance as Diakonoff does to military, religious and cultural factors, but devotes less attention to ancient society, while overall his theory is more diffuse, perhaps more all-embracing, but also less easy to apply to individual instances.

Diakonoff's book, then, occupies its own distinctive and very valuable position in the relatively small repertoire of works which offer a theory, rather than just a narrative account, of universal history. Indeed, it could be asserted that it sets out the most clearly argued and convincingly elaborated periodisation of human societies currently to be found in the scholarly literature. It is certain that its propositions will be keenly debated and that its ideas will inspire historians and sociologists to fruitful comparison, in whatever period or region they are working.

School of Slavonic & East European Studies,
University of London.

1. *Lineages of the Absolutist State*, London: NLB, 1974; *Passages from Antiquity to Feudalism*, London: Verso, 1978.
2. *The Modern World System*, 3 vols., New York: Academic Press, 1974–1989.
3. *Plough, Sword and Book: The Structure of Human History*, London: Collins Harvill, 1988.
4. *The Sources of Social Power*, 2 vols., Cambridge University Press, 1986–1993.

Preface

Throughout my life I have studied the socio-economic history of the Ancient World, and in recent years its social psychology as well. At last I arrived at a concept of how the historical process worked – at least in the period from Palaeolithic times to the end of Antiquity. It seemed to me that during this period the process consisted not of two phases as is assumed in Marxist historiography but of four regular stages of world-wide valence. The probable mechanism of change also seemed clear.

Then I asked myself whether this concept of the mechanism responsible for phase change could be applied to the later history of mankind. Although not an expert in the history of Middle Ages and the modern period, I tried nevertheless to trace an outline of the historical process during these phases, drawing on the work of a variety of authors. It appeared to me that the historical process after Antiquity could be subdivided into four more phases, each with its own mechanism of emergence and function. . . . The result was a short overview of the whole history of mankind, and of the laws governing it – not only economic and socio-economic laws but also socio-psychological ones.

For this overview of world history (perhaps too hastily conceived by me) I am solely responsible. A detailed account of my views as regards the first four phases can be found in my earlier published, less ambitious, work on more specific subjects. As regards the later phases, I have omitted all references in order not to make any of my colleagues answerable for my own, possibly faulty, conclusions.

In an earlier generation, H. G. Wells, who was not even a historian by training, offered an outline of the entire history of mankind. His efforts had some success, at least with the general public, I hope therefore, that this book too – written as it is by a specialist, at least as regards a certain part of world history – may be of some interest, and not only for professionals, but also for the general reader who is interested in history and has some elementary knowledge in the field. The historical periods and episodes which the existing handbooks expound in sufficient detail have been treated summarily, but those which usually are not to be found in popular handbooks on history, or which I felt to be especially interesting, are presented at greater length.

For inevitable minor – or perhaps even more serious – mistakes and omissions, I beg the readers' indulgence.

Introduction

Ahi quanto a dir qual'era e cosa dura Questa selva selvaggia ed aspra e forte
Che nel pensier rinnuova la paura.

Dante

Every science is cognition of a process or movement. A natural process usually has clear-cut phases of development, and may be oscillatory or variative, though delimited by certain physically conditioned constants and natural laws. Most processes do not develop in isolation but interact with others, thus causing apparent irregularities. One such process concerns the existence of the species Homo Sapiens. The task of a theoretically minded historian is to find out the common laws and regularities, as well as the causes and the phases of the process in question. We should also try to find the causes of deviations, and the origin of the particular forms of existence of the Homo resulting from the general laws.

The process of the history of mankind can best be likened to the flow of a river. It has a source; at the beginning it is no more than a brook, then come broader reaches; stagnant backwaters and off-shoots, rapids and waterfalls may occur. The flow of the river cannot be completely accidental but it is conditioned by many factors. These are not only the general laws of gravitation and molecular physics but also the particular qualities of its banks which differ in their chemical composition and geological structure; the configuration of its bends, which is conditioned by the soil and the environment; one current overlaps with other currents, and they carry different organic and non-organic admixtures. Whether the metaphorical analogy between history and the flow of a river is sufficient to allow us to suppose that the river of history will finally fall into a historical sea, or the historical process will be brought to an end by the intervention of some still unknown forces is something which it is difficult to prognosticate.

Through all these phenomena one can discern the action of certain main laws or regularities. But the regularities of the historical process which are discernible at present and are dealt with in the present book may be regarded as regularities in the Humean sense, i.e. an event may cause another event without there being necessarily an original link between them.

During the twentieth century Historians have tended to downplay the idea of regular laws of historical development; their task, as they conceived it, was to examine particular factors of this development, or to pursue the implications of a theory like the one put forward by A. Toynbee whose idea, in brief, postulated a sequence of crises and declines in civilisations which were more or less autonomous and causally unconnected. Such an approach is unproductive and has recently gone out of favour.

Western historical science of the later twentieth century empirically elaborated a certain general periodisation of social structures. Pre-industrial (Primitive, or Pre-Urban, and then Early Urban), and Industrial, after which it is thought that a Post-Industrial society has to emerge. Such a classification, to be sure, accords with the facts, and in this respect is acceptable; but it has the important drawback of disregarding the principle of causation; however, since Aristotle, science has been perceived in terms of cognition of causes; and in spite of the growing complexity of modern epistemological constructions, this definition of science certainly remains correct.

From the point of view of causality, the theory of socio-economic formations outlined more than 100 years ago by Karl Marx and restated (and partly distorted) in 1938 by Stalin,[1] has certain advantages. According to this theory, productive forces, i.e. technology in combination with its producers as a social category, develop so long as the relations in production which exist in the society satisfy their requirements. When this condition is violated, the development of productive forces slows down, bringing about an upheaval and a change of the relations in production, and thus one social epoch is replaced by another. Marx distinguished the following 'modes of production': the Asiatic, the Antique, the Feudal and the Bourgeois (or the Capitalist), these being 'the progressive epochs of the social formation'. The later Marxists applied the term 'social formation' not to the entire history of the social development but to each of the epochs which were now termed 'socio-economic formations'. They identified five such 'formations', viz. one pre-class formation (Primitive), then three class, or antagonistic formations (Slaveholding, Feudal and Capitalist), and, in the future, a Communist formation, whose first stage is Socialism.

When Marx said 'capitalism', he of course meant a mode of production in which the bourgeois minority exploits the working majority (the proletariat); he regarded this mode of production as a stage in the history of mankind which, as we now can ascertain, was correct. Not limiting himself to the proposed periodisation, Marx explained it by resorting to Hegel's idea of motive contradictions. For the three antagonistic formations, this motive contradiction was that between the exploiting and the exploited classes. The weakness of the Marxist concept lies first and foremost in the fact that no convincing motive contradiction had been found either for the first, pre-class society, or for the last, supposedly Communist formation.[2]

1. I am using the Russian edition of Marx's Collected Works which is more accessible to me: K. Marx, *Zur Kritik der Politischen Ekonomie*, in K. Marks and F. Engels, *Sochineniya*, 2nd edn, vol. 13, Moscow, 1959, pp. 7–8; cf. *Kratkiy kurs istorii VCP(b)* [by I. Stalin], Moscow, 1938, p. iv. The introduction into scholarly use of the notion 'Slaveholding formation' by Stalin (or his consultants) is mainly to be traced to V. V. Struve's works dating from the early 1930s.
2. Here I am referring to an inconsistency in the use of principles which a scholar has himself accepted as obligatory. If any movement is the result of a conflict of opposites, as taught by Marxism, then this is a natural law which has to be applied always, be it in physics, in cosmology, or whatever. However, in modern physical science movement is not regarded as a conflict of opposites. The attempts of Marxist philosophers to defend Hegel's concept of movement against the physicists must be regarded as futile. As we shall see below, also in history, the notion of movement as a conflict of opposites cannot be accepted.

Therefore, the Communist formation was conceived in terms of a completely harmonious future – an idea which goes back to Christian apocalyptic eschatology and does not tally with the materialistic explanation of the historical process.

At present, in the last decade of the twentieth century, it cannot be doubted that the Marxist theory of historical process, reflecting as it does the realities of the twentieth century, is completely out of date; not only because the hypothesis of a coming Communist phase is poorly founded, but also because of other errors, both theoretical and purely pragmatic. To Soviet historians of the antiquity, ever since the second discussion on the so-called Asiatic formation during the 1960s, it became obvious that the exploitation of slave labour in production was not the motivating factor of the ancient social 'formation'. Although doubtless there was a considerable number of slaves in Antiquity, and also in the early Middle Ages and later, it was only briefly in the history of the 'Antique' societies, especially in Rome during the Late Republic and Early Empire, that slave labour was a dominant factor in production. This secondary role of slave labour appears clearly in the works of L. B. Alaev, O. D. Berlev, E. S. Bogoslovsky, M. A. Dandamaev, V. P. Ilyushechkin, N. B. Jankowska, Yu. Yu. Perepelkin, A. A. Vigasin, K. K. Zelyin, and my own writings;[3] it also follows from a close study of the works by A. B. Egorov, G. S. Knabe, E. M. Shtaerman and many others.

But not only was the slaveholding 'formation' not slaveholding; the feudal one was not feudal. Marx introduced the term 'feudalism' for a certain stage of the historical process only because in the nineteenth century he could have had only very imprecise and vague notions of medieval society in Eastern Europe and in Asia. A feud (also called fee or fief) is a land-holding or a right of income which has been granted to a vassal by his suzerain on the condition of serving him in war and paying him a tribute. This was the system of organising the medieval ruling class characteristic of Western Europe before the epoch of the absolute monarchies, but the system, in this form, was not so usual for perhaps most of the other medieval societies outside the Western European political tradition. Therefore to call every medieval society 'feudal' means describing the whole world in terms of what happened in Europe. I do not think this term is worth preserving.

Unlike the feud, relations between labour and capital have been and are historically universal. However, while capital as such can exist in different historical 'formations', Capitalism as a system is, to be sure, a phenomenon which appeared only after Medieval society. But is it possible to use the term 'capitalism' to denote a society where not only the capitalists, but also the proletariat is in the minority, while the majority of the population is employed in the services sector? Such is

---

3. In the *History of the Ancient World* edited by I. S. Swencickaya, V. D. Neronova and myself (three Russian editions: 1980, 1982, 1989; an American edition of vol. I, Chicago University Press, 1992), the authors still maintained the concept of a slaveholding society, but mostly with certain reservations: thus, in the chapters written by myself, the exploited class of the ancient society is mostly characterised not as 'slaves' but as 'slave-type dependent persons', 'helots', etc.

the composition of the most developed modern societies. Western scholars call these societies Post-Industrial, and we must of course define them as Post-Capitalist.

Note that when Marx defined (in the first volume of *Das Kapital*) the ratio of the surplus value (approximately *c.* 100%), it was only a rough estimate. Moreover, from the third volume of *Das Kapital* we learn that this 100% is by no means totally consumed by the capitalist; they include the cost of renovation of the equipment (machinery), advertisement, land rent, repayment of credits, etc. If, as was recommended by the fanatical leaders of workers' groups, the capitalists were dispossessed of the surplus value, the new masters would, first, still have to deal with the cost of production; and secondly, the limited percentage of the surplus value which was the private income of the not-so-numerous capitalists, if divided between the numerous workers, would increase their wages only a little, perhaps less than by 1 per cent; but actually it would be necessary to spend it on paying not the workers but the administration, which now would have to fulfil all the organisational operations needed for production. This is what occurred in the new society built by the Marxists, where not only all the surplus value but a considerable part of the necessary produced value is consumed in this way.

Let us pose a question regarding the modern so-called 'capitalist' society: can the surplus value created by the labour of the few workers who belong to the proletariat suffice to support not only the class of capitalists but the whole giant service sphere? The amount of value of a commodity depends on the amount of labour which is socially necessary for its production. But for production, not only socially necessary is the labour of the turner working the metal with his lathe, or the stoker putting coal into the furnace, but also the labour of the inventor which has resulted in making the lathe and the furnace, and the labour of the scientist who created the possibility for the latter's inventions through basic research; that is, not only blue-collar but also white-collar labour is needed. And if the amount of the value depends on working time, then we must also include in it the time spent on creating the very possibility for the worker to labour at his job, including the time spent on fundamental research.

The Marxist theory of 'formations' in the form it was given by Marx and Stalin has another serious drawback as well: it does not even consider the mechanism of change from one socio-economic 'formation' to the next. But the apparent discrepancy between the development of productive forces and the character of the relations in production does not automatically bring about a change of 'formations'. To the question about the mechanism of change the Marxists of the nineteenth century and the first half of the twentieth answered, that such a mechanism is revolution, i.e. a violent upheaval: 'violence is the midwife of history'. This, however, from the point of view of world history, is incorrect. No violent upheaval divides Primitive society from Antiquity, nor Antiquity from the Middle Ages. As to Capitalism, this is a stage in world history which set in as the result of a revolution only in one country, viz. in France. In England the bourgeois political revolution occurred in the seventeenth century, the industrial revolution, i.e. the change from one system of production to another, occurred in the late eighteenth century and early nineteenth, but the real power passed to the bourgeois class only after the parliamentary reform of 1832, and even then not at once. In Russia, capitalism began taking root after the reforms of the 1860s; as for the bourgeoisie, this class might have come to power as a result of the revolution of February 1917 but did not. In Germany capitalism was the result of reforms, in America and Italy a result of war of liberation which cannot be termed a revolution in the strict sense of the word. And what about Egypt? Or Scandinavia? Or Thailand?

But whether or not we accept the doctrine of Marxism, the historical process in any case remains a natural process which has its own laws of development. History is a complicated unfolding of socio-economic factors in close connection both with technological and socio-psychological changes. If Marxism, one of the great doctrines of the nineteenth century, shows certain important limitations from the point of view of the twentieth century, this does not imply that we should immediately reject any Marxist statement and seek for all answers elsewhere, e.g. in Orthodox Christianity, although Christianity, of course, has its own theory of history, which, by the way, had a decided influence on Marxism, as well as the other social theories of the nineteenth century.

In our time, all concepts of historical development share, in principle, one important drawback: they are all based on the idea of progress, and of progress unlimited in time at that. This idea goes actually back to the Christian concept of the future as an immutable 'God's kingdom on Earth', which, in its turn, goes back to the historicism characteristic of Judaism, the ancestor of both Christianity and Islam.[4] Historicism was absent from Graeco-Roman philosophy, and from the philosophy of the Renaissance: we do not encounter it either in the works of Montaigne, or Spinoza or Descartes or Leibniz, and it exists only in embryo in the works of Francis Bacon.

Up to the eighteenth century all European thinkers regarded Classical Antiquity as the highest point of historical development. The idea of mankind improving everlastingly can be traced to the authors of the eighteenth-century *Encyclopédie* – to Diderot and D'Alembert;[5] but the concept of certain consecutive stages of an endless progress, in which the next stage after ours, a stage not yet reached by mankind, is to be the absolutely most perfect, was first formulated by Marquis de

4. See *Istoriya drevnego mira*, ed. I. M. Diakonoff, I. S. Swencickaya and V. D. Neronova, 3rd edn, vol. III, Moscow, 1989, p. 152 (the chapter was written using data supplied by S. S. Averintsev). Unfortunately, I had no opportunity to get acquainted with the work of Fr. Fukuyama.

5. We are (rightly) accustomed to regard the authors of the *Encyclopédie* as anti-clerical; but, perhaps it is worth while to remember that both Diderot and D'Alembert were pupils of Jansenists, i.e. of Catholics who were in opposition to the Pope's authority, and who stressed the importance of free will as against a general hopeless predestination. It is hardly possible to doubt the influence of Christian values upon the authors of the *Encyclopédie*.

Condorcet, who was active in the French Revolution. We find it in his posthumous work *Esquisse d'un tableau historique de progrès de l'esprit humain*, written in 1793, published 1795 (Condorcet died in prison).

From Condorcet the thread can be traced, first of all, to Saint-Simon, who regarded history as a sequence of positive and negative epochs, the positive factor gradually increasing. From Saint-Simon it can be traced to Marx. Another source of the idea of progress is the philosophy of Hegel, which influenced Marx most directly; in his younger years Marx was actually a Hegelian. As for Hegel himself, he began as a Lutheran theologian and the author of the book on the *'Spirit of Christianity'*. He was always a believer, although his philosophy, which developed only gradually, seemed to have lost its more obvious theological influences. Hegel had an enormous influence not only on Marx,[6] but indeed on all philosophical thought of the nineteenth century. Such influential philosophers of the first half and the middle of the nineteenth century as Auguste Comte, Herbert Spencer (for whom progress was, at least at the time, 'not accidental but necessary'), and John Stuart Mill, were all proponents of the idea of progress. The possibility of unlimited progress was something self-evident to men and women of the second half of the nineteenth century and the whole of the twentieth century, and this in spite of the law of conservation of energy formulated as early as the 1840s by Mayer, Joule and Helmholtz.

In the mentality of man the notion of progress is connected to basic social impulses, and it is necessary for cognition and reproduction. But we should not use this notion – from the field of social motivation – to evaluate the natural process as a whole, where unlimited progress, an eternal progress (which, of course, involves expense of energy) is a case of perpetual motion and contradicts the basic natural laws of conservation.

From the energy conservation law it follows, that accretions on one side are paid for by losses on another, i.e. each form of progress is simultaneously a form of regress: there is no progress without loss, and the more one progresses, the more one loses.

Historical changes can be observed most clearly in the realm of technology. Its development partly depends on how far the products of the environment and the society can at any point be exploited by man, and partly on the continuing development of the cognitive functions of the brain conditioned by its physiology. The

---

6. As is well known, Marxism has 'three roots and three sources', these being classical German philosophy (read: Hegel), English political economy (read: Adam Smith), and French Utopian socialism (read: Saint-Simon; Fourier did not play any major role). In our exposition we have not dwelt on Adam Smith. He also distinguished three stages in the development of natural economy: that of agriculture, that of manufactories, and that of international commerce. But (in Book IV of *The Wealth of Nations*) he pointed out only that the first stage was the most 'natural', and did not prophesy the advent of future social harmony. Therefore, for the correct appreciation of Marxist theory of history and its origins, only Saint-Simonism and Hegelianism are important.

possibilities of cognition are so far not threatened by extinction; cognition is not going to discontinue in the expected future, and for the time being it can be regarded as unlimited, although actually it is not; any unlimitedness is impossible as a matter of principle.

But when public figures and historians discuss progress, they are usually thinking not so much of the progress of thought and technology but of a progress of the human society as a whole, of the conditions of its existence, of the accessibility of material goods, etc. Here again an unlimited or even an uninterruptedly linear progress is hardly possible.

Therein lies hope for mankind, because unrestricted technological progress has already brought humanity to the brink of ecological hell, which neither Marx nor the other thinkers of the last century and a half had envisaged.

Marxist theory considers technology not *per se* but as a part of the productive forces which are thought of as manifestations of the human (personal) and material (technological) factors which realise the interaction between man and nature in the process of social production. But the development of personal relations in the process of production can (I should say 'must') be viewed not only in the realm of immediate productive activities, but also in the realm of social consciousness and the motivation of productive (and other social) acts, i.e. social psychology.

Therefore I shall try to identify the compatibility of each system of relations in production not with the complex category of productive forces, but, first, with the level of technology, and, secondly, with the state of the socio-psychological processes. The social activities of man depend on their socio-psychological evaluation. But this means that any passage from one type of economic organisation to another must be accompanied by a change in social values, even if the change does not involve the principles of social relations but is limited to ethnic or religious (ideological) changes, or even to differences inside the strata of society. What has been an anti-value must become a value, and what was a value must become an anti-value. Such a change cannot all at once involve the masses: in order to start them moving, emotional and strong-willed leaders are needed (this is the phenomenon called 'passionarity' by L. N. Bumilev).[7]

The mental realisation of the fact that the existing system of relations in production (or of the character of the state, or of the character of ideology) limits the possibilities for the development of productive forces does not immediately lead to a change of this system, whether forcible or gradual. Actually only the development of a new technology of the industrial society is impossible without a corresponding drastic restructuring of the relations in production; but also here the passage to a

---

7. In his book, *Etnogenez i biosfera zemli* (Ethnogenesis and the Earth's Biosphere), L. V. Gumilev suggests another explanation, which I think is wrong. Although one may agree with his definition of 'ethnic unit' as a phenomenon, the importance which the author ascribes to ethnicity in the creation of what he calls 'passionary situations', is very much overestimated.

new system is not always a social revolution, and is not always synchronised with a technological revolution. This is all the more true of the earlier systems of relations in production. The appearance of a metal ploughshare and a steel axe actually led to a change in the organisation of production, and even to the territorial spread of civilisations. But the same primitive ploughs were used without substantial improvements from the end of the fourth millennium BC (in Sumer) until the nineteenth century AD (for instance, in Russia). The change of the metal used for the ploughshare (steel instead of bronze or copper) did not imply any direct radical change in the state of the society. Also mining did not change radically from the beginning of the Age of Metal to the beginning of the capitalist epoch. In handicrafts, certain innovations (as, e.g. the invention of the vertical weaving-loom, the diamond drill, etc. etc.) are not directly connected in temporal terms with systemic changes in society. An important influence on the development of society was ascribed to the introduction of steel implements, which allowed to widen considerably the territory of tilled land. Of great historical importance was the progress in shipping. However, neither of these technological innovations can be synchronised with the changes in the socio-economic structure of the society of mankind as a whole; the results of these inventions were felt only very gradually.

There exists only one technological field where progress has a direct influence on the change of relations in production. This is progress in the production of arms.[8] Where there are no high quality arms, no class society can exist (and not even its forerunner, the stage defined by modern anthropologists as chiefdom society[9]). A warrior who is in possession of the kind of arms which can be produced at the stage of the Chalcolithic or the Bronze Age cannot organise mass exploitation of slaves of the classical type: for each slave with a copper or bronze implement an overseer would be needed. But one can exploit whole groups of classical-type slaves when the warrior has a steel sword, a steel coat of armour, a proper helmet and a shield. If in due time one had to abandon the exploitation of classical-type slaves, the reason would not be any kind of revolution in the productive forces (i.e. in technology), but the low productivity of slave labour. A warrior on horseback, with his horse covered with armour, and armoured himself, and, later, based in a new architectural invention, a fortified castle, could provide for the exploitation of peasants, who in the preceding epoch themselves made up the main mass of warriors. What brought about the end of the Middle Ages was not so much the great geographical discoveries (although certainly they played an important role), as the cannon which brought the role of the medieval knight to an end and made the industrial enterprise more important than the agricultural one, not to speak of the handicrafts. The nuclear bomb shall (if the human race survives) provide for the world-wide institution of post-capitalist society. This

---

8. This had already been noted by F. Engels in the apparatus to *Anti-Duehring*, not published in his lifetime.   9. On chiefdoms, see below.

shall, of course, itself be full of contradictions, and can by no means be regarded as a guaranteed future.

I should like to stress that changes in military technology do not of themselves cause a change in the relations in production (social relations). It is caused only by changes in technology in combination with a change in value orientation. And contrariwise, a change in value orientation will not produce a change in social relations, unless combined with an actual or imminent revolution in the technology of the production of arms.

Basing ourselves on these issues, we can distinguish eight Phases of the historical process, each of them characterised by its own system of social values (an ideology), and its typical level of military development. One Phase is divided from the next without a distinctive threshold, certainly not by a revolutionary upheaval, but by a transitional period of different duration, which continues until all the necessary symptoms diagnostic of the next Phase are developed. This period between the Phases we shall call Phase transition. While the progress in the production of arms expresses itself promptly in military events, which are the traditional and always spectacular contents of narrative history, socio-psychological changes underlie everyday life and are expressed in religion, lexical changes and works of art. In each chapter we have cited the most important artists and thinkers whose work provided for the necessary socio-psychological changes for the Phase in question; but to give a detailed account of their work or render the dramatic movement of their ideas through time fall outside the task and scope of our brief outline of the historical process.

Human creativity, in both fields, technology and ideas, is aimed to avoid 'discomforts', specific to each Phase but emerging always on the same natural basis. The effort of creativity, productive forces in the broadest sense, is made in quest of stability, of procuring the possibility of peaceful reproduction; but, being creative, they shall, at a certain point, inevitably discredit this stability. Then we can observe, on one hand, new technological inventions applied in the military field, and on the other, a change in current social values. The Phase transition has thus begun.

The unity of the laws of the historical process is made apparent also because they can be identified in Europe as well as on the other extremity of Eurasia: in the nearly isolated island chain of Japan which experienced neither the Crusades, nor the Turk or Mongol invasion; and also, e.g. in South America, and so on. These examples allow us to check the periodisation of the historical process as suggested below with a sufficient measure of strictness.

1   First Phase (Primitive)

For the earliest periods in the history of *Homo sapiens* only a technological periodisation is possible: the Palaeolithic period, the Mesolithic period (chiefly attested in the western part of the Eurasian continent), the Neolithic period. The actual life of the Late Palaeolithic man might have been observed in the instance of the aboriginal population of Australia; however, the very imperfect observations date mainly from the time when the societies of the Aboriginals had already been radically disrupted by the mass immigration to Australia from Europe from the second half of the nineteenth century. One of the most interesting pieces of evidence comes from a nearly illiterate Englishman, who was sentenced to transportation to Australia, fled from the colony and lived among the Aboriginals for decades, spending the end of his life in one of the towns of Eastern Australia. He told his story to a chance journalist. Scientific research, however, began only at the very end of the nineteenth century. It might seem that the Palaeolithic state of the Australian Aboriginals, at an epoch when Europe and America had reached the high level of capitalist development, might attest not only to social but even to biological backwardness. This is not the case. The epoch of the class development of mankind occupies no more than 1 or 2 per cent of the existence duration of the species *Homo sapiens sapiens*.[1] Thus a technological lag of only 2 per cent – let us say a

---

1. The problem of the development of modern man (genus *Homo*, species *sapiens*, subspecies *sapiens*) from certain preceding forms is still being discussed. If the hallmark of 'wise man' is the ability to create at least primitive tools, and to use fire for his own benefit, then already the so-called *Sinanthropus* of China must be regarded as belonging to the genus *Homo sapiens*; however, at present it is assumed that the *Sinanthropus* belonged to the same species (perhaps even to the same subspecies) as the Pithecanthropus in Indonesia, the Olduvia Man in Africa and the Heidelberg Man in Europe, who at present are usually subsumed under the denomination of *Homo erectus*, or *Homo sapiens erectus*, also called *Archanthropus*. The time of the latter's existence was the Middle Pleistocene (about 500,000–200,000 years ago); but at that period another hominid also existed (or still did exist), namely the *Australopithecus*; a late subspecies of the latter was also able to produce very primitive artefacts. Some scientists are of the opinion that the *Archanthropus* is the direct ancestor (through mutation) of modern Man, while others think that modern man is a mutant of the *Homo sapiens neanderthalensis* (the Palaeoanthropus). But the Neanderthal man is attested only from the period of the last (fourth) Glaciation, while the earliest Palaeolithic artefacts (Chellean and Acheulian) are by many students ascribed to the *Archanthropus*. If so, the *Archanthropus* should be regarded as the ancestor both of the Neanderthal and the Modern man. Then the intermediary type discovered in Palestine (Carmel, Qafzeh) should be regarded as hybrid. The problem is still debated.

speed of 10.2 seconds instead of 10.0 in a 100 metre run – is sufficient to account for a technological retardation of this scale.

The reason for it is not so much a minor diminishment in the speed of technological development, but rather a difference in whether the ecological environment had been more or less favourable. The Aboriginals arrived in Australia during the last glacial period which induced a low level of the World Ocean.[2] All of Indonesia was at that time a single peninsula joined to Indo-China, while New Guinea and the Halmahera island were a peninsula of the Australian continent. The narrow straits between Halmahera and Sulawesi, and between Sulawesi and Borneo (Kalimantan), then belonging to the Eurasian continent, were such as could be overcome on rafts which, seemingly, even Palaeolithic men were able to construct. (In the same way, over now-submerged land, man also reached Tasmania.[3]) On the continent of Australia there did not exist the necessary ecological (zoobotanical) requisites for the acculturation of cereals and fruit plants, and for domestication of animals.

Up to modern times, apart from Australian Aboriginals, the population of the subpolar and taiga region of Eurasia and America also belonged to the First Phase of primitive society. The reason was purely ecological: because in the zones in question there are no plants or animals which can be domesticated (even the reindeer is only semi-domesticated).

Note that in the first stage of the historical process (the Phase of early primitive society) there already existed a rudimentary exchange between the different groups of population, sometimes through many intermediaries over considerable distances. Obsidian and even flint for making Neolithic implements and arms could be acquired by exchange from afar.

In the Soviet school literature, what we here define as the First Phase, is lumped together with the Second Phase under the common name of 'primitive communal formation'. In this the Soviet authors follow rather Stalin than Engels, although the latter's book *The Origin of the Family, Private Property, and the State* is a classic for the

2. The same is true of the peopling of the American continent. This event seems to have occurred in the beginning of the last Glacial period through a then-existing isthmus between the Chukotka peninsula and Alaska (the level of the ocean being at that time lowered, and land appearing across the Bering straits). This isthmus cut off the cold Kamchatka-Kuril current flowing from the Polar Ocean; while from the South it was reached by the warm North Pacific current. The result was, that here sufficient verdure did appear, and the climatic conditions were generally quite favourable. Once having reached the American continent, the new settlers found more favourable conditions for development than those they had left in Asia.

3. Tasmania was a peninsula of Australia at the end of the last Glaciation, a period of low sea level. However, anthropologically, the extinct Tasmanians differed considerably from the Australian Aboriginals. It seems, their appearance here was due to an earlier migration across the Australian continent. An alternative hypothesis, supposing that the Tasmanians arrived from the New Hebrides, is untenable: the New Hebrides are surrounded by deep ocean waters, so that men could reach them not earlier than during the Neolithic Period, when the necessary boats (not just rafts) could be produced; but Neolithic man could not bring a Palaeolithic culture to Tasmania.

Marxists. However, Engels subdivided this 'formation' (a term not used by him) into two stages, which (following L. H. Morgan) he defined as 'Savagery' and 'Barbarism'. Engels' book is a brilliant but amateurish exposition of this outstanding American anthropologist's ideas. However, the works of L. H. Morgan are not the conclusion but the starting point for the exploration of primitive societies, and, in particular, of the very important factor in their social life, namely their systems of kinship reckoning.

The canonisation of the book of Engels led to Soviet social anthropology (ethnography) repeating elements of what was already a past stage in the development of the studies in primitive society. What Engels thought of the period of 'Savagery' – when men supposedly went through a stage of sexual promiscuity and a stage of group marriage towards the stage of pairing marriage – is not tenable. Promiscuity is attested neither in human societies nor even among the higher apes; as to group marriage, this phenomenon can be identified only with certain serious reservations (some primitive tribes have certain degrees of kinship which preclude sexual relations between men and women belonging to them, and other degrees of kinship where there is no such prohibition). But even in the most 'retarded' of populations known to us – the Australian Aboriginals – the prevalent type of marriage is not group marriage but cross-cousin marriage (a man takes as his wife the daughter of his father's brother or of his mother's sister). Although extramarital sexual relations (not inside the forbidden kinship groups) are not punished, a nuclear family actually does exist, which is in fact held together by the woman as the keeper of the hearth and the children. Note that the nuclear family is usually but not invariably monogamous.

We can affirm with a great degree of certainty that other, later, familial social structures (extended families, lineages, gentes, clans, etc.) are also developments of the nuclear family, and after reaching a certain critical dimension they dissolve into new nuclear families, which again create extended families, lineages, clans, etc. The external activities of the men of the clan depend to a considerable degree on the role of the women as the stimulus for men's activities, and even their aggression.

This is something we ought to keep in mind throughout history. Only by taking into account the nuclear role of the woman's function as the original mother and the stimulus of activity can we understand history as more than a series of male fights with mostly fatal results.

2   Second Phase (Primitive Communal)

The prehistory of civilisation first began in the Near East, where in the mountains surrounding the Fertile Crescent[1] were found wild cereals, and animals comparatively easy to domesticate: sheep, ancestors of domestic cattle, pigs and donkeys. Here also existed soils suitable for artificial sowing. The conditions were most favourable for the development of production with all the ensuing circumstances. On the American continent, the inhabitants of the more favourable regions had at their disposal such domesticable plants as Indian corn, potatoes, tomatoes, peanuts and cocoa-beans, but their cultivation demanded technical developments; therefore, a level similar to that of Sumer or Pharaonic Egypt was reached by the local population about 4,000 years later – a minor time span compared to the entire history of mankind.

According to the formerly accepted Marxist theoretical periodisation, until the beginning of 'class civilisation' (i.e. mainly in the dry subtropical zone), the whole territory inhabited by mankind was dominated by a 'primitive communal' mode of production.

A mode of production, by definition, depends on the type of property relations, on the type of the combination of labour power with the means of production,[2] on the forms of connection between the producers, the class structure of the society and the motives and goals of economic activity. In the case of 'primitive communal' society, we should of course drop the class structure of the society from the definition. But even with this correction, we actually cannot assign all the 'pre-class' (or 'pre-urban') societies to one and the same mode of production. Some of these societies were purely producing (in the economic sense, we must regard food-gathering, hunting and fishing, the making of drinks and the preparation of skins for

---

1. The Fertile Crescent is the name for the strip of land stretching through Palestine, Syria, Northern Mesopotamia and Iraq, between a half-ring of mountains, and a central zone of steppes and desert (now nearly totally desert).
2. Also, by definition, depending on the mode of exploitation of labour. However, Ilyushechkin has been able to prove that the number of possible ways of exploitation is limited, and which one of them is used does not depend on the social economic formation in question as a whole, but on differing and changing specific historical conditions; no one form is specific to Antiquity, say, or to the Middle Ages. Cf. V. P. Ilyushechkin, *Sistemi i struktury doburzhuaznoy chastnosobstvennicheskoy èkspluatatsii*, Moscow, 1980; and *Èkspluatatsiya i sobstvennost 'v soslovno-klassovykh obshchestvakh*, Moscow, 1990.

clothing and tents as forms of production – if we regard production as the process of creating material goods necessary for the existence and development of society: 'acquiring natural objects by an individual inside a certain societal form and through it'.)[3] But the later so-called primitive communal societies of the Second Phase of the historical process were not only producing but also reproducing. These were societies engaged in agriculture and animal husbandry. In the transitional phase from purely producing to reproducing societies, the means of production, the connection between the producers, the motives and goals of the economic activities – all of these change. The very structure of society changes: on the new level we may find the first indications of the existence of communities – a term which could not be applied to the small wandering groups of Palaeolithic Australians (including 5–10 persons), even though the groups of Palaeolithic men (like animals) had their own stable territories, and were also oriented towards rather sophisticated gentilic and marriage rules and contacts. But in primitive communities there emerged a different social structure which included the appearance of chiefs and men-at-arms. In the Anglo-American literature, and lately also in that of our country such societies are called 'chiefdoms'. The socio-psychological superstructure here is also different.[4]

The need for cognition is one of mankind's main physiological necessities. Encountering a certain phenomenon, man correlates it with the needs he feels and with the information about the means to satisfy them; the information may be estimated as favourable in regard to their satisfaction, or as unfavourable; at the subconscious level this, in any case, creates an emotion; but the evaluation is also made at the conscious level, and is made meaningful. However, we should not attempt to overestimate the impulse of primitive man towards finding meaningfulness in the surrounding world and society; note that making an object meaningful is impossible without a mental and linguistic generalisation. Meanwhile, the process of linguistic development is a slow one. Even as late as the beginning of the Third Phase (that of the Early Antiquity), mankind had not developed expressions for abstract notional generalisation. But what was actually wanted for the making sense of his environment were abstract generalisations of its processes. Hence, in the absence of a linguistic apparatus for abstractions, the only way to generalise was through tropes: correlation of objects as parts of a whole, by similarity, by contiguity, etc., all of which were felt of as a sort of identification. The world's phenomena are complicated, and one trope clings to another, creating a semantic series.

Even at the earliest stage of his existence, man could survive only by registering the causal connection of phenomena in his environment. A coherent interpretation of the world's processes, which could organise man's perception of them at a time

---

3. K. Marx and F. Engels, *Sochinenya*, 2nd edn, vol. 12, p. 713.
4. On this, in connection with the Second Phase of 'pre-class' or 'pre-urban' society, see I. M. Diakonoff, *Archaic Myths of the Orient and Occident*, Göteborg, 1994.

when abstract notions were absent (later they were not just absent but might actually be excluded), is Myth. This is a mental and verbal trace not only of what primitive and ancient man thought, surmised, believed or felt, but also of how he thought.

However, although in the notions of primitive man about the surrounding world, defining the causes was of paramount importance, the idea itself of a 'cause and effect relation' could not be expressed in a logically defined generalisation. In man's experience, cause was associated with his or someone's will. Therefore, unavoidably, any cause and effect relation was perceived as a willed act. At the same time, where there is a will, there must exist a willing principle – which, having a will, must also be in possession of reason. Thus, for the primitive and the ancient man, in every case of causal relations between socio-psychologically apprehended phenomena, a specific willing force is active; and behind the plurality of phenomena encountered by man during his life, there is a plurality of individual forces independent of man, i.e. deities. A deity may, of course, be considered as an explanation of the world's phenomena, but this rationalisation depends on faith, not on logically verified reasoning.

The life activity of man depends on certain socio-psychological impulses. For archaic man, the deities determine the character of the cause and effect relations, and thus also the possibility or otherwise of satisfying his social stimuli. Each stimulus can receive a number of different feasible answers (or mythologemes), but the number of the chief impulses (stimuli) is limited.

One of these is the reaction of search ('what is it?'), an emotional impulse which is induced by the positive or (more often) the negative character of a phenomenon. The reaction of search can develop into an impulse of cognition of what is new, but such a development stands in contradiction to the more characteristic impulse towards stability of man inside the society and the universe: the main rule, namely, 'to be as everybody' (which also predetermines the impulse towards mutual help), contributes to the creation of a consensus in human society, so important for its purposeful activity.[5]

Another impulse is that of satisfying hunger. Although this impulse is also emotional, it can only succeed as a social impulse (therefore, even in the most primitive societies, there was a division of labour, first of all of male and female labour: e.g. hunting and food gathering). Note that even at the earliest period in the history of mankind there was also a need for exchange.

Still another impulse is that of seeking to be defended, sheltered and loved.

Then there is an impulse to eliminate psychological discomfort ('injustice'). In history, this is usually the main reason for wanting social change.

Then there is the impulse towards aggression which is necessary for the survival

---

5.   But the impulse 'to be as everybody else' can also get an anti-progressive form: 'leave me alone' (this, for instance, is the social value from the point of view of a modern bureaucrat).

of man in an inimical world; it stands in connection with the more general impulse towards motion in general.

Then there is the impulse towards sexual satisfaction which, by the way, is closely connected with aggression (man has to achieve victory over his rivals and over the women herself): thus woman induces aggression.

Then there is the impulse to achieve physical success and glory.

Then there is the impulse to relaxation, to laughter, very important in the severe and strictly regulated conditions under which primitive and ancient man lived.

Then there is an impulse towards leadership, in order not to be 'as everybody' but to head them all. This impulse, as a rule, becomes clearly apparent and important in the critical moments of history. This is normally a male impulse.[6]

Each of these impulses must have had, in archaic social psychology, its own causal principle, a *deity*. The deity as interpretation of a cause and effect relation through a trope, creates around itself a semantic series. The local pantheons, if we abstract ourselves from details called forth by local conditions, can be defined as the causal principles of these impulses; but they differ according to the semantic series that are created around them, and according to the ensuing narrations, i.e. myths.

In the First Phase, that of the primitive society, there dominate, first, semantic series imagining the deity as similar to a certain influential type of persons, or to some important events or images in nature, actualised – in accordance with the trope of *pars pro toto* – with a certain animal, bird, or plant associated as totems with certain human groups; and secondly, a belief in the possibility of direct communion of man with the organising principle of the world through the medium of specially endowed members of the group (shamans, or medicine men and a comparable type of women).

During the Second (Primitive Communal) Phase of history, the deities are everywhere organised into definite pantheons; these remain as the socio-psychological base of the then existing societies also in the Third Phase (that of Early Antiquity): this is because the main mass of population in that Phase are the direct continuation of the population of the primitive social group.

It is important to note the following points concerning the mythological religions of communities: (a) they are local; (b) one of them does not exclude any other;

---

6. In history, women appear in social or military activities only as an exception that confirms the rule (thus Jeanne d'Arc, Catherine II, etc.). Therefore the reader of books on history may get the impression that history consists solely of boys playing. However, such 'plays' are made possible only when the home and hearth are protected, by women in the first place; the men are, as often as not, activated not to be 'unworthy of the kisses of the sweet ladies', as Pushkin puts it. The modern feminists are wrong in thinking that this situation is unnatural, being created by 'male chauvinist pigs'. Actually, this was the situation during seven historical Phases known to us; and if, in the Eighth Phase, women begin to acquire a position in society nearly equal to that of men – in socially necessary labour, in science and in politics – it is because this new situation is one of the diagnostic features of the Eighth Phase, and is non-characteristic for the rest of human history.

(c) they are not dogmatic; (d) they have no connection with ethic which develops independently in men's practical life as its organising principle.

Contrasting and opposed class ideologies are foreign not only to the primitive societies but also the ancient ones. Slaves have no conscious ideology of their own, while both the dependent and the independent population worship the same or typologically quite similar deities. Between chiefdoms and early states, no radical reappraisal of values, and hence no obvious social revolution, can be observed, but the evaluation of the relations between men and the deity does change. It is difficult to pinpoint the moment or the period of change, since the available sources do not allow us to investigate consistently any particular society both in the phase of a Chiefdom and in that of Early Antiquity. However, the very fact that a different structure of relations in production has emerged – especially the fact that the ancient society is already divided into social classes which differ as to their place in the process of production – allows us to ascertain that Primitive Society and the society of Early Antiquity are two different consecutive Phases in the development of the historical process, which are connected by a stage of Phase transition.

If there did exist not one Primitive Phase but two, then what did they differ in from the socio-psychological point of view? The First Phase is characterised by totemism and shamanism, the Second – by a genealogically structured pantheon headed by a divine 'chief' and his family (e.g. his wife and son), by important fertility and cults (involving human, animal and plant fertility), and also by the cult of a 'warrior-goddess' who, socio-psychologically, reflects the impulse of aggression. The faith is non-dogmatic and quite local (when changing one's habitation it is natural to start worshipping the new local gods; the myths are characteristically variable), and the religious beliefs are not connected to firmly established ethic norms.

In the First Phase groups of people are sufficiently separated from each other in space, and usually coexist peacefully, if we do not count occasional minor skirmishes, as e.g. occurring when women are kidnapped. The Second Phase corresponds to a richer society, where there is something to desire and what to defend; also the weapons are often much more effective. Engels calls his period 'military democracy' but does not count it as a separate 'formation'; he regards it as a stage in the development of one and the same 'primitive society'. The epithet 'military' is fit in a way: beginning with the Second Phase mankind entered an epoch of endless wars of all against all which continued throughout the Third Phase (Early Antiquity). In Babylonia of the second millennium BC you could not express the notion of 'foreign country', 'abroad' except by saying 'enemy country' – even in letters of merchant navigators sailing abroad with quite peaceful intentions.

However, we shall not use the term 'military democracy' – it is not an adequate designation for the stage of the development of society which we have in view. Not all chiefdoms were particularly democratic. Let us keep to the term 'chiefdom'. This implies a developed pre-class and pre-urban society. Its technological base is late Neolithic or Early Metal (production of picks, hoes and early forms of wooden plough). The social relations and all relations in production differ considerably from those which existed in the First Phase. Actually, although a chiefdom has many features in common with the Early Primitive Society, it also has privileged chiefs and social groups surrounding the chief, such as military leaders, priests, etc. However, these groups are not based upon law but remain informal. Therefore, alongside the council of chiefs with their body-guard, and alongside the priests, there also exists a popular assembly which unites everybody bearing arms. (Women speaking in the assembly and even at the council are also known.) The structured pattern of society, and at the same time a strict regimentation of everybody's life are the features which distinguish the Primitive Community Phase from the earlier Primitive Phase. Marx and Engels, drawing a picture of primitive freedom, were still under the influence of Rousseauist ideas. Actually, freedom of the individual was foreign to these Phases of human history, but the feeling of constituting a corporate body was strong.

However, there are a number of important features which are common to the First and the Second Phase of the historical process. Thus, both the First and Second Phases contain the feeling of an inviolable socio-psychological unity between the groups of men and women and the land which they occupy. No alienation of land is envisaged as possible. Then, although a certain privileged social stratum exists in the community, there is no exploited producing class to be contrasted with a reigning non-producing class. The agrarian production (including stock-rearing), as well as handicrafts, are the concern of the entire arm-bearing mass of the population. Slavery was known, but it was patriarchal slavery: the situation of a slave did not differ materially from that of a family member, because in any case only the head of the family had full rights; slave labour was not decisive in social production.

Many of the societies with a clan and/or tribal structure, which in Soviet scholarship are apt to be regarded as primitive were actually chiefdoms. Their structure could acquire different forms which cannot be reduced to the simple formula 'clan→tribe'. The economic unit in the Second Phase is usually a household kept up either by an individual (nuclear) family, or, when sons and grandsons with their wives and children appear upon the scene, an extended family.[7] But the extended family cannot be regarded as the legal owner of the land which it cultivates, since it is part of a larger unity, the lineage, which is bound by a more distant, real or imaginary (ritual) kinship. A lineage is not necessarily the same as a gens (clan), just as the familial household need not coincide with what we at present consider to be a family. Neither does a tribe, having its own chief, being governed by the tribal assembly, and delegating a tribal council, necessarily coincide with a lineage; moreover, there may exist tribal unions with their own governing bodies. The feeling of

---

7. Such an extended family cannot grow beyond the limits set by the conditions of the production process; when the normal limit is reached, an extended family is broken down into nuclear families, which either do not survive, or grow into new extended families.

the identity of men and women with their land is preserved at this stage. Although prisoners of war may (more or less sporadically) be enslaved, the society as a whole is not divided into antagonistic classes opposed to each other in the process of production. There are no big enterprises which require accounting, nor religious dogmas which need to be fixed in writing: hence writing is unknown.[8]

Perhaps the earliest chiefdoms which many others surpassed in their standard of living and came near to a society of the Ancient Phase (urban type settlements, temples) were those which were responsible for creating the Çatal-Hüyük type of culture in Western Asia Minor (*c.* 6000 BC). As was also the case with the actual Ancient Phase culture of Western Asia and the Nile valley, Çatal-Hüyük economics seems to have been based on the domestication of wild barleys and of cattle. The Çatal-Hüyük culture, as well as some other kindred cultures (Mersin, Jericho) perished during the sixth millennium BC, due probably to a prolonged spell of dry and hot weather, but their achievements were taken up on the Balkan peninsula, and their influence continued to spread.

In time, chiefdoms spread widely over Eurasia. The social structure of the first Indo-Europeans (possibly genetically connected with the Çatal-Hüyük culture) who constituted a certain dialectal continuum, seems to have been that of primitive communities. In a favourable natural environment (South Eastern Europe, as I am inclined to think) they had a highly developed agriculture, and reared stock for meat and milk; consequently, they achieved a comparatively low child mortality rate, and a rapid population growth. This led to a gradual dissemination of the Indo-European languages and cultures; their bearers passed them on to other populations in great parts of Europe and Asia; here the not-so-numerous First Phase primitive population groups merged with the Indo-Europeans, and themselves became the bearers of Indo-European type dialects and cultures, passing them further on.

Somewhat analogous events were happening (at a chronologically earlier period) in the history of the speakers of Afrasian (including Semitic) languages and also in that of the speakers of Sino-Tibetan languages, etc.

Much later, particular chiefdoms in different parts of the world also belonged to the Second (Primitive Community) Phase (thus, probably, Zimbabwe with the Monomotapa dynasty in South Africa, eleventh to fourteenth centuries AD, the 'empire' of the Zulus in South Africa, in the nineteenth century AD, the 'states' of Hawaii, Samoa and Maori in Oceania, and others of the same character). We do not know in all cases whether the societies in question had a distinct class which was

---

8. We do not take into consideration the archaic system of notation of objects which used specially made, three-dimensional tokens and was discovered in the Late Neolithic Period of the Near East by Denise Schmandt-Besserat. Before primary writing was invented, these tokens were in use all over the Fertile Crescent, which means they were understood all over a territory of many languages and dialects. They do not belong to writing as such, which is a sign system which fixes and reproduces speech.

exploited in the process of production (we are not talking of ethnically distinct and simply plundered groups), nor whether the extortion from a particular portion of the population was regular or irregular and occasional. When there is a systematically exploited class, and extortions are regular, then the society in question should be classed as belonging to the Third Phase, i.e. to the Early Antiquity. In America, most tribes in the taiga zone in the north, and the jungle zone in the south, probably also in the prairies, were still in the First Phase, but a number of tribes of the North American continent (the Iroquois, the Dakotas) seem to have been in the Second Phase or at the Phase transition to it. To the Second Phase, not the Third, belonged some important Amerindian populations, as e.g. the Hopi et al. (the Pueblo culture); the Aztecs and the Maya should probably be placed in the transition stage to the Third Phase[9] but the Andean ('Inca') civilisation seems to have belonged to the Third (Ancient Community) Phase proper of the historical process.

As to their technological base, the societies of the Second Phase were mainly agricultural and stock-rearing. The purely stock-rearing (nomadic) societies belong to a later period, and will be discussed below. The development of agriculture is based on achievements in metalwork: the hoe appears, then a primitive plough, the harrow, etc., and primitive metal arms: the dagger, the spear, a simple bow, a metal cap, a primitive shield.

9. The level of development of the Aztecs and the Maya may be compared to that of the Sumerians of the Proto-Literate Period, or the Egyptians of the Pre-Dynastic Period (c. 3000 BC).

3   Third Phase (Early Antiquity)

Since the exploited class is clearly shaped in contrast to the class of free-men (as yet undifferentiated), the system of governing the society becomes institutionalised, it receives a constant, generally recognised structure and an apparatus for coercion; in other words, it becomes a *state*. When, on the one hand, a clearly defined exploited class is formed, and on the other hand so too is the state apparatus, then the Second Phase of historical development is over, and the Third Phase begins – the Phase of Early Antiquity, the first stage of class society.

If we assume that a mode of production is dependent, first, on the character of property relations, and, secondly, on the type of the combination between the labour force and the means of production, then we must regard antiquity not as one mode of production (certainly not a slave-owning mode of production), but as two clearly distinguished phases. Conventionally, we will call these the Third Phase (the Early, or Communal Antiquity), and the Fourth Phase (the Late, or Imperial Antiquity).

The transitional stage between the Primitive Communal, or Second Phase and the Ancient Communal, or Third Phase begins with the creation of big economies. They are organised either for the maintenance of the cult of the main community deity, or for the chief with his entourage. Such a chief is in the Russian scholarly tradition termed 'czar', i.e. emperor (from Latin *caesar*); but their power was by means imperial, and they rather resemble the early medieval kings (*kuningaz*); this term is actually usual in the Western scholarly literature. One might also call them 'princes'.

The big temple (priestly) or royal economies were kept going by the labour of men belonging to a separate, working class different from the class of freemen. The latter included both an upper stratum and the main mass of warriors – agriculturists or stock-rearers; they differed in prestige and in their position in the administrative and/or genealogical structures, but there was no social division between the two strata.

The exploited class differed in origins. It could have been composed of the conquered aboriginal population (as in Sparta or Thessaly), or of those original inhabitants of the land who had been allocated to the chief (king) or to the temple. The number of actual slaves was not great. Of offensive arms, a warrior had only a spear with a copper spearhead, a short dagger, sometimes a rather imperfect bow with arrows; of defensive armour he had only a copper cap; there were no horses. (In the earliest Israelite poem, 'The Song of Deborah', Judg. 5, 10, twelfth century BC, the nobility is called 'those that ride on white she-asses', but usually they also fought on foot.) Under such conditions it was practically impossible to capture prisoners-of-war and to keep them in captivity; therefore a prisoner of war was killed by striking the back of his head with a hatchet, and only women and adolescents were kept alive. Inside the patriarchal family the captive teenagers became its junior members, and the women became concubines. The majority of the conquered peaceful population became part of the exploited class, especially in the state sector; but, with the possible exception of some ancient states, e.g. the 'Kingdom of Sumer and Akkad' (the third Dynasty of Ur), they were allowed to have their own family life, and they were not saleable. I have suggested the term *helots* for this class, aiming at convenience and conciseness, although I am aware that traditionally this term is applied only to Sparta, where the helots had particular features which had no analogies elsewhere in history.

The formation of an exploited class means that surplus labour is made possible; this does not mean, however, that the entire governing class lives exclusively at the expense of the surplus labour of the exploited class. A considerable part of the freemen continue to participate in production. The existence of free peasants and artisans which at the same time constituted the army is a characteristic ('diagnostic') feature both of the Third Phase and of the Fourth (that of Imperial Antiquity).

During the Third Phase (that of the Early Antiquity) as well as during the Second Phase (that of the primitive communities), all mankind was in a condition of constant and mostly armed confrontation between social units. With the advent of copper arms the quarrels escalated into war. Hence a powerful defence became a necessity; fortified towns emerged which were the centres of *nomes* – the minimal administrative and state units. Using aerial photography and a mass study of pottery finds, R. M. Adams and N. J. Nissen were able to show that, in the case of Mesopotamia and the lower Diyalah valley during the fourth and early third millennium BC, very small inhabited areas on the plain gradually disappeared, and the population densely behind the city walls increased. Small cities become the centres of settlement of the population, the administration, of the craftsmen, and for the storage and distribution of produce. Each 'city' was, as a rule, the centre of a 'nome'.

The social stages beginning with early antiquity were called 'class society' by the Soviet scholars, and 'urban society' by the Western scholars. I still think that the division of the society into classes is a causal phenomenon, while the emergence of cities is one of its effects. Hence the Marxist term 'class society' may be retained. In any case, what we are dealing with here are civilisations.[1]

---

1. From Lat. *civix* 'citizen', *civilis* 'civil, pertaining to city', *civitas* 'civil community, city'. The Early Antiquity is an epoch which distinguished between 'citizens' and 'non-citizens' or, according to Aristotle, 'freemen' and 'slaves by nature'.

The first class society (the Third Phase, or Early Antiquity) did not develop uniformly; it has different paths of development which are mostly determined by ecology. In Western Asia, where it arose earlier that elsewhere, we can establish the following main paths.

The best example of one path is the earliest period in Sumer. Economically, the Sumerian society was subdivided into two sectors. One included large economies, owned by the temples and by the highest officials of the emerging state. During the first centuries of written history, these economies gradually ceased to depend on the bodies of community self-government. The second sector consisted of land where the free population took active part in the bodies of community self-government; inside the territorial communities this land was possessed by the extended family communes headed by their patriarchs. In the third or fourth generation the domestic community tended to divide, but the divided communities still regarded themselves as kin; they might have a common ancestor cult, customs of mutual help, etc.

Later the economies of the first sector became property of the state, while in those of the second (communal-private) sector the supreme property in the land continued to be vested in the territorial community but was in the possession of the family heads; practically such possession differed from actual property rights only in that land could be used and administered at will only by members of the territorial community in question (a community of neighbours, of villagers, later also of citizens).

The community members, i.e. freeborn members of the households in the communal-private sector, tilled the land, as a rule, themselves, or only with the help of their family members. However, between the households, also between kindred households, there existed inequalities in property status. This depended upon the social position of the heads of the households (some might be priests, elders, etc.), from good or bad luck, from the ability to make use of one's means, because movables, unlike house and field, were the private property of each separate family member. Some families of community members were in a condition to use the labour of others – on the basis of the custom of mutual help, or by giving produce to their less lucky fellow members on loan; sometimes there were slaves, on whom more below.

As to the people settled on the land which later became the state sector, they could possess land only conditionally: it was given to them for subsistence and as payment for services or work, and given individually, for the nuclear, not the extended family, which meant that the sons and grandsons served separately from their fathers and grandfathers. Many workers of the state sector did not receive land at all, but only rations. But at the same time, there were also such men among the state personnel that could, according to the standards of their time, be regarded as men of substance, who owned slaves, and could employ the labour of others. These were officials, military figures, and skilled artisans. They were apportioned a certain part of what was produced by the agricultural workers in the temple or government economy. Sometimes they could ascend fairly highly on the service ladder; it was from among them that the administrators were chiefly recruited; some of them, not being owners of private land, could actually manage the economies in the state sector. But among people belonging to the latter there also were slaves and especially slave girls, who could be bought and sold.

Thus the society which emerged in the third millennium BC along the lower reaches of the Euphrates was divided into estates.

One of them included the members of free communities, who had a part in the community property in land, and had the rights of communal self-government; originally, they also had the right to take part in the election of the reigning chief.

Another estate included the members of the personnel in the temple or the ruler's economy, who were not owners of the means of production and had possession of land only under the condition of service or labour, or had no land possessions at all but only rations. But some of them were administrators.

Then there were slaves, who, as it were, did not belong to any estate, since they could be treated as cattle. However, for the sake of convenience, we may regard them as still another specific estate lacking civil rights.

In this way society was subdivided – as perceived socio-psychologically by the ancients themselves.

Let us call the reader's particular attention to the slaves who not only lacked ownership of the means of production but were themselves owned by those who exploited them: as if they were living instruments for production. The exploitation of slaves was pursued more comprehensively than in any other Phase in the historical process. The productivity of slave labour in the Third Phase, with its very primitive working tools, was not appreciably different from that of a peasant who was a member of the community – provided the slave was under constant supervision. The advantages of slave labour were that the slave was not allowed a family, while a labouring member of the community had to provide for a family from his ration or from the harvest of his plot. The slave's master found it more expedient to increase the rate of exploitation instead of feeding a slave family. This was profitable; at every possible occasion, in all epochs, slave-owners tried to keep other exploited persons to the level of slaves as well. But slavery as an institution has been studied mainly as it appeared in antiquity. Hence in Marxist historiography the economics of the ancient epoch was called slaveholding, and the unfree persons of the Third and the Fourth Phases were often termed the 'slave class in the broad sense of the word', which is hardly acceptable. Slavery is not diagnostic for any given Phase of the historical process.

Actually, in Early Antiquity, the maximal, 'classical' exploitation of slaves was, as a rule, unfeasible. It was rather difficult for a warrior, with the weapons then at his disposal, to enslave a male prisoner-of-war. To enslave completely a member of one's own community was also impracticable, because he would have kinship and cultic ties to other members of the same community, and they would come to his aid. Thus, for a period for more than 1,000 years community members in the valley of the Lower Euphrates obtained a periodical liberation of their fellow-villagers enslaved for debts. Even when a foreigner was taken prisoner in battle, it was not so easy and even dangerous to force him to work unless his living conditions were tolerable.

In the private households of the community members, prisoners could not receive a special share of land, nor was it possible to guard the prisoners at field work. Therefore the only feasible form of slavery was the patriarchal one. This means that from the captives brought from the enemy territory one took into the home either young girls (who could bear children for the slave-owners), or boys of that age when they still could get accustomed to the new surroundings, and feel they belonged to the new family. The slave-girls and the slaves were charged with the most onerous work in the house itself (such as moulding pots, caring for the cattle, spinning and weaving, cooking food, grinding the grain between two stones – which was an especially laborious task, etc.). In the field, the slave-boys and girls were allocated accessory work together with the members of the family: driving the oxen, weeding, reaping, herding the sheep – but ploughing and sowing were not to be entrusted to them. The labour of the slaves turned out satis-factorily not only because they always were under their owner's supervision; it was also because they took part in a process of production in common with their owners; note also that the difference in living conditions between masters and slaves was insignificant: the master and mistress of the house also had frugal meals and poor clothing. A small household, whether on 'one's own' (i.e. commu-nity) land, or on public (i.e. temple or palace) land, did not need many slaves, and could even do without any.

Temple land needed many labourers, but it was impossible to employ whole bands of slaves for field work – they would need too many overseers. Note that such land lacked a separate free 'boss' family who might itself have taken care of the ploughing and sowing. Usually, only women had slave status, while male pris-oners-of-war and the children of the slave-girls had the same status as the rest of the working personnel of the big estates. This personnel may have consisted of young brothers in poor domestic communities, of invalids, old men, fugitives seeking sanctuary and protection either at the temple or in the household of a neighbouring chief; this could have been caused either by the sacking of their native town or the consequences of a catastrophic drought or flooding. It is not impossible that a community might not only have allocated land for the temples and the chiefs but at the same time obliged a portion of its members to work in the temple or palace economies. A young Assyriologist, Chirikov, has pointed out that even under the third Dynasty of Ur, which is considered to be a period of the max-imum development of helot labour in antiquity, the workers on temple land did not labour throughout the year, but that one team, after a period of work, was suc-ceeded by another. Thus, whether the labourers in the economies of the state sector received only a ration, or also a share of the land, and despite their exploitation by non-economic coercion and their lack of a stake in means of production, they were still not actual slaves.

They were not necessarily prisoners-of-war, perhaps often they were locals. They had their own movables, sometimes their own house, a family and perhaps even some cattle – not as property but in conditional possession. Since they seem not to have been allowed to leave the economy where they worked, they are often called serfs. But since they had no property in means of production, they differed from the medieval dependent peasants because their dependence more resembled slavery. Therefore, to escape misunderstanding, we will use the term applied in Greece to state slaves settled on the land: helots.

Helots, as we understand the term, are equivalent, on state property, to patriarchal slaves.

The rulers of nomes or city-states, supported by the staff of prosperous state economies which they had seized, could organise numerous armed troops independent of the council, the popular assembly, and other bodies of community self-government. This allowed the rulers, aided by the bureaucracy consisting of their personal adherents, to create a unique royal despotic power, i.e. not limited by any other legal bodies; this power could extend to the whole network of irrigation canals in Lower Mesopotamia, the land between the Tigris and the Euphrates rivers.

Correspondingly, in the state sector there appeared a unified royal economy which was based on the labour of helots and engulfed the temple economies. However, this particular way of economic development made it possible for some private economies (although poorly attested in the documents) to survive inside the communal sector. But note that the level of their involvement in community exchange was low.

Since agriculture, which was the economic mainstay of the society, is seasonal, the weaker households could not manage without regular credits in kind received from more notable and rich economies. This led to the development of usury (a real curse which infested most societies of the Third Phase), and to chronic stagnation in economic development.

Moreover, subsequent history showed that maintenance of the state sector by its own official huge economy, using large numbers of slave-type exploited persons, was unprofitable, not only in the Third Phase, but in any Phase: it demanded too much unproductive expenditure for administration and surveillance. Beginning with the middle of the second millennium BC, the state started a new system of direct taxation, or the imposition of tribute upon the entire population.

A tax is not necessarily a form of exploitation, if it is levied to finance activities needed for the society as a whole; but in the case under discussion the tax was imposed to confiscate the surplus produce from the dependent labouring class.

Nevertheless, a difference between the state sector and the private-and-communal sector still remained, in spite of the fact that both sectors had more or less similar private economies which employed helot or slave labour. They differed in the type of property relations involved: possession of state land does not presuppose property in that land, while possession of community land presupposes a share in the communal property.

The most important form of exchange in Early Antiquity was international trade (often covering considerable distances through intermediary links). This trade was carried on, at their own responsibility, either by state agents or by family communities specialising in exchange, their members not being employed by the state. At any rate, the ones as well as the others, were closely connected with the nome state; but it did not so much control their international activities as ensured its income from them. The redistribution of produce went on in the towns or townships, where the state administration was at work. Inside the city community, exchange relations were mainly in kind; distribution was centralised by the state, and the inner market was underdeveloped.

Both on the inner and on the external market exchange often took the form of inequivalent 'mutual help', or of an exchange of presents, either equivalent, or inequivalent ('potlatch').

This was one path of development in the Third Phase (that of Early Antiquity). It was characterised by the coexistence between two economic sectors: a state sector, and a community-organised private one, the first one having the leading role. This path of development was typical for the lowlands of the Euphrates and the neighbouring valleys of the rivers Karun and Kerkhe (the ancient Elam).

The emergence of major economies led to the need for accountancy, and to the creation of writing, which later spread to the other Western Asian civilisations.

In lands which did not yield the abundant crops typical of the alluvial silt in the great river valleys, class societies formed according to the same general laws of development, but in other ways. First, the attainment of that higher technological level which could ensure the creation of surplus produce in agriculture, here required considerably more time. Note that along with the introduction of cereal farming other factors usually played an important role as well. Thus, stock-rearing, viticulture, cultivation of olives, ore extraction, etc. made it possible for neighbouring countries to take part, through exchange, in the extraction of surplus produce in the agricultural regions. Secondly, there was no need here to create labour-consuming and extensive irrigation and meliorative systems. Correspondingly, the role of the temples and the priest-chief was considerably reduced, and the community-organised private sector was far more important than the state or temple one. It is to be noted, however, that because these societies reached the level of class civilisation at a later period, Lower Mesopotamia and Egypt had the opportunity to exert a very strong influence, directed, among other objectives, specifically towards the strengthening of the authority of the local temples and of the royal power. The most ancient Western Asiatic societies which developed along the described path show very diverse signs of the interrelation between the state sector and community-and-private one: sometimes the one is stronger and sometimes the other. Moreover, where there did not exist extensive and manifold irrigation systems which could profitably be unified, there did not emerge monolithic despotic kingdoms, such as the kingdom on the Nile and the somewhat less stable kingdoms of Mesopotamia. Here the 'empires' (the Achaean, the Hittite, the Mitannian, the Middle Assyrian, the Egyptian 'empire' in Syria during the New Kingdom) were rather something like military coalitions, where the weaker urban or 'nome' states were obliged to pay tribute and render military assistance to the stronger central state. To this way of development belonged all the societies of the third and more especially the second millennium BC emerging in Asia Minor and in the countries gravitating towards the Mediterranean Sea (thus not including Lower Mesopotamia and the lowland of the Karun and the Kerkhe), and also the societies around the Aegean Sea in the Eastern Mediterranean region. In the beginning of the first millennium BC, the diverse societies of Western Asia and Asia Minor, of the mountainous parts of Western Asia, of Greece, and possibly Italy (Etruria and other minor states of Italy, including Rome) seem still to have belonged to the first type. The main part of the population in the Third Phase states (Early Antiquity) were direct descendents of the population as it existed in the Second Phase. Hence the socio-psychological proximity to primitive communal structures. The ideology of royal power slowly developed, and was based on the genealogical system of the communal pantheons and fertility cults. Little is known of the socio-psychological life of the exploited class, but we have no reason so suppose it stood in any opposition to the ideas inherited from the primitive communal past.

Contemporaneously with the main paths of development typical of the Near East during the Third Phase of the historical process, from *c.* 3000 BC emerged a specific Egyptian way of development. Upper Egypt is a narrow fertile strip along a single watercourse, the Nile; only in Lower Egypt is the Nile divided into a fan of channels, the Delta. It seems that just because the nomes of Upper Egypt adjoined each other, forming a continuous chain, squeezed in between the Nile and the rocky precipices on the border of the desert, there was no opportunity to organise many-sided political groupings, such as could, by making use of the rivalry and mutual enmity of the neighbours, warrant a sufficient independence to certain nomes having each its own self-government. Here collisions between the nomes inevitably led to their unification 'along the chain' under the dominion of the strongest, and sometimes to the complete destruction of any unruly neighbour. Therefore, already by the earliest period kings appear in Upper Egypt who are endowed with what amounts to despotic power over an individual nome and its neighbours, and later over the entire country. Later, Lower Egypt was also subdued. Most probably, a community-and-private sector may at first have existed in Egypt as well, parallel to the existence of a state sector (which included temple and royal lands, possibly also the 'houses' of the nobility); but if it had existed, it was completely absorbed at an early stage by the state sector. This does not mean that separate, economically autonomous economies did not emerge inside the state sector. Private slave-owning households developed on state land, and these private economies could draw labour force (helots) from the state funds, apart from their own private slaves. The working contingent had the duty to fulfil a certain task for the household to which it was allocated; they had the right to dispose of what was produced over and above the appointed task. Characteristic of Egypt was the strong development of the funerary cult; for the kings, especially during the Old Kingdom, there were erected giant funerary pyramids; the bodies of the noblemen were mummified in order to ensure them eternal life. The period of the Middle Kingdom (from *c.* 2000 BC) witnessed the elaboration of a system where the main mass of the labouring population was regarded as 'royal *ḥamw*'.[2] All of them, after reaching manhood, were allocated for life to different trades (including those of agriculturists and of different artisans, but also the trade of a warrior). Then they were distributed between the royal and temple economies; but the 'private' economies of the nobility (which mainly consisted of the administration and the upper priesthood),[3] also got labourers from among the *ḥamw*.

Apart from the *ḥamw* there existed also slaves proper, the *baku*; but their role in production was secondary.

This system experienced certain changes during the New and Late Kingdoms, the Hellenistic and the Roman period, but the principle of administering all the producing economies from a state centre remained. The introduction of iron implements and of more developed arms brought no change to the organisational principles. Therefore, although Egyptian history bore witness to certain changes in societal forms, on the whole it did not show real social progress. From time to time the bureaucratic system of administration brought about complete chaos (these are called Intermediate periods; such a period continued for 200–300 years between the Old and the Middle Kingdom, somewhat less between the Middle and the New, the New and the Late Kingdom, etc.) These chaotic periods are not what we call phase transitions, because the Egyptian way of development can with good reason be called a *cul-de-sac*. Such historical *cul-de-sacs* can also be observed at the later stages of human development, and not only in Egypt.

The difference between the Egyptian way of social evolution in antiquity, and the other ways of development, has also left its mark on the socio-psychological development of the Egyptian society. The Egyptian universe inverted the concept of the rest of mankind (the sky in Egypt is a female principle, the earth a male); and the fertility cult typical of the whole Third Phase acquired the form of a cult of death and of a life in death.

2. O. D. Berley, *Trudovoe naselenie Yegipta v epokhu Srednego tsarstva* [The Working Population in Middle Kingdom Egypt], Moscow, 1972. The word *ḥamw-* in the Common Afrasian proto-language denoted 'kinsman-by-marriage', or 'indirect kinsman'.

3. Analogous but not quite so developed was the system of exploiting labour in the Hittite Kingdom. Cf. the institute of *be* in Japan.

In the fifteenth century BC the pharaoh Ikhnaton attempted a religious reform, introducing a doctrine of a universal solar, supreme (and, as a matter of principle, unique) deity. This reform brought about a certain liberation in figurative art, which previously (and subsequently) developed within strict canonical limits. To Ikhnaton's time belongs the work of Djehutimes, a sculptor of genius. But Ikhnaton's reform did not survive him: from the socio-psychological point of view it did not promise anything positive.

On a world scale (inside the limits of the class societies), the third and second millennia BC were the period of social relations typical of Early Antiquity. But relations in production characteristic of the Third historical Phase did not necessarily originate inside the chronological boundaries of the classical Orient. Social development of the same type can also be observed much later in a number of regions of the Earth; in the tropical, mountainous and foothill landscapes this type may survive and even arise and re-arise as late as in the second half of the second millennium AD.

It is difficult to classify in detail, as belonging to specific 'ways of development', all societies which typologically belonged to communal antiquity (the Third Phase), except for those characterised above. However, we may note that to this Phase also belonged the following societies: in China, the state of Yin and all the following states preceding the Ch'in empire, i.e. up to the third century BC; in Japan, probably all the earliest states including the period of Nara (third to fourth centuries AD); in Europe, first of all, the Creto-Mycenean civilisation in the second millennium BC (and the Etruscan civilisation in the first millennium BC); but also many states of North and Eastern Europe which existed much later but belonged typologically to Early Antiquity: thus the Anglo-Saxon states until the eleventh century AD, the Scandinavian and Slavonic states until the twelfth century AD.[4] In Africa, typologically the states probably belonging to Early Antiquity were Malinke and Songai in the seventh to fifteenth centuries AD, the Hausa states (from the tenth to the eleventh centuries AD) and the states Congo, Bunyoro and Buganda (from the eighteenth century AD) et al.; in America, the civilisation of the Andes (the Incas),[5] and, with some reservation, perhaps the Mayan and the Aztec cultures.

---

4. However (because these north-eastern Ancient type states existed in an environment of Early Medieval states), inside them, beside obvious features of Early Antiquity (as, e.g. the presence of a class of free peasant warriors), were also in evidence typical Early Medieval features (thus, acceptance, at first rather nominally, of a dogmatic Christian ideology; beginning of exploitation of a part of the peasantry). On the border between chiefdoms and Early Antiquity (and also in an Early Medieval environment with all that this involved) may be placed the societies of Northern Caucasus before their conquest by Russia. These societies skipped some stages in their development, e.g. the Late Antiquity, and even – in the case of Norway, Iceland and Northern Caucasus – also the Late Middle Ages.

5. I regard the aboriginal civilisation in the Andes as belonging to the Third Phase (Early Antiquity), proceeding from the information supplied by the Inca Garcilaso de la Vega, *Comentarios reales ... de los Yncas*; part two, *Historia general del Perú*, 1608–1617. Russian translation, Leningrad 1974, part V, chs. 1–2. Some early American and African states lacked a written language.

All three or perhaps just the first two may be regarded as belonging to the Phase transition.

A considerable part of the Third Phase societies was surrounded by a mighty tribal (primitive communal) sphere, which finally grew in military power, nearly equalling that of the existing states. The history of this elemental power should by no means be neglected. But I would like to stress the fact that what I have in view has nothing to do with the mythical mass migrations of the Indo-European speaking tribes. I have already had the occasion to point out that the spread of Indo-European languages, connected or not with a definite culture, did not resemble the mass nomadic movements of the Huns or the Mongols. (Note that these latter belonged actually to the Fifth Phase, and, besides, did not bring about a spread of the language of the Huns or Mongols to the conquered territory.) I would like to repeat that the 'movements' of the population in Eurasia in the Second Phase were mainly a process of Indo-Europeanisation of the local tribes, which usually adopted the Primitive Communal structure instead of the former Early Primitive structures of the First Phase. Thus the Indo-European languages spread without migration by the tribes who spoke them.

In any case, movements of Indo-European speaking tribes have nothing to do with the fall of some ancient civilisations which we are going to discuss. The fact is that during certain historical epochs there are some striking cases in which the historical process comes to a seeming standstill, and then revives at certain critical points. What I have in view are the Indus and the Creto-Mycenean civilisations in Early Antiquity.

The states of the Indus culture probably had a Dravidic-speaking population. Their decline should probably be ascribed to a crisis in their bureaucratic structure which brought about economic chaos. The same phenomenon can be observed in Sumer at the fall of the 'Kingdom of Sumer and Akkad' (the third Dynasty of Ur) about 2000 BC; in Egypt at the end of the Old Kingdom about 2200 BC, and possibly in the Hittite Kingdom in the thirteenth century BC (the attacks by the 'Peoples of Sea' were responsible only for the culmination of a crisis which was due anyway). The Indus civilisation fell apart after the eighteenth century BC; only its remnants survived to the fifteenth to thirteenth centuries and perhaps later (Lothal, Kalibangan). The Creto-Mycenean civilisation fell apart towards the thirteenth century BC. The population of the states of this civilisation was partly aboriginal, partly Greek (Achaean); at present it is difficult to establish the role, in its fall, of some internal processes, or of invasions of new tribes, or of natural processes. Early in the fifteenth century BC a giant earthquake destroyed one of the important centres of Creto-Mycenean civilisation – the island of Thera (or Santorin), which was partly submerged in the sea;[6] the catastrophe caused irreparable damage to Crete, where the coastal plains were flooded, and the fields covered by hot ashes.

---

6.   This earthquake may have accounted for the origin of the legend about Atlantis.

It took about 150 years for Southern Mesopotamia to recover from the crisis, and a longer period for Egypt. But the fall of the Hittite, the Indus and the Creto-Mycenean civilisations opened the way to incursions into their former territories of a new primitive communal population which had nothing to do with their destruction.

In the case of the Hittite Kingdom the newcomers were the Proto-Armenians (the Mushki) who traversed the territory of Asia Minor during the twelfth century BC, and later the Phrygians in the eighth(?) century BC (both peoples came from the Balkans);[7] in the case of the Indus civilisation these were the Aryas whose appearance in Northern India is dated to around the fifteenth to twelfth centuries BC; in the case of the Creto-Mycenean civilisation, these were the Ionian, Dorian and Aeolian Greeks who moved southwards from their more northern original home between the thirteen and the eleventh centuries BC.

As is apparent from the social and legal terminology common – like some of the social institutions – specifically to Indo-Aryans and to ancient Eastern Iranians, they had already at the time of their common sojourn in their Central Asia homeland reached the comparatively high level of development typical of chiefdoms. It is difficult to judge the level of development of the Ionians and the Dorians at the period prior to their appearance in what is now called Greece. At all events, in both cases the population of India and of Greece entered, in this their new place of sojourn, the Phase transition from the Second (Primitive Communal) to the Third Phase (Early Antiquity). The Vedas (belonging to the early first millennium BC) draw a somewhat one-sided picture. The Homeric poems that probably received their final form in the eighth or seventh centuries BC, draw a rather realistic picture

7. The movement of Proto-Armenians into the Armenian Highland, and of Phrygians and some other Balkanic peoples into Asia Minor should not be regarded in terms of annihilation or the ousting of the other inhabitants of these regions, Hittites and Urartians. These remained in the same region but changed their languages for new ones. The languages of the newcomers adapted certain features of the substratum languages. Thus, Armenian, apart from borrowing a number of Hurro-Urartian words connected with local natural and social features to which the newly formed Armenian nation had adapted itself, lost the Indo-European differentiation between long and short vowels, and Indo-European tones, instead, from the substratum it adopted a fixed stress on the penultimate syllable; this again led to the loss of monosyllabic suffixed nominal and verbal flexions, or these were replaced by what originally were disyllabic flexions. Cf. I. M. Diakonoff, 'Hurro-Urartian Borrowings in Old Armenian', *Journal of the American Oriental Society*, 105 (1985), 597–603. Only after having assimilated the Urartians did the Proto-Armenians constitute the present Armenian people. The origin of Georgian is still a matter of conjecture, but it is quite probable that Georgian is collaterally akin to Indo-European, and it is not impossible that the first speakers of Proto-Georgian may have also descended from the men of the Çatal-Hüyük culture. The North Caucasian languages, including the languages Hattic, Hurrian and Urartian attested already in the antiquity, may belong to an ancient linguistic system originally spread through an area from Eastern Europe to the Caucasus and Central Asia during a period *c.* 10,000–8,000 BC.

The most obvious members of this linguistic system are the Western and the Eastern (not the Central) Caucasian languages, some linguists suppose that these are akin to the languages of the Yenisey valley, Tibet, and China.

of a society which had existed for three or four generations before that; thus they give us perhaps the most graphic picture of the chiefdoms.

Note that the new Early Antiquity which was formed in post-Homeric Greece differed very considerably from the Early Antiquity which before that had existed in the Near East. There the emergence of a state sector in the Third Phase was to a considerable degree called forth by the fact that the agriculture was based on an irrigation system, and the size of the typical economies was big. However, that was not the only reason for the emergence of a state sector: it was also the leading sector in the Hittite Kingdom, on Crete and in Mycenean Greece where irrigation did not play a major role. But all these civilisations perished just because the state sector was ineffective, and hence it was this sector which was most totally destroyed. In the next Phase, the state sector continued to play a major role only in a few regions, such as Sparta and partially Thessaly. In most of the Greek communities, which grew into city-states (*poleis*) much later that the fall of Mycenean Greece, a state sector did not, in any practical sense, emerge at all; there was a communal-and-private sector where, over time, the private households and artisan's workshops became dominant. The lack of a state sector induced the lack or abolition of royal power (not only of absolute power but even of a limited royal power), and the mass introduction of republican institutions in the Greek states.

The lack of big state economies and the mostly republican character of the state, where the entire free population could be politically active, allowed the polis world to free itself from the main burden of the Third Phase, namely usury. The system of crediting was strictly limited to trade (thus by Solon in Athens, 594 BC). This had a tremendous impact on social psychology. It was here that the notion of 'liberty' (*eleuthería*) was first evolved, meaning a complete independence of the individual; all forms of dependence, including dependence on royal power (instead of the self-government inside a city community, typical of Greece) were regarded as 'slavery' (*doulosýnē*). The situation was also favourable for the development of the Greek *poleis* because, first, they were already entering in the Iron Age, secondly, because they were in contact with the highly developed class civilisations, as well as with the sea-shore chiefdoms, which were involved in systematic trade. In the East, trade was hampered by constant difficulties created by the royal power of the bigger kingdoms (on which, see below); but, in the Mediterranean there were no obstacles to trade and private enrichment.

The mythology as well as the local character of the cults and a certain development of the ethical principles in religion were inherited by the Greeks from primitive communal tribes (the Second historical Phase). However, over time, mythology moved into the realm of fairy-tale, and scientific philosophy began to appear. At the beginning, like mythology, it used a metaphorical language, but then it began to evolve its own terminology, and – what was of cardinal importance for the further development of man – a scientific logic (Aristotle). Ethics were also developed as part of philosophy (Socrates). Although the ancient Greek state belongs, according to our classification, to the Third Phase (typical of which are small principalities), nevertheless the polis world was a society of quite a special type; its very peculiarity was conducive to its being able to influence the whole process of human history. Thus, in this case, the historical development led to the formation of a non-trivial branch.

In the first millennium BC the states belonging to the Third Phase were concentrated in the Eastern hemisphere. Their belt stretched from Spain (Tartessus) and the Mediterranean littorals (Phoenician and Greek colonies, the republics of the mainland and insular Greece and the Ionian states of Asia Minor, the Etruscan and other towns in Italy, the Philistine towns in Palestine), and over the entire territory of the Near East: a series of states in the Eastern Mediterranean and Asia Minor (Phrygia, later Lydia), the Armenian highland (Urartu), Mesopotamia (including Assyria), and then branching off to the Nile valley (Egypt and Nubia). Further on there were isolated early states or chiefdoms in Iran and in Middle Asia,[8] and the newly emerging states of the Early Antiquity type in India. The broad stretch of lands between the Black Sea and the Indian Ocean north-east of the described zone had not yet reached the stage of Early Antiquity. A second isolated region where the Early Antiquity had been reached lay in China, mainly in the valley of the Yellow River, later also on neighbouring territories. These were the states of Yin (Shang) with the typical ritual of killing off the mass of men taken as prisoners-of-war (fourteenth to twelfth centuries BC), then the state of Western Chou (twelfth to eighth centuries BC) and a whole conglomeration of Third Phase states in the eighth to fifth centuries BC. The economic base of these Chinese states was agriculture (only partly using irrigation) – the crops were sorghum, pennisetum and foxtail millet, and only secondarily barley and wheat; and stock-rearing – cattle, sheep, goats and pigs. The creation of the Chinese civilisation lagged behind those of Egypt and the Near East for about 1,500 years, which is not too long a period from the point of view of human history as a whole. Japan lagged still further behind.

The Phase of Early Antiquity in Japan is very poorly represented in our sources. It is certain, however, that the Bronze Age which signals that this Phase had begun, started not earlier than the second to third centuries AD. According to Chinese chronicles, as late as the sixth century the Japanese archipelago housed five separate states. Their unification by one 'queen' (a priestess?) may belong to the realm of legend.

8. Cultures preceding those which we may term civilisations, originating in the south of the Central Asiatic steppe zone, in the river zone of south-western Afghanistan, and in some cultural nuclei of Iran, shared the fate of the Creto-Mycenian and the Indian civilisations, changing their languages for that of the Indo-European newcomers, for reasons still unclear to us. (Probably, simply because the Indo-European newcomers, being better fed, were more numerous than the aboriginals.) Only the Elamite civilisation in south-western Iran, mainly in the valley of the Karun and Kerkhe rivers, did develop independently along with the neighbouring Mesopotamian civilisation.

Between the third and the eighth centuries there was a migration of new tribes from the Korean peninsula. In the sixth to seventh centuries there emerged a rather loose federation headed by a *tennō* (conventionally translated as 'emperor'); the federation included two centres of Japanese civilisation, Idzuma and Yamato, and a strip of the Korean shore, Mimana. From the fourth century, a single kingdom of Yamato was recognised, but the real power continued to belong to the local rulers, the heads of noble clans. Full-fledged members of the clans, including both the nobility and the rank-and-file free agriculturists, owned land and means of production as their property under the condition of being actual members of the community. Areas requiring irrigation, which were used for growing rice, were the property of the community. Non-members of the clan community, the *be*, were enlisted into professional organisations connected with the clans. The *be* had no share in means of production, they worked for the *tennō* and for the clan nobility, but some of them – namely the persons who headed the professional organisations – were, in fact, officials; a few of the *be* hold important offices at the court of the *tennō*.

The Japanese religion of the period is conventionally called 'early Shintoism'; but actually it was not an '-ism' of any kind; it was not a strictly formulated dogmatic religion; rather it was a series of local cults with a mythological interpretation of the world, characteristic of Early Antiquity in general. During the collective work on the rice fields the typical characteristic traits of Japanese mentality (as it also appeared in later epochs) gradually developed – a feeling of collectivism with features of conformism, co-ordination in the activities, and diligence.

From the sixth century, the Japanese lost Mimana; beginning with the seventh century Korea fell under the overlordship of China, and a migration of the Chinese to the islands started. To this period belong the first close cultural ties of Japan and China, and the influence of Chinese medieval ideologies on Japan, especially of Buddhism and Confucianism. Among the immigrants, there were a number of people who could read and write; at this period the Japanese adopted (with considerable difficulties) the Chinese hieroglyphic system to express their own language.

To all appearances, the Japanese society of this period should be classed as belonging to the Phase of Early Antiquity.

Summing up, we may note that the emergence of the Third Phase states stood in connection with a leap in the development of productive forces: production had reached a level at which surplus could be created, which was sufficient for the upkeep and servicing of a ruling class, the state and religious institutions. Once having emerged, this 'superstructure' has a tendency towards development and enlargement, which needs a further growth of the surplus produce. In the Second Phase, and especially in the beginning of the Third Phase, it actually grew incommensurably to what happened in the First Phase (Primitive), and we observe an extensive resettlement of the population, and growing numbers of new settlements over a greater territory. Can this be regarded as progress in the sense of more common good for more people? Surely not. This was an epoch of the growth of goods for a minority, and of growing impoverishment for the majority. At any rate, the growth of goods brought about constant (yearly) wars, which seems to have been the main stimulus for civilisation, if we understand it in the sense of creation of fortified towns as centres for the governing of the states, for handicrafts, and for the accumulation of food stores.

4   Fourth Phase (Imperial Antiquity)

The crisis of the societies of the Third Phase was induced by the fact that in each of these societies the growth of the surplus produce, began after civilisation's first brilliant success, to slow down and even come to a halt.

The productivity of labour had grown considerably during the Third Phase. This was connected with the introduction of irrigation in agriculture, but also with new achievements in the field of handicrafts: smelting of copper and later iron ore, elaboration of the technology of bronze, introduction of the plough, the potter's wheel, the weaver's loom, digging of irrigation canal systems, the invention of the first water-raising constructions. But later the productivity did not grow, and sometimes it slowed down. Thus, in Mesopotamian agriculture, because of the impoverishing and salinisation of the soil, which was the result of injudicious irrigation, the more valuable cultures (e.g. wheat) were ousted by the less valuable (e.g. barley). The growth of the ratio of exploitation has its natural limits: a certain improvement in hand-tools could not bring about any considerable growth in the output of manual labour.

Finally, the last reserve of the quantitative growth of the produce – natural population growth – was also being exhausted. During the Second (Primitive Communal) and the Third Phase (that of Early Antiquity), the growth of the population was considerable compared with the First (or Primitive proper) Phase, and we can observe an increase in inhabited places. But with the beginning of urbanisation we encounter the general law of all progress: one has to pay for it, and the cost begins finally to be higher than the benefit. The extreme congestion of the town population, in the absence of any kind of social hygiene, led to frequent epidemics and a high child mortality rate. The rate of survival under the conditions of primitive and early ancient society seems not to have exceeded, even outside the city walls, the average number of two or three children per one woman able to bear children, i.e. it was more or less sufficient for maintaining the existing population. But we must also keep in mind that wars were waged every year, and in some regions this could have catastrophic results (thus, towards the end of the second millennium BC the Canaanite civilisation in Palestine was virtually annihilated because of the merciless yearly devastation of the country by the Egyptian army; this led to a new settlement of Israelite tribes coming from the desert and steppe zone, and living in the Second Phase of historical development).

The states had to look for supplementary sources from which to extort produce.

Until the beginning of the first millennium BC there existed only three types of state: small 'nome' princedoms; unstable conglomerations of states, where the weaker paid a tribute to the central more strong state, and when required, sent military aid to it; finally, comparatively big kingdoms which united a whole river basin. The only more or less stable state of this type was Egypt (but periodically it fell apart as the result of a period of hyper-bureaucratisation of the system of requisition and redistribution of the produce). The general crisis of the societies of the Third Phase led to the need for drastic changes.

One of the methods of attracting resources from abroad was non-equivalent exchange: trade, of course, does not create produce, but it redistributes it, and one might try to redistribute it in such a way as to augment the income of the ruling class in the strongest states. In Early Antiquity there did not exist a constant and regularly active international market; hence the merchants bringing commodities which were especially needed in the agricultural societies, but were produced abroad, could protect fabulous profits. Most households (also the big economies) worked seasonally, and hence could not do without credit, but the credit took the form of usury. This could not bring about progress.

Some attempts were made to trade through the state administration. This method proved to be unprofitable: outside the country no control over the traders was possible, so that business abroad simply helped to organise superprofit; in the country itself control was ineffective because the administration was bureaucratic to the highest degree.

One might entrust international trade to private persons (which actually happened here and there during Early Antiquity), and to limit the role of the state to exacting a tax or tribute from it by the kings. This meant that the success or failure of international trade would depend upon the prudence or the greed of the princes, through whose territory the trade expeditions passed. But since at the heart of the crisis lay a feeling that the amount confiscated from the traders by the state was insufficient, sooner or later greed had to win. When the merchants began to be plundered too heavily, or the kings started robbing their trans-shipment points (as the Assyrian kings used to do), the merchants simply stopped trading (bringing the economies of the trading states to a state of decay or collapse), or they changed the trade routes to avoid the stronger kingdoms – from the Euphrates valley to Syria, from Syria to the island parts of Phoenicia, then to Carthage, and to the Greek *polis* world.

Now the task of the state became to raise the amount of produce exacted from resources abroad without recurring to trade, and this was what brought about the general emergence of empires. When they appear, we are already in a new historical Phase, the Fourth Phase, that of Imperial Antiquity. The passing to a new stage was accompanied by changes in technology (first of all, in the military field), in the structure of the state, and also in social psychology. There was no revolution between the two Phases, but there were conquests on a grand scale, which radically changed the structure of the societies in question; often these changes were brought about by outstanding leaders.

Such grandiose conquests became possible because of a very considerable technological leap, namely, from the Bronze to the Iron Age.

Iron is more difficult to smelt from ore than copper, and its moulding qualities are lower. Moreover, iron rusts more easily under the influence of air. Therefore, the technology of the production of iron was underdeveloped in Early Antiquity; we know only occasional iron objects dating from this epoch – mostly ornamental. In the second millennium BC the tribes of north-eastern Asia Minor had a monopoly in the production of iron, and the Hittite kings jealously retained this profitable monopoly.

After the fall of the Hittites around the beginning of the second millennium BC the export of iron ore was unimpeded; an 'Iron Road' emerged – from the deposits of that metal in north-eastern Asia Minor to the Greek cities on the south littoral of the Black Sea; and along the valley of the Euphrates to the Near East. But the secret of the extraction of metal from iron ore was soon discovered in other countries as well; it became known that iron ores are widely present over the surface of the earth. The ninth to seventh centuries BC saw the invention of the production of malleable iron with carbon additions which could be tempered into a sort of 'steel'.[1]

Only with the beginning of the mass production of steel can we declare the advent of the Iron Age. Steel tools made it possible to perfect the tilling of the soil, the clearing of forests, the construction of irrigation canals in hard soil, creating elaborate irrigation machinery; they revolutionised the handicrafts of the smith, the joiner, the shipbuilder and especially the armourer.

Instead of daggers, small axes and light spears, the infantry troops were now armed with big swords. Helmets now covered the cheeks, chin and neck, there was a complete body armour, steel leggings, steeled shields, more sophisticated bows and arrows. No longer was it possible for a man, taken prisoner and enslaved, to become, once he got a spade or a mattock, dangerous to his armed guard. Slavery was now much more common. Conquests became more vast and more durable.

Shipbuilding helped the Phoenicians and the Greeks to found maritime colonies, and facilitated sea warfare. Domesticated horses, first trained to follow the herd and for military use in Eastern Europe and behind the Urals, could now be found throughout the civilised countries, where first chariots and later cavalry were introduced. (Note that horses were not used as working animals, because horse-shoes were invented considerably later.)

The centres of emerging empires were not those regions that had been most developed in the preceding periods but those that were strategically most favourably situated, and had access to the roads which connected new production areas.

The first such region became Assyria on the Tigris.

---

1. The ancient carbonaceous iron we conventionally term steel was, of course, very different from modern steel.

Or, to be more exact, the first claims of being a 'world empire' in the first millennium BC were made by three countries in the Near East: Urartu, Elam and Assyria. Urartu had some success, incorporating all of the Armenian highland (Eastern Anatolia) and part of Transcaucasia. A hallmark of a new Phase of history was in this case the crowning of the local genealogical pantheons with the unique cult of the god Haldi common to the whole state. His temples, with the adjoined cattle-rearing economies (which ensured the offerings), were founded in every conquered valley – something that had no parallel in other early states.

Urartu soon fell, under the influence of different outside forces. Of Elam we know very little. But we know quite a lot about Assyria, which actually was the first 'world empire' encompassing, at its height, most of the civilised world of the epoch. In order to understand how it arose we should take into account the following.[2]

If from the point of view of the ruling class in an arising empire, the important thing was the greatest amount of appropriated produce, what actually mattered was ensuring reproduction on a larger scale, which is the only way to develop productive forces. But reproduction on an enlarged scale requires a certain stable ratio between the production of means of production and the production of consumer goods. All regions involved in the ancient civilisations, as well as the neighbouring ones, can be regarded from the point of view of their role in the division of labour between societies. The main agricultural countries produced mainly consumer goods (grain, textiles, etc.), while the mountainous and steppe countries mainly produced the means of production (metal, draught and pack animals, leather, etc.). The population of the agricultural regions of that time consumed very little meat; as to grain, wool and textiles, it could provide that on its own. For building purposes local clay and reeds were used.

For the regular functioning of the expanding social reproduction on the scale of whole major regions of the ancient civilisations, those of the first and the second type (or 'subdivision') had to be securely united by force. That exactly was the function of the empires. An empire at this stage would be a rather unstable organisation – the centrifugal forces were too strong; but it responded to a certain constant need, and in the place of a destroyed empire a new one emerged without fail. The first of these empires was the Neo-Assyrian which included all the Near East (Vorderasien), except Urartu and Asia Minor (ninth to seventh centuries BC); and later the Persian Achaemenian Empire founded by Cyrus; it already embraced all the territories from the Aegean Sea to the valley of the Indus, and from Egypt to as far as the Amu-Darya (Oxus) and even the Syr-Darya (Jaxartes, sixth to fourth centuries BC); later emerged the Hellenistic empires, beginning with Alexander of Macedon. To the same general type belonged the Mauryan empire in India (under the kings Chandragupta and Ashoka et al., fourth to second centuries BC), the

2. The following ideas have been first formulated by N. B. Jankowska.

empire of Ch'in (from the reforms of Shang Yang to the terroristic rule of the emperor Ch'in Shih Huang Ti, fourth to third centuries BC) and the dynasty of Former Han which succeeded it (founded by the emperor Liu Pang; duration from the third to the first century BC). Most of these empires were founded by outstanding leaders, striking personalities, although their individualities differed considerably; from blood-thirsty tyrants such as Ch'in Shih Huang Ti to patrons of sciences and culture such as Alexander and men who could be tolerant even having a cult of their own, such as Asoka. Their historical role was cruel in all cases and, in principle, rather similar.

An original and historically most important phenomenon was the Early Roman empire (first century BC to the third century AD); the late Roman Empire (third to fourth centuries AD) is a transitional stage to the next Phase of the historical process.

The economic sense of the emergency and the existence of ancient empires was, as have already been seen, constituted in the following terms. For a society, which at the end of the Bronze Age was in a state of prolonged stagnation, to make some headway against the everlasting chain of risings, changes, downfalls and further risings of minor states it was necessary to ensure a larger scale reproduction (without which no development of productive forces is possible) – and thus to reach a certain stable relation between regions producing consumer goods in plenty, and the means of production.[3]

In the mountainous regions the conditions for the development of agriculture were less favourable than in the regions of civilised river valleys. But at the same time, their specialisation in mining made them independent, for one thing, of the necessity of periodical investments, e.g. into grain for sowing, and also of draught animals whether or not pastures and forage were available for them. While any agricultural economy has to go through seasonal breaks in the production cycle (while unfavourable climatic conditions, like the long spell of droughts which started in the second millennium BC, could play havoc with agricultural cycles or even stop them for a long time), in the mining industry seasons play no role, and the only necessary expenditures are in the periodical renewal of the instruments of labour and the labour force.

In our time it would seem natural to seek to unify these regions in an organised international trade. However, between the second and the first millennium BC this was impossible. The sources of raw materials situated in the mountain regions ceased to be easily accessible, because the zones between them and the main producers of food (such as Egypt and Mesopotamia) were under the control of early but rather strong states. Since the kings were inclined to capture the trade routes

---

3. Although, from the point of view of the stock-breeders themselves, production of cattle is production of food for consumption (of meat), note that in the agricultural regions of the antiquity meat was mainly consumed during temple and other feasts. The stock-breeders produced draught animals and important raw material for handicrafts, while the agricultural regions had grain, wool, flax and cotton in abundance (the list of products differing from region to region).

and the trade centres by force, this proved a significant drawback in the development of international trade. At the same time the inner development of the regions producing mineral raw materials and timber was such that they were able to provide themselves sufficiently with food and textiles; raw material which formerly was exported for cheap prices could now be processed locally.

The mutual theft could not lead to reproduction on a larger scale all through the civilised world. A way out of the impasse was (as noted above) a compulsory forcible unification of the 'subdivisions' of socially important production, i.e. both the regions producing means of production, and those producing commodity goods. The empires, which from now on steadily replaced one another on the whole territory of the ancient world, had to solve this problem. During this period inner exchange in the empire began to play a most important role. This is reflected in the general phenomenon of the introduction of money (coins). Formerly, silver fragments had played an economic role mainly as a measure of value; only rarely were they used as means of payment. Now began an epoch not only of commodity exchange but of money exchange. Coins were invented in Lydia (Asia Minor) and became current in the Achaemenian Empire at the end of the sixth century BC, and nearly simultaneously in China (in the Chan Kuo period, i.e. even before the imperial age).[4]

There is a regularity also in the technological level corresponding to the Phase of Imperial Antiquity. Note the correlation between the dates of the emergence of empires and the dates of the mass introduction of iron (we do not take into account here the Mediterranean region which had a specific development):

	Mass introduction of iron	Introduction of an imperial state
Near East	eleventh to ninth centuries BC	ninth to eighth centuries BC (Assyria)
India	seventh to sixth centuries BC	fourth century BC (Maurya)
Egypt	sixth to fifth centuries BC	fourth to third centuries BC (The Ptolemies)[5]
China	fifth to third centuries BC	third century BC (Ch'in)
Japan	sixth century AD	seventh to eighth centuries AD (Nara)

The intervening 200 years correspond to the Phase transition from the Third Phase to the Fourth Phase.

Let us emphasise once more that the moving force was not the advent of the Iron Age in itself but, first, the necessary unification of the regions producing means of production with the regions producing consumer goods, and secondly, the introduction of early steel not only in the handicrafts but above all in the military field (steel swords, steel chain and plate armour, helmets).

4. However, in China coins were at first only a measure of value, only in the Imperial period they became payment media in circulation.
5. The dynasty of the Ptolemies was the first of the Egyptian dynasties in the first millennium BC, whose power was felt far beyond the limits of the Nile Valley.

The empires, or so-called 'world powers', differed essentially from the more or less important conglomerations of princedoms which had appeared in Early Antiquity. For one thing, the empires united by force territories which differed in their economics and their economic needs, in their geographical conditions, and their cultural traditions. Secondly, if the big state conglomerations of the earlier Phase did not, on the whole, disrupt the traditional government structure in the different conquered countries, the empires, on the contrary, were subdivided into new uniform administrative units (districts, satrapies, provinces and the like). The state as a whole was ruled from a single centre, while any autonomous units remaining within the empire were (at least at the beginning) of quite subsidiary importance; the empires aimed at bringing them down to the level of their usual territorial administrative subdivisions; this, however, did not at all mean that the empire endowed the inhabitants of the new provinces with the rights enjoyed by the inhabitants of the conqueror or nuclear state.

The early empires, being huge mechanisms for plundering a number of tribes or nations, could not have been very stable structures, because plundering was only a form of simple re-distribution, and hence could not sufficiently ensure reproduction on a larger scale and the development of productive forces. The robbing policy of the empire contradicted the needs of the constituent regions for a normal division of labour between them; as pointed out above, the trade routes were soon moved to regions outside the empires – into the Phoenician-Graeco-Roman *polis* world, or to the 'silk' road not normally controlled by the Chinese Empire (first century BC to second century AD) etc.

The more the empires grew, the less stable they became, but after the fall of an empire, another arose immediately. In the Near East Assyria was followed by the Neo-Babylonian and the Median empires, then came the Achaemenian empire, the Seleucid, the Roman, and the Parthian; in India the Maurya empire was succeeded by the Kushan empire (second century BC to fourth century AD), and this was again succeeded by the Gupta empire (fourth to sixth centuries AD); in China the Ch'in dynasty (third century BC) was quickly followed by the Han (second century BC). The incessant rise and fall and rise of empires came about because the forced unification of the regions producing means of production with the regions producing consumer goods was vital during the whole epoch of Imperial Antiquity.

Gradually it became apparent that over and above the armed forces and the imperial administration, another mechanism of importance was also needed. It was aimed at ensuring the actual functioning of reproduction on an ever larger scale under the conditions of the then existing productive forces and relations in production; at the same time, this mechanism had to be guaranteed from arbitrary imperial intervention. The mechanism in question developed gradually, at the earlier stages meeting firm resistance from the army and the administration who regarded it as damaging to the empire's monopoly on political power; nevertheless it grew and prospered, if not to the same degree in all the different empires of the ancient world. This mechanism was provided by a system of independent self-governed cities that were centres of handicrafts and trade inside an integrated empire. Here, absence of too strong a royal interference in the cities, and privileged taxation, created favourable conditions for the development of a commodity economy and for the considerable enrichment of the ruling class; the prevalence of peace within the empire secured links between regions producing raw material and the regions marketing consumer goods.

In Western Asia this process is already clearly apparent during the Achaemenian empire (sixth to fourth centuries BC), but it receives an especially strong impulse after the conquest of Alexander in the fourth century BC, when the Greek model of the *polis* was introduced in the Orient (although here it was subject to the superior authority of the empire). A network of *poleis* continued to exist, gradually decaying, all through the period of existence of the Hellenistic empires, created by Alexander's heirs: the Ptolemies (in Egypt and outside Egypt), the Seleucids (in the Near and, partly, the Middle East), and the Arsacids (in Parthia and Armenia); it existed also under the Romans. Egypt was influenced by the *polis* system less than the other empires, mainly retaining the archaic features of state bureaucratic exploitation. Self-governing republics were known as far to the East as India, where they were established under the Mauryas, but here the imperial authorities failed to make use of them, and they soon withered away. In China under the Han empire the group of population concerned with trade and handicrafts was given a certain leeway, and a considerable growth of cities could be observed, although in no way can they be compared with the Parthian Hellenophone *poleis* as to the degree of independence they could enjoy; however, the Chinese cities (especially in the earlier period) were a stabilising factor in the exchange between the regions producing means of production, and those producing consumer goods. In India and China the lack of a *polis* system was conducive to an earlier fall of the ancient type empires, and the passage to the Early Middle Ages.

The main exploited class in the Phase of Late (Imperial) Antiquity, both at its earlier and its later stage, was not so much the slaves alone, as a broader part of the population differently known in the various empires (thus they were *laoi* in the Hellenistic empires, *śudras* and *dasyui* in India, *ch'ien-min* in China, *coloni* in the Roman empire).[6] Slavery existed in both ancient Phases, as well as all through the following Phases of history, but nearly always played a secondary role (except for a few regions and a few periods).

It is not apparent whether the slaves by themselves should be considered to be the main exploited social class, or whether they were a specific stratum of the class of ancient dependent men and women which conventionally we have called helots.

---

6. The term *coloni* began to be applied to the main exploited population only in the late Roman Empire. In the Early Empire, the main exploited group, at least in Rome itself and in Italy, consisted not of coloni but slaves.

The people belonging to this class were obliged to create surplus produce for the benefit of the ruling class (the latter often assuming the form of a military aristocracy or of a bureaucracy). The produce could be collected either directly, or in the form of taxation[7] (thus in Kassite Babylonia in the second half of the millennium BC, later in Assyria, in Han China, etc.); or else in the form of a métayage (quitrent) or corvée. If it was confiscated in the form of tax, then it could be distributed in some other way among the ruling class.

Conservation of the *polis* system was characteristic of the mightiest (and richest) empire of the Late Antiquity, viz. the highly developed Roman Empire. Its most important feature was that its conquests were made not by a king as in some traditional state but by the *polis* (*Urbs*) Rome itself. The main prerequisites for the transformation of the Roman city republic and its territorial dependencies into an empire were created by the conqueror and dictator Julius Caesar (killed by the republicans in 44 BC), and by his successor Augustus, the actual founder of the Roman Empire. Both of them (as well as a long series of their successors) were traditionally considered to be republican magistrates. The main Mediterranean countries were conquered by Rome during its republican period; and even after the creation of an empire by Caesar and Augustus, the *polis* system continued to be the mainstay of its structure.

Making use, with reservations, of the *polis* system (and even extending it to new territories) contributed to a stability which left the Roman empire without rural competition from its Indian and Chinese opposite numbers in Late Antiquity.[8] The citizens of the *Urbs* (Rome itself) were in a privileged position, but as the subordinated *poleis* gradually lost their independence, and their institutions became no more than empty formalities, their more outstanding citizens also received Roman citizenship, till at last in the year 212, under the emperor Caracalla, this citizenship was actually granted to all freemen in the empire. Hence the notion of citizenship, as it emerged in the Greek *polis* world in the middle of the first millennium BC, lost its specific sense: Roman citizenship finally began simply to mean being a Roman subject and paying taxes to the Roman state. This, as we shall see below, was the first step towards the next, Fifth, Phase of human history.

The most important feature which distinguishes the Late (Imperial) Antiquity Phase from the Middle Ages is the stable preservation of personally free peasantry (the peasants, although paying taxes and being obliged to do military service, were not the property of any person or state organisation); also the city dwellers were free. Antiquity does not end with the end of the exploitation of slaves (they

---

7. We have already pointed out that taxation cannot always be regarded as exploitation (e.g. not when the taxes are used for socially necessary aims); but, of course, it *may* be a form of exploitation.

8. The lack of a *polis* system based on private property as if representing community property, was the reason for the direct retention of two economic sectors in China throughout the Phase of Late Antiquity.

continue to be exploited in the Medieval Phase, the Capitalist Phase, and under the condition of the so-called 'developed socialism' as well). Antiquity comes to an end with the end of personal liberty.

Can we regard Late Antiquity as a mode of production different from that of the Early Antiquity (i.e. as a different Phase, or, in Marxist parlance, 'formation')? The level of development of the productive forces and means of coercion (i.e. of arms) in Early and in Late Antiquity respectively was quite different: in Late Antiquity it was based on a completely new technology (namely, on that of the Iron Age, implying also the appearance of the early form of steel). The character of the exploitation of the lower class was not very dissimilar from Early to Late Antiquity, but it has been shown by V. P. Ilyushechkin that any form of exploitation is not strictly bound to one certain Phase of historical development. From my point of view, the forms of property did differ: typical of Early Antiquity is a juxtaposition between palace and/or temple property on the one hand, and communal-cum-private property on the other; and a quasi total absence of regular taxation;[9] while typical of Imperial Antiquity is, first, the existence of state property as opposed to private property; and secondly the fact that the freemen were to a different degree divided into estates (cf. the *varnas* of India: priests, warriors, other 'twice-born', i.e. enjoying full rights as opposed to those who have diminished rights or none at all; in a *polis* of the Late Antiquity, enjoying of the right of citizenship was, of course, an attribute of belonging to a certain estate as well). Each estate had different property and civil rights, and even an exploited class (sometimes including the slaves)[10] might not have been totally devoid of property in the means of production or, at least, of the possibility of their stable use. That Imperial Antiquity is one of the regular Phases of the universal historical process can be seen from the fact that it appears in all parts of the Old World and nearly synchronously, from the Atlantic Ocean to China and probably to Japan. We need not stress that the political superstructure in the Imperial Antiquity is also different from that of Early Antiquity.

Imperial Antiquity is separated from Early Antiquity not by a social upheaval from below (i.e. by a popular revolution), but by a regular Phase transition, during which all the necessary prerequisites of the new Phase were being created (such prerequisites were 'steel' arms, imperial ideology, new forms of the exploitation of labour, and of the organisation of the ruling class).

According to the traditional Marxist theory, the passage to a new historical Phase should have been preceded by a violent popular revolution. One might regard as such the forcible conquests, by the new empires, of societies of the Early Antiquity

9. Thus, there was no regular taxation in second millennium BC Mesopotamia; there were regular mobilisations of the populace for the purpose of irrigation projects (obligatory for the entire population), and sundry irregular requisitions.

10. Slaves in the Neo-Babylonian and the Achaemenian empires, while remaining the property of their owners, were allowed to organise production of their own, to lend money on interest, to own slaves themselves, etc.

type which were happening all over the civilised world. But if this is to be regarded as a revolution, it was certainly not popular but imposed from above. This means that we are not to seek for its direct socio-psychological mechanism in the ideology of the masses – they kept everywhere to the inherited ideas – but in the psychology of the emergent imperial ruling class. Although in religion previous pantheons persisted in most empires, and even a tolerance of those neighbouring cults which differed somewhat from one's own, we also observe the emergence of at least one new cult, e.g. the typical cult of the empire's capital. But there is another important innovation: the supreme deity was now regarded as reigning over a celestial empire, while the other deities constituted his retinue. This happened in most parts of the Near East and in the Roman Empire. In China the cult of an impersonal but animate divine 'Heaven' began to oust the local archaic cults even before the advent of the imperial period. In several countries the earthly king was deified.

But if imperial revolutions happened despite the will of the people and without their knowledge, nevertheless *because* of them the popular masses acquired certain new socio-psychological impulses which had far-reaching historical results.

The complication of technologies and of social relations in Early Antiquity had already led to the understanding that the cause-and-effect connections were not merely mythological. The socio-psychological need for being defended, for 'fairness', was felt as unsatisfied. The fatal question 'Why so?' emerged more and more urgently. It can be heard in the literary masterpieces of the antiquity – still half-suppressed in the Babylonian 'Epic of Gilgamesh', more loudly in the great poems of 'The Innocent Sufferer' and 'The Babylonian Theodicy', and in the Biblical 'Book of Job' (first millennium BC). It can be traced barely perceptibly in some, on the whole very archaic, Vedic hymns composed in India about the same time. Later the Indian region saw the evolution of a doctrine of individual salvation consisting of the liberation of oneself from the slavery of the sensed world and the 'recognition' of the eternal principle of existence (the Upanishads, seventh to second centuries BC?).

But the matter was not limited to that: there emerged new, universal, non-local doctrines, for which *the* God (the ethical principle) was of paramount importance. In the beginning, the existence of deities was either negated (as in early Jainism of the seventh century BC, preached by Jnatriputta, or Natapputta; the Jainists regarded extreme asceticism as a way to liberation from evil); or a very secondary role was ascribed to the deities, as in early Budhism, founded by Siddhartha Gautama (the Buddha) in the sixth century BC. According to the teachings of the Buddha – who disapproved of the traditional division of the Indian society into estates – ethically correct behaviour leads finally to a personal liberation from the world's suffering (namely in the *nirvana*). Those who have attained the possibility of such liberation, could deny themselves the nirvana and become *bodhisattvas*, who are capable of helping the suffering ones (this notion seems to have evolved in Buddhism somewhat later). The Buddha himself preached orally; the voluminous Buddhist canonical scriptures go probably back to the third to first centuries BC.

Buddhism was a proselytic doctrine, i.e. it did not confine itself to a specific human group, but actively sought adherents.

In China during the rule of the Chou Kingdom (twelfth to eighth centuries BC) there were already signs that the archaic mythological religion was dying off; the end of the sixth and/or beginning of the fifth century BC is the time of Confucius, whose doctrine for the first time made moral principles (*jen* – 'humanity') the base on which the ideas of society should rest. This notion did not, however, imply an indiscriminate love of all humankind, but assumed, first of all, love of the family and reverence for the mother and especially the father; then this love spread hierarchically to the head of the clan (and, later, to the lawful chief) and, finally, to the sovereign. But all this was centred on a sort of cult of the nuclear family as the base of all structures of human society. The Confucian family was not necessarily thought of as monogamous, but the wives were not recluses of a harem (as was later the case in Islam): all of them could freely converse with the outer world, and had the right to be esteemed as befits married ladies.

In its original form Confucianism was more a philosophy than a religion (although it implied a cult of the supreme Heaven, and also allowed for the cult of other deities); it was a *Weltanschauung*, and even a way of life.

In Iran and in the neighbouring regions of Central Asia, at a very early period – actually at the very beginning of the change from chiefdoms to early kingdoms – the doctrine of Zoroaster (Zarathustra) was formulated in the hymns of the Gāthās. It contains certain postulates which are supposed to establish social justice. But the essence of Zoroastrianism were certain formal principles: prohibition of mass sacrifices of cattle, a cult of 'the clean elements' (water, fire and fertile soil) with the concomitant prohibition of burning corpses (that were considered ritually unclean), or burying them in the soil. At the same time, Zoroastrianism promised a *post-mortem* reward to the righteous (who pass to Paradise over the bridge Chinvat, which is of a hairbreadth narrowness), and also (possibly at some later stage in the development of the doctrine) the coming of a saviour and a future reign of social harmony. The date of Zoroaster is not certain (eighth to seventh centuries BC?). Much earlier dates have been suggested (by M. Boyce and E. E. Kuz'mina).

A very special case was the situation of the inhabitants of the Kingdom of Israel in Palestine, and particularly of the Kingdom of Judah which had preceded the Israelite state, and continued in existence after its fall. The prohibition on the worship of gods other than the god of tribal union, Yahwe, dating from before the formation of the state, finally led, as a result of the prophetic movement (Hosea, seventh century BC, Isaiah and his school, eighth to fifth centuries BC, Jeremiah, sixth century BC, et al.), to the concept of One unique God. The cult of this unique God (Judaism) was based, apart from certain ritual regulations, on the ethical doctrine set forth in the 'Ten Commandments'. These were very similar to the commandments of the Buddha, and they formed the basis for future European ethics. Later, perhaps under the influence of Zoroastrism, there developed in Judaism the doctrine of the future coming of 'The Anointed' (*mmāšīaḥ*, Messiah) from the dynasty of the second king of all Israel, David; it was the Messiah who was to establish the absolutely harmonious and eternal kingdom for the Israelites; but some of the prophets, beginning with Jeremiah, visualised this Messianic Kingdom as one which would unify all nations of the world.

As was usual in antiquity, the Jews were, with few exceptions, literate.[11] The doctrine spread easily among them, and the sermons of the prophets were written down. Their selection and editing belong mainly to the fifth to second centuries BC; the final form was attained by the Biblical canon (Hebrew *Tanakh*, the 'Old Testament' of the Christians) at around 100 AD.

Beginning with the second century BC new trends in Judaism made themselves felt; now its ethical side was increasingly stressed. In the beginning of the first century AD Jesus[12] appeared, who put aside the ritualistic aspect of Judaism and gave a wholly ethical aspect to the belief in One God the Father. Jesus either declared himself, or was recognised by his disciples to be, the 'Anointed One' (the Messiah, Jewish *Mashiah*, Greek *Christos*), who had been promised to the Jews by the prophets.

The appearance of the supposed king of an eternal Israelite kingdom was felt as politically dangerous both by the Romans dominating Palestine at that time, and to the official Jewish élite who hoped for peace with the Roman authorities; and Jesus was executed by crucifixion. However, his adherents declared that he was resurrected and had ascended to heaven, so that in the Last Days he will come 'to judge the living and the dead, and his kingdom will have no end'. The adherents of Jesus regarded themselves originally as part of the Jewry; the vigorous activity of Paul from Tarsus was needed to formulate the Christian doctrine dogmatically, to make it proselytic and to extend it all over the Roman Empire – at the beginning, among groups of Jewish refugees, then also among the lower groups of the general population, and finally to all of it.

The events of the process of creation of early Christianity, and its ideas, were written down soon after the events themselves, but the final canon of the 'New Testament', including four histories of the life of Jesus (the Gospels), as well as several letters (Epistles) of Paul and some other apostles, and the Apocalypse, a poetic vision of the end of the world and the establishment of God's Kingdom on Earth, received its final form between the fourth and seventh centuries AD.

All ethical doctrines of the ancient peoples had an oppositional character, and later on, in an appreciably remade form, most of them played a role in the socio-psychological validation of the transition from the Phase of Imperial Antiquity to the Medieval Phase of the historical process.

---

11. It is very important to stress, that both in Early and (especially) in Imperial Antiquity, and different from the period of Middle Ages, literacy was widespread among the entire free population everywhere.

12. For Christian readers, I want to stress that I am trying only to relate the outline of the historical events, not to touch upon subjects that belong to the realm of faith.

In the Mediterranean area, the ethically coloured teaching of the Greek philosopher Socrates, who put himself to death according to the sentence passed by the judges (fourth century BC) made an impression only on a few of the philosophising 'intelligentsia' of the time; cults of the traditional type, characteristic of the numerous *poleis* and kingdoms of Early Antiquity, continued their existence. This way of the development of ideas was continued by the preservation (although, with time, in increasingly formulaic terms) of *polis* structures inside the Hellenistic kingdoms and the Roman Empire. However, the late Empire saw the emergence of several different 'religions of salvation': Hermetism, the teachings of the Orphics, Gnosticism, Mithraism. But none could compete with Christianity in the degree to which it corresponded to the psychological needs felt by the majority of the population.

As to the official attitude of the ancient empires towards the ethico-dogmatic religions, it differed depending on the circumstances. For the Assyrian and the Neo-Babylonian empires it was sufficient to restructure the traditional mythology after the manner of the imperial administration on earth (we know very little of the attempt to launch a religious reform made by the last Neo-Babylonian king Nabonidus). The Median and the Achaemenian empires adopted Zoroastrianism – probably in a very distorted form; it is possible that it presupposed a belief in a latter-day Saviour; it probably dated from a period later that the life of Zarathustra himself. But at the same time, these empires not only allowed the functioning of archaic local cults, but actually encouraged them. The Hellenistic and the Roman empires preserved the archaic type cults and provided a cult of a major deity protecting the Empire; a cult of the deified emperor was also generally accepted.

Since Buddhism perceived resignation to one's lot as a virtue, and preached salvation only through inner self-improvement, it was rarely persecuted by the state.

Moreover, the Buddhists actually could, in fact, be better subjects for the monarchs who were building their empires – more complaisant, more satisfied with life than the unruly Indian Brahmanists – adhering to traditional Indian mythologies and traditional cults; the Brahmanists were divided into rigid estates (*varnas*) at loggerheads with each other, partly embittered, partly desperate, and often no longer corresponding to the socio-economic structure existing in the society. That is why the Maurya dynasty adopted Buddhism as its official dogmatic religion (permitting, however, the existence of archaic Brahmanist cults, and later the Hinduist cults, which had developed from Brahmanism; sometimes they permitted and sometimes persecuted the Jainists); note that a certain tolerance was not incompatible with the spirit of Buddhism. Something similar occurred also under the Kushan dynasty. Buddhism did not reign supreme in India; ancient cults were preserved, and these, after being subjected to a long and arduous religiously-philosophical elaboration, produced, towards the beginning of the next historical

Phase, new, authoritative teachings of Hinduism. As to Buddhism, it was – in forms ever changing with time – pushed away to the periphery: to Tibet,[13] later to Mongolia, to China, to Ceylon,[14] to Burma, to Japan.

No concept of *polis* citizenship like that originating in the Hellenistic and Roman world arose in China. The greatest degree of rights was enjoyed by the members of the bureaucracy. For this reason ideological development here assumed forms other than in the West. If Buddhism did not contradict the interests of the new, imperial structure of the ancient societies, neither did the early Chinese Confucianism. The philosophy of Confucius (*c.* 551–479 BC) was an answer to the discomfort common to the epoch of Early Antiquity which was due to the obvious impotence of impulses for fairness and justice; but it did not give any recipe for achieving justice (either teleologically or here-and-now, at least for the individual); instead it attempted to mitigate this discomfort: 'The ruler must be a ruler, the subject must be a subject, the father must be a father, the son must be a son.' During the imperial period of the antiquity, Confucianism, especially as treated in the writings of Meng-Tzu (Mencius, fourth to third centuries BC), remained an unofficial teaching.

The local archaic cults which corresponded to the socio-psychological needs of the Second historical Phase (the Primitive Community) and the Third Phase (Early Antiquity), became unfit for the interests of state power in China at a very early date (already in the Chan Kuo epoch, sixth to third centuries BC). At the beginning of the Han dynasty a cult of an impersonal Heaven was central for the whole empire, and the emperor himself appeared as 'The Son of Heaven'. However, this did not exclude the existence of different cults of secondary importance, either of archaic, or Taoist, or Buddhist origin.

Because of the great importance ascribed by the Confucians to the utter stability of moral principles which are passed from the ancestors to their descendants, they regarded five archaic books received from early antiquity as canonical. The most important of these were the 'Shu Ching' ('The Classic of Traditions'), and the 'Shih Ching' ('The Classic of Poetry'), a collection of very ancient poetry, drastically edited and purged of archaic mythology. Normative for the Confucians were works ascribed to Confucius himself, as well as to some of his later followers.

In parallel with Confucianism there developed the doctrines of Taoism; they were mutually influenced one by another. Canonical for the Taoists was the book 'Tao-te ching' which is supposed to date from the fourth century BC or earlier. It was ascribed to the great ancient holy wise man Lao Tzu himself.

13. Buddhism of the Maháyana persuasion (Tibet, Mongolia, China, Japan) differs considerably from the original teachings of Siddhartha Gautama: the Bodhisatvas have become deities; other deities also appear. The Theravada persuasion is more archaic; it was prevalent in Ceylon, in Burma, Thailand, and Cambodia.

14. The state founded on the island of Ceylon is now officially called Sri Lanka, which is the Sanskrit pronunciation of the island's name (pronounced [si-long] in the local Indo-Aryan language, Sinhalese); Sanskrit, as a sacred language, is acceptable both for the Buddhist Sinhalese, and for the latter arrivals, the Hinduist Tamils (belonging to the Dravidian linguistic family).

One should not confuse philosophic Taoism and religious and magical Taoism. The philosophy of Taoism is thought to have been founded by the half-mythical Lao-Tzu, but it was more profoundly developed in the works of historically attested thinkers, Chuang Tzu (fourth century BC) and Liu An (second century BC), the latter being the author of the book 'Huai-nan-tzu'. Central to the philosophical Taoism is the concept of the *Tao* – the Absolute of Being. Man's aim is 'non-action' (in other words, not doing anything 'unnatural', the natural life of man not infringing upon the *Tao*); this means humility, satisfaction in one's life, one's weakness, lack of inducement towards a career, towards knowledge. As to ritual, the artificial ordering of society, war, taxation, official morals – all this was repudiated by Lao Tzu. Chuang Tzu added the concept of existence as perpetual change, but, according to him, actually 'All is One'; a man must be 'the fellow of nature', and 'the friend both of life and death'. According to 'Huai-nan-tzu', existence is like running water: the beginning was non-existence; out of *emptiness* emerged the *Tao*, but it also created the material world; the world created the material forces; the female principle *yin* joined the male principle *yang*, the negative with the positive; these principles dominate the universe. The Taoist cosmogony, and specifically the teaching about the *yin* and *yang* was, by and large, adopted by Confucianism; very strong, too, was the influence of Taoism on the Chinese forms of Buddhism, more especially on that variant of Buddhism which is usually designated by the Japanese term *Zen*.

In parallel to philosophical Taoism developed religious and magical Taoism. Partly urged by the survivals of some very ancient cults, it was formulated through the tenets of Chung Taoling, a great magician and healer, the founder of a long line of teachers. Basing their reasoning on the same principle of *yin* and *yang*, the religious and magical Taoists at the same time inclined to ascribe an individual deity to nearly all phenomena of the world. The main aims of a Taoist were to achieve happiness, health, many children and long life. About the seventh century AD developed a system of magical acts and attitudes which were supposed to bring these good things of life to every believer, and to manifest the principles of 'essence', 'life force', and 'spirit'. These acts and attitudes included control of breathing, a certain diet, ablutions, meditation, sexual limitations and physical exercises (all this was to a considerable extent borrowed from Buddhism); and also the use of certain medicinal drugs and magic objects, which later favoured the origination of alchemy, including attempts of turning quicksilver to gold.

Now a few words about Japan, which lagged somewhat behind the other countries.

In spite of its situation, Japan, of course, had contacts overseas with Korea and China, and the latter's influence was important. However, iron arms were introduced to Japan only from the sixth century AD on; it was only then that a society of the Fourth Phase – that of Imperial Antiquity – began to be formed here. In Japan this Phase was not of long duration, because the continent was already living in the

Fifth, Medieval Phase, and the Japanese authorities strove to copy the continental patterns.

In the late sixth century the most influential clan of magnates, the Soga, promoted a new ruler of the country, Shōtoku (593–622 AD). The Soga and Shōtoku himself planned to create a state system after the pattern of the then ruling Chinese dynasty of Sui. Buddhism was introduced as an official ideology, but with an admixture of Confucian ethics. This ideology, official though it was, could never oust the different more ancient beliefs, which only at a much later period received the more distinct general form of 'Shintoism'. In 603 Chinese-type hierarchical ranks were introduced at court. In 607 an official embassy was sent to the Chinese court; and it was followed by groups of scholars and priests who were to be educated there.

As a result of a struggle between the different clans, the Soga disappeared from the scene, and the dominating force became another clan, the Kamatari Fujiwara; at that time one Kotoku became *tennō* (emperor). His supporters enacted in 645 the so-called 'Taiku reform', which resulted in the *tennō* receiving enormous power and being deified; private property in land was converted into state property, the nobility receiving offices in the imperial administration and land allotments from the emperor. (The offices were given not after an examination, as in China, but according to the influence of the clan in question.) The army was formed by conscription. According to law, each third man of the age between twenty and sixty was to serve either in the army, or – in peace-time – in workers' detachments. It was not possible to implement this reform as planned, especially in the outlying regions. By the eighth century private estates of the aristocracy had appeared. Rich Buddhist monasteries emerged.

The first permanent imperial capital, Nara, was founded in 710. From this time on, Japan may be regarded as being an empire. An imperial post service was organised, money was coined. The foundations of historiography were laid, and poetry was composed.

Towards the beginning of the ninth century, under the *tennō* Kammu, the capital was moved from Nara to Heian (not Kyoto). At that period the peasants began to flee from state land, and to supplicate for positions in noble houses.

The Nara period, however short (it lasted only about 100 years), can be defined as a period of an underdeveloped, inconsistent Fourth Phase (that of Imperial Antiquity), cf. such diagnostic features as iron arms and tools, centralised state, deification of the monarch, introduction of an official religion (viz., Buddhism; however, the relations between the state power and the Buddhists seem to have been rather uncertain).

Summing up, we may state that characteristic of the Phase of Late (Imperial) Antiquity is the more or less active introduction of certain cults aimed at strenthening the empire, and even at deification of the monarch; this supports the effectiveness of the socio-psychological need of 'being as everybody'. The former mythological ideology was not completely ousted; instead, it was being adapted to the new imperial conditions, but continued to exist everywhere (less in China than elsewhere). Note that at the same time the peasants and the artisans, although taxed, continued to be free and armed. This was the reason why the archaic, originally community cults continued to exist. At the same time, under the influence of the need to get rid of 'injustice' (which was felt the more as the strength of the central state power grew), among many groups of the population there appeared new ethico-religious doctrines. They were preparing a socio-psychological crisis of the social structures existing during the epoch of the Imperial Antiquity. They led up to the emergence of a new historical Phase, but did not as yet acquire a dogmatic form.

And finally, let us say a few words about the cultural and scientific achievements during both Phases of Antiquity. Above we have mentioned the development of technology during the Phase of Imperial Antiquity. But the most important achievement of antiquity in general was the separation of the scientific, non-emotional cognition from mythological cognition. First, this had already occurred in the *polis* world during the Phase of Early Antiquity: here, more than anywhere else, conditions for the freedom of thinking had been created. For the first time we can observe a divorce between philosophy and religion – a phenomenon characteristic chiefly of the classical world, which gave birth to philosophers who influenced substantially the advanced thinking both in Europe and in Western Asia. Between the sixth and the third centuries BC these were Heraclites, Socrates, Plato, Aristotle, Epicurus, and, in the imperial period, Epictetus, Seneca and even the emperor Marcus Aurelius (at that period the philosophers were mostly concerned with moral philosophy); later appeared the religiously philosophic teachings of the Neo-Platonics. History as a science has its roots, first and foremost, in the works of the Greek Thucydides (fifth century BC).[15] China also had its great historians, such as Ssu-ma Ch'ien (second century BC) and Pan Ku (32–92 AD), who were also the founders of Chinese literary prose. The same historical Phase also bred the Chinese philosophers. The teachings of Confucius (sixth century BC) were originally philosophical; probably one must regard also the half-mythical Lao Tzu (date unknown) as an early philosopher. An outstanding materialist philosopher, actually hardly belonging to the general Chinese tradition, was Wang Ch'ung (first century BC–first century AD).

In India one might also name some outstanding personalities, some of whose ideas can be said to have gone beyond mythology. However, here philosophy seeking for the cognition of the world did not exist apart from a mythologised, if not simply mythological system of thought.

During this Phase, science in the narrow sense of the word, as an unemotional cognition of the world's phenomena, also begins to appear. During the imperial

15. Somewhat earlier, in the work of Herodotus, history was still a branch of entertaining literary narration.

epoch we can name, first of all (as a result of the existence of the *polis* world!) the Greeks: Theophrastus (botany, fourth to third centuries BC), Euclid (geometry, third century BC), Archimedes (mathematics and mechanics, third century BC), Hippocrates (medicine, about 400 BC), Hipparchus (astronomy, second century BC), Hero (inventor of automata, first century AD), Ptolemy (astronomy; also the founder of scientific chronology, second century AD), Galen (medicine, second century AD). Although the activities of all these scientists belong to the Imperial Phase (the Hellenistic and Roman periods), they were all representatives of the *polis* ideology. The works of Euclid and Archimedes had the greatest influence on European sciences right down to the nineteenth century AD. In Babylonia we can name one scientist, Kidinnu (Kidenas, astronomy, fourth century BC), in India, a genius of grammatical science, Panini; in China between the periods of Chou and Han there were considerable achievements in geometry, astronomy, mathematics and medicine, but unfortunately we do not know the Chinese ancient scientists by name.

Note that the scientific discoveries of the Imperial Antiquity epoch, whatever their significance, never found any practical application. Although technology (including its military branch) did develop (cf. the siege techniques of the Assyrians, the improved Scythian bows and arrows, the introduction of cavalry, but also the invention of silk in China), there were no drastic technological changes. The main working tools were inherited from Early Antiquity (substituting iron for bronze), and their technological improvement was not substantial. Theoretical science did not become a productive force.

Among the arts of antiquity the most important were figurative arts and poetry; also drama (in Greece, in Rome and India). Prose (mainly historical) appears later: in the seventh to sixth centuries BC in Judaea, in the sixth to fourth centuries in Greece, in the third to first centuries in China. The poets of antiquity (Homer, Catullus, Ovid, Virgil) have not lost their force for even a modern reader, but this is a branch of intellectual life which we cannot dwell upon in this short historical overview.

Most important for the future history of mankind was the creation of ethical doctrines, which either acquired religious force (as was the case of Buddhism and Confucianism), or were religious in origin (late Zoroastrianism, Judaism, Christianity). They were responsible for a socio-psychological revolution which was the mechanism that finally brought the Ancient Imperial Phase to its end.

5   Fifth Phase (the Middle Ages)

Modern historical terminology and periodisation is usually (at least in this country) based on the experience of Europe alone: as to the Asiatic societies, the Marxists class them by 'formations' quite mechanically; certain forms are explained as 'feudal', although very often in these societies a feudal class in the European sense did not exist.

Actually, during this particular segment of the historical process it was Europe that differed considerably from the rest of the world, while the Asiatic ways of development were typical. The peculiarity of European development was partly conditioned by the tradition of ideas belonging to Imperial Antiquity; the breaking with the traditions of *polis* structures and ideology was an immensely slow process; moreover, the historical situation in which the crisis of Imperial Antiquity took place was very specific. The specificity of the situation was created, first, through the occupation of considerable territories which had already passed both the Chiefdom Phase, and the Early as well as the Imperial Antiquity, by Germanic and Slavic Late Primitive chiefdoms which at that time were going through a very mobile stage; and secondly, by devastating intrusions of nomadic hordes.

But before we examine the causes, the prerequisites, and the peculiarities of the next, Fifth, Phase of the historical process, as it developed among the agricultural and industrial population, it is advisable to dwell (very shortly) on the peculiar nomadic variety of the human race.[1]

The division of labour between agriculturists and artisans, on the one hand, and the cattle-breeders on the other goes back to the Second (Primitive Communal) Phase. However, until the camel and the horse were domesticated, the cattle- (or, mostly, the sheep-) breeders could move about only near to the rivers or sources of water. At the same time – for instance in Mesopotamia – there existed a successful system of stall-and-camp maintenance of cattle which involved either seasonally sending cattle to grass in the swampy reed-lowlands, or, in the mountainous regions, a seasonal system of keeping cattle on distant mountain meadows. As to the purely stock-rearing societies which had appeared on flat land, they remained,

---

1. In this chapter we also discuss a typologically distinctive variant of the historical process, namely nomadic society. Note: the place and time of the domestication of the horse has not been determined, but South-Eastern Europe and South-Western Asia in the second millenium would be a fairly good guess.

during the phases of Primitive Community and Early Antiquity, still very much dependent on the handicrafts of the settled population. This led to a development of exchange of produce but also to periodical intrusions of the cattle-breeders into the territories of the settled population. The cattle-breeders did never travel more than one or two days' marches from water; they never lost touch with the agriculturists, and easily returned to agriculture if the situation was favourable for that. A good instance are the Near Eastern Aramaic and other Semitic tribes described in the 'Book of Genesis' of the Bible.

The dromedary camels were domesticated in Arabia and the neighbouring parts of the Near East about 1000 BC: horses were known in Europe at a very early date. However, societies totally oriented towards riding (not towards using chariots which were technically unwieldy and not very effective for military use) appeared in the steppes of Eurasia also about the beginning of the first millennium BC.

A society which was in transition from a half-sedentary state to a fully nomadic one, seems to have been that of the Scythians in Eastern Europe; under this heading we also subsume the Cimmerians, as well as the Massagetae, the Sacae, the Sauromatians and other Iranian-speaking nomads, from the steppes bordering on the Black Sea (the Euxine) to the steppes in the foothills of the Altai, the Pamir and the Kopet-Dagh. Not all of them were actually nomads; certain agriculturist tribes co-operated with nomads proper. While the Scythians introduced important military-technical innovations (e.g. the famous Scythian arrows with light bronze arrowheads, and the tactics of mounted raids against enemy infantry), their real impact on the development of the neighbouring sedentary societies was still very limited.

Not only did the real nomads not engage in any agriculture of their own; perhaps even more important is the fact that they could not organise handicrafts of their own. It is true that the Scythian mounted detachments included arrowsmiths who knew how to cast bronze arrowheads in special small portable mould-forms (the metal having been part of the plunder); but they had no developed forging, pottery and other handicrafts,[2] so that the Scythians depended on the surrounding settled population. But the agriculturists had their own cattle, and hardly depended on the nomadic cattle-breeders (thus, a great demand for war horses began to be felt only in the first millennium BC; on their own land, the agriculturists employed oxen, and also donkeys). With the onset of the Iron Age the nomads became badly in need of the artefacts of the settled smiths and other artisans. Settled neighbours became more and more a necessity, and since the nomads had not enough produce for equitable exchange they actually became parasitical on the settled population. Periodical conquests of agricultural regions by the dwellers of the steppes hindered normal development.

---

2. The famous 'Scythian gold' had been ordered by Scythian chiefs, but manufactured by Greek goldsmiths.

The situation reached a crisis when the contrast between the standard of living of the numerically increasing nomads, and that of the settled population became very marked, while the nomads still were unable to organise production of arms for themselves (not to speak of objects of luxury). The civilised regions had passed to a commodity-for-money type of economy, and they were less and less in need of an exchange in kind with the nomads. The settled handicrafts in nomad-dominated territories experienced a regression.

There began an offensive of the nomads. If up to then we could class their societies as Primitive Communities, now they aggressively intruded into the life of societies that were at different historical phases, also in the phase of Imperial Antiquity, which was richest in material goods. Such intrusions, followed by the creation of nomadic 'empires',[3] were later known in Africa (cf. the 'empire' of the Fulani[4] in Western Africa), but the mightiest – and the most destructive – nomadic 'empires' were those which not only were based on cavalry but where the entire male population were mounted warriors armed with bow and arrows. A culture of the Iron Age, an elaborated shooting technique and a mass employment of cavalry may seem to indicate that the nomadic 'empires' belonged either to the phase of Imperial Antiquity, or even to some later stage of historical development. But actually it is more probable that the nomads followed a completely distinctive way of development inside the framework of both phases, that of Imperial Antiquity, and Middle Ages.

The impact of the nomads on the development of these phases in the history of mankind – it mostly assumed the form of certain local regressions in the smooth onward movement of the process – will be discussed below.

However, I would like to note at once – against the opinions of Maria Gimbutas and other authorities of the nineteenth and twentieth centuries, but in accordance with the later findings of C. Renfrew and J. P. Mallory – that the most ancient Indo-Europeans living in the fifth to third millennia BC, i.e. long before the Iron Age, although already acquainted with horse-drawn chariots, never were nomads. Their movement across Eurasia (presumably via the Balkans) was not a military invasion, but a slow spread, caused by a fall in the child mortality rate and, consequently, by an increase in population growth. The reason was that the population speaking the Indo-European proto-language changed to a diet of milk and meat, and had a sufficiently developed agriculture (growing barley, wheat, grapes and vegetables). The surrounding population which lived in the Early Primitive Phase, and thus was by far not so numerous (the population numbers after the

---

3. The artificial unions created by nomads and stretching over huge spaces, can be called 'empires' only conventionally: they were not the result of a necessity to unite regions producing means of production with regions producing objects of consumption, as is typical for actual empires.

4. The Fulani were wandering stock-breeders; they had no cavalry, and they belonged to the Iron Age; they were able to create an 'empire' of only short duration, but it markedly influenced further developments in the regions in question.

change from Primitive to Primitive Communal Phase tend to multiply by two orders of magnitude), adopted the agricultural achievements of the Indo-Europeans, and at the same time also adopted their language; thus the further movements involved not only the original Indo-Europeans but also tribes who had adopted the language and the mores, the latter including the Primitive Communal stage customs which the Indo-Europeans had evolved.

As to the nomadic intrusions, these were of a different type. The earliest, these of the Sacae and the Scythians, had little influence on the development of the historical process on a world scale.

The invasion of the Huns in the third to fifth centuries AD (which involved also the Iranian-speaking Alani whom the Huns had displaced from their original habitations), swept over the territories of the Primitive Community Phase tribes, and those of the Ancient Imperial civilisations. However, the Hun warriors were far less numerous than the local populations, and their invasion petered out, leaving no noticeable traces either in the languages, or in the anthropological type, or in the culture of the countries involved.

The Mongol invasion (which happened in the thirteenth century AD, when Imperial Antiquity had been long left behind) was far more formidable. We should take into consideration the fact that also the Mongols were reared on a meat and milk diet, and therefore experienced a considerable growth of the population; but, unlike the speakers of Indo-European dialects, they were nomads, and the growth of their numbers led not to their gradual spreading out but to powerful inroads, and to a considerable increase of the Mongols' pressure against the more highly developed peoples of the neighbouring countries. Of all the nomads, it was the Mongols (and their successors, mostly speaking Turkish languages) who made the greatest impact on the fate of the subjugated population, and that for the longest period (from the thirteenth to the seventeenth centuries); the impact mostly amounted to constraining the developing of the non-nomadic regions. However, the Mongol potentates (their 'emperors') did not necessarily destroy the existing state structures, but sometimes made use of them for exploiting the conquered peoples. The Mongol conquests were begun by Jenghiz Khan (Temuchin).

It is important to note, that the impact of the conquering Mongols was felt unequally in the different regions. In Russia, after the first invasions, the Mongols left, and their power was manifested only in the fact that the Russian princes had to go and pay their homage to the Khans, and to get from them a *yarlik* (permit) to reign; they also had to pay a more or less considerable but usually not absolutely ruinous tribute. But it must be pointed out that the regularity of the payments was ensured by continuous inroads into Russia. More catastrophic was the Mongol conquest of the prosperous kingdoms and cities of Central Asia. On the one hand, the Mongols installed their own henchmen, and hence the butchery and the plundering were more efficient; but on the other hand, more complicated relations with another important power took shape, a power which was also nomadic by its origin, namely that of the Turks; this ended in a merger of Turks and Mongols, and in some cases also of the local population.

Quite different was the result of the Mongol conquest of China. Here Kublai Khan, Jenghiz's grandson, founded an actual empire in the proper sense of the word. The Mongols made up only the upper stratum of the class ruling the Chinese society, the latter continuing to develop at more or less the same pace as before.

We shall have more to say on the Mongol nomadic empire in another connection.

The surplus population having flowed out of Mongolia proper, the society there acquired a more stable nomadic structure.

As to the movement of the Turks into the eastern (today Chinese) part of Central Asia, it can be traced more easily than the slow and gradual outward flow of the Indo-European languages; at the same time it was somewhat less aggressive than the Mongol invasions. The most ancient of the known Turkish tribes combined stock-rearing on distant mountain or steppe pastures, or even nomadic life, with some agriculture. Beginning with the sixth century AD, and then during several centuries, some of their tribes or groups of tribes moved both to the East and especially towards the West, capturing minor states, where they introduced their own dynasts who based their power on Turkic troops; at first to begin with, the local population was merely a source of plunder but finally the invaders easily mixed with it.

Since all Turkic dialects were very similar, Turkic soon became the *lingua franca* for both the eastern and the western part of Central Asia, for large parts of the territories along the Volga, Eastern Transcaucasia, and later also Asia Minor. The local population – the Khorasmians, the Medians, the Aghwani (also called the Caucasian Albans), the Greeks, etc. – continued to exist but changed from their original languages to Turkic. The same happened to those Mongols who had moved into Central Asia.

The Turkic languages reached the Black Sea region, but the physical anthropological features symptomatic of the Mongoloid race can be observed to diminish the farther we move to the West, and they virtually disappear when we reach the Turks of Anatolia (Asia Minor). Thus, what really happened was the assimilation of the Turks with the local population which, however, adopted the Turkic language.

Now, leaving aside the nomads, let us turn to the general characteristic features typical of that phase of the world historical process, which followed the Fourth Phase (that of Imperial Antiquity).

In principle, all historians agree that now begins the history of the Middle Ages (as one traditionally terms the period in the West), or of feudalism (a term used in our country in compliance with Marxist theory, according to which feudalism is the last but one 'antagonistic formation', immediately preceding capitalism).

The first diagnostic feature of the fifth, Medieval Phase of the historical process, is a change in ethic norms, which acquire a dogmatic and proselytic form (becoming official from having been oppositional). The state, and a highly organised, inter-state and above-state church ensured that the population adhered to prescribed norms while normative ethics was now regarded as sanctifying the social establishment as it existed in the world of that epoch (or, better, in a certain huge social super-entity).

The time of tolerance was over; in a number of societies the expression of ideas which differed from the established doctrine was punished with death. The dogmatic religions were mainly based on the social motivation 'to be as everybody else', and on a strict suppression of the motivation of 'looking about for what's new'.

There was no important progress in the technology of arms, but the arms became the exclusive property of the members of the governing class alone; thus it can be said that a serious change took place in the military field.

Another diagnostic feature is, as already mentioned above, the exploitation (mainly or even exclusively), of the peasantry, i.e. of that part of society which in the Third and the Fourth Phases provided the mass of personally free warriors, subordinate only to military discipline. War now became the occupation and privilege of the ruling class.

In order not to return to the question later, we may note here that it is difficult to explain the medieval wars by socio-economic causes. Nearly all of them (and this is also true of many a war both in the previous and the subsequent periods) can be explained most easily, from a socio-psychological point of view, as the result of the incentive to aggression inherent in man. To conquer and subjugate a neighbour was prestigious, and gave satisfaction to the social impulse towards aggression, which in Rome was partly satisfied by gladiatorial fights, and at the end of the Seventh and in the Eighth Phase was to be achieved by, for example, football and hockey matches, as well as by the excesses of teenage gangs – a real calamity in the modern big cities in the West and in the East. In the Middle Ages, a powerful motivation was the emotional perception of military glory, both for the individual and for the state. Contending for glory was, no doubt, a strong inducement (e.g. for the generals) already in the antiquity, but in the Middle Ages it became institutionalised as *the* criterion of the dignity of man.

The Middle Ages witnessed some progress in military techniques (castles, crossbows,[5] armour for horses, 'Greek fire', etc.).

Typical of the beginning of this phase was the land-ownership of 'magnates', who apart from their property right also enjoyed judicial and executive power. The number of persons subjected to exploitation increased. The living standard was lowered (even for the ruling class).[6] International trade became less

---

5. A crossbow, or arbalest (*areballista*), was a steel bow on a wooden stock, the bow-string drawn by a winch. The crossbow was invented very early in China, but appears in the Near East and in Europe only in the eleventh century; it was a typical weapon of the crusaders. Castles were first constructed in Europe about the same time.
6. Compare the comfort of a villa of a rich Roman in the second and third centuries AD with the discomfort of a castle, the cold and unsanitary dwelling of a Western European feudal lord in the thirteenth to fifteenth centuries.

important, commodity–money relations decayed (in some places coins no longer even circulated). Positive sciences ceased to exist, philosophy was completely ousted by theology. The religion which had become dominant in a given territory determined regional mental and moral idiosyncrasies. Art, and especially poetry and painting (e.g. icon-painting) continued to be important.[7]

Note that although the subjects treated by the artists and the tastes in art change from period to period, figurative art as such (as regards its impression on the onlooker) does not 'progress': the Palaeolithic scenes of mammoth hunts are in no way inferior to the Assyrian scenes of lion hunts; the portrait of Nefertiti created by the Egyptian sculptor Djehutimes in the fifteenth century BC, is in no way inferior to the Gioconda created by Leonardo da Vinci in the fifteenth century AD; an ornament of the Neolithic period or of the Muslim Middle Ages does not make less impression than the abstract art of a Kandinsky. Of course, in the periods of strict predominance of a dogma, art too is bound by it; nevertheless, Gothic cathedrals and Orthodox icons do not lose their emotional impact in our own 'enlightened' age. But on the whole, in the Fifth, Medieval, Phase of history there was no progress in the usual sense of 'more good for a greater number of people'. This epoch was a step further, but not 'up'; this particular phase of history (the early period of the exploitation of peasantry) often shows us a picture of regression, especially in Europe, where it is justly called 'the Dark Ages'.

We will regard as 'Medieval' the period beginning with the third to fourth centuries AD in Europe, with the first century AD in China, with the eighth century AD in Japan (and in the other regions of the world, in each at its own special date).[8]

Just as had been the case with the economy of the states of Early Antiquity, the

---

7. Figurative art and, to a lesser degree, poetry (especially lyric) cannot but be influenced by the dominating ideology; but possibilities of engendering emotional co-experience by artistic means are broader than the limits allowed by ideology. The difference lies in the fact that although ideology is also based on primeval spontaneous and emotional socio-psychological impulses, it is nevertheless a specific form of expressing such impulses that can be (and are) controlled, and, to a certain degree, rationalised; while emotion as such is a phenomenon common to the species *Homo*, and cannot be rationally controlled (only its manifestations may ideologically be directed). It is hardly possible to connect the contents of lyric (i.e. the most emotional) poetry with the evolution of historical Phases, although one may connect with it the evolution of its forms.

8. The Fifth Phase had not been reached in the Australian-Polynesian region, while in Africa it extended only to the northern part of the continent (from Sudan and Ethiopia to the Maghreb – Algeria and Morocco), including, of course, also Egypt. We shall discuss these countries together with the Near East. As to Latin America, after the invasion originating in societies of the Fifth and Sixth Phases, (these were to be introduced on top of those of the First to Third Phase), it experienced an equivalent of the Third, Fourth and Fifth Phases and, before reaching the Sixth, was confronted with capitalism of the Seventh Phase. Notwithstanding the archaism of the Phases it was going through, it is inconvenient to describe their history before the description of America's discovery; therefore, we shall dwell on Latin American history in an addendum to chapter 6. As to North America, here the Sixth and the Seventh Phases were transplanted from Europe, ousting the local Second Phase. For this reason we shall discuss the history of the United States together with that of Europe.

economy of the Ancient Empires finally reached the limit of its positive growth. In antiquity – also in the Imperial Antiquity – there always was a tendency towards maximal exploitation of the unfree class; periodically the exploitation of actual slaves was being intensified. This happened under the later Roman republic, and in the Roman empire during the first and second centuries AD; the same can be observed in the Chinese empires of Ch'in and the Elder Han. But in the course of time it always turns out that slave labour has a low productivity. Excessive centralising of the administration, which was being felt even in the Roman Empire but especially so in China, also hemmed the development of productive forces. Big landowners, who appeared in all empires, strove for maximal independence. The progress in military techniques, and the ruin of the free peasantry, living as it did under the conditions of natural economy and feeling the impact of strong development of commodity–money relations, made it possible for the big landowners to exploit the peasants. Military matters were being entrusted to a professional military élite – in other words, to the landowners themselves, and to military troops organised by them. Centrifugal forces were increasingly felt inside the empires, and this brought about their fall. On top of it all, certain specific local phenomena became important.

Thus, for instance, the development of Europe was, as it seems, atypical. The reason for this was that European societies had spread over great areas, and had already passed both the Early and the Imperial Antiquity Phases, but just at the moment when most of Europe was to pass to a new historical Phase, its societies clashed and merged with others still on the level of early chiefdoms. Here more than anywhere else in history, is the Eurocentric mentality out of place, if we wish to achieve a correct classification of historical Phases. Therefore I shall begin the exposition of the features of the new, Fifth Phase of the historical process from the opposite side of the Eurasian continent, namely from China (not Japan, because here the change of Phases encountered some delay).

In China the impulse towards social changes and thus to the end of the Fourth Phase of the historical process (that of Imperial Antiquity) was triggered by the 'reform' of Wang Mang, who for a short time had wrested the power from the Han dynasty (5–23 AD). He declared himself a partisan of the 'true' Confucianism, but actually is perhaps to be regarded as a follower of the Legalist school, which had already inspired Ch'in Shih Huang Ti. Formally, Wang Mang attempted to return to an 'ideal' social structure (that of Antiquity), and to combat the unrestrained corruption of the bureaucracy. But actually this was an attempt to bring imperial centralisation to the last – and in fact unattainable – limit.

He regarded all land in the empire as state land, and decided to subdivide it into small, equivalent plots, disregarding the traditional communal structure of agricultural economic units; at the same time the tax on land was raised. Moreover, all slaves were declared state property. Trade, and especially slave trade, was greatly hampered by Wang Mang's attempts to make it 'just'. Natural resentment was ferociously suppressed: punishment for a 'crime' meant slavery not only for the 'criminal' himself but for five whole families (perhaps an extended family?). Thus hundreds of thousands of people were enslaved, and a significant proportion perished during deportation or in places of conviction. Money credit – which meant usury – was also entrusted to the state. All this resulted in a severe crisis and a dizzying inflation. The symptoms of a Phase transition became more and more apparent.

Wang Mang had chosen a most unfavourable moment for his reckless reforms. The strong hordes of Hsiung-nu nomads were a significant menace; they had occupied huge territories and cut off the 'Silk road'. China itself experienced a tremendous natural calamity – the main river, the Huang-Ho (Yellow River) changed its course throughout the first century AD. All over the country there were mutinies, the most important being the insurrection of the 'Red-brows'. Wang Mang suffered a defeat, and committed suicide. After that, the survivors of the Han dynasty had to fight with the 'Red-brows' for several years.

With the coming of the Later Han dynasty to power (in 29 AD), the transition of China to a new, namely the Fifth Phase of world history had begun. Of course, it was the result of such inner contradictions of the Imperial Antiquity that had already been apparent in China: the crisis was inevitable, but the preceding Phase might still have continued for a while had its end not been speeded up by the activities of an individual tyrant.

Under the Later Han not only the corrupted bureaucracy was re-installed (while the land returned to private ownership), but also the beginnings of 'magnates' landholding' can be observed: the richest of the landowners – the so-called 'powerful houses' – took under their 'patronage' the weaker agricultural households, probably receiving from them some gifts in kind, but paying their taxes to the state, the agriculturists became personally dependent on the magnates, their patronage actually amounted to the peasants being bound to their parcel. The magnates arrogated to themselves the right of jurisdiction over their peasants. The system of economies belonging to magnates with all-embracing power including public-law functions, led to the decay of money circulation and to the rebirth of barter.

At the same time, enslavement for crime by the courts became one of the important sources of slavery. Nevertheless, the latter could no longer play a major social role. The magnate economies lacked sufficient means of coercion for the exploitation of slaves *en masse*.

The emperors attempted to retain and even to strengthen the centralised administration, and to stabilise the taxation, but the sum of the incoming taxes fell. During the first half of the second century AD catastrophic inundations of the Yellow River continued; Northern China was invaded by a new wave of nomads, the Hsien-pi. In an indirect relation to this, another important process took place, which became possible because techniques of bed-cultivation of land (especially of rice-plots) had been introduced: hence, a number of the 'powerful houses', together with their dependents, began a migration to formerly uninhabited (because swampy or densely wooded) spaces in Southern China.

Should we regard the period when the Later Han dynasty ruled, especially the latter part of the period, as the last stage of the Imperial Antiquity Phase, or as a part of the Phase transition towards the Middle Ages? Changes in the type both of the productive forces, and of the relations in production seem evident. We might regard as revolutionary the internal war which brought about the fall of Wang Mang, but it has already been pointed out that a forcible upheaval is not necessary to diagnose the arrival of a new historical phase.

It seems more convincing to say that the transition towards the new, Fifth Phase of human history, the Middle Ages, was completed under the Later Han. Apart from the 'magnates' landownership, an important diagnostic feature is the appearance in Han China of a normative, dogmatic doctrine. Its base was a new version of Confucianism, as formulated by the philosopher Tung Chung-shu, a counsellor of the Han emperor Wu-ti; this doctrine amounted to the justification of the emerging new social and state structure.

Tung Chung-shu united the Confucian doctrine with the doctrine of the male (positive) and the female (negative) principle, the natural-philosophic notions of *yang* and *yin*, whose combination constitute the entire plurality of the world's phenomena (the notions of *yang* and *yin* seem to have been originally introduced as a systemic conceptual base in Taoism).

It is important to point out that it was Tung Chung-shu's idea to employ in administrative positions men who had graduated from a special academy for the study of the Confucian doctrine. This system of choosing administrators was widely used in the later periods, and was for centuries decisive for the essential type of Chinese society. Already under the Former Han (from 136 BC) 'examinations' had been introduced; later, Confucianism as interpreted by Tung Chung-shu was established as the official doctrine of the empire. But the society had as yet not quite severed the ties with the traditions of Antiquity, which made possible the philosophy of another great thinker of the Late Han period, Wang Ch'ung (1st century AD). Although he seemed to base his reasonings on the same Confucian premises, his position was materialistic; he was the one who for the first time raised the question of the necessity of experimental proofs of postulated truths.

The strengthening of the 'magnates' landownership, of course, led to the weakening of the state power, and to the disorganisation of the empire. In 184 AD there began a great insurrection of the 'Yellow Headbands' directed against the empire and, basically, against the Confucian teachings. It was not actually a peasant rising: the 'Yellow Headbands' did not aspire to a re-allotment of land; they only confiscated food and other necessities, under the guise of charitable and military needs. They were defeated, but among the magnates themselves there was no unity. Simultaneously, there were more intrusions of nomads, the Hisung-nu and

Hsien-pi, and later of some others who succeeded in creating a separate 'Chinese' dynasty in the north-east.

The middle of the third century AD saw the beginning of the period of the 'Three Kingdoms' (Wei, Wu and Shu). Typical for the period is the strengthening of the 'powerful houses'; on their land settled their so-called 'guests', who actually were landholders deprived of any rights, and in servitude for debts. The society ('the folk', *min*) was now divided into 'low folk' (*chien-min*) and the 'good folk' (*liang-min*); between the fourth and the sixth centuries appeared the doctrine that Heaven itself has instituted the division of men into 'aristocrats' (*shih*) and 'common people' (*shu-jen*). The slaves and the household servants did not belong to either group. The ruling class itself was in the process of being subdivided. The magnates had armed troops of their own, and the status of warrior was hereditary. The imperial authorities tried in vain to resist this process. At the same time, the impact of the nomadic tribes from the outside increased, and so did the migration of the Chinese towards the South.

The period of internal strife continued from the beginning of the third century AD to the end of the sixth century. But it is to this period that belong the lyrics of the great Chinese poet T'ao Yuanming (365–427 AD). A short-lived re-creation of the empire occurred in the 580s (the Sui dynasty); at that period, by the use of forced labour *en masse*, the system of canals joining the valleys of the Yellow River and the Yangtze was improved, and the imperial cities Lo-yang and Ch'ang-an were reconstructed. The Great Wall against the nomads, first built under Ch'in Shih Huang Ti, was renovated (although it actually never was a real barrier for nomadic inroads). Some conquests were made outside of China; among other campaigns, there was a rather unsuccessful war against the Turks, who are for the first time in history mentioned in this context. (This happened in Eastern Mongolia, where the first Turkic 'kaghanate' is mentioned around the 550s.)

The immediate continuation of the Sui empire was that of the T'ang dynasty, which was founded in 618 AD by Li Yuan. There is no doubt that both these dynasties were medieval in structure, although at the same time it may be noted that slave labour still existed. It is characteristic that under the T'ang dynasty the taxes were collected in kind (under the Han, all taxes except the land-tax were collected in money). At the same time, the social structure which had developed under the Later Han, was retained under the T'ang. The history of the T'ang period is full of wars with outside forces (the destruction of the Eastern Turkic 'kaghanate' in 630 AD, defeat of the Western 'kaghanate' in 657 AD, conquests in Indo-China and in Korea). One may also note that there were destructive rivalries between Chinese generals and certain groups at court (the most influential being the eunuchs).

At the same time, we may regard the T'ang epoch as the heyday of the Medieval Phase. The centre of the empire was gradually moved from the Yellow River basin to that of Yangtze, where the population greatly increased in numbers; the reason was the success of rice cultivation and bed agriculture (which later proved most important for the development of the Chinese national character, patient, enduring the thoroughgoing even to details). Rice cultivation was being spread also northwards. The population grew, internal and external trade was being developed; a number of foreigners appeared in China, bringing to the country new doctrines: Buddhism (as early as the first century AD), Christianity, Zoroastrianism and Manichaeism (on which see below). But, in spite of the successes in trading, commodity-money circulation in the cities did not develop to any great extent; money circulation was made difficult by the existence not only of state mints, but also of private mints. The eighth century saw the introduction of bankers' endorsed cheques, the so-called 'flying money'. In the twelfth century the first mass of paper money was issued.

Law was being codified.[9]

Bureaucracy continued to be the mainstay of the empire. The serving literati began to make itself felt as the leading force in society, although the influence of the big landowners also grew immensely. The system of examinations, which had been tried already earlier, was more actively introduced under the Sui and the T'ang dynasties; but the bureaucrats were mainly recruited from the same landowning aristocracy; even without submitting to examinations, it rivalled the importance of the bureaucrats in the country.

The emperors of the T'ang dynasty patronised at first Taoism and then, later, Buddhism; but Confucianism continued to play the leading role in China's ideological life. As the examination system became more and more elaborate to reinforce the administration, the study of Confucian literature grew in importance.

From the beginning of the Middle Ages, it was actually Confucianism which was the leading ideological force in China, although its influence could rise or decline periodically. In this respect the role of Confucianism was somewhat analogous to that of Roman Catholicism in Europe and of Islam in the Near East. But although Confucianism was an official and obligatory doctrine, it did not resemble a religion as we are accustomed to define it. Thus, Confucian doctrine tolerated, more or less,

---

9. The discovered laws of the Ch'in and Han period have as yet, to my knowledge, not been sufficiently studied. The T'ang code, which was a model for Chinese lawyers up to the late nineteenth century, is by no means comparable to that of Justinian, or to the Sasanian Code. The 'legalists', adherents of 'Fa', who thought it necessary to introduce systematic laws, uniform for everybody – especially criminal laws – had been discredited by supporting the policy of Ch'in His Huang Ti; as to Confucius, his opinion was that one ought to foster virtue which does not require written laws but only discretional judgement. In bureaucratic China legal thought had little stimulus for development, and we might state (somewhat simplifying the problem), that the T'ang code was actually not much more than a list of 'crimes' (including civil infringements of the law), and a table of main punishments (the majority being rather inhumanely cruel), and tables of their mitigation with regard to the status of the defendant in the bureaucratic hierarchy, or to his nobility rank (in this the code followed the dictum in 'Li-chi': 'Punishments do not rise to chiefs, rituals do not descend to the common people'). In short, in order to act as judge, an official did not want any legal education: it was sufficient to move the index finger along the list; medieval China did not know the principle of equality in the controversy between persecution and defence.

the functioning of other different religious doctrines (Buddhism and Taoism first and foremost), provided they did not infringe upon the order of the established state, and did not disagree with Confucian ethics. Ideological dissent was discouraged to a certain degree. But at the same time, Confucian ethics was gradually assimilated both by the Buddhists and the Taoists, becoming a way of life.

Literacy was widely spread among those who were in any way connected with the administration. The mass demand for classical Confucian literature led to the invention of book-printing in the ninth century AD (at first from engraved boards – so-called xylographed books, published in thousands of copies; especially numerous were the editions of Buddhist books).

As to the general level of technology in production, there was little progress, except in bed agriculture. (Since the eighth century tea was cultivated in this way.) In the military field we may note the introduction of tower architecture and the improvement of armour, not only for men but also for the horses.

A great achievement of T'ang culture was its literature. In prose development took place mainly among the more 'utilitarian' genres: history, philosophy, prosaic disputes on moral and philosophic subjects. Prose fiction first appears as translations of Buddhist books, but in the ninth century original works of different prosaic genres also appeared. But most important was lyric poetry; it was the glory of the T'ang period (Li Po, 701–762 AD, Tu Fu 712–770 AD, Po Chü-i, 772–846 AD); also T'ang figurative art is remarkable.

We may state without exaggeration that T'ang China was a most brilliant example of a flourishing society of the Fifth, Medieval Phase.

The Sung dynasty which followed, as well as the Mongol Yüan dynasty, I would attribute to the Sixth Phase.

In Japan the Medieval Phase begins with the transfer of the capital from Nara to Heian. The transformation of all land to state domain proved impossible. The system of 'estates' (shōen) belonging to noblemen spread over the country. At the same time, the tennō becomes more and more a figure of ritual, while the real power devolved upon the noble clans heading armed troops, the most important being the clan of Fujiwara. In the middle of the twelfth century bloody feuds start between the clans Minamoto and Taira; in 1192, the chief of the victorious clan Minamoto, one Yoritomo, was declared 'commander-in-chief' (shōgun). From that time on, the country was actually being ruled by a shōgun, and only in comparatively rare cases, by the emperor, tennō. The latter's role remained mainly ritual during the Medieval and Post-Medieval phases.

The social structure of Japan, as it had developed over the twelfth to sixteenth centuries, is very similar to Western European feudalism, and we can with certainty characterise it as belonging to the Fifth (Medieval) Phase. The shōguns found their support in a feudal military estate, the busi; the rank-and-file members of it were called samurai. They remind one of the European knights both in their arms (their body armour was very like that of the European knights), and in their notion of personal honour (if honour was involved, and there was no way to be avenged, a *samurai* was supposed to commit suicide by *hara-kiri*). The dependence of the peasants on the estate of warriors was similar to serfdom.

The prevailing religion was Buddhism (in a new, more easily understood form; Zen Buddhism, based on intuitive inspiration, played a great role). As we have already mentioned, in contrast to Christianity, Buddhism is not intolerant; it is ready to accept any deities, regarding them as having, like the humans, each its own *karma*. Thus Buddhism did not exclude the traditional Shinto cults. It is actually due to the fact that Buddhism is tolerant that the Japanese Middle Ages, in contradiction to the European, brought not a decline in the art of literature but an efflorescence. The novel by a lady of the court, Murasaki Shikibu, the 'Tale of Genji', written in the early eleventh century, belongs to the finest works of world literature. Lyric poetry blossomed, in the characteristic laconic forms of the *tanka*.

The attempts of the Mongols to conquer Japan using the Chinese navy (in 1274 and 1281) failed, partly because of a typhoon but also because of a resolute defence on the part of the Japanese.

After deposing the *shōguns* of the Minamoto clan, the emperor Daigo II reigned from 1318 to 1339. He seized power with the help of the Ashikaga clan, a rival of the Minamoto; after that, Ashikaga was predominant in Japan for more than 200 years. Under the Ashikaga, Japan formally recognised its vassal allegiance to the Ming dynasty in China. (It was always thought in China that there existed only one independent state in the world, namely the Chinese Empire; all others were vassals, either loyal or rebellious.) Japan took over the duty of fighting pirates on the sea, for which it was paid by the Ming government; Ming coins became accepted as common currency in Japan.

The Ashikaga period (1335–1587), as well as the preceding one, did not differ much from the European Middle Ages. Towards the end of it, a city bourgeoisie began to develop. From the late sixteenth century Japan entered the Post-Medieval Phase.

In India, the lack of a historiographic tradition, and the fact that the moist climate is unfavourable for the preservation of documents are among the reasons why the historian has great difficulties in reconstructing the deeper lying historical processes. Therefore, here we shall dwell mainly on the socio-psychological and the ideological side of historical development.

The Maurya empire (fourth to second centuries BC) supported Buddhism, but no hindrance was put in the way of development of other doctrines. During this and the following period were written those canonical books which later became the ideological expression of Indian medieval thought, namely, the ideology of Hinduism.

A scholar once said: 'Hinduism is not a religion but a way of life.' To a certain extent this is true.[10]

---

10. This definition is, of course, still more applicable to Chinese Confucianism, which of course became a way of life.

Although the Vedic hymns addressed to the ancient Indian deities were always sacred for the Indians, and still are read during religious gatherings, the medieval Indian religion, which was destined to oust Buddhism, was actually quite unlike the Vedic religion. Just as Buddhism and Confucianism were philosophies before they became religions, so also the base of Hinduism was a religious-philosophic doctrine. If we leave aside the Puranas (which originally were verse commentaries to the Vedas, but in the surviving parts they are, as it were, a bridge between the Vedic religion and Hinduism), the real basis for future Hinduism were the Upanishads. Exploring the essence of existence, they find it not in matter, the vital principle, the mind and reason or logical cognition but in 'blessedness' (anánda) which can be attained beyond the limits of reason. Then the Upanishads turn to the notion of átman ('the being Oneself') and state that it is universal consciousness, which exists both in man himself and outside of man. Our inner 'I' is identical with the universe (bráhman);[11] therefore, in the relation of man to man 'he is also thou'. Brahman, being universal, has no positive definition, only a negative one ('not that', 'not this', etc.). But the universe is made apparent by the endless unfolding of a picture of outside phenomena (māyā). Man is saved, as in Buddhism, by liberation from all that is sensual and personal.

The date of the composition of the Upanishads is unknown, but they seem to have antedated the appearance of Buddhism, which suggested more simple and more intelligible solutions to the religious-philosophical problems of the Upanishads.

Subsequently, the philosophy of the Upanishads was developed in the so-called 'six doctrines' (Darshanas), of which the more ancient (the Sankhya, the Yoga) were already known to the Buddha, while the latest belong to the early Middle Ages. All of them are sometimes embraced under the term Vedanta (lit. 'The Conclusion of the Vedas'), but it is more usual to apply the term Vedanta only to the latest of the Darshanas, the works of the philosophers Shankara (ninth century AD), Ramanuja (twelfth century) and Madhva (thirteenth century).

The recognition of a unique common principle which lies outside cognition, and which is the Bráhman (the whole world being only its manifestation), opened the way for the retention of polytheism, since each deity can also be regarded as a manifestation of the Bráhman. There appeared a concept of avatars, i.e. of manifestations of the deities in different forms or persons (even down to animal and phallic forms). The text most important for all Hinduists is the Bhagavad Gita, a poetic interpolation into the great Old Indian epic, the Mahābhārata. The first commentary on the Gita was written by Shankara. The poem has the form of a dialogue between the hero Arjuna whose soldier's duty requires killing his own

11. Note that one should distinguish between, first, the philosophical notion bráhman (neutral); second, brahmán (masculine), a term which denotes a social estate (a varna), and, third, Bráhma (masculine), the name of the supreme Deity of Hinduism.

kinsmen, and his charioteer, who actually is an *avatar* of the god Krishna, who again is an *avatar* of one of the supreme gods (or, according to certain Hinduist teachings, the only superior god) – Vishnu. The dialogue turns into a discussion of the moral problems of Hinduism. One of the most important of Krishna's assertions is the following: 'Whatever god you worship, I answer to the prayer.' (Compare the Ten Commandments of the Bible: 'Thou shalt have no other gods before me.')

Thus, Indian religious practice permits all forms of worship (present-day Hinduists also revere Christ); being, as it were, monotheistic in its philosophy, it permits in practice all forms of polytheism.

The doctrine stated in the *Bhagavad Gita* contributed to the fact that inside Hinduism there appeared very different trends; the most important but by no means the only ones being Vishnuism and Shivaism. All trends recognise Brahma the Creator as the highest deity, who sits at perpetual rest somewhere on the Himalayas. The cult of Shiva is cursorily mentioned in the Vedas; it seems to go back to the Harappan civilisation, and to have belonged to the Dravid aboriginals of the Indian subcontinent.[12] Several hymns to Vishnu are introduced into the Vedas; both cults became dominant in Hinduism only in the medieval period. Female deities play an important role in Hinduism.

A very important element of Hinduism is the concept of *dharma* which is man's forever pre-ordained lot implying his *karma*, which literally means 'doing' ('activities'). The *karma* doctrine presupposes a perpetual migration of souls; it asserts that man's happiness or unhappiness depends on his actions in this or in one of his previous lives, and that one's evil actions spoil one's *karma* in one's next rebirth; a similar doctrine also exists in Buddhism.

The notion of the *dharma*, man's unalterable and eternal lot, is central to Hinduism. It is also the base of the 'estate' system which defines the overall character of Indian society from the Middle Ages and indeed down to the present times.

The castes cannot be regarded as a later subdivision of the Vedic 'estates', the *varnas*, although it is true that there do exist brahmanic (priestly) castes. It is possible that a certain but not determinant role in the formation of castes was played by the process of interaction between the northern Indo-Aryan population and the southern Dravids. The castes as a system developed the beginning of the Christian era. At the early stage they were closed units, though it may have been in the power of the head of the state to transfer a person or a whole group from one caste to another. In the final form of the caste system a caste was neither a social nor a professional unit. There still exist exogamic castes where marriages inside the same caste are prohibited; there are groups of people who cannot receive food from another caste; there are castes specialising in activities prohibited to members of

12. However, the name of the deity Shiva is not Dravidian, originally this was not a proper name but an Indo-Aryan epithet of the deity in question, whose name has not been preserved.

other castes such as castes of butchers, barbers, scavengers, etc. Members of such castes are usually 'untouchable' for the members of other castes.[13] The members of a caste, whatever it is, share a common *karma*.

Characteristic of Hinduism, in contrast to the religion of the Vedic period, is the belief in transmigration of souls, the prohibition of sacrificing life – any life (unless your *karma* is to be a warrior); strictly forbidden is the slaughtering of cows which are regarded as sacred. Recitation of the holy texts and other rituals are relegated to the family circle; the temple is the abode of a deity which can be visited for prayer but is not a place of public worship in the European sense of the word.

We have given considerable attention to a description of Hinduist beliefs and the Hinduist caste system because, unlike other medieval societies, Indian society had not evolved a unique, compulsory, religiously dogmatic system. It seems that here no heresies were of any danger because the caste system itself disunited people, so there could not be any threat for the existing social and state structure.

In technology, including military matters, the Indian society was more or less at the same level as the other medieval societies. The reasons for India's passing over to the medieval phase are not quite clear because the sources are inadequate, but one may suppose that they were not much different from those that can be established for other regions.

A most important phenomenon in the history of India during this phase was the conquest of a part of the country by the Muslims and the introduction of Islam there – but this problem will be discussed below in connection with Islam.

Turning now to Iran, we may begin by stating that the Parthian Empire (third century BC–third century AD) can legitimately be compared to the Elder Han in China, and the following Sasanian Empire (third–seventh centuries AD) to the Later Han (and also, following V. G. Lukonin, to the T'ang dynasty). Some *poleis* still existed in the Parthian Empire, although their existence was rather precarious. In religious matters the authorities were tolerant to a considerable degree, notwithstanding the fact that the dynasty and most of the nobility adhered to an archaic form of Zoroastrianism. The integrity of the empire was at times disrupted by the appearance of local competing dynasts. The type of armaments was not unlike that in use in the Roman and Han Empires (but by the Parthian period there were already professional mounted warriors clad in chain-armour, the so-called *cataphractarii*).

Under the Persian Sasanian dynasty independent cities perish; in their place appear administrative centres, royal military headquarters ruled by royal servants. Now predominant in society was the landownership of 'magnates', and the borderline between a big landowner and a small sovereign was not easily discerned. At first (during the third century AD) the Sasanian state was more like a confederation of several separate kingdoms, but later it tended towards centralisation. The society

13. One of such castes were probably the gypsies (*rómani*), who left India in the fourteenth or fifteenth century – ultimately for Europe.

was clearly divided into four estates: the priests (the magi), the warriors, the officials and the landowners; the latter estate also included the artisans, merchants and physicians. The division into estates did not fully correspond to the existing class division: the ruling class included not only the warriors but also, at least partly, the scribes. Moreover, the military estate was subdivided into royal kinsmen (*vaspuhr*), magnates (*vazurg*) and the rest (*azat*, which means 'free, freeborn'). There was a stable court hierarchy where each rank differed by costume. The land was divided into the *dastakert* which belonged to the king, the *shahr* belonging to minor kinglets and the land of the cities (the latter land existed only in the western part of the empire, and mostly in the early period of its history). The exploited peasantry contributed either to the *dastakert* or the *shahr*. The Fire temples owned great riches.

Under the Sasanians, Iranian law was codified; it constituted an elaborate and well-reasoned system.

The ideological base of the Sasanian state was the religion of Zoroastrianism as reformed by stricter tenets. The cult of fire was central, but the introduction of a cult of the Sasanian king also began to develop. Just as Confucianism was reformed under the Elder Han by Tung Chung-shu, so Zoroastrianism was reformed under the Sasanians in the middle of the third century AD by Kartir (and then once more towards the end of the century). But just as Buddhism, Taoism and other doctrines were tolerated under the Han dynasty, so also under the Sasanians existed certain oppositional doctrines with which the Zoroastrian government established a *modus vivendi*. This was the case of the Jews, the Christians, and, in the earlier years, of the Manichees.[14] However, Mani, the founder of Manichaeism, was finally put to

14. Manichaeism, a dogmatic religion with its own scripture, was founded by Mani (215–274) in Babylonia. Mani was acquainted with Zoroastrianism, Christianity and Judaism, with different Gnostic and mystical doctrines. He regarded himself as 'the seal of the prophets', as the final religious teacher; his 'apostles' spread his doctrine to Iran, Central Asia and even China, to Egypt, North Africa and Asia Minor. The dogmatics and mythology of Manichaeism were very complicated. According to Mani, the good and evil are inherent in everything that exists, and they are in constant struggle. The Devil has invaded the world of Light. The soul of man may yield to evil by ignorance or negligence, and this postpones its acceptance in Paradise (instead, it can return to the world, or to hell, depending on the Higher Judgement). The believers were required to shun the world, to lead an ascetic life, to confess, to keep fasts, etc. Spreading during the Fifth Phase, in an epoch when all civilised countries already had their established dogmatic religions, Manichaeism was harshly persecuted nearly everywhere. It was practically wiped out in Rome and Byzantium in the sixth century, in Iran earlier still (here Mani himself died in prison); in the Arab Caliphate it was wiped out in the tenth century, in China it was prohibited in the eleventh; in Eastern Turkistan it held its own until the fourteenth century. Mani himself taught about a Creator who is in a state of struggle with a Creator of Evil, but some of the western Manichees (the Christian-Manichaean sect of Paulicians in Syria, and Asia Minor, seventh to ninth centuries) believed that the World was made by the Evil Creator, who is struggling with the Good One. This doctrine was resurrected in the tenth century in the creed of the Bogomils which spread in Bulgaria, Serbia, Bosnia and Italy. There was a connection between the Bogomils and 'heretic' Albigenses in Southern France; the latter were one and all killed off by Christian feudal 'crusaders' in 1209–1244. The Bogomils probably embraced Islam after the Balkans were conquered by Turkey in the fifteenth to sixteenth centuries.

death, and the Manichees went underground. Later Manichaeism was banned in China as well. As for Christianity, initially it was persecuted in Iran as the religion of the Byzantians who were enemies of the Iranian state, but was made legal after 451 when the Eastern Christians refused to endorse the Byzantian Nicene Creed and formed new Christian churches – the Monophysite and the Nestorian. After that the Christians of the Sasanian Empire became self-governing in regard to their inner religious and civil law affairs. A similar status was achieved by the Jews, who were numerous in the cities and villages of Sasanian Babylonia. The head of the Christians and their representative before the Sasanian government was the patriarch, the head of the Jews was the *rēsh-gālūtā* ('Head of the Exile'). Both were responsible for their co-religionists paying taxes. The artisans and the merchants also had their separate 'heads' according to their religions.

As to the level of technological development, the Sasanian Empire had made little progress compared to its predecessors with the exception of warfare and what seems to have been a cavalry consisting of 'knights'; it was the mainstay of the country's military forces based on fortified cities and castles. International trade played an important role; a route passed northward towards western Central Asia (here new states of the Early Antiquity type had emerged; Zoroastrianism in a form slightly different from that existing in Iran, as well as Manichaeism had been adopted); from there the route continued to meet the Chinese 'Silk Road'; another route, towards the South, was the 'Incense Road' to South Arabia and hence over the sea to India. The trade was mostly in the hands of Aramaic ('Syriac') Nestorian Christians, and also in the hands of Manichees and non-orthodox Zoroastrians (the Sogdians, in the valley of the Oxus River, modern Amu-Darya). Settlements founded by these groups of traders were to be found all along Central Asia as far as the borders of China, and overseas, on the shores of India. It seems the merchants attempted to keep their main storage places out of reach of the Sasanian Empire. The Iranian nobility did not personally take part in the trade, but there is no doubt that it made good profit from it.

In spite of it being an empire, the Sasanian state, just as was the case with the Later Han, must be regarded as belonging to the Middle Ages, not to Imperial Antiquity.

The fall of the Sasanian Empire will be described below in connection with Islam.

The typological similarity between the Late Roman Empire, Sasanian Iran, and the Empire of the Later Dynasty of Han is considerable; we might disregard the dissimilarities as minor, were it not for some specific circumstances, partly due to outside events.

In the Roman Empire, technology did not change materially during the period which had elapsed from the Early to the Late Empire, and this is also true of the military techniques; but with the new centuries the structure of the army changed appreciably. If earlier it was the free proprietors of land who were called up for military service, now gradually emerged a new type of professional army consisting of hereditary warriors. A peculiarity of the Late Empire was the retention of the system of cities (no longer called *polis* but *municipia*); their inhabitants (*municipals* in the earlier period, *curials* later on) continued to use slave labour, while outside the city lands, the labour of *coloni* (dependent tenants) was mainly used. As to the slaves, they received the right to a *peculium*, which meant unlimited possession of means of production and other objects, which, however, remained the property of the slave's owner. Thus the difference between slaves and *coloni* was minimised. At the same time, the muncipals were burdened by *liturgies*, i.e. public duties of building and keeping up public constructions (bath-houses, hostels, roads, water-mains, etc.); these were to be performed gratuitously. Formerly an honorary responsibility of the richer members of the *polis*, the liturgy had evolved to become a form of oppressive taxation.

There had never been a 'royal' or 'imperial' economic sector in the Roman Empire (since the Empire had not been created by a monarch but by the *polis* of Rome collectively). So land was divided into the municipal – which, in principle, was owned by city dwellers – and the exempt, which included big economies, called *saltus*; it also included peasant communities (especially in the outlying regions). Although the different emperors tended to be inconsequent in their actions, the main trend was towards trying to eliminate the difference between municipal and exempted land. The curials tended to be stratified, a minority being medium-level landowners, and the majority merging with the exploited class. Already in the third century AD the population of the Empire was being unofficially subdivided into the *honestiores* and the *humiliores*, and in the fourth to fifth centuries it was legally subdivided into the *potentiores* and the *inferiores*; thus the Phase transition to a medieval structure of society can be regarded as having been completed (cf. the similar terminology in third/fourth century China).

The most important phenomenon in the economics of the Late Roman Empire as it evolved between the third and fifth centuries AD was the landownership of the magnates, the latter uniting property right to land with administrative and later also judicial power. Since the lands of the magnates were vast, the 'inferiores' here had an easier life, and city dwellers migrated *en masse* to the saltuses, so that the cities decayed. Within the magnates' land, natural exchange dominated; money did not disappear, but the coins were being devalued (for instance, silvered copper coins replacing silver coins).

The powers-that-be tried for a long time to sustain, in the realm of ideology, the ancient cults of the *poleis* (with the obligatory addition of the cult of the reigning emperor); under the emperors Decius (about 250 AD) and Diocletian (284–305) bloody mass persecutions of Christians occurred. However, the staunchness of the Christian martyrs helped to strengthen their oppositional doctrine. Their strength lay in the negation of ethnic and social barriers (as Apostle Paul put it: 'There is neither Jew nor Greek, there is neither bond nor free, there is neither male nor female: for ye are all one to Christ Jesus', Gal. 3); and also in self-discipline, in generous mutual aid, and even help for outsiders, not to speak of the hope which it gave to the despairing population of the Roman Empire (moreover, Christianity also spread to regions outside the Empire). Finally, the imperial authorities decided it would be more useful to adopt the new doctrine instead of trying to kill off its adherents. By that time Christianity had spread to the majority of the population, and under the emperor Constantine (in 313 AD) it was introduced as a dogmatic doctrine obligatory for all the subjects of the Empire (though the old religion was formally forbidden only in 381). An attempt by the emperor Julian to create an alternative universal religion based on the traditional Graeco-Roman cults (361–363) failed. There followed persecutions of 'heathens' (a notorious case was the atrocious murder in Alexandria of the Neo-Platonist woman philosopher Hypatia by a rabble that seems to have been incited by the patriarch Cyril, renowned for his persecution of all kinds of differently minded persons). (Later he was canonised as a saint.)

The movement of anchorites – persons who fled to the desert to escape the acts of violence committed by the local bureaucracy, at first in Egypt in the first to second centuries, and then also elsewhere – developed, after the victory of Christianity, into a movement of Christian monks: they settled, in order to save their souls, in uninhabited places (hermitages), e.g. in deserted towers, etc., and there they began to organise monastic communities. The monks, following as they did Christ's teachings most closely, especially the demand for chastity, were highly respected by the believers, and it was primarily from them that the leaders of the Church were selected. There even existed an opinion that monastic life was the sole path to salvation.

Christianity now evolved a hierarchy of its own: there were the *diakonos* ('servant, helper'), the *hiereus* ('priest'), the *episcopos* (bishop, lit. 'surveyor'), and the *patriarchēs*, a title which was conferred on the supreme bishops. The patriarch of Rome, called the *papa* (pope), was uppermost. The dogmatic base of the Christian faith (the 'Creed', *Credō*) was approved by special meetings of the hierarchs (the first and the most important was that of Nicaea, 325 AD, with the still unbaptised emperor Constantine presiding; that of Constantinople, 381 AD, when the authoritative Nicene Creed was formulated more fully, and that of Chalcedon in 451 AD). In the final form of the Creed, as adopted, for example, by the Eastern Orthodox Church, there is an addition from the so-called Apostolic Creed, stating that the organisation of all Christians is the Church, which is indivisible, holy, catholic (i.e. universal), apostolic (because the apostles received divine grace from Christ, their disciples from the apostles, and so on to the last *hiereus*), and finally, orthodox, i.e. the only correct Church in its teaching. All points of the Creed were so formulated that each refuted a certain 'heresy', since the different interpretations of Christ's teaching were by that time many. Some of the 'heretic' doctrines were suppressed, others developed into separate churches.

For someone today accustomed to differences in opinions, there is a hair-splitting quality to the theological disputes both in the early Middle Ages and in the

Post-Medieval period. The reason was that the Christian hierarchy took it upon itself (because of 'apostolic grace') to decide on subjects not discussed in the Gospels, and thus, it would seem, the province of God alone. Such, for instance, was the fourth-century controversy between the adherents of the idea of Christ being *homoousios* 'of one substance' with God the father, and adherents of his being *homolousios*, 'of similar substance'; or, as late as in the seventeenth century, the controversy between the Jansenists and the Jesuits on the comparative importance of man's free will and divine grace for the redemption of sins and the salvation of sinners: the Jesuits emphasised grace, while the Jansenists relied on free will. The discussion resulted in some heads being chopped off. Each of such discussions (and they were many) had, of course, its political reasons, and the suppression of 'heretics' assumed the most savage forms.

The emperor Constantine, breaking once and for all with the Roman *polis* traditions, transferred the capital of the Empire from Rome to Byzantium on the Bosporus straits between the Black and the Marmara Seas (330 AD); the new capital received the name Constantinople (now Istanbul), and the new Eastern Roman Empire received the name Byzantium, although Rome also continued to be regarded as a parallel capital of the Empire unto the end of the fifth century AD. The last emperor to attempt to resurrect the Roman Empire in its former extent was Justinian (527–565), who also led a long and useless war against Sasanian Iran.

The fate of the Western Roman Empire, on the one hand, and of the population of Eastern Europe north of Byzantium, on the other, was connected with specific phenomena which at first seem not to conform with the outlined schema. Actually, they underlay the same laws of Phase transitions: the possibilities of development of the society are, under the existing state of the 'productive forces' (i.e. mainly of the technology), exhausted; in social psychology there appears a complex of 'injustice'; the existing relations in production are restructured (from above or from below), especially as regards the technology of arms. Such a process is repeated in every Phase of history, but it is not synchronous in the different regions of the world. It depends on differences in the natural environment, and the availability of resources necessary for the introduction of new arms, and on the growth of the level and quality of consumption. It is important that at some periods and in different places of the Earth societies of the Fourth or the Fifth Phase have contact with societies that still are in the Second or the Third Phase, or with nomads. This leads to non-typical situations with a very serious historical outcome.

The population of the forested taiga zone in Europe, north of the Alps, and west of the Dnieper river basin persisted into the first centuries AD at the level of chiefdoms. This was caused by natural conditions (only comparatively small spaces could be cleared of forest for arable land, and especially for cattle pastures).[15] Part of the

---

15. It may be important that the horse began to be used for ploughing and as a draught animal: this happened late in the first millenium AD, when (at first in the lower reaches of the Rhine) heavy draughthorses were first bred, and at the same time horse-shoes and the horse-collar were invented.

taiga population was still living, in fact, under the conditions of the First Phase. Meanwhile, the lively exchange with the Roman Empire furnished the tribes with a technology characteristic of Imperial Antiquity or even of the Phase transition to the Middle Ages. This leads to a surplus in population growth and to a unique phenomenon: namely, to mass migration of formerly settled tribes to the south, towards the borders, and even into the territory of the Empire itself (the Roman and later the Byzantium Empire). The migrants belonged to two sub-branches of Indo-Europeans: the most important were the Gothic-Vandal and the Central Germanic tribes (comprising the Alamanni, the Franks, etc.); some migrants were groups of Slavs. The first contacts between Rome and the 'Barbarians' (actually the Germanics) were incidental, and the aggressors were the Romans; but then a certain pressure of the Germanic tribes against Rome's frontiers began to be felt. Possibly because of the growing number of the *coloni* and the falling number of freeborn soldiers in the Empire, imperial authorities began to feel a shortage in military forces, and decided to allow the 'Barbarians' to settle within its frontiers in the capacity of *foederati* (allies), using them freely in their own armed forces. In the later centuries of the Empire, the Roman army became less and less 'Roman'.

A portion of the Germanic tribes invading Roman territory adopted Christianity (not in its orthodox Catholic form recognised by Rome, but in the form of Arianism: the Arians regarded Christ as a man who only after his birth was incarnated as God). Those migrants who had not adopted Christianity restructured their religious ideology: instead of Donar, the supreme thunderer-god (a situation typical of chiefdoms) they accepted as supreme the originally minor wanderer-god Wotan, whom the Romans identified with their own Mercury. Having reached the level of social development when a class division of society was possible, the Germanic tribes started to create their chiefdoms, and later their kingdoms on both sides of the Roman Empire boundary. Thus Early Antiquity type kingdoms arose in Northern Africa, in Spain, in what is modern France and in the territory between the Rhine and the western tributaries of the Dnieper. Atypically, they combined features of Early Antiquity with those of the Early Middle Ages, because, on a world scale, it actually was an epoch when Early Antiquity had outlasted its term.

Julius Caesar (first century BC) writes on the Germanic tribes in his 'Commentaries'. He mentions their attempt to cross the Rhine in Gaul (a country corresponding to modern France and Belgium, which by that time had already been conquered by Rome). If we believe what Caesar has to relate about these tribes, they must have still lived in the First Primitive Stage. Nearly 150 years later these tribes were in more detail observed by the Roman historian Tacitus, and from his description it is quite apparent that these tribes had by that time reached the Second, Primitive Communal Stage.

In the first half of the first millennium AD, during a period preceding the creation of their first states, the Germanic and the Slavic tribes formed tribal unions – unstable ones to judge from the change in their names and localisation in the

Roman sources. In their original places of habitation these tribes were mainly agriculturists, but during their migration they became cattle breeders. The first Germanic states were formed as extensive but unstable conglomerations, not unlike the African empires of the Zulu and the Fulani in the nineteenth century AD. The territories occupied by the Barbarian kingdoms tended to change quickly, and could even move for hundreds of miles away from their original location. We are not going to dwell on the changes in their fortunes. This is politically a very complicated story, and it seems advisable to point out only a few of the more typical cases.

Consider, first of all, the Goths and their near kindred the Vandals. Living in the Iron Age, all Germanic tribes had iron arrow- and spearheads, but their armament was, on the whole, as described above for the beginning of Early Antiquity. The homeland of the Goths was southern Sweden,[16] a region which is still called Götland (and cf. the island of Gotland nearby). The Germanic tribes of Scandinavia had a long time ago mastered the art of seafaring, so that the Goths could, in their boats, perhaps in the second to first centuries BC, pass to the southern shore of the Baltic Sea. Here – roughly from the Jutland Peninsula in the direction of the Vistula River, and not very deep into present-day Germany – lived the kindred tribes of the Vandals. Moving on from this territory, the Vandals made a huge march, including the traversal of the Balkans, the sack of Roman cities in Italy, and the creation of a kingdom, first in Spain (Andalusia), and later in Northern Africa. This Vandal kingdom was conquered by the emperor Justinian – or, to be exact, by his general Belisarius – in 534 AD.

In the first century the Goths, who seem to have been the most advanced of the Germanic tribes, created a more or less stable kingdom on the Vistula; in the third century they succeeded in forcing the Roman army to leave the completely Romanised province of Dacia (present-day Romania); but the main direction of their movements was towards the East. It seems that Slavic tribes played a considerable role in the Gothic kingdom, because Slavic languages retain many Gothic words, reflecting cultural borrowings: thus *khleb* 'bread' (from an earlier *khleiba* from Gothic *hlaifs*, or, rather, from the more ancient form *hlaibhaz*), which meant 'bread baked in an oven (and, probably, made with yeast)', as different from a *l-iepekha*, which was a flat cake moulded (*liepiti*) from paste, and baked on charcoal.[17]

---

16. Note that often only a part of the population migrated. Thus, a part of the warriors of Central Sweden (the Suiones) went away with the Goths, the rest remained to become Swedes; a part of the Goths also remained in Southern Sweden, where they were called 'Gauts' but assumed the Swedish language. A part of the Central Germanic tribe of the Suevi (Suebi) was caught up in the movements of the Vandali, and at a later period founded a short-lived kingdom in Portugal; another part, the Swabians (Schwaben) still exists as a part of the German nation. The Saxons partly went away to Britain together with the Angli, but most of them stayed in Germany.

17. The same nominal stem *hlaibh*- has been preserved in modern English as 'loaf'; cf. 'Lord', from ancient *hlafweard* 'bread-keeper'.

Another such Slavic word is *izba* 'wooden hut', the usual habitation of the Slavic peasant in the forest zone, from an earlier *istubā* from Gothic *stubā* (cf. German *Stube* 'room', English *stove*). The word was usual for a dwelling heated not by an open fire under an aperture in the roof as in the more ancient Indo-European *domus* (a term still retained in Slavic for 'house' or 'home' in a general sense), but by an oven. The Gothic *kuningaz* 'chief' (English *king*) has been preserved nearly without change in the Baltic languages (Estonian *kuningas*), and was received into Slavic as *küne(n)z(i)* 'prince, kinglet'. Of Gothic origin is the word *kaupaz* 'merchant' (from Vulgar Latin *caupo*), hence Old Slavonic *koup(iti)*, Estonian *kauba-*, Russian *kupit'*, German *kaufen*, English *cheap*). Such close relations between Slavs and Goths are the more remarkable if we take into consideration that there are practically no words in Russian which can be shown to be borrowed from the language of the Norman (Vaering, Varyag) dynasty which actually ruled in Russia in the ninth to eleventh centuries AD.

The Goths moved towards the east as far as the Black Sea and the Crimea, where the Gothic language was preserved as late as the seventeenth century (later the Goths were assimilated by the Crimean Tatars). Vulgar Latin, on the other hand, was preserved in Gothic Dacia, later evolving into the Romanian (Rumanian) language.

Any further movement of the Goths towards the East seems to have been brought to a stop by the Iranian-speaking tribe of the Alani (whose language and traditions are continued by the present-day Ossetes in the Caucasus). It was probably then that the Goths became divided into two branches, the Ostrogoths in the East, and the Visigoths in the West. The most famous of the Ostrogothic kings was Ermanaric; tales of him later spread among all Germanic tribes, even including the Anglo-Saxons. But Ermanaric also encountered an enemy which proved to be invincible, namely, the Huns.

The Huns were a mighty, numerous and warlike tribe, Mongoloid from the point of view of physical anthropology, either Mongol or Turkic by their language; it is not impossible that they were identical with the Hsiung-nu of the Chinese sources. For the same reasons which usually lead to migrations of nomadic tribes, they started a powerful movement towards the West, incorporating the tribes they met on the way into their own hordes; this happened to a considerable part of the Alani (the rest moved towards the Caucasus). Ermanaric, failing to achieve victory over the Huns, committed suicide (in 376 AD?).

The remainder of the Ostrogoths and all Visigoths moved, with their families and cattle, towards the West; the Ostrogoths settled as *foederati* on Byzantian territory, and later passed all through the Balkans and Greece, finally invading Rome, where their chief, Theodoric, succeeding another Germanic leader, Odoacer, became king of Italy (493–526). Formally he was supposed to obey the Byzantian emperor. In the kingdom of Theodoric the Romans were not allowed to bear arms, and also some other of their rights were curtailed. The Ostrogothic reign over Italy was of short duration. Meanwhile, between 376 and 507 AD the Visigoths made a fantastic journey: from the Dnieper to near the walls of Constantinople, thence to Greece including the Peloponnese peninsula, then towards the North along the Adriatic, then to the South through the Apennine peninsula as far as the end of Calabria, then to Southern France and to Eastern Spain, then back to France unto the valley of the Loire. Being thrust back from there, they (probably already Romanised as to their language) returned to Spain where they founded a stable kingdom which existed until 711, when it was destroyed by the Arabs. On this journey the Visigoths sometimes stopped for ten to fifteen years, only to continue on their path until they finally settled in Spain.

It should be kept in mind that it was not only the Germanic tribes of the Gotho-Vandalic group who were constantly on the move; the same happened to the tribes of the Central group. Thus the Franks and the Burgundians[18] invaded Gaul (which still had not become France), and settled there; the Angli from modern Schleswig, along with a western group of the Saxons and a part of the Jutes invaded Britain and settled there; moreover (something that was not very usual for Germanic tribes), they apparently tried to destroy the local population, thus forcing the Celtic nation of the Britons to retire to Wales and Cornwall or to flee overseas to Brittany (Bretagne; the local population of Gaul had been Romanised by that time). Of the other Germanic tribes, the Langobards (Lombardians) stayed in Italy and were Romanised there, the Helvetii stayed in modern Switzerland. This is far from being a complete account of the Germanic tribes.

The Huns, throwing the Goths off the plains of Eastern Europe and driving a big wedge into Central Europe via Visigothic Dacia, reached the frontier of the Roman Empire along the Danube, making devastating raids into Roman territory.

Attila, the 'king' of the Huns, who acquired despotic power, imposed a huge tribute in gold on the Byzantine Empire. He traded in prisoners taken during his raids, and had pretensions to imperial rank; but invading Gaul, he suffered a crushing defeat from the allied forces of the Romans and the Visigoths of king Theodoric in the battle of the Catalaunian plains (450 AD, near modern Châlons-sur-Marne). However, the Huns did not stop their inroads, but after the death of Attila in 453 they were destroyed in wars with the Goths and especially by internal warfare.

We have already mentioned that the Huns left no trace in the European population, either in physical anthropology or in the languages.[19]

---

18. The Burgundians probably also originated from the Baltic; from their tribal name is derived the name of the island Bornholm; ancient *Borgundarholm*.
19. We have omitted the history of the Avars (the Obri) who repeated the movement of the Huns in the sixth to seventh centuries. The Avars settled in Pannonia (the future Hungary) and in Dacia. There were also other waves of nomads coming from the East (the Khazars, the Bulgars). Connected with these is the appearance of the Hungarians (Magyars), a tribe akin to the Khanty and Mansi now living along the Orb and the Irtysh rivers; the Magyars were torn away from their homeland by a nomad migration. The number of Hungarians that had settled in Pannonia was not great, however the local Slavonic population assumed their language.

Naturally, under the described conditions the existence of the Roman Empire (at least of the Western Empire) actually became a fiction, so that hardly anyone noticed when the last Roman 'emperor', the young Romulus Augustulus (enthroned by his adroit father, a former counsellor of Attila) was dethroned by the Germanic leader Odoacer.

The sixth century witnessed the last major masterpiece of Ancient thought. In the 530s, on the initiative of the emperor Justinian, Roman law was codified (we have already noticed that similar codifications had been achieved in Sasanian Iran; in China the first attempts at codifying laws were made under the Ch'in and the Elder Han dynasties, but the juridical system influencing all later legal activities in China, was created under the T'ang in the seventh century AD). The greatest merit which belongs to the compilers of Codex Justinianus – and especially to their leader Trebonianus – lies in the fact that a coherent system of legal thought was made possible, a system of legal definitions which had a tremendous influence upon all later European law until this day (least of all was British law influenced). And in spite of the fact that the Codex Justinianus actually appeared in the early Middle Ages, it was the result of the legal thought of the Imperial Antiquity.

The fact that it was not nomads who moved into the Roman Empire but tribes which had originally been settled gave a quite unique historical colouring to a whole series of events during that age. The kingdoms arising in the early period of the Middle Ages retained certain features of the Early Antiquity type. Note that the composition of the population in the countries conquered by the Germanic tribes did not change drastically. The main mass of the inhabitants of France, Spain and Italy continued to use dialects of 'Vulgar Latin', and the contribution of Germanic dialects to the new languages developing out of 'Vulgar Latin' – French, Spanish, Italian, etc., – was not very important. The history of these countries did not start from scratch – it was mainly the history of the same population which inhabited them in Antiquity.

Discussing the movements of the Germanic tribes, we should take notice of the specific role played by their Scandinavian group, often described as Normans, but actually calling themselves *Vaerings* (Russ. *Varyagi*), i.e. 'inhabitants of the offshore islands'; locally also called Danes, Norsemen (North-men) or Rus (Ros). The latter seem to have originated from Northern Sweden, where their name is preserved in a local toponym (Roslag, cf. Tröndelag inhabited by the Trönds in Northern Norway, and Danelagh (Danelaw), the habitat of Scandinavians in Eastern England); the Finnish name for Sweden is still Ruotsi to this day. As to the Danes and the Norsemen, these names were only at a comparatively late stage assigned to the inhabitants of Denmark and Norway respectively; at an earlier stage the two terms were used indiscriminately for Western and Southern Scandinavian tribes.

The Scandinavians occupied spaces either formerly totally uninhabited or but thinly populated – such as Northern Norway, Iceland, Greenland (with a 'colony' on the shore of North America – Vinland), the Faeroe Islands, the Shetlands, the Orkneys, the Hebrides – or attempted to conquer territories that were already inhabited by other Germanic or Celtic tribes (Denmark, Eastern England, a part of Ireland, Normandy, i.e. Northern France; the inhabitants of Normandy, even when French-speaking, are often specifically called Normans, but we shall use the term only in the sense of Scandinavians). They became Romanised in Normandy, Slavicised in Russia, and ousted from most of the islands (except the farthest) by Celts and Anglo-Saxons. The Normans raided also the southern shores of Western Europe, including the Mediterranean, but for the most part did not try to settle there.[20] Moreover, they sailed upstream along the rivers; they also sailed down the Volga to the Caspian Sea (the 'Rusi' in the history of Azerbaijan who brutally raided the slores of the Caspian, were, of course, Vaering Normans). It was also they who traced the 'Way from the Varyagi to the Greeks' mentioned by the Russian 'Primary Chronicle' – and afterwards 'protected' it – by taking tribute from passing merchants. Objects and documents left by the Scandinavians have been found in the Neva valley, near Novgorod, and in Belorussia.

A movement not unlike the Germanic in the West was that of the Slavs in the East of Europe. The centre of the original settlement of the Slavs seems to have been the territory from the middle reaches of the Dnieper to the Vistula (first century BC–first century AD and later). As we have mentioned above, the Slavs had been a rather stable part of the Gothic Kingdom. Its fall and the intrusion of the Huns, as well as causes similar to those that had, somewhat earlier, led to the migrations of the Germanic tribes, directed the movement of the Slavs – to westward (partly to areas left by the Celts and the Germanic tribes), to the north-east (where they spread among the rather sparsely settled Fenno-Ugric tribes, occupying nearly all the taiga forest zone in Eastern Europe), and to the south, into Byzantine territory. Important in the early history of the Slavonic tribes was their clash with the Avars, or Obri in the sixth to seventh centuries, and with the Turkic tribe of the Bulgars moving somewhat later from the Volga westwards. Finally, both tribes dissolved in the Slavonic population ('perished' as the Russian 'Primary Chronicle' puts it). Only the Ugrian tribe of the Magyars (originally from the Volga basin) survived in Hungary.

Thus there were several waves of nomads moving towards the West from the central parts of Asia: Huns, Ugrians, Turks, Mongols. The reason may have been over-population in the cattle-rearing region and/or a long period of drought in the Eastern Asiatic pasture zones during the fifth to ninth centuries.

As for the Slavs, from the fourth to fifth centuries, preserving mutually

20. Still, they founded and maintained for a time a kingdom in Sicily and Southern Italy.

understandable dialects, they were divided into the Venedi in the West, the Sclavini in the South, and the Anti in the East.[21]

In some places there appeared Slavonic chiefdoms, and sometimes even rather extensive kingdoms. But the chiefdom phase became predominant among the Slavs at a somewhat later date than among the Germanic tribes, therefore dynasties originating from outside the Slavonic area played here a certain role: thus the Normans (Rus, or Vaerings) – in Russia, the Turkic Bulgars who had been ousted from the Volga by the Khazars – in the Balkan region. The Norman and the Turkic elements were totally assimilated by the Slavs, both as regards the language and the culture, not leaving even traces as did the Goths. Nevertheless, the contention that there never were any Normans in Russia is patiently jingoistic. Along the 'Way from the Varyagi to the Greeks' have been found Scandinavian Runic inscriptions, as well as Scandinavian archaeological objects; the Greek sources name in parallel the 'Russian' (actually Norman) and simultaneously the 'Slavonic' (actually Slavonic) names of the rapids on the Dnieper; the first Russian 'princes' (*knyaz'* *kunenzi-*, 'kings') – the term is Germanic – have easily identifiable Scandinavian proper names: *Ryurik* (=Hrörek), *Oleg* (=Helgi), *Igor'* (=Yngvar), *Olga* (=Helga), *Svenald* (=Sveinveld), *Askold* (=Háskuld), *Volodimer* (the last name, in the form *Voldemar*, *Valdemar* was borrowed by the Normans form the Celts, and later Slavicised to *Vladimir*). Of the two dozen or so names of Russian envoys arriving in Byzantium in the eleventh century, only three are easily identifiable as Slavonic, but many are Scandinavian. Moreover, the Russian 'Primary Chronicle' says: 'Thus were these Varyagi called "Rus", as others are called Swedes, Normans, Angles and Goths; thus also these.' But soon the Varyagan stratum was absorbed by the Slavic ethnic mass, just as it absorbed the Merya (Mari) the Ves' (Vepsi) and other Fenno-Ugrian tribes. On the deeds of prince Oleg, the 'Primary Chronicle' has this to say: 'And he had with him Varyagi, and Slavs, and others who were named Rus.' The cultural connections of Slavonic Russia were extensive. Vladimir II Monomach (1113–1125) notes in his reminiscences that 'My father, sitting at home, learned five languages, since therein lies honour from foreign lands.'

The Turkic (Bulgar)-speaking dynasty in the Balkans survived as such somewhat longer than the Norman-speaking dynasty in Russia; like the Norman 'Rus', the

---

21. This subdivision goes back to Greek historiographic tradition but does not conform with the usage inside the Slav world itself. Thus the Estonians and the Finns call the Russians and Belorussians *Vene*, i.e. Venedi, while according to Greek tradition they ought to be considered as Antae. However, it is probable that both terms have a common origin, from an ethnonym (not necessary an autonym), *Want-. Thus the name of the city Vyatka (now Kirov, formerly Khlynov), and the name of a Northern Slavonic tribe, Vyatichi, are both derived from a more ancient *Wanti. The city was called 'Antian' because it was situated in a non-Antian, i.e. a Fenno-Ugrian environment. The Slavs themselves divided all tribes known to them into *Slovene* (from *slovo* 'word') who spoke a comprehensible language, and into *Niemcy* (from *niemŭ* 'mute, dumb', i.e. not comprehensible). In modern Russian *Nemcy* means 'Germans', *Slovene* has been changed to *Slaviane*, from *slava* 'glory'.

Turkic Bulgars left their name to the country where they had reigned, but its language also remained Slavonic.[22]

The movements of the Germanic and the Slavonic tribes through Europe came to an end in the seventh century (but the spread of the Slavonic speech to the East continued for many centuries to come).

There began a period which saw the emergence of new, more stable states, none of which, however, was a 'national' state in the sense of being connected with the speakers of one particular language. In the West, only Britain and Pannonia changed their language (from Celtic to Anglo-Saxon, and from a Romance language to the Ugrian language Hungarian). The Franks, the Burgundians, the Visigoths and the Langobards were absorbed by the population speaking the 'Vulgar Latin' of the Roman Empire. Meanwhile, the population of the Byzantian empire was completely Slavicised, except for the Rumanians and the Greeks. Latin continued to be the written language in the West of Europe; in the East, the written language was mostly Greek, although the Goths and, since the ninth century, the Slavs as well evolved their own alphabetic scripts.[23]

After the Great Migration – actually from the eighth to the ninth centuries – Western Europe returned to the normal medieval way of development, and reached its highest stage, which in world scholarship is usually called 'feudalism'. Typical of feudalism were knights, with their chain armour or, later, cuirasses, with their armoured horses, long swords and their bow and arrows (from the twelfth to thirteenth centuries, crossbows). During the same period developed a system of castles (at least one castle in every important feud – supposed to be unassailable). Dominating the field of ideology was a dogmatic form of the Christian religion in its Roman Catholic variant, with rigid and even savage suppression of any kind of oppositional doctrines.

The foundations of the social structure typical of feudalism were laid under the second Frankish dynasty, that of the Carolingians, who ruled in the eighth to tenth centuries over considerable territories in what now is France, Germany and Italy.

The feudal system was based on feudal benefice extending to land (as well as to other sources of income), and on certain obligatory personal relations. A benefice was not property. The holder of a benefice was a vassal of a person of higher rank (his suzerain), to whom the vassal owed certain services and his personal loyalty. His suzerain might at the same time be the vassal of somebody else. To maintain himself, a vassal knight had to be the suzerain of no less than fifteen to thirty

22. The Bulgars were a Turkic tribe, possibly speaking a language akin to modern Chuvash on the Volga. A part of them was pushed off to the Balkans by the Khazars in the seventh century. But perhaps the majority of the Bulgars, whose kingdom originally was situated between the Kuban and the Don, moved northwards and settled along the Volga and the Kama, where their kingdom survived until the Mongolian conquest in the thirteenth century.

23. The Germanic tribes had had a primitive alphabet since the third century; this was probably borrowed from northern Etruscans in what now is Switzerland. But this alphabet (Runic) was mostly used for magic and funeral purposes.

peasant families. Military affairs were entrusted exclusively to the knighthood which constituted a separate estate; the peasants were not supposed to wear arms. Besides the fiefs (feuds) were also preserved some allodiums, i.e. land whose owners were no one's vassals except the king's. Often the suzerains had also judicial rights over their vassals – if they had enough power to put their rights into practice.

The feudal system took form for the first time in the Frankish Kingdom. It did not exist as such in Britain,[24] in Scandinavia or in Russia, where each landowner, even if he tilled his own land himself, was entitled to be armed; where a *thing*, or a *vieché*, or other forms of popular assembly continued in existence, as well as other institutions characteristic of Early Antiquity, and only a part of the peasantry (the *smerds* in Russia) was exploited and restricted in their rights. There also existed slaves (*kholops* in Russia), but their labour was of little importance.

No feudal (vassal) system existed in Russia. Theoretically, local princes were subject to the Grand Prince whose kinsmen they were; such local princes had their apanages (*udiel*), but they changed them every time one of them died, each prince moving from the less important *idiel* to a more important one; the prince holding the most important *idiel* was Grand Prince. This system was introduced in the eleventh century, but there was no real possibility of keeping to it strictly. Just like the Western feudal system, it led only to bloody internecine strife, and to a division of the apanages into 'sub-apanages', which produced something similar to the Western feudal system – not in the economic but only in the political sense.

Like Russia, Poland and Scandinavia had missed the stage of Imperial Antiquity. Here the historical development assumed other forms.

The beginning of Poland as a state under the Piast dynasty (eleventh to twelfth centuries) resembled that of the Russian state: here too emerged one Grand Prince (from 1025, king) who divided his land between his sons; similar also were the debates over the question of seniority inside the dynasty. This led to attempts of the German Holy Roman Empire to conquer the country (under Frederick Barbarossa, 1157); German traders, handicraftsmen and peasants penetrated into Polish territory. A devastating raid of the Tataro-Mongols occurred in 1241; however, there were no painful after-effects. The main problem was the constant wars with the northern and north-eastern enemies: the chiefdoms of the Prussians[25] and the

---

24. The feudal system was introduced in England after the Norman conquest by William I in 1066. The Normans in question were a dynasty of Norman (Norwegian) origin which had captured Northern France (Normandy), and by the eleventh century had been long since Romanised (i.e. they spoke a dialect of French); and they already professed Catholicism.

25. The original Prussians (who should not be confused with the Germans living in Prussia, who also are called Prussians) were a group of tribes belonging to the Baltic branch of the Indo-European linguistic family; at present, to this branch belong the Lithuanians, the Latgalians and the Latvians, while formerly there also existed such Indo-European Baltic tribes as the Old Prussians, Yatvingians, Semigalians, Curonians, Selonians, Galdinians, etc., spreading from Prussia to a region near modern Moscow.

Lithuanians. Against them, prince Konrad Mazowiecki called in the knights of the Teutonic order – crusaders who had returned from unsuccessful campaigns in Palestine (on which see below) – and suggested to them a crusade against the Baltic 'heathens'. The Grand Master of the order, Hermann von Salz, declared the German emperor Frederic II to be the suzerain of all territories conquered by the crusaders. Since that time there long co-existed in the Baltic region a German gentry and nobility, and a local peasantry with its own languages and culture. As to culture, Lithuania was the most isolated region; no form of Christianity could take root here under the Lithuanian king Gediminas and his descendants.

The development of Scandinavian countries began from the level of Early Antiquity, which gradually developed into the Middle Ages, bypassing the stage of Imperial Antiquity. Slavery died out early; the peasantry was divided into freemen who were entitled to be armed, and 'land-hirers', i.e. leaseholders. In 1380 Norway was united with Denmark, which developed more or less on the same lines as the neighbouring German feudal states (but the Danish politico-economic situation did not extend to Norway). Sweden also began from Early Antiquity: peasants were represented in the Riksdag (a sort of parliament) along with the nobility, church-men and citizens as late as the sixteenth century.[26]

In England also, Early Antiquity dominated until the eleventh century; feudal-ism was introduced here by the conqueror from Normandy, William I (r. 1066–1087). On the whole, England developed according to the medieval type, but it is important to note that free peasantry did not disappear, while the gentry, in union with the city-dwellers, extorted from the king the 'Great Charter of Liberties';[27] a parliament representing the estates was constituted in 1265. The Post-Medieval Phase began around the fifteenth to sixteenth centuries. On the main events in the history of England we shall dwell further on.

Since we are discussing general processes of development of mankind, it is nei-ther interesting nor productive to dwell on all the different stages of the appear-ance, growth and decay of the different and numerous state structures in medieval Western Europe. Their existence always depended on the specific arrangement and placing of the different forces involved; in no case did the limits of a state coincide

26. Later Sweden embraced the doctrine of the Lutheran Reformation, and the kings confiscated vast ecclesiastical lands, which gave a stimulus to a post-medieval development. Mining and other industries flourished, hired labour was used widely. From 1680, an absolute monarchy was established (Charles XI, 1670–1697, Charles XII, 1697–1718). There was a period when Sweden had conquered all the coasts both in the northern and the southern part of the Baltic Sea. Even after having lost its external territories, Sweden continued to develop in the same direction as Europe in general did, namely, towards capitalism.

27. The Magna Carta – the Great Charter of English liberties (1215) – contains a provision which was of major constitutional importance for all the future history of England: namely, that 'No free-man shall be taken or imprisoned, or disseized, or outlawed, or exiled, or in any way destroyed, nor will we go upon him, nor will we send upon him, except by the lawful judgement of his peers or by the law of the land ... To no one will we [i.e. the king] sell, deny, or delay right or jus-tice' (clauses 39–40).

with the spread of a certain language, or certain ethnic features. Therefore we shall dwell only on one characteristic phenomenon which played a major role in the history of medieval Europe – on the creation of an empire by Charles I (Charlemagne).

In the late eighth century, in the course of wars typical of the feudal period, Charles, the king of the Western Franks, succeeded in uniting the kingdoms and tribes from the Bay of Biscay to the Adriatic, and from the North Sea to the Mediterranean; moreover, he also exacted tribute from Slavonic tribes and princes all along the eastern frontier of his empire.

At that time, the Roman pope Leo III was greatly concerned about the fate of Roman Catholicism: the crown of the emperors continued to be in the hands of non-Catholic Byzantium, which was still considered to be the only heir of the Roman Empire; taking advantage of the fact that the power in Byzantium had passed to the empress Irene, a monstrously cruel usurper, the pope declared the imperial throne vacant, and promised it to the Christian sovereign who had the greatest power to defend the Roman faith and the pope himself, namely to Charles, king of the Franks. In 800 AD, the pope crowned Charles as emperor. Of course, the new-born empire had already begun to disintegrate in the times of Charlemagne's son, Louis the Pious; but the principle of a union between the Pope and an Emperor (selected from among the Frankish kings, later from the Saxon or other Germanic kings), remained; all sovereign rulers in Central Europe, in Burgundy and Italy were regarded as imperial vassals, and had to be invested by the emperor, the emperor himself being crowned by the pope. This situation continued for a very long period; it survived the Crusades, on which we shall dwell below.

The relations between the individual emperors and the individual popes ranged from very friendly to most inimical, but the whole history of Europe was influenced by the fact of the existence – whether in union or in opposition – of the papal and the imperial power. In time, the title 'Roman Empire' was changed to 'The Holy Roman Empire'; when, in the fifteenth century, the Empire's Italian possessions were all lost, and the coronation of the emperors by the pope was discontinued, the 'Roman Empire' became 'The Holy Roman Empire of the German Nation'; in any respect, its monarch continued to be titled 'Caesar' (*Kaiser*), 'Emperor'.

Here we ought to dwell on what was meant by 'nation' at that epoch. Latin *natio* is derived from *natere* 'to give birth to'. Hence *natio* came to mean 'birth'; that which is born; descent, gender; degree of kinship more distant than family or local community'. Thus, this term did not have the connotation now usual in Russian, viz. 'a historical community of men, perceived by themselves as such, and based on the commonality of territory, language, political and cultural traditions, which are the result of lengthy common existence, and thus developing common traits of mentality'. The English definition includes 'forming a society under one government', which is much nearer to the medieval meaning of the term. Nation in the Russian sense of the word did not exist until the Sixth or even the Seventh Phase of the historical process.

The proselytic principle which lies at the base of all ethico-dogmatic religions (the contrasting of the 'rightly believing' to the 'wrongly believing') favoured the policy of conquests of the main medieval kingdoms (cf. already the campaigns of Charlemagne against the Western Slavonic 'heathens', and the Crusades: not only to Palestine, but from the thirteenth century to the Baltic region as well). Wars between individual feudal lords did not contribute to strengthening of the ruling class as a whole, and tended to destroy the enslaved peasantry; once the productive possibilities of the Medieval Phase were exhausted, there developed a stalemate which could be solved only by the creation of new relations in production. But this required an alternative socio-psychological ideology, and fundamentally new arms.

We shall later return to the Late Middle Ages in Europe and Russia, and to the most important processes which evolved there; but now we shall turn to the Eastern Roman Empire, which has already been mentioned in connection with the Slavonic migration.

The characteristic of the Late Roman Empire as given above is just as applicable to the early Byzantine Empire until the seventh century; it developed in the same direction. But note that already from the end of the fourth century old cities were subject to agrarianisation, and the new cities emerged mainly as administrative centres. As to the living standard, Byzantium's was higher than that in the countries formerly belonging to the Western Roman Empire; the country led an extensive trade with Iran, with Arabia, and even with China.

The Roman Empire had once stretched from Spain and Britain to Syria; but the history of the Late Roman Empire, and the early history of the Byzantine Empire as well, were interrupted by periods of break-ups of the original territory, and the creation of competing 'empires', and of new, mostly unstable, states.

The seventh to eighth centuries saw the creation of a new system of military-administrative regions (*themes*), and a new estate of warriors (*stratiotes*; the warriors and their horses were not armoured). The *stratiotes* corresponded to the Western European knights and to the Japanese *samurai*. At the same time, the dependent peasantry was organised (partly under the influence of the Slavs who had settled in the Byzantine Empire) into village communities. Also during this period it happened that internecine strife occurred, always based ideologically on some supposed religious grounds. In the middle of the ninth century the Byzantine Empire, having lost much of its original territory, evolved into a strong centralised state; in the eleventh to twelfth centuries there developed a system of conditional 'feudal' land-holdings, with a 'seigniorial' system of exploitation of the peasants, who at the same time were taxed by the state. One may note a new growth of cities and a development in commodity–money relations. During the eleventh to thirteenth centuries Eastern ('Orthodox') Christianity, headed by the Byzantine patriarch, separated from the Roman Catholic Christianity headed by the pope – the patriarch of Rome.

One might have expected a new flourishing of Byzantium on the lines of the Chinese T'ang dynasty, but this was hindered by the constant intrusions of Slavs, Normans and of Western European crusaders (the latter being a most destructive factor), and then by Turkic military inroads (those of the Seljuks).

We have noted above (and we are going to return to this again further on) that for a transition from one historical phase to another, a radical change in social psychology, in ideology and in *Weltanschauung* is needed. But this alone is not enough: the change must coincide with a revolution in technology, first of all in the production of arms. A great part of the Old World had, during the Fifth Phase, experienced a radical change in the dominating *Weltanschauung*, but this did not lead to any phase transition. This change in the philosophy of life was of course the outcome of a socio-psychological stress, which it helped to alleviate, but since there was no novel technology of arms, there was no sufficient stimulus for the passage to a new Phase.

The change in question was the introduction of Islam. The new doctrine was launched in Arabia by the prophet Muhammad (570?–632); it was, to a certain extent, based on Judaism and Christianity which by that time had penetrated the country. Muhammad was a native of Mecca, a centre of trade between the Byzantine Empire and the shores of the Indian Ocean, a trade which at that period was of considerable importance. Having been persecuted in his home town, he fled to nearby Medina, which became the centre of diffusion of a new religion, *Islam* (its adherents being called *Muslims*, or Moslems).

In contradistinction to other founders of new religions and religious-philosophical systems (to Zarathustra, the Buddha, Confucius, Jesus, Paul), Muhammad was not only an ardent proponent of his doctrine but also a warrior, and this made a serious impact on the whole development of Islam. In order to introduce Islam, Muhammad himself, at the head of his followers, conquered Mecca and a considerable part of the rest of Arabia. Under his successors, the caliphs, not only the new religion but also the new state power spread abroad, at first to the Fertile Crescent (the Near East), but soon as far as to Spain (with an attempt to invade Gaul) in the West, and as far as the Indus and beyond the Indus, to the Oxus (Amu-Darya) and beyond the Oxus in the East. One could say that the conquering force was not so much the Arabic troops as the doctrine of Islam itself.

In contrast to Islam, Christianity made very strict moral and dogmatic demands on its followers and advocated the idea that only through a complete renouncement of the world and of human passions (if possible, in monastic life) can a person be saved; Islam also differed from Zoroastrianism with its complicated taboos and the doctrine of obligatory non-defilement of the clean elements (an obligation which it was difficult to observe). Islam differed from these religions in that its burden was easier to bear. Instead of learning by heart the very complicated Credo whose aim was to refute everyone of the conceivable heretic variants of Christianity, it was required of a Muslim only to know and to repeat a short formula: 'There is no god except God (*Allāh*), and Muhammad is the Messenger of God.' In Islam different doctrinal currents did appear, but none of them was deemed unorthodox; even the main division of the Muslims into Sunnites and Shi'ites is based not on the essence of the doctrine but on the recognition of the legality or otherwise of the Sunnite caliphs – successors of the prophet (Omar or 'Ali?), and on details of the interpretation of the oral tradition. Muslims do not regard the Jews and Christians as heathens (as Christians regard the Muslims), but as people having had an incomplete revelation: anyway, they, too, are 'People of the Book'; Moses and Jesus being regarded as predecessors of Muhammad.

The main requirements of Islam can be listed in a few lines: an oral assertion of the Unity (i.e. not Trinity) of God, five daily prayers with ablution, paying (over and above the state tax) of a 'poor rate' (*zakat*), a fast in the month of Ramadan, and, if possible, a pilgrimage to Mecca; and from the point of view of theology, a belief in the One God, in angels, in the written revelation, in the prophets, and the Last Judgement. We may also count as one of the main requirements of Islam the *Jihād*, religious war against the unbelievers, and for introduction of the orthodox doctrine. It is true that at a later date the Muslim theologians decided that the *Jihād* can be carried out not only by arms but also by thought and by oral preaching.

Besides elimination of socio-psychological discomforts, which is the aim of every mass ideological movement, Islam satisfied the drive towards leadership, aggression and even the sexual instinct. While Christians strove to minimise it, Islam not only requires no monastic continence but even recommended polygamy (a man, if he is able to maintain them, is entitled to four lawful wives and an unlimited number of concubines). Even in Paradise, an Islamic righteous man may enjoy intercourse with numerous 'pure fair ones', the houris, with each of them once for every day of fasting in the month of Ramadan, and for each good deed. (At the same time adultery involves corporal punishment.)

No wonder that Islam spread like fire. The Arabic tribal troops invaded the Near Eastern countries of the Fertile Crescent under the caliphs Abu Bakr (632–634) and Omar (634–644); internecine wars between the different tribes broke out immediately, and lasted throughout the reigns of the caliphs of the Omayyad dynasty (660–750). Nevertheless, the capital of the Sasanian Iran, Ctesiphon (in Mesopotamia) fell in 637, and in 657 the last Sasanian king Yazdigerd III perished (near Merw in southern Central Asia); in 645, 12,000 Muslims seized Egypt, in the 670s, and again in 717, the Muslims laid siege to Constantinople, in 676 the Arabs invaded Khorezm, in 709 they captured Bukhara, in 710 the Arabs reached the Atlantic, in 711–712 they seized the greatest part of Spain, and even made an (unsuccessful) intrusion into the centre of Gaul where they fought the Franks, etc.

The Arab conquests continued until the second quarter of the eighth century. As early as 655 they made an overseas (!) raid against Cyprus and other Byzantine dependencies, and later to Sicily. Clearly, this needed sailors, and these sailors must have been Muslims, but they hardly could have been Arabs. Thus, by the middle of the seventh century, not only Arabs but also those in the local population were Islamised.

The arms of the Arabs were no stronger than those of the Byzantine and Sasanians – it appears, in fact, that they were somewhat weaker: a spear, a sword (or a sabre), a bow and arrows, a rather small shield, a spiked helmet with a shoulder-mantle of chain-mail, a chain-armour; the horses were mostly unarmoured. The Arabs had no siege machinery (but they had incendiary devices); nevertheless, the cities opened their gates.

All the newly converted were freed from paying the *jizya* (an additional capitation tax levied from 'infidels'), which was a strong argument in favour of embracing Islam.

Land ownership relations in the Caliphate were rather simple. Not counting the uncultivated and uncultivable lands (*sawafi*), all the land was distributed as property (*mulk*), subject to a tax (*kharaj*). The caliph himself could have a *mulk*; spiritual and charitable institutions (for instance, the *madrasahs* – religious schools) had land specially assigned to them as a gift (*waqf*). Beginning with the ninth to tenth centuries important military and non-military personages received the right to collect tax from certain specified lands – *iqta*. No feudal hierarchy was recognised by Islamic law. The *kharaj* was collected from all incomes, including that of the city-dwellers – the traders and artisans.

No clergy as an estate emerged in Islam. The nearest parallel with Christian clergy were the *'ulama*, ('the learned; the scholars', sg. *'alim*), i.e. men who had received education at a *madrasah*. The most revered of the local *'ulama* would preside during the collective prayer, and (if needed) preach a sermon. This person presiding over the prayer was an *imam*, although *imam* could also be a purely honorary title. Some 'scholars' were allowed by tradition to interpret points of religious doctrine and laws – these were the *muftis*. And last, a *cadi* (Arab. *qāḍī*) 'judge' also belonged to the *'ulama*, but was usually appointed by the state. No special ordination was needed for the Muslim *'ulama*, and no special grace reposed on them. The term *mullah* (of later origin) can be applied to any of the *'ulama*.

In the legal field the Muslims are guided by the *shariah*. But *shariah* is not 'law' in the Western sense of the word, because it regulates all activities of man, in the everyday, in the legal, and in the religious sense. Any action or inaction is either ordered by God, or recommended by God, or has no legal importance, or is censured by God, or is completely prohibited by God. It should be noted that the rules established by the *shariah* are not based on laws introduced by man but on revelation which is supposed to originate with God himself. Therefore the *shariah* is based on the Koran (*Qur'an*, a collection of the Prophet's sermons pronounced at different unspecified occasions), on the canonical tradition (the *Sunna*) and on the agreement of opinions among the interpreters. These opinions are checked (in the same way as in the Talmud) through a special intricate system of juxtaposing them by analogy (*qiyās*). Since, anyway, not all arising questions can be covered by the *sharīah*, the *'ādah*, or the local customary law, is also made use of. The *sharīah* is regarded to be divinely inspired and just as obligatory as the Koran; in practical life it is even more important that the Koran, since, different from the utterances of the prophets in the Old Testament, and from Paul's epistles in Christianity, Muhammad made little reference to the ethical contents of the ideas of 'good' and 'evil' but centred his sermons mostly on Faith as such.

The divine inspiration of the *sharīah* makes it rigid; with time it grew more and more archaic. It is actually their following the *sharīah*, as well as the easiness with which the Muslims turn to the *jihād*, ('the Holy War') that makes the image of the Muslims among other peoples to be perceived as that of limited, backward and aggressive men. However, we have already pointed out that the appearance of Islam during the seventh to eighth centuries in the Near and Middle East and in Northern Africa was felt by the population as a social alleviation of their life. A very interesting and not fully explained phenomenon was the quick and mass change by the local population not only to a new faith but also to a new language – the Arabic; note that the absolute number of Arabs to arrive in the region was comparatively not great. It is true that for the most part this language change happened in countries which formerly had used Afrasian languages which were distinctly akin to Arabic; it did not occur in Iran, in Central Asia, in India or in Indonesia. But all over the Muslim world Arabic became the living language of the educated group of the population.

The Caliphate continued to exist under the dynasty of the Omayyads (with the capital in Damascus) until the eighth century, and under the dynasty of the Abasids (with the capital in Baghdad) until the thirteenth century. At the same time, different amirates and sultanates were constantly emerging – states typical of the Middle Ages, unstable and not corresponding to any ethnic units. Some declared themselves caliphates, as, e.g. the Shīite (or, more exactly, Ismaïlite) caliphate of the Fatimids, with a centre originally in Tunis, and later in Egypt (tenth to twelfth centuries).

The Islamic civilisation gave birth to a number of outstanding philosophers, historians and physicians; less important were the achievements in literature (except poetry); and, because of the ban on 'idols', figurative arts disappeared (but ornamental and architectural art flourished).

The Arabic philosophers were acquainted with Syriac (Aramaic) and Greek (Neo-Platonic) commentaries to the works of Plato and Aristotle; but Plotinus (often confused with Plato) was more influential. Note that not all Arabic philosophers were actually Arabs. The most notable were al-Razi (868–923?), Avicenna (Ibn-Sinā, 980–1037), al-Biruni (973–1050?) and Averroës (Ibn-Rushd, 1120–1198). The first of them was a Persian, the second and the third were Khorasmians,[28] the last was possibly an Arabised Spaniard. For al-Razi, God was the soul of the world, but beside

---

28. The Khorasmian language was one of the Iranian languages, akin to Ossetian (Alan); the Khorasmians, who dwelled in the lower reaches of the Oxus (Amu-Darya), later merged with the Uzbeks, and partly with the Tajiks.

Him there existed matter, time and space; in the question of matter al-Razi was an atomist not too distant from Democritus and Epicurus. Avicenna thought that intellectual cognition was so powerful that it supplied the only way for understanding even the superiority of prophetic revelation; Averroës maintained that truth was unique, and could be attained through philosophy as well as through faith. Biruni, a thinker endowed with wonderfully encyclopaedic knowledge, was on the whole inclined to a certain tolerance in religious matters. Al-Razi and Avicenna were also the greatest physicians of their time; Avicenna contributed a great deal to different sciences. The remarkable thinker Ibn Khaldun (1332–1406) should also be mentioned. He was a historian with a theoretical disposition, regarding the development of human society as a natural process; he was the first to attempt an explanation of the cause of historical events by sociological and climatic factors.

The material and cultural standard of living in Islamic countries during the ninth to thirteenth centuries was considerably higher than in Europe which was an out-of-the-way region and had grown rather wild. But in Spain the Muslim society reached maximum prosperity (eighth to ninth centuries; in Granada it continued to exist until 1492). Here a dynasty of Omayyad caliphs continued in existence, while in the Near East it was ousted (in 750) by the Abbasids. Trade and industry flourished in Muslim Spain, as did philosophy – both Muslim (Ibn-Rushd), and Judaic (Ibn Gabirol, Maimonides, both writing partly in Arabic); also poetry flourished, both Arabic and Hebrew. As a rule, neither the Christians nor the Jews were persecuted. During the so-called Reconquista (the re-conquest of Spain by the Christians, eleventh to fifteenth centuries) the former Muslim territories in Spain returned to the rule of the Christian feudal lords.

The Reconquista was a conquest of the rich by the poor, which explains the incredible savagery of the Christian conquerors. After the Reconquista there followed the forced conversion of the Muslims (the 'Moors') and the Jews to Catholicism with plundering of their personal property, which led to a mass migration from Spain to Northern Africa, to the Balkans and to the Netherlands. Not content with that, the Spanish authorities began persecuting the newly converted in the same way, after which many of them fled, also then returning to their original faith.

At the very beginning of the Reconquista the inquisition was at its worst. (However, the Grand Inquisitor was appointed to Spain only in 1483). The word 'Inquisition' spells horror throughout the centuries because of its inhuman system of questioning, tortures and public burnings; but as to its victims, twentieth century executions have been responsible for a thousand times as many. Nevertheless, the results of the annihilation of the most valuable fund of genes are felt in Spain to this day,[29] while the standard of living in Christian Spain fell

29. Cf. the incomparably greater number of outstanding scientists, scholars and writers in neighbouring France during the seventeenth to nineteenth centuries, although the population number of France is (and was) only about double that of Spain.

from the eleventh century on, and reached the lowest mark in the fifteenth century.

In countries where Islam existed undisturbed, further development was slowed down for other reasons, viz. the Crusades, the Mongol and the Turkic conquests.

The formal cause of the beginning of the Crusades was the fact that the leader of the Seljuk Turks, Toghrul-bek, who had already taken possession of the greater part of Iran and Middle Asia, and his son Malikshah, who both had received the title of *sulṭān* from the Abbasid caliph, invaded first Byzantine Asia Minor and then Syria and Palestine which belonged to the Abbasids themselves (1071–1092). Thus they blocked the then existing constant flow of Christian pilgrims from Western Europe to Jerusalem. But a more important cause was that after the spread of Christianity to Scandinavia, the Baltic coast and Hungary, the inroads of the Vikings and the nomads into Europe had stopped, a certain order was introduced in the feudal states there, and some of the warlike troops belonging to the knights felt themselves unemployed.

In the European historical tradition, the organisation of the Crusades is regarded as a period of religious and spiritual upsurge. It is true that religious propaganda roused passions: it is known that even children tried to undertake a 'crusade' of their own. But actually, the crusaders (so-called after the sign of the Cross they wore on their breastplate or on their shield; the Arabs called them 'the Franks') were united into a poorly organised force more fit for robbery than for organised war. In our time they might have been called gangsters: what they wanted first of all was plunder and, as a rule, nothing was sacred to them; they were not over-anxious to get exactly to Jerusalem; sometimes they created their fiefs on the way to it, for instance in Western Armenia, in north-western Mesopotamia, on the eastern shore of the Mediterranean Sea. At the same time, they often waged war between themselves.

The First Crusade received the blessing of the pope, who hoped that it would help to mend the breach, which at that time had not yet been officially recognised, between the Roman Catholic and the Greek Orthodox churches. The occasion was an application from the Byzantine emperor Alexius I for help against Toghrul and his Seljuks. The march began in 1096 and went on in two directions: through Hungary, and through Albania. Instead of the expected reinforcement, Alexius found he had to do with undisciplined gangs followed by thousands of pilgrims and a large, disorderly rabble. The emperor made them swear an oath of allegiance to himself, and to promise that they should re-conquer Asia Minor and the city of Antioch in Syria on his behalf, and that the territories which they seized there – as well as in Palestine – should in the future be vassal dependencies of Byzantium. However, the newcomers began almost immediately to plunder the countryside, and then skirmishes broke out between the crusaders and the Byzantine troops; as soon as the knights left Asia Minor for Syria, Alexius reestablished his power over the land vacated by them.

Antioch was captured by the crusaders, but no sooner had this been achieved than a struggle developed between two pretenders to this principality. When, finally, the crusaders reached Jerusalem in 1099 (it was then in the power of the Egyptian Fatimid Caliphate), they could capture it only after a prolonged siege. Baldwin I was declared King of Jerusalem.

As the result of the First Crusade, there emerged a number of Christian principalities and counties (which were subdivided into numerous baronies). They stretched from the Gulf of Aqaba on the Red Sea to the south-eastern part of Asia Minor. Here a feudal system was created after the Western European pattern. The domains founded by the crusaders were in constant hostility between themselves and against the surrounding Muslim states. They acted very unwisely and unsuccessfully; making pogroms was one of their favourite activities; the greatest was launched in Jerusalem itself. In the new states there were created certain half-monastic orders of knights: the Templars[30] and the Hospitallers of St John.[31]

The Second Crusade (1147 AD) was provoked by the capturing of the County of Edessa (on the Euphrates) by the Muslims, who declared a 'Holy War' against the 'Latin' states in the Eastern Mediterranean region. The crusade was headed by Louis VII, King of France. Instead of attempting to regain Edessa and to get hold of Antioch, the pious king moved towards Jerusalem. After visiting the Holy City, the crusaders decided to plunder Damascus, but failed to seize it; the Second Crusade came to naught, if we discount the fact that it finally triggered off a 'Holy War' of the Muslims against the Christians. It was waged by the rulers (*atabeghs*) of Mosul and Haleb (Aleppo) – Imad-ad-dīn and his son Nūr-ad-dīn who also succeeded in controlling Fatimid Egypt. After Nūr-ad-dīn's death in 1174 the actual power passed to his general Salāh-ad-dīn (Saladin). He managed to capture Jerusalem in 1187; the rich Latin feudal lords bought their freedom from Saladin and returned to Europe, the poor Latins remained. Saladin did not persecute the Eastern Orthodox and the Monophysite Christians, nor the Jews, but exterminated the knights of the Orders.

The Third Crusade (1189 AD) was headed by the French King Philip II Augustus and the English King Richard I Coeur de Lion (who was a vassal of King Philip II in regard to his possessions in Normandy and in other parts of France), and also by King Guy of Jerusalem (who had been taken prisoner by Saladin but set free upon his word of honour, which he broke immediately). But Philip Augustus, having taken one fortress, returned to Europe, leaving Richard alone to face Saladin (meanwhile Guy, expelled for the second time from Jerusalem, founded a kingdom of his own on the island of Cyprus). Richard succeeded in seizing the Palestinian harbours, but left Palestine in 1192.

30. The Knights Templars, who managed to be rather independent of the local sovereigns, amassed great riches during the Crusades, and employed them for usury, provoking envy of kings and popes. This was their undoing: in the beginning of the fourteenth century their Order was dissolved, their gold was confiscated, and many knights were executed.
31. From the sixteenth century on, the Order of the Hospital of St John of Jerusalem was usually termed the Maltese Order.

Strangest of all was the Fourth Crusade (1199). It had been planned by Thibaut II, count of Champagne, but his crusaders lacked ships for going to Palestine. They asked the Doge of Venice for ships; he promised to supply them if the crusaders first re-conquered for him the city of Zadar (in modern Croatia) which had been occupied by the king of Hungary; and, secondly, if they helped the Venetians to instill a pretender friendly to them on the throne of Byzantium. The crusade turned into a disorderly destruction of the Byzantine empire; Constantinople was sacked in 1204, and a new 'Latin Empire' was declared. The Byzantine managed to regain Constantinople in 1262, but the Byzantine Empire never regained its former power and prosperity.

The further history of Asia Minor and the Balkans in the fourteenth to nineteenth centuries belongs to the history of Turkey and its dependencies.

After the first four Crusades, there still were the Fifth Crusade (1218), the Sixth (1227) and the Seventh (1244). The Fifth amounted to a siege of the Egyptian harbour Damietta (Dumyat), the Sixth – to a short-lived (for six years) restoration of the Kingdom of Jerusalem, and to a ten-years' internecine war between the knights themselves; and the Seventh to a senseless war with Egypt.

The Crusades brought the Muslim world nothing but perhaps such animosity against Christians as had not formerly existed. It was as if they had made Islam more rigid, making any difference of opinions inside it unacceptable. This happened at a period when the drive of the Mongols and the Turks from Central Asia had begun, and the heyday of the Arab successes was over. For the Byzantine Empire, the Crusades brought about the end of its power and prosperity; for Europe, they brought more intolerance, which led to anti-Semitic and anti-heretic pogroms,[32] but also made Europeans acquainted with the higher culture of the Near East. As a historian (H. S. Fink) puts it, 'ships which set out from western European ports carrying men and goods in bulk, such as grain, timber and horses, had on the return journey space to sell cheaply. Hence the freight rates on all types of eastern luxury goods were lowered. Spices, fabrics of all kinds, tapestries, cushions, rugs, drugs, fruits, sugar, jewellery, perfumes, glass and fine ('damask') steel products came to the west in larger quantities than ever before.' The sale of all this merchandise led to the enrichment of the merchants and of the nobles, and hence to the intensifying of exploitation of the serfs and to the replenishment of the exchequers of the feudal domains. The trade and the necessity of transporting the pilgrims contributed to the rapid growth of usury and of credit in general; both Italian merchants and Templar knights were involved.

To the east of the zone harassed by the Crusades, the following events occurred.

During the Islamic conquest the Arabs had put up their garrisons in the most important cities, first in Iran – in Nishapur, Merw and Heart, and then in Middle

---

32. Cf. the barbarous extermination of the Albigenses, the semi-Manichaeans of Provence in Southern France, during the years 1209–1244.

Asia: in Bukhara and Samarkand, after they had been conquered by Qutaibah Ibn Muslim (705–715 AD). At first the Arabs did not worry the local Zoroastrian nobility, the *dehkāns*,[33] but later, with the local population increasingly Islamised, mixed marriages began to occur; from this developed the creation of a new, 'Persian' nation and of the Persian language, which became the means of communication for nearly the entire population to the east of Iraq (Mesopotamia) and further eastward to the Hindukush mountains and the borders of India.

The Viziers of the Abbasid Caliphate were recruited from the Persian family of Barmakids. The eastern part of Iran – Khorasan – became the centre of opposition to the Abbasids in Baghdad; the opposition leaders – princes and military chiefs – were, however, themselves of Abbasid origin. In Khorasan there emerged independent states headed by Takh-ir (originally an Abbasid governor) and his kinsmen (821–875). Then there were wars of the type usual for the Middle Ages, between different pretenders to state power on changing territories; in their struggle an important role was played by Islamic religious dissenters – Shiïtes and Kharijites. After the fall of the Takhirids the power in Eastern Iran passed to Ismaïl, the founder of the Sunnite dynasty of Samanids (late ninth century), and in Western Iran, to the Shiïte dynasty of Buids (945 AD).

While conquering the basins of the Oxus and the Jaxartes (the Amu-Darya and the Syr-Darya), against serious resistance of the local Sogdian and Khorezmian nobility, the Arabs first came into contact with Turkic-speaking tribes who had, as early as the pre-Sasanian times, begun their movement from East Turkistan into the steppes of what now is Kazakhstan and Kirghizia (Qyrghyzstan).

Unlike the Mongols, the early Turks seem not to have been completely nomadic; they may partly have engaged in agriculture or, at least, seem to have made use of the labour of the local agricultural population. We have not enough data for deciding whether their first states could be classified as belonging to the Third, the Fourth or the Fifth Phase, but anyway they already had their own system of writing borrowed from the Sogdians, who, in their turn, had borrowed it from Aramaic Nestorian Christians. The Turkic 'kingdoms' had constantly to hold their own against Primitive and Communal Primitive tribes, which leads us to surmise that these 'kingdoms' were stable enough as medieval kingdoms go.

Thus, at the period of its highest development the Turkic khaganate (552–745) dominated a territory stretching from the Amu-Darya (Oxus) to China. It had been founded by a tribe (or tribes) that were the first to be named 'Turks', and which probably had early broken off from the movement led by the Huns. The geographical centre of the Turkic tribes was at first the Altai mountain region, and later the upper reaches of the river Orkhon (a tributary of the Selenga river) in Mongolia.

When the Turkic khaganate fell apart, an Uighur khaganate arose (about 750–840). It was established by another group of Turkic-speaking tribes which later

---

33. At a much later date, the term *dehkan* was used to denote the peasants of Iran and Central Asia.

seem to have assimilated a minor group of Indo-European speakers inhabiting Eastern Turkistan (they are usually – but inexactly – termed Tocharians); owing to this assimilation, the modern Uighurs, from the point of view of physical anthropology, are more Europoid than Mongolian.

Beginning with the ninth century the Muslims bought Turkic, and also Caucasian and even Slavic prisoners of war and slaves, and sold them to the central regions of the Caliphate, where they sometimes were used to form military troops of *ghulāms*, or *mamlūks* – a military guard which was the better suited for the local rulers because it had no local roots. Later the Mamluks (also called Mamelukes), founded a dynasty of their own in Egypt.

At the same time, warriors recruited from Turkic tribes began to seize power in important Islamic centres. Such a new state with a Turkic military elite emerged in Khorasan with its capital in Ghazni (now in Afghanistan); then the Turks destroyed the kingdom of the Samanids in Iran. Some of the Oghuz Turks were re-settled to Khorasan by Mahmud Ghaznawi (eleventh century), who was a great conqueror and robber. In 1020 his Kingdom stretched from Mawerannahr (the region between the Amu-Darya and the Syr-Darya) to Punjab on the Indian subcontinent; his raids led to mass plundering and pogroms. The successors of Mahmud were, however, ousted by another conqueror, Muhammad of Ghor, who penetrated still further into India with his Afghans; as a result of his conquests a Muslim sultanate was created at Delhi. In the rest of the Indian territory persisted medieval Hinduist states.

After the death of the conqueror Mahmud Ghaznawi, Toghrul-bek and Chaghry, two chiefs of the Seljuk tribe of the Oghuz Turks, defeated the Ghaznawi army, and began conquering Western Iran, Iraq and later Asia Minor. The Seljuk Malikshah who ruled in Baghdad (his vizier was the eminent Persian statesman Nizam al-Mulk) created an empire which included Syria, Iraq and all of Iran. Its provinces were dealt out to Seljuk chiefs as their *iqtā* (see above). But after Malikshah's death his empire was torn asunder by local leaders (*atabeghs*); and also by other chiefs of certain troops or tribes. This was the period of the crusaders' invasion, which we have discussed above. As to Central Asia and Iran, here too new states emerged, although these were ruled by Turkic dynasts; at the same time, there was an invasion by Turkmen Oghuz tribes; much fertile land was turned into pasture.

In spite of all these important and bloody events (typical of the Middle Ages everywhere), the period from the ninth century on witnessed the flourishing of scholarship, science and literature. We have already mentioned Avicenna and Biruni, but now we have also to mention the great Persian epic poet Firdousi.[34] His

---

34. At present, Firdousi belongs both to the Persian, and the Tajik literature (the difference between literary Persian, or Farsi, and Tajiki is negligible). But during the Middle Ages, *Tajik* was a term for Arabs who had settled in Central Asia, while the ancestors of the Tajiks of today were called either simply 'Iranians', or *Farst*, i.e. Persians. The Persian-speaking part of the population in Afghanistan calls its language *Dārī* (formerly it was termed *Farsī-Kabulī*). The speakers of that language are colloquially called Tajiks.

'Book of Kings' (*Shāh-nāmā*) though, formally, impeccably Muslim, had nevertheless a certain anti-Arab and anti-Turk bias. History became an eternal feud between Iran and Turan.[35] No wonder the book did not have success with Mahmud Ghaznawi, to whom it had been dedicated. The 'Book of Kings' by Firdousi is witness to the fact that Persian self-consciousness had been born. For Firdousi, the great past was represented by the dominion of the mythical Zoroastrian Kayanid dynasty and the historical Zoroastrian Sasanid dynasty. It is interesting to note that the Achaemenid Empire had completely disappeared from historical memory.

The Turks, conquering lands which had been inhabited by peoples speaking languages of the Iranian branch of Indo-European (Khorezm, Sogdiana, Bactria, Media, Persia, etc.) took wives from the local population and merged with it, both culturally and – in many parts of this territory – also linguistically. However, great parts of Siberia, and of present-day Kazakhstan and Kirghizia in the East, of Southern (now Iranian) Azerbaijan[36] and of Asia Minor in the West, as well as some of the tribes of the Eastern Caucasus – originally speakers of either North-Eastern Caucasian (Alarodian) or the Iranian dialect of the Alani – gradually also adopted Turkic dialects, beginning with the nobility and later extending to the whole population.[37] One of the reasons why the Turkic language was so widely adopted was that it is very easy to learn; at the same time, the Turkic dialects did not differ very much, and this provided for mutual understanding in all countries of the belt between Eastern Turkistan and Asia Minor.[38] At the same time, it should be pointed out that the emerging states in Iran and Middle Asia were no more 'national' than the other medieval states.

Now we have to discuss a most important event which greatly influenced the

35. *Tūra* (pl. *Tūrān*) was one of the nomadic Iranian tribes mentioned in the Avesta. However, in Firdousi's poem, and in the later Iranian tradition generally, the term *Tūrān* is perceived as denoting 'lands inhabited by Turkic speaking tribes'.

36. Until the early twentieth century, the term *Azerbaijan* (a late form of the term *Atropatēnē*, derived from the name of Atropates, satrap and later king of Western Media at the end of the fourth century BC) was used solely for the Turkic-speaking regions of North-Western Iran. When, in 1918–1920, the power in Eastern Transcaucasia (Shirvan, etc.) was taken over by the party of Musavatists, they gave to their state the name 'Azerbaijan', hoping to unite it with Iranian Azerbaijan, or Azerbaijan in the original sense of the term; that territory had a much greater Turkic population; the Musavatists relied on the state of complete political disintegration of Iran at that period, and hoped easily to annex Iranian Azerbaijan into their state. Until the twentieth century, the ancestors of the present-day Azerbaijanis called themselves *Türkt*, while the Russians called them *Tatars*, not distinguishing them from the Volga Tatars. The Azerbaijani language belongs to the Oghuz branch of Turkic; the Volga Tatar language belongs to the Kipchak branch of Turkic.

37. This probably happened latest of all (in the eighth to fourteenth centuries) in former Shirvan, and in the neighbouring regions of Transcaucasia which now are part of the Azerbaijan Republic.

38. In this Turkic resembles Medieval (literary) Latin, Neo-Hellenic (Greek), Church Slavonic, Ancient Common Scandinavian, Persian, Sanskrit (and some other Indian languages), literary Tibetan, Chinese and Japanese. The popular dialects, often originating from the same linguistic sources, were more apt to be a factor dividing a nation than uniting it.

whole historical process, namely the Mongol conquest. We have already dwelt briefly on its causes; now we shall have to discuss it in some detail.

The Mongol conquest had an impact on Islamic civilisation considerably more destructive than the impact of the Crusades.

Ever since the formation of nomadic tribes in this part of the planet, the territory of Southern Siberia and present-day Mongolia has been the starting base of Mongolian excursions into neighbouring countries. These nomads spoke different Uralo-Altaic languages, either Turkic, Mongol or Tunguso-Manchu; little is known of which tribe belonged to this or that language group.

The first cause of the military expansion of the Mongols in the early thirteenth century to the East and to the West under Jenghiz Khan (the name is also spelled Genghis, Chinggis, etc.) must, to my mind, be sought in the excessive growth of the stock-rearing population in the Mongolian steppes. But the grand scale of the Mongolian conquests was more due to the fact that the Mongol army, as it moved in different directions, incorporated other nomadic or simply stock-rearing populations, especially the Turkic, so that finally it became Mongol only in name (and as regards its ruling dynasty).

During the reign of the Han emperors, China experienced incursions by certain tribes, probably anthropologically mixed, the Hsiung-nu,[39] possibly Turkic as to their language; it is surmised that their descendants were the T'u'küe, who certainly were Turks, and lived in Western Mongolia from the seventh century. As early as the first century, the Hsiung-nu divided into an Eastern and a Western group; it is possible that the Western Hsiung-nu (probably with an Ugrian admixture) were identical with the Huns who invaded Europe in the second to fifth centuries.

From the beginning of the Christian era, and especially in the second and third centuries, the main nomadic opponents of China were the Hsien-pi, possibly of Mongolian origin, who, like the Hsiung-nu, created a short-lived but vast 'empire'. In the fifth to sixth centuries we learn of a large nomadic union of the Juan-Juan who waged war against the Chinese, the Turks and the Uighurs; later the Juan-Juan moved westwards, and some authorities identify them with the Avars, or the Obri who appeared on the Middle Danube as reported above. In the tenth to eleventh centuries the Mongol-speaking tribe of the Khitan (Kitai), seizing the north-western part of China and Manchuria, founded the Liao empire, which even had its own writing system. Another empire, His-Hsia, was founded in the eleventh to thirteenth centuries between China and Tibet by the Tanguts, a Tibeto-Burman tribe; they also had a developed writing system of their own. From 1115 to 1234 still another empire existed in Manchuria and in some of the northern regions

---

39. Although it is possible that this term reproduces the name the Huns used to denote themselves, the identity of the Hsiung-nu with the Huns is by no means proven; the Chinese traditionally construed here a play on words: *hsung nu* meaning 'evil slaves', *hung nu*, 'submissive slaves'.

of China. This empire was founded by the tribe of the Jurchen, belonging to the Tunguso-Manchu linguistic family. In all these states the ruling dynasties were of nomadic origin; the military élite was often nomadic as well, but the main population usually lived not only as cattle-breeders but also as agriculturists. The land was tilled either by the Chinese, or by certain tribes or groups of the conquerors themselves. Part of the population had converted to Christianity of the Nestorian persuasion which had been introduced here by Syriac (Aramaic) merchants. In the Sinkiang region there was an Uighur kingdom; the Uighurs had by that time, as mentioned above, merged with the Indo-European 'Tocharians'; farther to the north-west reigned the Kara-Khitans. Nearly all of western Central Asia and a considerable part of Iran belonged to the empire of the Khorezm-Shahs, whose capital was Urgench (now in Uzbekistan). The Khorezm-Shahs were a dynasty of Turkic origin but with an Iranian culture and strong Muslim traditions. They had risen by struggling against another Turkic group, the Seljuks. According to the standards of the Middle Ages, their kingdom was a flourishing one.

This was the historical background for the creation of the great Mongol nomadic empire. The Mongols, under the designation of Meng-ku, or Meng-ku Ta-ta (i.e. 'Mongols', or 'Mongolo-Tartars') are mentioned for the first time in China under the T'ang dynasty. The Mongols in the strict sense were a purely nomadic tribe dwelling to the south-east of Lake Baikal and in the basin of the river Selenga. Here began the exploits of the Mongol chief Temujin, the future Great Khan Jenghiz; after his great military successes he began to entertain thoughts of World domination (the real extent of the world was, of course, unknown to him).

West of the Mongols, and of the Selenga valley, lived the Christian Turkic tribes of Naimans and Keraits, who probably exploited Chinese immigrant agriculturists. It is possible that the ethnic name Ta(r)tars was first used to designate these particular tribes. By 1206 the Keraits and the Naimans had been conquered by Jenghiz and had become incorporated not only in his empire but also in his army. This explains why in the East and South the hordes of Jenghiz were termed 'Mongols', while in Russia they were called 'Tatars' from the very beginning.[40]

The invincibility of the Mongols seems inexplicable.

However, their military power was based on their strong and numerous cavalry, the riders being excellent archers; the army of the Mongols had a highly developed

40. Later the term 'Tatars' became the name used to denote themselves by Turkic-speaking tribes of different origin, predominantly of the Kipchak, and sometimes of the Oghuz branch. Thus, the term is applied to the Tatars of Kazan, who were the main population of the Golden Horde in the Middle Ages, and, at present, of the Republic of Tatarstan on the Volga, and also settled outside that republic; the Siberian, or Chernevye Tatars; and a number of other ethnic groups. The Crimean Tatars, who in the fifteenth century had created a strong Crimean Khanate but were exiled from the Crimea by Stalin in 1944 and are now attempting to return, are the result of merging several Turkic groups into one people: tribes of the Crimean steppe (Oghuz branch), Osmanli Turks (also of the Oghuz group), a part of the Nogais (Kipchak branch), as well as a part of the Turkicised local population, including Goths, Greeks, Genoese et al.

intelligence service. Enlisting military and other experts from different peoples, the Mongols were able to capture fortified cities, something that other nomads were unable to do. Moreover, the devastation perpetrated by the Mongols had such a psychological influence on neighbouring populations that opponents who could have offered resistance surrendered in order to receive quarter.

As mentioned above, by about 1206 Jenghiz had overcome the Naimans and the Keraits and included their troops into his own army. Then he succeeded in gaining recognition of his overlordship from the Tangut kingdom of the His-Hsia; subsequently he captured a part of the territory belonging to the Chin dynasty in Northern China. Terrible incursions into Central Asia then began. In 1218 there was a devastating war against Khorezm; Bukhara, Samarkand and Urgench were captured and totally destroyed. The advance detachments of the Mongols, headed by Jebe and Subaday, marching through Georgia and Armenia, bypassed the Caspian Sea and, proceeding along the Caucasus, invaded Crimea and Russia (1233, the battle of Kalka, now in the Donetsk oblast of the Ukraine). The Russian princes, acting unwisely and without any co-ordination, were utterly defeated and captured, their troops and they themselves were brutally slaughtered; prisoners were executed.

But even the defeat of the Russian princes in the battle of Kalka was not so tragic as the massacre of the peoples of (Western) Central Asia. Its aftermath was felt there for centuries, because the irrigation systems as well as the cities were destroyed.

The king of the Tanguts did not agree to take part in a Mongol campaign against Khorezm, with the result that the Mongols launched a punitive expedition against His-Hsia; the fact that Jenghiz died during the campaign made the Mongols only more ferocious; not only the kingdom of the Tanguts but the entire Tangut civilisation was annihilated.

By 1227 the Mongols reigned supreme from Central China to the forests of Siberia. Sometimes they enslaved whole peoples – and dealt the slaves out to their military leaders. Jenghiz Khan regarded himself as elected by Heaven for dominating the world – an idea which may have been borrowed from China. His counsellor, Yeh-lü Ch'u-ts'ai, a Khitan, dissuaded him from turning all Chinese territory into pasture for Mongol cattle. In any case, though, the administrative system on conquered territory was totally destroyed: Jenghiz felt that his arms were best served by military leaders, not administrators; it seems, however, that he had educated counsellors: Uighurs, Khitans, and Nestorian Turks. The Mongol military leaders collected tribute from the conquered population through tax-farmers, and were not at all interested in its social or political traditions. However, this did not prevent them from occasionally entering alliances with traditional kingdoms. Thus, in 1243 (i.e. after Jenghiz, who died in 1227) the Mongols destroyed the Jurchen Chin empire and captured its capital K'ai-Feng – and did that together with the troops of the Southern Chinese Sung dynasty!

The Mongol empire was regarded not as the personal property of the Great Khan but as the property of his clan. It was impossible to manage as a single entity, although a highly developed system of messengers did exist. But when the Great Khan tried to administer from a single centre, his messenger had to spend months (if not years) to get from one end of the empire to the other.

Therefore, during Jenghiz Khan's lifetime the Mongol Empire had already been divided into allotments for his sons, called *ulus*. The original Mongol territory went to Tului (he died before his father and was succeeded by his son Möngke); Ogadai received Western Mongolia (the territory of the Naimans); Chagatai received the lands of the Kara-Khitans and the eastern parts of Central Asia; Juchi (and after his death in 1227, his son Batu) was allotted Western Middle Asia and south-eastern Siberia (the future Golden Horde).

In 1229, at the Great *quriltai* (meeting of the Mongols), Jenghiz Khan's third son, Ogadai, was proclaimed his successor as Great Khan (1229–1241). The capital of the Empire was to be Karakorum on the river Orkhon in Central Mongolia. During the thirteenth century this capital grew into a rich city with churches, mosques and Buddhist temples.

Covening a *quriltai* and arriving at the necessary decisions demanded much time, and after the death of a Great Khan it was usual for his widow to rule. After Ogadai his son Hüyük was elected (1246–1248), and then Möngke (1251–1259); but after that there followed a struggle between the different pretenders to Jenghiz Khan's heritage.

The devastating Mongol conquests continued after Jenghiz. In 1236 the imperial authorities decided to conquer the western part of the world, and the charge was entrusted to Batu. He destroyed the kingdom of Volga Bulgary in 1237, and in the same year he devastated the Russian city of Ryazan together with nearly every inhabitant, and set out to conquer one Russian princedom after the other; only a very severe winter and the following violent thaw saved Novgorod. After the sack of Kiev by the Mongols in 1240, the Russian princes discontinued their resistance.

The Mongols moved further on to Galacia and Volhynia, to Poland, and got as far as Silesia, but did not continue their march further into Germany. Instead they struck against Hungary, accusing it of harbouring the Kumans, a Turkish tribe which had fled before them from the Southern Russian steppes. Batu was hindered in making further offensive by the news of the Great Khan Ogadai's death, since he hoped to be elected in his stead. Unsuccessful in this quest Batu retired to his *ulus* (to Sarai-Batu, near modern Astrakhan), where he died in 1255. His brother and successor, Berkè, founded a new capital on the Volga, Sarai-Berkè. Here he embraced the Islamic faith. The new kingdom, the Golden Horde, spread from the river Irtysh in Siberia to the Crimea, to the lower reaches of the Dnieper and even the Danube; but the Russian princedoms were not directly incorporated in the Horde proper; as already mentioned, the princes were obliged to pay a tribute to the Khans and to get a *yarlik* (permit) for ruling their princedom. From time to time the willingness of the princes to pay was sharpened by brief Tatar raids. The last raid was that of Tokhtamysh Khan in 1382, although in 1380 Dimitry Donskoy, the Great Prince of

Muscovy, had been able to rout the Tatar army of Mamai on the field of Kulikovo. But it was only Ivan III who stopped paying tribute to the Tatars in 1476.

The Golden Horde's income depended not only on tributes but also on caravan trade between the Crimea and Russia, on the one side, and Middle Asia, on the other. During the fifteenth century, the Golden Horde disintegrated, and independent Muslim kingdoms were formed; of these, the Astrakhan, the Kazan and the Siberian kingdoms were conquered by Ivan the Terrible of Russia (1533–1584), but the Crimean Kingdom survived nearly to the end of the eighteenth century.

Another direction of the Mongol invasion after Jenghiz was towards the Middle and the Near East. For this a separate, fifth *ulus* had been founded for Hulagu, the brother of Möngke. Hulagu started his campaign in 1255; in the next year in Northern Iran he annihilated the influential warlike sect of the Assassines (Hashishin),[41] and then attacked Iraq. Orthodox Shïites and even Christians supported Hulagu against the Sunnite Abbasid caliph al-Mustasim (Hulagu's wife was a Christian of the Monophysite persuasion). Baghdad was conquered by the Mongols in 1258 and totally devastated; the caliph was killed. Hulagu – whose army by that time included many Oghuz Turks – also made inroads into Syria; he captured Haleb and Damascus; he also fought with the Egyptian troops of the Mamluk dynasty but was defeated. The centre of Hulagu's empire was established in Iranian Azerbaijan, where he founded the dynasty of the Il-Khans. To the end of his life Hulagu remained nominally dependent on the Great Khan. He died in 1265, and at his burial a ritual massacre of maidens required by the Mongol tradition was committed. His second successor, Ghazan-Khan (1271–1304) was brought up as a Buddhist but later embraced Islam. Through his able counsellor Rashid ad-Dīn he introduced an orderly administration in his empire, which can be called feudal even according to European standards: he dealt out land as *iqtā* to Mongol warriors, and confirmed the already earlier introduced serfdom of the peasants.

The contemporary Great Khan, Kublai (1260–1294) had meanwhile settled not in Karakorum but in Khanbaliq, i.e. in Peking (1264). The Golden Horde and the empire of the Il-Khans were still, though only nominally, subordinate to him.

Of course, the Mongol conquest of China meant much bloodshed and devastation (there also followed unsuccessful attempts to conquer Japan, Burma, etc.). In China, however, the Mongol élite submitted to Chinese civilisation. Both Kublai

---

41. The Assassines (from Arabic 'hashish-eaters') were a terroristic group belonging to the Islamic sect of Ismaïlites, an extreme branch of Shïites. The Ismaïlites regarded their hereditary Imams as the living incarnation of the Deity. The Imam interpreted the narcotic-induced dreams of the Assassines as visions of Paradise, which shall be opened for those who despise death in fulfilling their terroristic task (which was interpreted as *jihād*). The organisation of the Assassines was created by Hasan Ibn Sabbah about 1090 AD, and had its centre in the Alamut castle in Northern Iran. The Assassines performed acts of terror (led from Syria by their chief, the Old Man of the Mountain) mostly against Sunnite Seljuks, but also against the Egyptian Fatimids – whose Shïism was regarded by the Ismaïlites as insufficiently orthodox – and against the crusaders.

himself and his successors regarded themselves as Chinese emperors, although keeping to traditions introduced by the Mongols (such as Mongol names being used along with Chinese ones, or the ritual of election of the Khan).

The economic and cultural progress of China which had begun under the preceding Sung dynasty continued during the Mongol rule (the Yüan dynasty). Paradoxically, the fate of China under the Yüan dynasty was completely different from that of the other countries conquered by the Mongols. The reason was that the historical Phase which the conquerors encountered here was not the Fifth but the Sixth, the Post-Medieval, while in the other countries of Asia the Mongol conquest did not lead to any new Phase, whether as regards the type of arms or the type of ideology (which practically remained unchanged – some minor innovations inside Islam were of no significant import).

Even in Russia, which had suffered comparatively less from the invasion, the Mongol conquest slowed down historical development quite noticeably; but in Western and Eastern Central Asia, in Iran and in the Near East, this conquest was a real catastrophe. All the Middle and the Near East, and later also India, were economically thrown drastically backwards, and for many centuries (actually, down to the nineteenth century) were trapped in the Fifth, Medieval Phase.

What followed here was typical of the Middle Ages: endless wars, dynastic states with unstable, movable frontiers, not connected with any particular ethnic entity, nor dependent either on the self-consciousness of their population, or on physico-geographical conditions. Nearly everywhere Turkic tribes were active, often only half-nomadic; they introduced their own dynasties (the Kara-Koyunlu, the Ak-Koyunlu, the Qyzylbashs). Also important were their religious affinities – there were Sunnite, Shïite, and Ismaïlite dynasties.

We shall now pause on a few historical lines of development which had important consequences. All of them were connected with the more successful conquerors – who often were also the cruellest ones.

Timur the Lame (Timur-i Leng, Tamerlane, 1336–1405) belonged to a tribe which was considered Mongol but had been Turkicised. He was a descendant of Chagatai through his mother, and from 1361 he had a military administrative position in Mogulistan – one of the successor states of Chagatai's *ulus*. (Later Mogulistan coincided with Eastern Turkistan, or Sinkiang in China, but at the period in question it also included Western Turkistan, or Mawerannahr.) Timur began in alliance with other military leaders of similar rank and power, but afterwards placed himself in military opposition to them; he suppressed the anti-Mongol movement of the Serbedar Shïites who were supported by the remaining city population of Central Asia and Khorasan (*Serbedars* was a pejorative designation of the lower groups in the Shïite movement; the left wing of the Serbedars, headed by a spiritual order of dervish mystics, demanded social equality). Then Timur seized Samarkand, made it his capital and in 1370 declared himself an amir ruling for the Jenghizids; then he started a series of campaigns which led to atrocities unheard of even in those times.

Thus, after he captured Serakhs, the stronghold of the Serbedars, Timur ordered the bricking up of 2,000 men in the fortress wall.

The victories of Timur were due not only to his mastery as a general but no less to the terror he inspired into his adversaries. After having captured Khorezm and destroyed its capital Urgench, he continued, during the years 1380–1390, to subjugate, plunder and murder the populations of Iran and Transcaucasia. In 1389–1395 he utterly defeated the Golden Horde, plundering Sarai-Berkè and other cities. In 1398 he invaded India and captured Delhi where a Muslim dynasty had been in power. Then he waged war against Bayazid I, sultan of Turkey, and took him prisoner in the battle of Ankara in 1402. Marching through Asia Minor he reached the shore of the Aegean Sea, and in 1403 expelled the Hospitaller (St John's) crusader knights from Smyrna (Izmir) which they had held until then.[42] Subsequently Timur planned a campaign against China (his idea was to restore the Jenghizid Empire), but he died soon after the beginning of the campaign.

Not all territories that Timur traversed were added to his kingdom. Thus, he left Asia Minor, the Golden Horde, and Delhi, keeping for himself only the Punjab in India. And in any case, Timur, like all other medieval conquerors of such scale, had to divide this empire between his sons and the sons' sons, which naturally brought about internecine wars. Nevertheless, the core of Timur's empire was still intact under Shahrukh (1409–1447), Ulugh Begh (1447–1449) and Sultan Husein (1489–1506).

In spite of the military losses sustained by the population, the empire left by Timur to his descendants was very rich. In Samarkand, in Bukhara, in Herat there lived great scholars, architects and poets; Ulugh Begh himself was an outstanding mathematician and astronomer; he built an observatory renowned in the Middle Ages, but its building was the reason why he was murdered by Muslim fanatics. It is characteristic that in a state of that size architecture had pride of place among the arts: magnificent residences were a necessity for such mighty rulers. The architectural glory of Samarkand and Bukhara goes back to Timurid times.

Towards the beginning of the sixteenth century the empire of the Timurids broke up into several domains quarrelling with each other. In 1504 Babur, reigning over Fergana, was expelled by nomadic Uzbeks headed by Muhammad Sheibani-Khan (the founder of the new Uzbek dynasty in Western Central Asia),[43] and founded for himself a stronghold in Kabul. From there he made vain attempts to regain Bukhara and Samarkand before starting a series of bloody campaigns to India. In 1525 he seized the sultanate of Delhi and founded the dynasty of the Great Moguls. Barbur left interesting memoirs.

---

42. The main base of the Knights of St John was the island of Rhodes, which they occupied from 1309 to 1522. After that, they settled on the island of Malta (cf. n. 31).
43. Muhammad Sheibani was a descendant of Juchi, a grandson of Jenghiz Khan, and he claimed to continue the Jenghizide traditions. However, his main population base were not Mongols but Turkic tribes of Kipchak, Qarluq and Oghuz origin, who later became absorbed in the Uzbek nation (their medieval literary language was Chagatai).

He was not the first Muslim conqueror of India. The first was the above-mentioned Mahmud Ghaznawi (971–1030) who had reached the Ganges but retained only the Punjab. In 1206, after a long period of conflict, the military leader Qutbaddin Aibak founded a sultanate at Delhi. Five Muslim dynasties ruled here between 1206 and 1526 (when Delhi was conquered by Babur), and some of them had pretensions to rule over the whole of India; but none of them was as powerful as the Great Moguls (1526–1857).

The most outstanding of the Mogul emperors was Akbar (1556–1605). The tax he exacted from the peasants was three times less than that before his reign, he abolished the *jizwa* tax collected from Hinduists, began to enrol Hinduists in the army, restrained the influence of the *'ulamā*, cherished the idea of creating a universal religion which could be acceptable to all his subjects. These tendencies, however, were curtailed by Akbar's successors, especially Aurangzeb (1678–1707), who were fanatical Muslims.

After the death of Aurangzeb, the morally decadent Muslim aristocracy could no longer claim to be dominant in India.[44] Along with Muslim domains, India contained a number of domains belonging to Hinduist *rajas*, who were constantly at war with one another – and with the Muslims.

The Empire of the Great Moguls was a typical medieval state whose frontiers did not correspond to any ethnically or physico-geographically defined regions, but – as is usual in such cases – which depended on the outcome of internecine conflicts, and on the success or lack of success in each individual campaign. The empire grew rich on plunder from the regions under its sway, and could pay poets, miniature painters[45] and architectural geniuses (as evidenced by the masterpieces of Delhi, Agra and Samarkand). But under the Moguls there was no sign of a change to a new Phase of the historical process. Although the Timurids had a primitive sort of firearms, namely the arquebus, this alone was not sufficient for a passage from the old Phase into a new one. There was no sign of the formation of new classes in the society, and there did not appear any kind of alternative socio-psychological features.

It is remarkable that during the epoch of Arabic conquests Islam was easily and quickly adopted by local populations, while this was by no means the case during the Timurid conquest of India. Only the population of Sindh (the valley of the Indus) and of Punjab embraced the Islamic faith (as did the population of Bengal, modern Bangladesh, conquered by Muslims about 1200 AD). But even in the Punjab part of the population later converted to a new religion, namely the doctrine of the Sikhs, which was a monotheistic religion introduced in the late fifteenth century.

---

44. The last Great Mogul, Bahadur Shah, was deposed by the British. However, the real power of the Great Monguls actually lasted only to the beginning of the eighteenth century.

45. The Islamic prohibition of figurative art as giving occasion to idolatry was somewhat mitigated in eastern Moslem countries: if the figures were flat, they were not regarded as idols. Hence the abundant development of miniature-painting in Iran, Central Asia and India.

It seems that the Hinduist caste system satisfied the need for 'being protected, being among one's own', and a new doctrine which could better correspond to the social wants of the population was not forthcoming.

The history of medieval Iran presents us with the same well-known nauseating paradigm of everlastingly warring and changing unstable domains with uncertain frontiers; they mostly had Turkic dynasties. In the fifteenth century the leading role passed to the adherents to the spiritual dervish order Safawiyah, whose main military support was a group of Shïite Turkic tribes, the Qyzylbashs.

Having rebelled against the Ak-Koyunlu, the Qyzylbashs, headed by Ismaïl I Safawi (1500–1524), conquered the whole of Iran, a region which extended almost to its present-day limits but also included the south-western part of modern Afghanistan, and also present-day Armenia; and in the seventeenth and early eighteenth centuries also the present-day Republic of Azerbaijan and, at times, Georgia. Shïism was declared the official religion. The empire of the Safawids proved so stable that it lasted from 1500 to 1722 when it was overthrown by an insurrection of Afghan tribes; this led to a new series of internecine wars, which continued throughout the eighteenth century.

Like the other post-Mongol states of the Near and the Middle East and of India, Iran (Persia) can be classified as feudal in the Western European sense of the word. The system of *tiyul* was dominant, which meant that royal servants received the right to collect, by way of a feudal rent in their own favour, a tax from certain territories. Later the *tiyul* was transformed into a grant of land. Until the fifteenth century another system preceded that of the *tiyul*, namely the *soyurgal* system (which had spread not only to Iran but also to Iraq, Central Asia and the Golden Horde, and under the Mogul dynasty, also to India). The *soyurgal* was granted for military service, and its possessor was entitled to collect taxes, while himself being immune from taxes and from administrative and juridical responsibility (of course, subject to royal favour).

Despite the nightmarish conditions of the Middle Ages, cultural life continued. Muslim architecture is famous throughout the world; we have already tried to explain the reasons for this. The religiously-philosophical current of Sufism played an important role in the life of medieval Muslim society. It was based on metaphysical principles and practised a rule of obedience, which meant that disciples (*murids*) under the preceptorship of an elder (*murshid*, or *pir*) were being prepared for an ascetic way of life (*tariqat*) which implied self-extinction, and led to the gradual mystic cognition of God and a final merger with Him. The Sufis strove towards mystical 'illumination' through ecstatic dances, prayer formulas, and mortification of the flesh. There were Sufi spiritual orders, and even monasteries of a type (*hanaqa*). The Sufis played *tariqat* above the *sharïat*, and for a long time were persecuted by the orthodox Islamic *'ulamā*.

Although Sufism, at most, led from the insupportable real life only into a mystically coloured cognition of it, this doctrine inspired remarkable poets (or gave to them the possibility for self-expression): Sa'adi (1210?–1292), author of lyrical and larger poems of humane moral contents, and of prose; Jellal-ad-din Rumi, an outstanding Sufi leader and the author of poetical proverbs (died in 1273 in Asia Minor); Hafiz (1325–1390?), one of the world's greatest lyrical poets with a well-earned world renown.[46] Some remarkable epic poetry in the Persian language was produced (Nizami, 1141?–1209?),[47] along with satiric poetry (Zakani; died in 1370). However, a poet could exist only through modest patronage and therefore had to write eulogistic poems. In prose, the most important genre was history, the authors being paid by the rulers.

We must do justice to the moral fortitude of the medieval thinkers, scholars, poets and artists who acted at a time which could not have been worse for creative efforts. Today, much of what they have done can still excite and gladden our hearts.

However, after the fifteenth century, all poetry written in Persian was imitative. There was nothing new that could be imparted to the reader – society had begun to stagnate.

Across the globe medieval societies display a monotonous picture of unstable state formations, whose contours depend solely on rude and violent military force. As we have already pointed out, the Middle Ages are a historical trap. Of course, inside medieval society, as at all other times, men and women enjoyed everyday life; they were born, loved and died (either naturally, or by being murdered by their rulers); but only in lyric poetry, whether Chinese, Arabic or Persian (especially Sufi poetry), and perhaps in the prejudiced dynastic histories do we find some intellectual traces of this life.

We shall leave aside the Indo-Chinese peninsula, Burma and Indonesia, where more or less similar processes were going on (but my sources here are rather insufficient). But before we turn to societies where signs of a new Phase were apparent, it seems advisable to dwell in some detail on one more peculiar society, namely that of the Ottoman Empire.

From the eleventh century, Turkish tribes speaking Oghuz dialects began to infiltrate Asia Minor.

As in all similar cases, we are not to suppose that the newly arrived tribes replaced the former population. They replaced only the ruling stratum of the society: in the main, the inhabitants of Asia Minor after the eleventh century were agriculturists of Greek (and partly Armenian) origin, who gradually were being Turkicised, and who, in their turn, had been descendants of Hittito-Luwians and other ancient inhabitants of Asia Minor, who had adopted Greek as their spoken language while living under the Roman Empire. At first – beginning with the

46. The expression of living human feelings could, if need be, receive a mystic interpretation. This is why the great poet Hafiz could allow himself, e.g. the following lines: 'When a Turki girl of Shiraz holds my heart in her hand, I can give away Samarkand and Bukhara for just her one black mole.'
47. Nizami lived in Ganja, a Turkic (Azerbaijani) speaking city, but he wrote in Persian.

eleventh century AD – only the ruling élite of Asia Minor was Turkic speaking. However, mixing with the local population, this élite influenced its mentality in the direction of more conformity with the mentality of the steppe-dwellers. Note that the term 'Turks' has two meanings: originally, it meant all tribes speaking Turkic dialects; at present, it is currently used in the sense of 'Turkish speaking population of Anatolia and the modern republic of Turkey'. Note also that the first Turks settling in Anatolia did not often settle in the cities, and some of the cities continued to be Greek into the twentieth century. On the peninsula lost from the Byzantine Empire several Muslim Turkish domains emerged. In such cases the dynasty and the military élite were typically Turkish, with the Greek agricultural population becoming Islamised and gradually Turkicised. From the tenets of Islam the Turks acquired for themselves first of all the doctrine of *jihād* (or *ghazawat*; those who waged a 'holy war' were called *ghazi*). Armed groups gradually pushed back the Byzantines and settled all along the frontiers of the Byzantine dominions and of Armenia Minor, conducting a never ending terroristic 'war'. Most of the new Turkish amirates in Asia Minor were engaged in internal affairs, and only Osman I, amir of the little domain of Söghüt in the north-west of the peninsula, made use of the *ghazi* movement for expanding his territory. For this, the Osmanli (or Ottoman) government took on the role of propagators of Islamic orthodoxy.

Expanding the territory necessarily meant storming enemy cities, but this required prolonged sieges, and the Ottomans lacked siege techniques. In Osman I's lifetime they managed to capture only Brusa (1326 AD), but his successor Orkham seized Nicea (Iznik) and Nicomedia (Izmid) as well, and also annexed the neighbouring Turkish amirate Qarasi.

In 1354 the Ottomans made an important acquisition, capturing the town Gallipoli (Gelibolu) on the European shore of the Straits of the Dardanelles. This gave them a key to the Balkans, where the political situation was extremely grave: here there co-existed Venetian possessions spread along the coast of the Adriatic, fragments of the former Latin Empire of the crusaders, districts which had fallen away from Byzantium, three Bulgarian and several Serbian principalities, and also what had survived of the Byzantine Empire, mostly along the Sea of Marmara and Bosporus (with its centre in Constantinople), and also along the southern shore of the Black Sea. Moreover, the residual Byzantine Empire, like all medieval states, was constantly pulsating, now shrinking, and now expanding.

The Turks had earlier crossed the Dardanelles, taking part in the wars that were being waged to the West of the straits, acting as allies of this or that parties; but after having secured a stable base in Gallipoli, they could start a regular conquest of the Balkans. They seized Adrianople (Edirne) and southern Serbia. The frontier from which the *ghazi* started fighting moved inexorably towards the North. In 1386 Sofia was captured, in 1389 Serbia experienced a crushing defeat on the Kosovo field, and the Serbs recognised the superiority of the Ottomans (however, the

Turkish sultan Murad I fell in battle); Murad's son, Bayazid I, conquered the whole of Bulgaria in 1393, and repulsed a Franco-Hungarian counter-offensive in 1396.

Thus something like the skeleton of an empire had been created, but actually the Ottomans controlled only the main communications, the river valleys, etc. Most of the population of the empire were Christians, some parts of it were ruled by Christian vassals. Bayazid made his goal the spread of orthodox Islam throughout the empire, also introducing Muslim administrators, judges, etc. For this, he lacked a sufficient number of reliable Muslim statesmen in his amirate, so he decided to conquer the remaining Turkish amirates of Asia Minor with the help of Christian contingents and of janizaries (the *ghazis* refused to wage war against their co-religionists).

Who were the janizaries? Over and above other levies from their Christian subjects, the Ottomans introduced a levy in boys (*devşirme*). The children were converted to Islam, received a military and spiritual schooling and were included in the infantry corps called the janizaries (Turkish *yeni çeri* 'the new troops'). For a very long time, the janizaries were forbidden sexual relations with women; isolated in their barracks both from the Christian and the Muslim population, lacking normal family life and human connections, with conscience completely numbed, the janizaries became an obedient and cold-blooded tool of the Ottoman sultans. Having the janizaries, the sultans did no longer want the *ghazis*.

Some of the exiled amirs of Asia Minor called in Timur for help; as we already know, he invaded the peninsula, and in 1402 gained victory over Bayazid in the battle of Ankara. After a raid through Asia Minor, Timur went away, and, as might have been expected, internecine strife broke out between the three sons of Bayazid, of whom Mehmed I was victorious. He continued the policy of subjugating the amirates, but now not by military force but by diplomacy, diplomatic marriages, etc. During the fifteenth century the amirates gradually became incorporated into the empire.

The sultan Murad II started *ghazawat* anew in the Balkans (including Morea, i.e. the Peloponnese peninsula). In the winter of 1443–1444, the independent Christian rulers of Serbia, Walachia and Poland, headed by the Hungarian king János Hunyadi, started a 'crusade' against the Ottomans, but Murad, having broken the resistance of the last amirates of Asia Minor, prevented the 'crusaders' crossing the Straits with the help of the Genoese fleet; they were defeated in 1444 near Varna, and finally routed in 1448, again in Kosovo.

The next sultan, Mehmed II, captured Constantinople in 1453. Artillery was used in the siege for the first time in a serious engagement (immovable siege-artillery had been known since the end of the thirteenth century, but was rarely used). Mehmed rebuilt the city according to his own ideas, making it a new great Muslim capital, Istanbul. In 1456 he besieged Belgrade – but to no avail. But in 1458–1460 Mehmed II captured Athens, the Greek principality of Morea and what remained of Serbia, and during 1463–1484 Bosnia too was overrun; many noble Bosnians embraced Islam and were among the most valued *ghazis*. In 1461 Mehmed II conquered Trapezus (Trabzon), the last remnant of the Byzantine Empire which had survived since the thirteenth century.

The Sultan of Bayazid II (1481–1512), after having fought off the challenge of his brother, continued to make conquests, occupying Herzegovina and areas around the mouth of the Danube and the Dnieper (which made contacts with the Crimean Khanate possible); in the Adriatic, he wrested from Venice five districts of considerable consequence. He also founded a strong Turkish navy.

Rivalry developed between the Ottomans and the empire of the Mamluks.

Originally, as mentioned above, the Mamluks were prisoners of war sold into slavery in Muslim countries after sundry internecine conflicts in Russia, the Caucasus and Central Asia. The Abbasid caliphs used them as warriors; Mamluk troops became an élite force, and gradually they developed into a sort of military caste. The Fatimid sultans of Egypt (969–1181) organised a Mamluk army, probably in order not to be reduced to recruiting soldiers from neighbouring countries inimical to Egypt; Saladin also made use of them. Then the Mamluks gained power in Egypt; Mamluk sultans also ruled neighbouring countries (1250–1517), such as parts of Libya, the whole of Syria and Hijaz (in Arabia, with the sacred cities of Mecca and Medina). In 1485–1491 there was a conflict over Syria between the Ottomans and the Mamluks. The war came to nothing; meanwhile a new danger for the Ottomans arose in the Safawids of Iran, who were responsible for Shïite propaganda in Asia Minor and in those regions which were disputed by the Sunnite Ottomans and Mamluks. A Shïite insurrection broke out in Asia Minor.

Meanwhile, during the rule of Bayazid II a war broke out between his sons. It was customary for a sultan to send his grown-up sons into sundry provinces to study statesmanship, but it was also customary for each new sultan to execute all his brothers and their sons. This was why armed struggles inevitably broke out in the lifetime of the ruling sultan. In this particular case, one of the sons, Selim, was allied to the khan of Crimea, while another son, Ahmad, relied upon the support of the army fighting to suppress a Shïite insurrection. Ahmad seemed clearly to have superior forces, but the janizaries decided for Selim; Bayazid abdicated in favour of the latter. Ahmad was defeated and killed by Selim I in 1513, and after that Selim inflicted a defeat upon Ismaïl Safawi.

Selim I the Grim appears to have been an efficient general; he defeated the Mamluks and in 1516–1517 captured not only Syria but also Egypt. This made him sovereign of Hijaz as well with its sacred cities of Mecca and Medina, which later made it possible for the sultans of Turkey to declare themselves caliphs. The conquests also continued under Selim I's son, Suleiman I the Magnificent. He captured Belgrade in 1521, defeated the Hungarians in 1526 and declared the new king of Hungary, János Zápolya, his vassal. But Ferdinand Habsburg, the archduke of Austria and brother of Charles V, emperor of the Holy Roman Empire, also laid claim to the Hungarian throne. This led to a war in 1531–1532, during which the

Ottomans besieged Vienna. The result was that Suleiman created for himself an advantageous position in the north-west, establishing a series of vassal states: the Crimea, Moldavia, Walachia, Transylvania and Hungary. After this, Suleiman waged three wars against Safawid Persia, occupying the Armenian Highland (now called Eastern Anatolia by the Turks).

Suleiman had also important victories on sea. In 1522 the island of Rhodes was besieged; the knights of St John had used it as a base for their piratical raids; now, after the siege, they had to shift their base to the island of Malta. The famous Arab corsair Kheir-ed-Din Barbarossa who had taken possession of Algeria, entered Suleiman's service (he became the local chief at Gelibolu and a member of the sultan's council). Besides Algeria, another corsair state was also founded in Tripoli (in Libya). Hungary and the Habsburgs were also involved in the fight for supremacy in the Mediterranean (the Habsburg emperor Charles V was also king of Spain; later the crown of Spain was inherited by his son Philip II); France also entered in the war – but against the Habsburgs, and hence on the side of Turkey.

In 1571, the Christians achieved a victory over Selim II at the battle of Lepanto off the coast of Greece (it was the greatest of the sea battles in the era of galleys); however, differences of opinion between the allies induced Venice to cede Cyprus to the Turks. The next major war (1582) was between Turkey and Persia; they fought for southern (at present Iranian) Azerbaijan, for Shirvan and Daghestan. In 1590 the threat of the Uzbeks to invade Khorasan forced the shah Abbas I to cede Georgia, Shirvan, Azerbaijan and Lurestan to the Ottomans.

Under Mehmed III and his son Ahmed I there was war once again with the Holy Roman Empire; in 1606 a peace was concluded with Austria, and in 1611 with Persia. Ahmed I, who was a pious man, abolished the custom of killing the brothers of the new sultan; it was decided that in the future they could be kept singly in special pavilions or 'coops' from which women were forbidden. One of them might eventually become sultan. Henceforth it was usually not the sultan's son who inherited the throne, but one of his brothers, who lacked any experience in statesmanship; as a result, depositions of sultans by the viziers and janizaries became not uncommon.

We have reached an epoch when Europe already had passed into the Sixth Phase, the Absolutist Post-Medieval one. In Turkey, however, the most important signs of this Phase are not yet visible, despite Turkey's huge territory and hence large internal market and its possession of fire-arms (cannons and arquebuses) – a symptom of the coming Sixth Phase. City handicrafts (including the production of arms), as well as trade, were in the hands of Greeks, Venetians and Armenians, and Turkish society as such was wholly oriented towards war as the main source of income.

The state was a consistently structured military and bureaucratic machine. Deviating from my usual practice, I shall try to describe it in some detail, just to show the great differences which exist between societies which in our country have been lumped together as 'feudal'.

The sultan was surrounded by janizaries who had been trained under the supervision of white eunuchs; the ladies of the harem were supervised by black eunuchs. The chief supervisor of the harem (with the title of *agha*) was also in charge of the property granted for spiritual needs (*waqf*); only through him could the sultan be addressed. Of the officials of the 'inner service' most important were the members of the council (*Divan*): it included the Grand Vizier who, subordinate only to the sultan, ruled in practice over the whole empire and its armed forces (later sultans did not head the army themselves); but the court of the sultan and the *'ulāmā* were not subordinated to the vizier. From the same 'inner circle' originated the highest officials of the country – the commanders of the navy, the military judges, the treasurer, and also the provincial governors (*beylerbey*), and others. From the sixteenth century, the empire was ruled not by the sultan's divan but by that of the vizier, the 'Sublime Porte'. Ranked below the officials of the 'inner service' were those of the 'outer service', who were partly recruited from the janizaries. These officials included the commander of the janizaries, of the artillery and the cavalry, the chief of the commissariat, the chief gardener and others. Eunuchs played an important part in Turkish society; they served in the harems, and were also entrusted with different administrative duties, where they could not be dangerous for the sultan since they were incapable of founding rivalling dynasties. Castration, especially of prisoners of war, was widely practised; it had to be done in childhood, before puberty, otherwise impotency could not be guaranteed.

Beyond the sultan's court, the beylerbeys and the rulers of regions subordinate to them had their own councils (*divans*) and were actually feudal princes; each had his own troop of feudal cavalry, the *sipahi* (sepoys). The most profitable fiefs (those bringing more than 1,000 ducats a year) were called *hass*; they belonged to the sultan's kinsmen and the highest officials; an income of 200 ducats and more was received from the *ziamet* fiefs; an income of less than 200 ducats was received from *timars*. Thus, it was not an administrative, but a military feudal system, and the districts were military. This system did not extend to some Kurd, Arab and Christian territories, nor to the vassal states (Crimea, Moldavia, Walachia, Transylvania). The merchants of Dubrovnik (Raguza) in the Adriatic paid a tribute but were self-governing. Local administrators were the *qāḍīs* (judges applying the rules of *sharīat*), and the treasurers. Taxes from the grass roots were mainly received by the regional rulers and spent on their services and sepoys, while the sultan's treasury was replenished from other sources of taxation, namely from customs duties, tributes and military booty. Most of these incomes were spent on the army and the navy. The navy consisted mostly of galleys; the oarsmen were chiefly convicts and prisoners of war, while the warriors on the galleys were janizaries and sepoys. Behind the troops of the regular army followed irregular and unpaid bands of bashi-bazouks who lived exclusively off the plunder.

Although there was no further growth of the Ottoman Empire after the eighteenth century, the system created by the sultans survived until the middle of the nineteenth century. Even during the Crimean war (1853–1856), Turkey differed but little from what has been described above (the galleys were replaced by frigates and ships of the line).

I have dealt with Turkey in greater detail than other state formations of this Phase because it is a good sample of what a medieval society would look like at its fullest development. In particular, it is a graphic rejoinder to the idea that the passage from Antiquity to the Middle Ages constituted progress in the sense of being more beneficial for a greater number of men and women.

If we discount architecture (Sinan) and some handicrafts (as, e.g. carpet-making which, it may be noted, was also characteristic of many regions to the east of Turkey, including India), Turkey did not achieve a great deal for world culture. Noteworthy are the voluminous records of the traveller Evliya Çelebi (1611–1683). Turkish poetry was imitative and influenced mainly by Persian poetry. An original mystic poet who retained the formal Turkish traditions was Yunus Emre (d. 1320). Most poets wrote not only in Turkish but also in Persian and Arabic. A remarkable philosopher-poet with a pantheistic tendency was Nesimi (1369–1417). He was accused of heresy and flayed alive. The most important sixteenth-century poet, Fizuli, wrote in the classical genres introduced by the Persian poets.

Meanwhile, different parts of Western Europe witnessed the growth of cities which gradually achieved a degree of independence. International trade was concentrated here, together with the production of handicrafts organised in the new form of manufactories. New classes emerged in the cities – the bourgeoisie and the working class. Gradually, the bourgeoisie began to compete with the feudal lords, and it strove to free the workers from dependence on the feudal class, since it was difficult to recruit labourers from among bonded peasants. All this led to a crisis of medieval society; in Europe it began during the fourteenth to fifteenth centuries. But in Italy, from the 1280s, independent cities had already appeared – 'communes', with a republican or, at least, elected administration.

The wars constantly waged by countries in the Middle Ages led to a situation in which the production of arms (especially defensive), the building of all kinds of military constructions (e.g. castles) and imposing temples and monasteries, the making of rather elaborate clothes and footwear (with and without spurs), could not be satisfactorily accomplished inside the knights' agricultural estates. External trade became vital, and in Western Europe it was facilitated by the proximity of overseas civilisations (for the Italian communes these were mainly Islamic countries: Asia Minor, Palestine, Egypt and 'Barbaria', i.e. Northern Africa; for the northern European cities, they were Britain, Scandinavia and Russia). The distances were manageable even for comparatively primitive ships.

Therefore, as early as the Fifth Phase, even before the Crusades but especially after them, new centres for handicraft industries and for export appeared in Western Europe.

Each handicraft was kept secret from the uninitiated – this was a necessary measure for safeguarding the well-being of the craftsmen. Each trade was united in a special closed organisation – a guild, which included both full members (masters), and subordinates (apprentices). After primary training, the latter were often sent into the world in order to receive and to pass on new practical skills. They often travelled considerable distances but the European apprentices, who were bound by a religious oath, did not leave the bounds of the Catholic Christian world.

The apprentices were not opposed to the masters as one class to another; a successful apprentice could become a master himself. Of course, there was a considerable difference between the two groups as regards their means, but the emergence of two opposed classes, a bourgeoisie and a class of hired workers devoid of property, belongs to the Sixth Phase, and is closely related to the development of some prospering artisans' shops into bourgeois manufactories, on which more below. Both the appearance of manufactories as a typical social feature, and the formation of new classes belong to the new, Sixth Phase of the historical process; however, in the Fifth Phase cities as centres of trade and industry had already begun to play an important historical role, especially in Northern Italy.

As late as the eighth century a considerable part of Italy still lay under the dominion of the Byzantine Empire, most of the eastern region, including Venice, Ravenna, Bari and the Apulian peninsula, as well as certain important points in the south-west including Amalfi and Salerno. Moreover Sicily, Sardinia and Corsica were to remain in the empire for a long time to come. Northern Italy, having been conquered by the Langobards (Lombards), was taken over by the Holy Roman Empire, and after its division under the heirs of Charlemagne, several independent states appeared in this region. The more important cities were more or less self-governing. They were also centres of trade and of church administration. The rulers of the cities, gradually achieving independence, assumed the title of dukes or (in Venice) Doges.[48] In Central Italy over time emerged a specific region in which the pope was not only the spiritual head but also a lay sovereign.

The need for investiture to take place in Rome presented certain difficulties for the Holy Roman emperors. Note that in addition to the imperial title, which required a papal investiture, there was another title, 'King of Germany';[49] moreover, wars usually decided which of the quarrelling German feudal lords would

---

48. The Doges were elected for life by the 'people' – actually by the upper stratum of the city population.

49. The title of Emperor of the Holy Roman Empire was not hereditary; nor was that of King of Germany; each new Emperor had to be elected by a body of the most influential feudal lords, the 'electors' (*Kurfürst*); but to receive the title of emperor the recognition of the pope and an investiture by the pope were necessary. The most telling episode showing the conflict between the emperors and the popes was the reign of emperor Henry IV (1084–1106). Having been excommunicated by Pope Gregory VII, he – at that time (1077) already King of Germany – had, in order to be pardoned, to repent his sins barefoot and on his knees, before the pope who was at that time resident in Canossa Castle. But excommunicated again, he captured Rome and was there crowned emperor by his own henchman, the antipope Clement III. Later his activities involved wars and various adventures, and a series of reverses. It was only the family of Habsburg that routinely produced Roman emperors from the fifteenth century.

receive the imperial crown. Hostilities accelerated during the rivalry between Otto IV, duke of Bavaria from the family of the Welfs (emperor from 1209 to 1218), and Frederick II of Swabia, from the family of the Hohenstaufens (emperor from 1218 to 1250), whose ancestral home was the castle Waiblingen. The rivalry between Otto and Frederic coincided in time with the efforts of Pope Innocent III to organise a secular papal state in Central Italy. Innocent III at first tended to support Otto, but towards the end of his life he was obliged to recognise Frederic as emperor. A pro-papal party of Guelfs and a pro-imperial party of Ghibellines (the names originate from 'Welf' and 'Waiblingen') had already emerged, first of all in Florence. Later, in Italian cities, followers of these parties deeply hostile to each other, still called themselves 'Guelfs' and 'Ghibellines', but their connection with a pro-papal or pro-imperial policy was not always evident.

Meanwhile, in the late ninth century, Norman pirates, with the blessing of Pope Nicholas II and headed by Robert Guiscard, and later by his brother Roger, seized Apulia, Calabria and also Sicily which at that time had a considerable Arab population. Roger patronised both the Byzantine and the Roman church and tolerated mosques. The authority of the Norman dynasty, which at times extended not only to the islands of the Mediterranean Sea but even to the coast of Northern Africa, continued until the era of Frederic II of Hohenstaufen, who practically annexed Sicily to the Holy Roman Empire. But in 1265 the pope bestowed the crown of Naples and Sicily on the French prince Charles of Anjou. Meanwhile, the Normans had become partly integrated with the local population of Sicily, and partly resettled to the Byzantine empire as mercenaries, while the Arabs emigrated to Africa. Thus, Southern Italy developed in a way quite different from that of Northern Italy. Its main conflicts were now with Spain: the kings of Aragon had seized Corsica and Sardinia, and later became established in Sicily and in Naples.

In 1474 the marriage of Ferdinand, King of Aragon in the eastern (Catalan) part of the Pyrenean peninsula to Isabella, Queen of Castile, led to the creation of a unified Spanish kingdom. America was discovered during the reign of Ferdinand and Isabella, a matter we will return to below.

After Ferdinand and Isabella, the Spanish throne passed to their grandson, king Charles of Habsburg, who became Charles II, emperor of the Holy Roman Empire; subsequently (1519) the Spanish and Italian possessions of the Aragon dynasty also passed to the Habsburgs.

Let us now turn to the history of Northern Italy. The traders and artisans, defended by the strong walls of the cities, valued their independence highly, but had no cavalry of their own; therefore, they hired *condittieri*, i.e. leaders of mercenary knights who had deserted one or other of the dynastic parties. At the same time, self-governing bodies (*communes*) were established inside the city-walls. The interaction of the condottieri and the communes gave rise to the North Italian city-states with leaders which the emperors of the Holy Roman and the Byzantine empires regarded as equals to the kings of France and Naples. The Northern Italian cities differed in their constitution: they might be ruled directly by the commune, or by a *signoria* – a board representing the most noble and rich families of the city – or by a duke (in Venice, by an elected Doge), or by a hereditary noble dynasty (as, for instance, the Medici family in Florence), whose leaders bore the title *pater patriae*, or *magnificent signor*; but in the European genealogies they were regarded as equal to monarchs.

There were a great many Northern Italian communes, and one commune often was dependent on another. The most important communes were the habour cities of Venice and Genoa, and Florence, which lay inland.

Venice dates back to the Great Migration, when many inhabitants of Northern Italy, fleeing the invasion of the Langobards in 568, settled on the shore of a vast lagoon along the coast of the Adriatic Sea near the mouth of the River Po. For a long time the commune which grew up was dependent on the Byzantine 'exarchate' of Ravenna, but the German Roman emperors also had a claim to it. Venice was officially regarded as a republic, but actually it was an absolute monarchy for the lifetime of the Doge elected by the estates – which, in the earlier period, also included the common people. However, the rules of election changed more than once. The Doges did not found dynasties.

Obstructed from the mainland (the food was procured from the sea and the small mainland district of Treviso), Venice turned towards overseas trade supported by naval warfare. Its first attempts to get further into the Adriatic and beyond were cut short by the plague of 1349.[50] Later, by the treaty of Torino, the spheres of interests at sea were divided between Venice and Genoa. Venice tried to avoid confrontation with Turkey, but waged wars in Italy and on the Istrian peninsula, acquiring new territory. While the Turks were destroying the Byzantine Empire (which had lost its lands in Italy during the eleventh to thirteenth centuries), Venice extended its domains, founding colonies on the islands and shores of the Adriatic and in the Aegean Sea, and also on the island of Cyprus. Oriental handicrafts and agricultural produce poured into Venice, bringing it the wealth it was to be famous for.

Genoa, on the western shore of the Apennine peninsula, had already become an independent commune during the decline of Charlemagne's empire. Volunteers from all strata of the population (the *compagna*) furnished the state with arms, with capital and labour. The state itself was ruled by consuls who were replaced from among the gentry and the more prosperous citizens. Dominating sea trade in the western part of the Mediterranean, Genoa, like Venice, grew very rich and proved a

---

50. According to tradition, the plague was imported from Central Asia; it broke out among the Kuman troops besieging Kafa (Feodosia) in the Crimea in 1347. The besieging warriors threw corpses of those who had died of the plague into their opponents' midst, and later Genoese ships brought the infection to Europe. Central and Southern Europe suffered most heavily, but the epidemic reached also Northern Africa, Britain and even Norway, where the population of some valleys died out totally. The epidemic receded in the early 1350s, but it broke out again several times during the fourteenth century.

magnet for those in search of a living or gain. At the beginning of the thirteenth century it already had *c.* 10,000 inhabitants. If the Oriental and Byzantine trade of Venice allowed its merchants to cater for Italy and the Holy Roman Empire, Genoa's merchants also catered for Italy, and moreover, for France and even for Spain. Among the Jews who had fled the atrocities of the Reconquista in Spain many settled in Genoa. The Genoese occupied Sardinia and Corsica, and created a whole net of semi-dependent colonies on the Mediterranean shores of Europe. But in the eastern part of the Mediterranean Genoa could also successfully vie with Venice. The Genoese took part in the Crusades, their considerable losses compensated for by the advantageous sale of the booty. In 1261 the Genoese made a peace treaty with the reborn Byzantine Empire; this opened for them the Marmara and the Black Sea. Pera, a suburb of Constantinople, became a Genoese colony; part of the Crimean coast with its centre in Kafa (now Feodosia) was owned by Genoa. In addition to trade and handicrafts, the Genoese also went in for credit business. However, in the fifteenth century, a crisis in Europe (which is to be discussed elsewhere), and the beginning of an era of colonial conquest, led to a change in the direction of the main trade routes, and in the relative importance of the economic centres. Genoa's power began to wane, and in 1421 it was joined to the dominions of the duke of Milan; in 1443 its Crimean possessions were seized by the khan of Crimea.

Florence, whose origin goes back to Roman and even Etruscan times, played an important role under Charlemagne and the Carolingians, and was the centre of the military district of Tuscany (ancient Etruria). During the conflict between the pope and the emperor Henry IV at the beginning of the twelfth century, Florence supported the pope, using that pretext to increase its own possessions, and soon began to install its own local authorities in the neighbouring towns. At first, the commune of Florence consisted of autonomous parochial groups of craftsmen and tradesmen, but later they united, constituting the Florentine commune which was headed by six or eight consuls, and had an assembly of 100 'good men' (i.e. noble, rich men). Over time, neighbouring villages and castles were annexed, union treaties were concluded (e.g. with Pisa). Emperor Frederick I Barbarossa tried to seize Tuscany, but in vain; finally he acknowledged the sovereign right of Florence over it.

The quarrels between the leading noble families of Florence led to the institution of the neutral high office of the *podestà*, who at first was a local inhabitant but from the thirteenth century was either invited from elsewhere or imposed by the emperor. Being involved in the political life of all Italy and even of the whole empire, Florence took part in the embittered struggle between the Guelfs, supporting the emperor Otto IV (and the papacy), and the Ghibellines who were on the side of the emperor Frederic II. The course of military events led to the flight of the Guelfs from Florence, and then to their total expulsion in 1248; their homes were destroyed and their property confiscated. In 1250 the eminent merchants of

Florence set up, alongside the *podestà* and his council, a specific government official, the *capitano del popolo* ('captain of the people'); the Guelfs again came to power. In 1252 a local golden coin, the florin, was issued, which soon became a generally accepted currency in Italy. In time, the Ghibellines would be reinstated but this situation lasted only until the conquest of the city by Charles of Anjou, the king of Naples, in 1266. The 'captains of the people' were then replaced by 'captains of the Guelf party'; now the Ghibellines had to flee.

In order to put an end to internecine strife, Pope Nicholas III intervened. The office of the *podestà* was restored, but with a *capitano* set beside him, charged specifically with 'keeping the peace': there were also two councils and a signoria of 100 men, led by eight 'good men', among whom both the Guelfs and the Ghibellines were to be represented. But this was not the final reform: the most influential of the guilds demanded the right to participate in the administration. Six of their representatives were introduced to help the *capitano*, who now received the title 'defender of handicrafts and arts'. Then, in 1293, an act which gained representation in 'Ordinances of Justice' was introduced against the nobility; the lesser guilds, the signoria and the nobles were excluded. To implement the new order, the office of a 'gonfalonier of justice' was introduced. The end of the thirteenth century and the entire fourteenth century were full of strife between the different groups of commoners and the Florentine nobility. On account of being a Ghibelline, the great poet Dante was exiled for life from Florence (in 1301).

Notwithstanding all these inner political disorders, Florentine handicrafts and trade thrived; a number of Italian cities (mainly in Tuscany) submitted to the rule of Florence or were subjugated. The city's might and riches were based on the production and export of wool and woollen stuffs from the world's first manufactories. A manufactory was a vast workshop (or a net of workshops) belonging to a master (or a nobleman) – the capitalist who invested in the manufactory. The workers were not apprentices but hirelings with no rights of their own. In this structure the labour of fifteen workers became specialised, making it more productive than in a simple workshop. But exploitation also grew since the worker was bound for life to a single working operation.

The heyday of Florence was interrupted by a pandemic ('The Black Death', 1349). However, the city-state soon recovered, and even conducted military campaigns until 1378. That year saw a rising of the Ciompi, for the most part workers who were dissatisfied with the dismissal of a liberal gonfalonier. This insurrection can be regarded as the first political action of the working class. The government established by the Ciompi survived until 1382.

The Florentine bourgeois republic flourished despite its involvement in different kinds of strife.

In 1417 Giovanni Medici became gonfalonier; in 1429 he was succeeded by his son, the immensely rich Cosimo; thus the political power in Florence passed to the dynasty of the Medici, which continued to hold power for 300 years.

Although its territory was small, and its rulers did not assume ducal or royal titles,[51] Florence in the fifteenth century was one of the great fifteen powers of Europe; being related to Florence's ruling house by marriage was considered an honour for European kings.

We have dwelt upon the history of Venice, Genoa and particularly Florence because it was actually here that we can with certainty state that the transition to the Sixth Phase of the historical process was first achieved. The first symptom was the creation of two new classes in addition to the main classes of the medieval society (landowners and dependent agriculturists): namely, a class of capitalistic entrepreneurs and a class of hired workers.

The second symptom of the Sixth Phase – a stable 'national' absolutist state – did not emerge until later in Italy; however, Tuscany under the Medici may be regarded as such a state in embryo. It should be noted that it was the Tuscan dialect which later became the basis of the national common Italian language.

Yet another diagnosic symptom of the Sixth Phase can be seen in the existence of alternative socio-psychological tenets. In Italy of the twelfth to fifteenth centuries, such a symptom cannot be detected. It is true that Catholic dogma was no longer followed quite so strictly, a point which is particularly evident in figurative art; such art continued, it is true, to cater mostly for religious needs, and only gradually turned away from the prescribed Byzantine canon of the icon. The frescoes and the stained-glass panels of the Florentine artist Cimabue (1240?–1310?), although comprehensively and originally conceived, clearly show their continued dependence on Byzantine prototypes. Giotto (1299–1337), another Florentine, is regarded as the founder of the 'New (Italian) Style' in the art of painting; he introduced perspective in place of the Byzantine flat surface, but he too, in a certain sense, continued the icon tradition. However, the painting schools of Florence continued to evolve, and for a long time this city was the place where the best masters of painting studied (as in the case of the Venetian family in Bellini).

In these artistic developments the image of man – heroic or humble, but always alive – was paramount. Here we should mention the sculptor Donatello (1386?–1460); one of the greatest figures of the Italian Renaissance, Leonardo da Vinci, painter, sculptor, musician, poet, architect and scientist (1452–1519); Michaelangelo, a universal master in the arts, the author of the famous giant statue of David in the Piazza della Signoria in Florence, and the painter Rafael, a genius in the art of harmonious pictorial imagery (1489–1520). The work of these outstanding artists shows that a new era had begun, when 'one could think otherwise'; although apart from pictorial art and architecture these tendencies are not conspicuous (they were, to a great extent, conditioned by the needs of the luxurious and by no means saintly lives of the popes and other Catholic prelates). Even the famous scholar Pico della Mirandola (1463–1494) who, as it was rumoured, 'knew all there

51. Alessandro Medici assume the title of duke only in 1532.

is to know and also something else', who was acquainted with Greek, Arabic, Hebrew and Latin authors, was still limited in his thinking to theology connected with late (mostly Arabic) Platonism and Aristotelism.

The same can be observed in literature. Up to the end of the thirteenth century what was written consisted of undistinguished chronicles, verse compositions of the troubadours and trouvères, and of course, numerous theological treatises. The fate of Pierre Abelard (1070–1142), an outstanding philosopher, logician and theologian, was remarkable. For a liaison with a gifted noble young lady, Héloïse, he was punished by her father (whether in the spirit of Christianity I do not know) by castration. Both lovers took monastic vows.

To the beginning of the fourteenth century belongs the so-called 'sweet new style' in lyrical poetry and, of more consequence, the great epic, the *Divina Commedia*' of Dante (1265–1321), in which he depicted, with compelling, imaginative force and poetic mastery the inhabitants of Catholicism's Inferno, Purgatory and Paradise. Characteristically, when seeing the sadistic and, moreover, eternal tortures of the sinners in Hell, Dante himself weeps out of pity for them; but Dante's God is devoid of the least degree of compassion, and is indeed very unlike Jesus of the Gospels.

Another great medieval writer was the lyrical poet (less an epic poet and historical philosopher) Petrarch (1304–1374). Only Boccaccio (1313–1375), author of the lively, merry and ironical *Decameron* – a collection of novellas, reflecting not so much the social as the private (and love) life of the epoch – can perhaps be regarded as something more than a medieval writer.

In the twelfth to fifteenth centuries, Italy had not yet entered the new historical Phase because it had not created an alternative ideology to that on which the Middle Ages were based; but it was preparing such an ideology. A certain substitute for a new ideology was the sharp decline in the prestige of the popes, and thus of orthodox Catholicism as a whole. The court of most of the popes, supposed to be Christ's vicars on Earth, was remarkable for the greatest luxury, depravity, and open corruption. Although elected, as a matter of principle by a Curia consisting of the most highly ranked Christian prelates (cardinals), it actually so happened that the pope was in fact elected by only those cardinals who could be present in Rome; not uncommonly the wishes of some secular sovereign were decisive in the election of a new pope; and it was the pope who ordained the cardinals.

The pope Clement V (1305–1314), a Provençal by birth, ordained a number of French and Provençal cardinals, and was under constant pressure from the French king Philip IV the Fair. Clement V left Rome and set up the papal throne at Avignon (in the south of modern France). The Avignon popes were wholly dependent on the French kings. They stayed there until 1377. Then 'The Great Schism' occurred. There appeared two Curias, and two popes, one pope cursing the other as an 'anti-pope'. Even a 'counter-anti-pope' appeared. The Schism continued until 1417. A further important element was the practice of selling 'indulgences' – remissions of sins which were to be punished in purgatory (not in the Inferno); the money filled the papal treasury but sometimes also the treasury of secular powers. From all this it is apparent that during the thirteenth and fourteenth centuries the Catholic world possessed neither an alternative ideology nor even a more or less respectable official one. And individual humane and selfless monks such as St Francis of Assisi (1182–1226), who actively preached love not only for humans but for all creatures, did not help to save the situation.

A strong role in the resistance to an alternative ideology was played by the monastic orders, in spite of the fact that they were traditionally very much respected (the Benedictines, the Cartesians, etc.), and by the pauper monastic 'fraternities' (the Dominicans, the Franciscans, the Carmelites, etc.), but especially by the Inquisition, introduced by the Dominicans. The strict rules of the monastic orders served to strengthen the authority of the Catholic Church.

The works of the early 'humanists' (thirteenth to fourteenth centuries) should not be confused with the influential movement of the High Renaissance which already belonged to the Sixth Phase. The essence of the early 'humanism' was the following: since state frontiers constantly moved during the Middle Ages, there was a need for common languages to facilitate understanding across the frontiers. These were living languages that were in constant usage, at least in intellectual practice, but, of course, they differed from the vernacular forms: this was Latin for Western Europe, Church Slavonic for the Balkans and Russia, Arabic for all Islamic countries – and, specifically for the eastern Islamic countries – Turkic, and also Persian; Hebrew for the Jews (spread across very different countries); Sanskrit for India; literary Chinese – first Wen-yen, later Pai-Hua – for the Han (Chinese) and partly for Japan. Of course, since these were living languages (at least, in a certain milieu), they were changing, and the Latin of Dante's *De Vulgari Eloquentia* would probably have horrified Cicero.[52] A scholarly movement for the restoration of Cicero's Latin, as well as for reading and studying Greek authors of the Classical period in the original, emerged in Italy between the thirteenth and the fifteenth centuries. It became possible because of the mass flight of Byzantine Greek scholars from the Turk invasion. The early 'humanists' were mostly university professors and clerics (some of them even became cardinals). In no way did they influence the social development of Europe, but they prepared the way for the humanists of the fifteenth to seventeeth centuries. These will be discussed in the next chapter.

In some other parts of Europe the first signs of a new Phase also made themselves felt. There were an increasing number of independent cities in which international trade, and handicrafts developing into the manufactory form were concentrated.

---

52. Note that the 'spoken' Latin of the medieval educated élite differed greatly from the popular Romance languages (Portuguese, Spanish, Provençal, French, Italian, Moldavian, etc.); these had developed from the 'Vulgar' Latin spoken by the common population of the late Roman Empire, which was very unlike the Latin of Cicero, Caesar or Horace. Dante, in his treatise, attempted to recreate a 'lingua franca' for the educated Europeans.

New classes were developing: the working class and the bourgeoisie, the latter beginning to compete with the feudal class. This brought about a crisis, and not only in Italy. In this period lands around the North and the Baltic Seas saw the emergence of the Hanseatic Union of self-governing independent trading towns headed by Lübeck and including, among others, the cities of Antwerp, Hamburg, Stralsund, Visby (on the Swedish island of Gotland), Riga, Reval (Tallinn) and dozens of others. The farthest Hanseatic cities were Utrecht in the West, Dorpat (Tartu) in the East, and Erfurt in the South. The Hanseatic League had its offices in Bergen (Norway), Bayeux (Normandy), London (England), Novgorod and Pskov (Russia). Inside the frontiers of the Holy Roman Empire the privileges of city self-government were confirmed by law or by treaty. But, as already mentioned, independently of the Hanseatic League there existed guilds of artisans (as well as merchants, barbers, surgeons, etc.); the guilds regulated production with respect to technology and working conditions, as well as relations between masters and apprentices.

An important centre of developing capitalism was Flanders (a region now divided between Belgium, France and the Netherlands). From the twelfth century, and particularly from the fourteenth to fifteenth centuries, its cities of Ghent, Ypres, Brügge, Antwerp, Amsterdam were important centres of international trade; here (and also in England, on which see in the next chapter), bourgeois relations in production were formed not only through trade but also in industry, e.g. in the wool industry.

Historically perhaps the most important achievement of the late medieval cities in Western Europe was the invention of firearms; their introduction fulfilled the prerequisites for the rise of the Sixth, Post-Medieval Phase of human society. Now it was necessary for alternative socio-psychological motives, as well as a sphere in which they could be applied in the form of stable 'national' states.

Meanwhile let us turn to Eastern Europe.

After a long period of medieval internecine wars, Poland was re-united in the fourteenth century by Wladislaw Lokietek and his son Kazimierz III the Great. During his reign, Poland, like other European countries, experienced the pandemic of the plague ('Black Death', 1348–1349).

The Polish rural population had no inducement to settle in towns. Kazimierz III was concerned by the increasing establishment of Germans there, fearing, not without reason, that the increasing influence of the German Hanseatic League might bring about territorial claims of the Holy Roman Empire; hence he decided that Jews would be far more preferable as town-dwellers since they were not backed by any outside political force. Thus Kazimierz invited Jews to Poland, who since then and until the German Nazi genocide of Jews in 1939–1945 and the activities of Wladislaw Gomulka in 1967, were an important part of the country's population.

After the destruction of Jerusalem by the Roman emperor Vespasian and his son Titus in the year 70 AD, and especially after the failed rebellion of Bar-Kokhba in

135, the Jews had been expelled from Palestine, and they spread all over the Roman Empire. Nowhere were they allocated land (later, the European states prohibited Jewish landownership by law); therefore, the Jews were always city-dwellers practising handicrafts and trade; rich Jews also practised usury. Under the conditions of fanaticism raised by the First Crusade (1096), a mass massacre of Jews began in Germany which was to be repeated throughout the following centuries. Therefore the Jews accepted Kazimierz's invitation; he even allowed them to form a sort of parliament of their own (the *Kahal*) with judiciary and taxation powers in regard to co-religionists. However, in the seventeenth century, especially during the Polish–Ukrainian war, the Jews were massacred both in Poland and in the Ukraine; hundreds of thousands perished. Nevertheless, a Jewish self-government continued to exist in Poland, although in a very curtailed form, right through to 1764. The Jews brought to Poland their dialect (Yiddish) which belongs to the Germanic branch of the Indo-European languages.[53]

The Polish society of the twelfth to fourteenth centuries consisted of peasantry (mainly leaseholders), an upper stratum of nobility (the magnates), and numerous gentry (*szlachta*); a group of related families of the gentry had a common coat of arms. The *szlachta* were originally free warriors typical of the Early Antiquity – but developed into a European-type medieval gentry sharing some privileges with the magnates. In its struggle against the magnates, the *szlachta* acquired for its sessions (called *seim*) the right to control royal power (from 1505), and later also the right to elect the kings.

The Polish Kingdom, although strengthened under Kazimierz III, and extended by acquiring some land formerly belonging to the Teutonic knights, was nevertheless not yet a 'national' state. A son of Kazimierz was elected King of Bohemia (Czechia), and later of Hungary; another son of his became Great Prince of Lithuania. Such dynastic stunts were very frequent in the medieval history of Europe: thus, the popular king of the Czechs, Charles IV (Wenceslas) was a son of the German duke of Luxembourg (later king of Bohemia) and a Polish princess; his first wife was a French princess; for a time he lived in Italy, fought against the English together with the French in the battle of Crecy (1346 AD), and was crowned emperor in Rome.

There was a growth in towns during the reign of Kazimierz III, whether the population was Polish, German or Jewish. A land-leasing system was dominant in agriculture.

53. Later, when Poland was divided during the reign of Catherine II of Russia, most of the Polish Jews became subjects of the Russian Empire. They were not allowed to leave former Polish territory ('the Pale'), and settle outside the cities. The Jewish ghettos became a breeding ground for hopeless penury. The only persons who were allowed to leave the pale were either Jews who had decided to embrace Christianity, or rich merchants ('merchants of the first guild'), later also persons who had managed to acquire university education (practically, only lawyers and medical doctors), or who had served twenty years in the army as privates, and also prostitutes.

The most important event in the history of Poland was the union with Lithuania, a princedom which included not only lands inhabited by Lithuanians proper, but also that part of ancient Rus which is now called Belorussia. The dynasty of the Gediminowiczi was Lithuanian, the nobility and the peasantry were partly Lithuanian but mainly Belorussian.

After Kazimierz III, Poland was temporarily ruled by Louis, son of the Hungarian king Charles Robert who was descended from the Neapolitan line of the house of Anjou, and then by his daughter, Jadwiga (from 1384); in 1386 the Polish magnates married her to Jagiello, Grand Prince of Lithuania, who embraced Catholic Christianity and received the name of Wladislas II. The union with Lithuania made Poland a great power. Lithuanian and Belorussian nobility began to embrace Catholicism, and it became Polonised. The greater part of the local peasantry continued to be 'Russian' (i.e. Belorussian or Ukrainian) and Orthodox Christian; the rest were Lithuanian and Catholic. The Polish authorities tried a compromise, in 1506 introducing a separate Uniate Church which preserved the Eastern Orthodox ritual but had to recognise the supremacy of the pope in Rome. However, the original Eastern Orthodox Church retained an important position.

In Russia during the fourteenth to sixteenth centuries the Great Princes of Muscovy managed to build up a strong absolutist state, with a sufficiently constant and stable territory, and with symptoms of national self-consciousness. Ivan III (1462–1505) declared Moscow to be 'the Third Rome' and assumed the title of Tsar (i.e. 'Caesar'). Russian society of that epoch cannot be defined as belonging to the Fifth Phase – from the point of view of world history it had already passed it – but the Sixth Phase had not been yet fully established; society was, as it were, temporarily stuck between the two Phases.

The landowning class in Post-Mongol Russia did not constitute a monolithic noble estate, and, unlike Western nobility, did not form a chain of feudal dependence (where a baron served a count, a count served a duke, etc.). The titles were hereditary. Apanage princes continued to exist among the descendants of Ryurik and the descendants of Gediminas; their possessions went back to the Kiev Russian system of apanages (*udiel*): inside his own apanage, each prince was the legal head of his princedom – subject, however, to the supreme sovereignty of the Great Prince. Nobility titles (not princely ones, as a rule) could be awarded by tsars at will, but in actual fact genealogy was always taken into account: descendants of Ryurik came before the descendants of Gediminas, the latter came before the descendants of Tatar or Caucasian immigrants of princely rank; also military and political merits of the ancestors were important for evaluating the rank of a person. The highest nobility were *boyars* who had a seat in an assembly, the *Boyar Duma*, which was being convened by the tsar for consultations. But a member of the Duma was not necessarily a prince (whose ancestors had been sovereign rulers); also boyars who were not princes could be members, and vice versa: certain princes did not rank as members of the Duma. A considerable part of the time was spent by the

Duma in arguments about the seniority and merits of the members' ancestors; such seniority gave a member the right to 'sit above' the members of some other family, if it was decided that the latter had less merit.

Besides the boyars, there existed so-called 'boyar's children' and gentlemen of different rank (*dvoryane*).

Sometimes the tsars would, at their discretion, convene a *Zemski sobor* (Estates General), a sort of parliament including as well as the boyars the higher clerics, representatives of the cities, and some arbitrarily appointed representatives of 'free' peasants (legal serfdom did not exist until the seventeenth century, but peasants were usually in a dependent position towards their landlords because of debts, military duty, etc.)

The rule of Ivan IV the Terrible (1533–1584) proved a new obstacle to further development. Attempts to depict his reign as progressive cannot be taken seriously. From the time of the historian Karamzin in the early nineteenth century, Ivan the Terrible has usually been represented, first of all, as a sadist, a bloodthirsty exterminator of old princely and boyar families. He certainly was that; the opposition of the princes and boyars to the Muscovite absolutism ended in the most ferocious reign of terror. However, still worse for the country was what Ivan did to the peasantry. Having divided his empire into the 'Zemshchina' ('main-land, country-land') on which he re-settled the traditional landholding nobility, and the 'Oprichnina' ('separate land'), which was given to his private followers, favourites and executioners, he started a programme of re-settling of peasants from the 'Zemshchina' to the 'Oprichnina' and vice versa, which led to tremendous losses in life and to the deprivation of the peasantry of any belief in a stability of their status (an element of this feeling of instability was later to become inherent in the Russian national character). Then Ivan IV put a finishing touch upon the 'deeds' of Ivan III: these two tsars not only conquered but totally exterminated the free cities of Pskov, Novgorod and Khlynov (Vyatka). Hence the development towards the Sixth Phase was made impossible. Citizens of Novgorod were hanged all along the highway from that city to Moscow. After that, the Terrible Tsar, who had lost the 'window to Europe' which Pskov and Novgorod had opened through their Hanseatic connections, instead of attempting to 'open' it again involved himself in an unprofitable and protracted Livonian campaign, which developed into a war with Poland, Sweden and Denmark, and this again brought about losses in life and prestige. Moreover, the period from 1597 to 1649 witnessed the emergence of peasant serfdom in Muscovy – except for its northern parts and Siberia, and later also for the Ukraine, which was annexed by Muscovy as a result of the insurrection of the *hetman* Bohdan Khmelnitsky against Poland (1648),[54] as well as for the semi-independent Cossack republics in the South. Then followed civil war and Polish occupation.

---

54. This insurrection was followed by most bloody massacres of Catholics, and especially of Jews.

It is obvious that at the beginning of the rule of the new Romanov dynasty (1613), Russia was far behind Western Europe (and China), and was only just moving towards the Post-Medieval Phase. The 'Code' ('Ulozhenie') of the Tsar Alexei Mikhailovich is typologically similar to the Sasanian and the T'ang codes. From the point of view of jurisprudence it is better founded than the T'ang code but worse than the Sasanian code. An all-Russian market was in formation, to be sure, cities with their trading and artisans' population grew, and the first manufactories appeared, but for the most part they exploited serf labour; thus it cannot be said that a working class and a bourgeoisie had appeared. Neither were there any signs of an alternative ideology – the Old Believers were oriented towards the past, not the future.[55] Of firearms only primitive cannons and arquebuses were known. During the reign of Tsar Alexei (1645–1676) muskets still had to be bought abroad. Education was in a deplorable state.

My observations so far have been confined to the Eurasian continent (Africa and Australia will be mentioned later). It is now time to turn our attention to the great continent lying between the Pacific and the Atlantic oceans.

We mentioned America at the beginning of this book in connection with the evaluation of the Phases of the historical process which its aboriginal inhabitants had reached before their contact with the Europeans. It is my belief that some of the American Indians had not left the First Phase (those in the polar zone and partly in the taiga zone of North America, and in the jungles of what was to become Latin America); some of them had reached the Second, or Chiefdom Phase (thus the most important tribes in what now is Canada and the USA, many of the tribes of Central America), or were at the border between the Second and the Third Phase (the Aztec civilisation in Mexico; possibly also the Mayan civilisation in Southern Mexico, Guatemala and Salvador); and the Third Phase had certainly been reached by the Inca civilisation of the Quechua and Aimara in the Andes.

---

55. After the fall of the Byzantine empire in 1453, the Russian tsars began to claim the right to 'pro- tect' all peoples of the Greek-Orthodox Christian persuasion living in the Ottoman empire. Meanwhile, the Greek patriarch of Constantinople still continued to be regarded as the head of all Orthodox Christians; it was only in 1589 that the Muscovite sovereigns managed to found a patriarchate in Moscow. In this connection there arose the necessity to introduce uniformity into the text of the books used in church service, and into religious rituals, which appeared not to have been identical as practised by the Greeks and the Russians. The unification was entrusted to the Muscovite patriarch Nikon (from 1652 on). It met with bitter opposition in Russia, where it was believed that the Greeks had been 'Turkicised', and that real Orthodox Christianity has been preserved by the Russians alone; the main difference between the 'Nikonians' and the 'Old Believers' was that the first made the sign of cross with three fingers and the second with two. A cruel persecution of the Old Believers began; their main spokesman was the archpriest Avvakum. His invectives and memoirs, written, perhaps for the first time, not in Church Slavonic but in a fine, expressive popular Russian, were the beginning of the new Russian literature. Avvakum was burned at the stake for heresy, but also Nikon was exiled to a far-off monastery: tsar Alexei was interested not so much in putting an end to religious discord as such, as in establishing the right of the Russian tsar to decide on the ecclesiastical policy of the Orthodox Church, both in Russia itself and abroad.

In typical histories, the events in America during the period between the discoveries of Columbus, Cortés and Pizarro, and the coming into being of the United States of America, are, for all practical purposes, omitted. Nevertheless, from the theoretical point of view it is vital to understand the development of society in the Americas, especially Latin America (Southern and Central), from the end of the fifteenth century to the early sixteenth, and from the end of the eighteenth into the early nineteenth – a period about which our knowledge is usually very scanty.

The historical process here had important peculiarities, and it might be surmised that there was a qualitative leap from the Early or Late Primitive society directly to Capitalism. But this could happen only if the cultures of the First to Third Phases had been more or less annihilated, and if the Europeans living in the Sixth and Seventh Phases had to begin their history in the New World from the point at which they were when they left their homeland. But if this may be taken as a nearly (not completely) adequate picture of what had happened in the USA and in a part of Canada, it is not an adequate picture of what happened in Latin America, where (except for the Caribbean islands) the aboriginal population had not been exterminated, although European conquest brought about great losses in life and in material and cultural values.

We have suggested that, in the history of man, there exist eight phases, which differ in their level of technological development (specifically in the technology of arms), in their structure of relations in production, and in their socio-psychological orientation (their ideology being either mythological, or ethico-dogmatic, or pluralistic). Does the history of America corroborate our hypothesis? Answering this question is tantamount to asking whether our hypothesis is applicable to the history of any association of living creatures feeding on biological products – whether on this planet or any other planet, in another galaxy, or even in our own but at a distance more than 100 light-years from us.[56] It is obvious that the Phases of the historical process are not synchronous in Eurasia and in Latin America; the question is, can similar Phases be observed in both regions? Does there exist a common rule for the development of the Phases of the historical process wherever it is going on?

The American continent was settled during one of the Glacial periods by a population which wandered over an isthmus where now the Bering strait is (this isthmus came about because of the low sea level during the Glacial period). It was also visited by Europeans before Columbus. Thus the Norman colonies in North America (Vinland) and in Greenland paid a tithe to the pope as late as the twelfth century, and there is a map showing Greenland and Vinland which dates from the middle of the fifteenth century; a ship from there arrived in Scandinavia in the

---

56. All stars inside this radius have been registered by astronomers, and none has the parameters needed for the existence of inhabited planets around it. The most long-lived creatures could reach the nearest inhabitable planet, even if they flew for many generations. Inhabitants of other planets can be struck out of fantastic literature, if it pretends to be 'scientific'.

early fifteenth century. But the honour of discovering America belongs to Columbus.

Cristobal Colon (or, in Italian, Colombo; Columbus in Latin), as well as his family, is regarded as Genoan, but his native tongue was Spanish, and his letters to his brother and sons are written in that language. His given name, Cristobal or Christopher, shows that he was a Christian and a Catholic, but it remains unexplained why in the fifteenth century a family of Spaniards should settle in Genoa which was by no means friendly to Spain. Perhaps the solution first suggested by S. de Madariaga is correct: according to him, Columbus belonged to a family of Marranos, i.e. Spanish Catholics of Jewish origin who often secretly practised the religion of their forebears; because of that, Columbus' ancestors had to flee to Genoa to evade the Inquisition.[57] However, only a minority of the Marranos returned to Judaism.

In popular publications it has been stated that Columbus, pondering his idea – using the spherical form of the globe to conquer the treasures of Eastern Asia[58] not by an eastward campaign but directly from the West crossing the Atlantic ocean like St Brandan of the legend – made use of the works of the Portuguese prince Henry the Navigator and other scholars.

In his expeditions, Columbus based himself, first of all, on the sayings of the prophet Isaiah who mentioned far-away 'islands of the sea' (XI, 10–12), and on the apocryphal Book of Esdras. A historian has once justly said that Columbus arrived at the firm conviction that Asia lay to the west of Europe 'by reading, meditations, intuition and miscalculation'. Once he had arrived at the idea, he made frantic efforts in order to find supporters – supporters, of course, such as could help him financially. As can easily be imagined, he did not find much support from men of common sense, although in his quest he managed to spend a lot of his own and other people's money. At last, he struck pay dirt: in 1486 he had an audience with the Spanish queen Isabella, an *exaltée* woman and a fanatic, perhaps a paranoiac like himself. She raised the money for Columbus' voyage by somewhat untoward means. But even the money might not have brought about the result he wished were it not for the fact that he received help from the experienced sailor M. Alonzo Pinzón (who agreed to be second-in-command in Columbus' expedition), and from his brothers.

---

57. Columbus is first mentioned under the years 1472 or 1473 as a corsair serving René of Anjou, a pretender to the throne of Aragon and Naples; and then in the year 1476, in reports of a battle between the Portuguese and the Genoese fleet, where he fought on the side of Portugal. It seems he also took part in a sailing expedition in the Northern Atlantic; but the existence of land there was in any case known before Columbus.

58. Usually it is thought that Columbus was seeking India. However, *Las Indias* (in the plural) was at that period a common designation for all countries east of the Moslem lands. Actually, Columbus was looking for Japan (Marco Polo, the great traveller of the thirteenth century, mentions *Zipango* as the farthest country away in the Indian Ocean. This is a transcription of Chinese Zhipen-Kuo, a name for Japan employed alongside the more usual Nihon-Kuo, Nippon).

On the seventy-first day after sailing from Palos the *Santa Maria*, the *Pinta* and the *Niña* arrived at the island in the Bahama archipelago which Columbus named San Salvador. The ships were rather small: the whole expedition consisted of fewer than 100 men, and the *Niña* had a crew of only seven. The landing at that obscure islet was made with all possible solemnity, with gonfalons and crosses, in showy armour (for those who possessed it). Of course, it was a disappointment that instead of the presumably rich and civilised inhabitants of the fabulous Zipango, the land of gold (see n. 58), the conquistadors were met by 'savages' clad (at best) in loin-cloths. But they were met by them reverentially, as deities arising from the Eastern ocean. Unfortunately, some of the Indians had golden ear-rings and other trinkets, and by the end of Columbus' procession with cross and banners his men began to tear the ear-rings out of the women's ears, and to drag the naked girls behind the near-by bushes.

After staying for a short while on this wild island, they continued their voyage further westwards where they discovered the big islands of Cuba and Hispaniola (now Haiti). There the standard of living of the aboriginal inhabitants was somewhat higher: in Hispaniola gold was mined, and Columbus' crew started plundering on a bigger scale (many of the sailors were former pirates and convicts). Columbus took Cuba again for Zipango, but made his base not there but on Hispaniola where he founded a small settlement, San Domingo.

In March 1493 Columbus returned to Spain. His account was a sensation. He was immediately dispatched back with seventeen ships carrying 1,500 settlers and missionaries.

A certain diplomatic complication arose. After Vasco da Gama's voyage around Africa in 1498 'the Indies' were declared to be the possession of Portugal. The sailors were little bothered that the lands which they had discovered possessed their own administration systems, and their own traditions and religions. For declaring a country to be Portuguese it was sufficient to get a blessing of the pope. It is true that the pope gave his blessing only on condition that the inhabitants embrace Christianity, but the new conquerors were not much concerned with such details; sometimes they began their contacts with the local inhabitants by immediately baptising them.

With Portugal everything was all right, but now it appeared that Spain also had pretensions to sovereignty over 'the Indies'. Moreover, the idea that the Earth was spherical had begun to win support. According to the Treaty of Tordesillas in 1494, the possessions of Spain and Portugal were to be divided by a line drawn from pole to pole 370 leagues (about 2,500 km) to the west of the furthermost island of Cape Verde Islands. The Western Hemisphere was being divided, so to say, blindly, and it became apparent only later that the Tordesillas line crosses the continent of the 'Indies' (actually South America) through what now is Brazil.

Meanwhile, from the Spanish point of view, Columbus had but little success: the income in gold was small, the aborigines fled to the mountains or perished. King Fernando of Aragon reduced the privileges of Columbus, and finally replaced him by Bobadilla; the latter's success, however, was no more remarkable, and from 1502 to 1507 Hispaniola was ruled by Ovando. He founded new settlements; forbade the turning of aborigines into slaves, but approved of their forced labour by shifts. By that time, only few aborigines were left alive on Hispaniola, so the Spaniards started discovering new islands and new shores, where they continued to plunder and murder. Attempted evasion by the aboriginal inhabitants was punished with mass burnings. Easier forms of execution were applied if the victims agreed to undergo holy Baptism before their death. It should be noted that mortality among the new colonists was also high – more than 50 per cent – with many people dying of illnesses from which the Europeans had no physical immunity. Sometimes too, but not often the colonists were killed by the local inhabitants. Note that the colonists were practically all male, so the aboriginal women were raped.

When Columbus again sailed in these seas in 1502–1504, he was just one of the many sailors active around the Caribbean archipelago. During the expeditions in the Caribbean Sea between 1500 and 1542, all the islands and shores were mapped and partly plundered (and the local population often killed off), from Florida to about the site of present day Vera Cruz in Mexico (among other things, the mouth of the Mississippi was discovered in 1539). About the same time, Ojeda and Nicuesa (and after they perished, Pizarro and Balboa) followed the coasts of Costa Rica (at that time rich in pearls), of Panama and partly of Columbia. The Italian scholar Amerigo Vespucci was a member of Ojeda's expedition; later he published a book about the newly discovered lands, which were named America in his honour. In 1513 the first European sighted the Pacific Ocean. According to tradition, this was Balboa; but his discovery did not keep a rival from executing him 'for treason' (treason against whom?). Towards the beginning of the 1540s not only had all of the Caribbean Sea been explored but the courageous searchers for 'golden cities' had traversed all the most important pathways in the south of the future United States, and the shores of Northern Mexico and Southern and Northern California; in some places settlements were founded.

Bypassing the part of the South American mainland which, according to the Tordesillas treaty, was left to Portugal, the Spaniards nevertheless found land: the steppe regions around the valley of the Rio de la Plata (Paraná) – this is now Argentina – which lay to the west of the treaty line. In 1526 an Italian sailor in English service, Cabot, sailed up the river. He found there was no passage to the Pacific here, but he was able to bring back some nuggets of silver.[59] The Paraná basin was later explored without bloodshed by Irala. This region (in what now is Bolivia) contains the rich silver mines of Potosí which seem to have been already known to the Incas. In the new region the towns of Buenos Aires (later the capital of Argentina) and Asunción (later the capital of Paraguay) were founded.

The attitude of Queen Isabella to the enslavement of her new subjects vacillated.

---

59. *Rio de la Plata* is Spanish for 'River of Silver'.

By the beginning of the sixteenth century such slavery was prohibited, and those already enslaved were to be liberated except (!) for cases of cannibalism, mutiny or resistance to Spanish colonisation and Christianisation. The aborigines of the islands in the Caribbean Sea gained little from these 'privileges' for the excellent reason that by the 1540s–1550s none was left alive. Slaves captured in Africa were imported. On the continent of America, the Spanish 'New Laws' of 1542 introduced, instead of slavery, a so-called 'commendation'. Each Indian was 'commended' to a certain Spanish owner, and the latter had the right to call the Indian in to carry out necessary work; the Indian could spend only his spare time in working for his own household. The Hispano-American 'commendation' can be likened to the ancient 'helotry' (in a broad sense). Subsequently the prohibition on slavery was not always observed.

Meanwhile, there began a period of a Spanish offensive against the continental Indian proto-states and states: Mexico, a state of Aztecs about the site of the modern city of that name, the state of the Maya in Central America, the proto-state of the Chibcha in Columbia, and the state of the Incas in the Andes.

The first conquest was made by Hernán Cortés. Rumours of the riches of the Aztec empire had reached Velásquez, the conqueror of Cuba, and he sent Cortés to reconnoitre and, if possible, to conquer it; he also supplied him with considerable resources. Cortés set out in 1518, after having first quarrelled with Velásquez. He founded the settlement Vera Cruz on the shore of Mexico, and the 'senate' of this newfangled 'city' commissioned Cortés to conquer Mexico in the name of King Charles I (the emperor Charles V). Through his agents, and through his Indian mistress Malinche who served him as interpreter and informer, Cortés knew that the Aztecs worshiped a deity of light, the (white-faced) Quetzalcohuatl, and that therefore the whiteness of his own face induced a superstitious fear in the Aztecs. He moved towards the capital of Mexico, the lake city Tenochtitlan below the volcano Popocatepetl. In the middle of the city was a stepped pyramid – a temple. Hundreds of Spanish armoured infantrymen, dozens of cavalrymen and a thousand tribal warriors who wanted to break from the yoke of Tenochtitlan, besieged the Aztec capital for nearly a year. In 1521 the half-ruined city surrendered to the Spaniards. The king, Montezuma, died a prisoner; then the last king of the Aztecs, Cuautemoc, was captured, and afterwards was accused of conspiracy and hanged.

Soon after his victory over the Aztecs, Cortés got the upper hand over a neighbouring Spanish warlord and started conquering Guatemala. Meanwhile Mexico passed into the power of the enemies of Cortés; he went back to Spain in order to plead his case. In spite of all his deeds of doubtful honesty, Cortés was regarded as the noblest and most just of the conquistadores. After his departure, the land of Mexico (including territories later included in the USA) became the site of long internecine wars. In 1524 the helper and friend of Cortés, Alvarado, began the conquest of the Maya kingdom on the Yucatan peninsula.

In the same year 1524 the Spaniards invaded the countries of the Andes. The invaders, led by Pizarro, were tempted by the legendary riches of Peru. Finding that he was confronting a state of considerable strength, Pizarro returned to Spain for reinforcements. A new campaign started in 1532, and next year Pizarro received further reinforcements led by Almagro. More than two years were needed for the conquest of the kingdom of the Incas; during this time Pizarro had founded the town of Guayaqil as his military base on the sea-shore. Shortly after this, war broke out between Pizarro and Almagro, the result of a failed attempt by Almagro to conquer Chile. In the course of the war both generals perished. After a period of civil war, the leadership of the troops was entrusted to Valdivia. The campaign proved to be most difficult, but Valdivia managed to conquer northern Chile (in its southern part he was unable to quell the courageous tribe of Araucans).

A result of the conquests in South and North America was that the Spanish territories came in contact with unconquered tribes both on the outside (to the north of Mexico, in Florida, in Chile), and inside (to the south-east of Peru, the former kingdom of the Incas, in what now is Paraguay and around it). To contact these tribes and, if possible, to Christianise them, monastic missions were sent to their borders. These missions consisted of Franciscans and especially Jesuits. The latter started large-scale economic and civil reorganisation, and managed to baptise great numbers of the forest Tupi-Guarani tribes. As it happened as soon as the Indians lost contact with their enlighteners they very often returned to their traditional beliefs (just as did the other Indians all over Latin America).

Towards the middle of the seventeenth century the Jesuits managed to create a theocratic republic in Paraguay – a republic which was markedly superior to the neighbouring territories in its standard of life and organisation. However, in 1773 the Jesuit Society was temporarily dissolved, and the republic of Paraguay was turned upon by aggressive neighbours.

The middle of the seventeenth century saw the creation of a sort of Spanish empire, which embraced most of Southern America, Central America, Mexico (including territories later lost to the USA), the islands of the Caribbean Sea, and, at least formally, Florida. To rule this empire from Madrid was a practical impossibility, considering the then existing means of communication. A special imperial structure was therefore created: the entire American territory belonging to the king of Spain was divided first into two vice-regencies (New Spain and Peru), and later into four: New Spain (including Mexico, the Caribbean and Central America); New Granada (including the present-day Venezuela, Panama, Columbia and Ecuador), Peru (also including parts of present-day Bolivia and Chile), and La Plata (which included all other South American regions, i.e. the modern Argentina, Uruguay, Paraguay and parts of modern Bolivia and Chile).[60]

60. In the first half of the sixteenth century, Venezuela (on the southern shore of the Caribbean Sea) was a base for those who sought pearls along the coasts, and for expeditions looking for the fabulous city of Eldorado, believed to be a fantastically rich country. Charles V borrowed a very great sum from the German bankers' firm Welsers, and gave Venezuela; they held it until 1546, but not having received sufficient profit, did not renew their concession.

The vice-regencies were divided into 'reigns', or actually officially 'kingdoms', although normally they more resembled the ancient Roman procuratorships; a 'king' was aided by an executive and an *audiencia*, a judicial-cum-administrative body (the ideas of Montesquieu about the division of powers were first published only in 1748). The *audiencia* included *oïdors*, lit. 'listeners', who were both police inspectors and judges at once.

The main function of the executive and the *audiencia* was to keep the 'kings' from acquiring independence of a feudal type. The 'king' presided in the *audiencia*, listened to its advice, had the right of patronage over the church, was in charge of all matters concerning the Indians, and led the armed forces of the 'reign'.

The viceroys, although ranked above the 'kings', were more strictly controlled from Madrid and by their own *audiencias*.

The more outlying regions were entrusted to 'captains-general'. The 'captains' were appointed by the king of Spain directly, but the orders from Madrid went through the viceroys.

Besides the 'captaincies', there were also smaller 'presidencies' which had no military power.

All the *audiencias* had broad judicial powers and, moreover, the power to control their own 'captains' and 'viceroys'.

The lowest administrative body was the community (*cabildo*); it could be 'open', i.e. including all landowners of the community, or it could have a more narrow form. In practice, the communities had considerable administrative and even military possibilities, and sometimes defied the higher authorities.

In addition to all these administrative bodies, the following institutions also existed: the *visita* which included controllers who were supposed to be able to inspect any person at all without previous information; and the *residencia*, a permanent controlling body with public sittings.

The land fell into different categories.

First, there was the *economienda*-land settled by the Indians 'commended' to certain of the conquistadores and to their descendants; these were obliged to ensure that the Indians were converted to Christianity and subject to Spanish civilisation. Often the conquistadors took over the power and the functions of the former Indian chiefs; the 'commended' Indians had to labour for them. The *encomienda* system began to die out about 1600 AD; the responsibilities of the conquistadores devolved upon the '*corregidores* of the Indians'. It was they who formed the Spanish colonial nobility.

Secondly, there was land of the Spanish settlements, and of settlements created according to Spanish pattern, but inhabited by Indians; they were also headed by '*corregidores* of the Indians'.

For the most part the population of the emerging cities was Spanish.

The social difference between the local inhabitants and the Spanish was gradually reduced, especially in the region of the Andes and the Aztec civilisation, after the Christianisation of the local nobility – although actually it was not very deeply

Christianised. The local nobility enjoyed a certain esteem, and a marriage of a Spanish settler with an Aztec or Quechuan lady not only did not lower his social status but could even bring him more esteem. Many Indian peasants cultivated Spanish (and colonial) crops, and the difference between them and the peasants who had emigrated from Spain diminished.

At this point it is appropriate to ask how we should evaluate the events which occurred in that huge region of the Earth which we call Latin America from the point of view of our theory of Phases of the historical process.

In America from the sixteenth to the seventeenth century the peculiarity of the historical events consisted in a population reared in the Fifth Phase or living at the borderline between the Fifth and the Sixth Phase and the encounter between a population living in the Third, Second and even the First Phase. What could the result be? Could the Fifth and the Sixth Phase pull the Second and the Third up to their own level? Before answering this question, we should take account of the fact that the local population, although with heavy losses, did survive, being Christianised (rather superficially), and was gradually beginning to use spoken Spanish. If we postulate such a 'pulling up', I think we would be overestimating the importance of external influences in the historical process as a whole. We have already encountered the inverse situation, when the Mongols or the Turks, living in the Second or, at the best, in the Third Phase, invaded territories whose population belonged to the Fifth Phase. It is true that they did delay the process, but they did not force the conquered population out of the Phase to which they had belonged. This is true of purely military invasions which were not accompanied by any new alternative socio-psychological motives, nor were they induced by any advantage in arms. The same is also true of such invasions which were based on an alternative ideology but not on advantage in arms (as that of Islam). It would seem that in America the situation was quite different: there was an invasion of forces which had a great advantage both in arms (horses, steel armour, steel swords, and at least some kind of firearms), and in having an alternative ideology (Christianity). This, however, does not mean that the invasion could achieve a passage from the border between the Second and the Third Phase directly to the beginning of the Sixth (although we have observed in Scandinavia and in Russia that one could pass from the Third to the Fifth Phase).

Actually, there is a crucial difference here. In the latter two cases the alternative socio-psychological concept could alleviate the continuing discomfort. But in Latin America there had been no discomfort which would require a socio-psychological revolution, especially in the form of a proselytic and ethico-dogmatic religion, which (at least in the first generation after the conquest) was itself perceived as a burden, as a discomfort. The introduction of a new obligatory religion was accompanied by turning the 'believers' belonging to the local population (i.e. of free members of a tribe, or citizens of a state of the Early Antiquity type) into slaves, or, at best, into helots. Of course, the local tribes experienced all kinds of discomfort, but they had no real socio-psychological alternative of their own, nor the arms necessary to defend themselves.

The fact that slave-owning relations in production at first prevailed over helotry in Latin America (i.e. over the *encomienda*) can easily be explained: two or three Phases more 'developed' than the aboriginal inhabitants, the conquistadores were correspondingly better armed and could introduce a more harsh system of exploitation. At the same time, the absence of an alternative social psychology which might have been able to mitigate the discomfort and the low productivity of slave labour – and the latter can exist in all Phases of history – explains the fact that in Latin America slavery was soon abandoned for the *encomienda*, which is equivalent to helotry or to the ancient colonate. Therefore, the 'states' founded by individual conquistadores in the first half of the sixteenth century in Latin America – by Cortés, Pizarro, Montejo, Valdivia and all the others – are surely to be classed not as belonging to the Fifth, Medieval Phase, but to a specific form of the Third, communal-and-slavery Phase (note the *cabildo* institution). Let us remember that most of the population of the conquered continent lived in the First and the Second Phase, while the Third was also beginning for the Incas, the Mayas and perhaps the Aztecs. Thus the period of foreign domination during the sixteenth century is certainly to be regarded as a continuation of the Third Phase.

However, the social and state structures of New Spain during the seventeenth and eighteenth centuries were already very similar to forms which had developed in the Old World during the Fourth Phase: the same type of all-embracing empire, levelling, as it were, all its inhabitants, who were entrusted into the power of proconsuls, propraetors, procurators – now called viceroys, 'kings', capitanos. Attendant on them were councils of the nobility (*audiencias*) with limited rights, and below them were town or village councils (*cabildo*) with still less rights. We may observe the same legal inequality between the newcomers (who can be compared to Roman citizens) and the aborigines ruled by the newcomers (i.e. by the corregidores and the captains of the Indians). We can also observe here the attempt by typical tribal groups to preserve self-government inside the empire.

The whole empire had a common official language which was also the language of mutual understanding – the Spanish language.

But all this means that the 'war of liberation' in Latin America of the early nineteenth century, although using slogans borrowed from the French Revolution and Napoleon, actually introduced only the Fifth Phase of the historical process. The lofty French idea of liberation certainly inspired Bolívar and his companions-in-arms (and rivals); but this is no indication that the results achieved in Latin America could be the same as in Europe: on the new continent, the social situation which took shape after Bolívar, correlated with his ideas in the same ratio as the politics of the medieval popes correlated with the great ideas of Jesus and Paul. Theoretically, the result should have been the creation of medieval type states, constantly at war, with unstable and changing frontiers.

The discomfort which led to Bolívar's (and the other leaders') revolution was mostly felt by the creole population, i.e. the population whose origin and native language was Spanish but who had grown up on Latin American soil and who felt that this was their native country. And this native land was ruled either directly from Spain, or by officials who had come from Spain – sometimes being exiled from there – and had come for a short while, just to get a spring-board for promotion in the mother country. The revolution of Simon Bolívar (from 1810), famed as the liberator of Latin America, was, first of all, a purely creole[61] one, because the aboriginal population was indifferent to it; and, secondly, its spirit was more Bonapartist than revolutionary: we observe the same brilliant victories on one front, defeats on another, new brilliant victories, further defeats and, finally, an imaginary triumph of the Bolívian idea after his death.

Bolívar not only had supporters and imitators but also rivals, but they had a common aim: to liberate Latin American land from 'alien', i.e. Spanish administrators, and to bring the creoles to power.

Practically, Bolívar, in spite of all his revolutionary pathos, could only perpetrate the Fourth Phase of historical development. The alternative ideology of creole domination was not sufficient to move the population of the continent towards the Seventh Phase, which was actually what Napoleon tried to do. The creole empire fell asunder even before the death of Bolívar (1830). The new creole states, such as Venezuela, Columbia, Ecuador, Peru, Chile, Paraguay, Argentina, Uruguay, although nominally taking on a republican if not actually democratic form, were, in actual fact, medieval (belonging to the Fifth Phase), with their constant *pronunciamentos*,[62] with their nominally elected but seldom changed 'presidents' or *caudillos* ('führers'), with unstable and by no means national state frontiers, with their military-administrative élites and the peon[63] peasants. A specific characteristic was contributed to the Latin American society by the great mass of Negro slaves bought from African chiefs and slave-merchants; their traditions went back to the First

61. The word *creole* means 'home-born'. All persons of European descent born on the soil of former French, Spanish or Portuguese colonies in America, Africa or West India were called 'creoles' as distinct from those arrived from Europe only a short while ago. Later, first in Brazil and then in other European colonies, 'creoles' became the name for negroes who had lived there for no less than two generations after their ancestors had been imported from Africa and sold; also mulattos were called creoles. In this sense 'creole' and 'creole languages' is used in linguistics.

When we speak of a creole population (in the original sense of the word) in the Spanish dominions in America, we should keep in mind, that with each generation the number of metises (*mestizos*) grew: the *mestizos* were the offspring of marriages and illicit liaisons between creoles and aborigines. By the eighteen and nineteenth centuries, not counting negroes and mulattos, the majority of the Latin American population consisted of *mestizos*, while the (white) creoles were regarded as a social élite few in numbers.

62. A *pronunciamento* is a declaration of a change in the character of political power (e.g. from elective to dictatorial, or to a new ruler after the preceding has been deposed).

63. A peon is a peasant or agricultural worker, labouring for a landowner as payment for his debts (spurious, as often as not). Typologically, a peon, especially in the seventeenth to eighteen centuries, was more like a Fifth Phase serf than like a Fourth Phase *colonus*. More than half of the agricultural population consisted of peons; there also were free agricultural workers; a part of the Indians continued to live in independent rural communities (*ejidos*), typologically similar to those of the Second Phase.

and Second Phases; culturally and linguistically they didn't merge either with the local aboriginal population or with the local creole one.

What ensued was not the Sixth, Post-Medieval Phase of stable absolutism, but the Fifth Phase of feudally split society, of unstable frontiers and constant war. The most horrible war was not one of those in twentieth-century Europe but that in Paraguay in 1864–1870.[64]

The conditions in Brazil developed somewhat differently. Discovered in 1500 by the Portuguese sailor Cabral, Brazil became a dependency of Portugal according to the formal interpretation of the Tordesillas treaty of 1494, whose authors did not dream of the existence of land here. The coasts were explored, and the newly discovered capes and rivers were named by Amerigo Vespucci in 1501. But settlement began only from 1533. The entire coast of Brazil was divided on the map into fifteen 'captaincies', and each of the pieces of land was given in possession to Portuguese nobles and courtiers receiving the title of *donatários*. They were encouraged to found cities, to deal out land, to appoint officials, and to collect taxes from the population. The king of Portugal kept for himself the right to collect customs dues, and the monopoly in trading in Brazil-wood.[65] Of the *donatários* two were especially successful: de Sousa in the south who organised the lucrative trade and explored an extensive territory; and Pereira in the north, in the region of Pernambuco, where he converted most of his territory into a huge plantation of sugar-cane. In 1549 the lands of Brazil were subjected directly to the Portuguese crown. An important role was played by the Jesuit missions, whose activities here were more successful than in Paraguay. They managed to get a law promulgated in 1574, which prohibited the forced labour of the Indians; instead, they had to submit to 'voluntary' agreements. It seems the Indians had begun to flee into the interior, and all of this, of course, resulted in the importation of negro slaves from Africa.

In 1555 the French attempted to found a colony of their own in Brazil; one idea

64. From 1610 on, Paraguay constituted a sort of republic of the Jesuit Order. In the beginning, the Jesuits were not only baptising the Indians, but they cared for their interests, and taught them agriculture. However, all the soil was declared property of the Order; the unaccustomed heavy labour of the Indians as farm-hands, the frequent epidemics and riots resulted in a catastrophic reduction in the numbers of the Indian population. In 1768 the Jesuits were expelled from Paraguay. After that, the country was ruled by most cruel dictators; the territory of the country was extended at the cost of neighbouring regions. The country grew richer, and attracted enterprising persons. By the middle of the nineteenth century Paraguay was ready to enter the Capitalist Phase, but its situation was made difficult by the absence of an outlet to the sea and by conflicts with Brazil, and also with Argentina, where the quarrel was about access to the use of the Parana River. The aggressive policy of Paraguay's dictator, F. S. López, triggered off the destructive war of 1864–1870 against the 'triple alliance' of Brazil, Argentina and Uruguay; during this war, partly because of the military actions and political reprisals, partly because of hunger, Paraguay lost nearly 70 per cent of the female, and nearly 90 per cent of the male population. In Europe these events went on more or less unnoticed. Jules Verne's *Captain Grant's Children*, travelling across Argentina in March 1865, did not notice the war between Argentina and Paraguay.

65. Brazil-Wood (*Caesalpinia*) furnishes a red pigment, and is a fine wood for making furniture, etc.

was to create a haven for Huguenots who were persecuted in France. But this colony proved to be unprofitable: moreover, a bitter struggle broke out between the Huguenots and the local Catholics. The French were ousted by the Portuguese governor-general Mem de Sá, who founded on the site of the former French settlement the city of Rio de Janeiro.

During the seventeenth century, the coast of Brazil was attacked by the Netherlands navy (at that time Portugal, and hence also Brazil, were subject to Spain which conducted a war in the Netherlands).

The greatest importance for Brazil was the discovery of rich gold deposits in 1693, which led to a new wave of immigration. At the same time Brazil, widening the interpretation of the Tordesillas agreement, began to extend its dominion over the Amazon lowlands and the regions bordering on the Andes. Moreover, the Portuguese made constant intrusions (*bandeiras*) into the Spanish lands in the west of the continent.

The local Indian population of the lowlands and the jungles, not numerous from the outset (it lived in the First Phase of the historical process), was gradually elbowed out to regions unfavourable for colonisation. Nevertheless, here and there mixed marriages occurred, and in a number of regions one of the Indian dialects, Tupi-Guarani, was accepted as a lingua franca along with the Portuguese, which was the common language for all colonists, including workers on the plantations, cattle-breeders, miners, and also the Indians, and the negro slaves employed on the plantations and in the mines.

However the Portuguese never appeared as an organised ruling class: the mixed nation which now is called Brazilian (including, since the nineteenth century, numerous Germans, Italians, Arabs and others) is less than any nation in the world inclined towards national prejudices; marriages between the whites, the blacks and the Indians are usual, so that among the modern Brazilians it is not easy to find persons who might regard themselves as pure descendants of the first Portuguese settlers; and this process of mixture began as early as the seventeenth century.

Although the change of the Phases was not so clear-cut in Brazil as it was in New Spain, nevertheless we can safely assign Brazilian society from the sixteenth to eighteenth centuries to the Third Phase ousting the First, and to the first steps of the Fourth Phase.

The further history of Brazil was rather peculiar. The Portuguese royal family, exiled from Lisbon during the Napoleonic wars, changed its capital for Rio de Janeiro; later Brazil formally seceded from Portugal but retained the form of an empire (1822). The royal, and later the imperial, government introduced certain measures for modernisation and even liberalisation of the country's political life (protection of external trade, parliamentary government, etc.); however, at the same time, in the leading branch of economic life – agriculture – a purely slave-based system was paramount. Slavery was finally abolished as late as 1888, and in 1889 the emperor Pedro II was dethroned, and Brazil was declared a republic. This political revolution was a form of moving Brazilian society from pretty much the Fourth Phase to nearly as high as the Seventh.

And what happened to the aboriginal population of Latin America? For the most part, those who had lived under the conditions of the First Phase totally disappeared. Just a few years ago the last inhabitants of Tierra del Fuego died out; the last aborigines of the basin of the Amazon are perishing, the result largely of the mass felling of the tropical forests. Those who lived in the Second Phase have for the most part undergone a process of metisation, and few of them have retained their original languages. One exception is the Tupi-Guarani which is a literary language in Paraguay alongside Spanish; its dialects are still in use in some of the neighbouring countries as well.

As was to be expected best preserved are the languages of those people who had already reached the Third Phase before the Spanish conquest. More than a million people speak Aimara in the frontier regions between Peru and Bolivia; there is a literature in Aimara. The Quechua (or 'Inca') language is spoken by about 10 million people (many of them are, of course, bilingual) – mostly in Peru and Ecuador, but also in Bolivia and (in small numbers) in Chile and Argentina. There is a literature; newspapers are published.

Some groups of the peasant population in Mexico and Central America preserve dialects which belong to aboriginal linguistic families.

Spoken Arawak dialects are still alive among the scanty and quickly disappearing tribal groups in the jungles of Brazil, Columbia and Venezuela, and spoken Carib dialects – in Guyana and the neighbouring regions. On the Indian population of North America, see below.

In relating the history of Latin America, we have exceeded the limits of the Fifth Phase of the historical process. Let us point out once more that the most characteristic feature of the Fifth Phase was the lack of any appreciable forward movement except, in a very limited degree, in the field of technology (first of all in the technology of arms), and none at all in the standard of life. Note also, that lack of appreciable headway is typical of the First Phase (the Primitive), the Third Phase (the Early Antiquity), and the Fifth Phase (the Early Middle Ages). This happens partly but not wholly for ecological reasons. Sometimes entire civilisations die out and there are also cases which deviate from the main line of development, and even entangle the line of development, so that unravelling it becomes difficult.

A study of the Fifth, as well as the other odd Phases of historical development shows plainly that the historical changes are heterogeneous and often contradictory, the movement can be differently directed, and may allow of whole millennia of recession without noticeable advance.

Typical of the Fifth Phase were obligatory dogmatic doctrines, any derivation being punished, as often as not by death. The discomfort tended to become chronic and insurmountable; it was felt by the peasants who were in total thrall to their lords, a power practically not limited in any way; every day a peasant might await the ruination of his home by war, by the lord's ill will, by eviction, by murder, not to speak of the Turkish devshirme. The masses of the agricultural population were those who least of all could count on a comfortable life. The end of the Fifth and the beginning of the Sixth Phase were marked by peasant uprisings on a huge scale.

But the landholders also felt a discomfort – first of all, because of the lack of any kind of stability. Today you might have to pay tribute or yield military service to one lord. Tomorrow you might have to serve as a warrior for some other lord. Each form of destabilisation boded ill for one's property, family and one's own life.

At the same time, through the Middle Ages a very strong impulse towards aggressiveness was maintained, quite openly in the class of landowners, who regarded it positively, as a 'desire for glory'.

6 Sixth Phase (the Stable Absolutist Post-Medieval Phase)

As soon as we pass to the Sixth Phase of the historical process, we encounter a terminological difficulty. There is no doubt that so-called 'modern history' (which in Europe lasted from the sixteenth century to the nineteenth) is a separate Phase of the historical process. However, the term 'modern' is, for several reasons, undesirable. Since a considerable part of humanity is already experiencing the Eighth Phase, how can we call the Sixth Phase 'modern'? We certainly have to invent another term. Above, we regarded the societies traditionally termed 'Primitive' as belonging to the 'Primitive' and the 'Primitive Communal' Phases, and the societies traditionally treated as 'Ancient' we have subdivided into 'Early Antiquity' and 'Imperial Antiquity'. In both cases we introduced to the names of the Phases with even numbers an additional defining feature, referring to the type of the societal organisation but not to the type of production itself, or, in Marxist terminology, not to the 'basis' but to the 'superstructure'. Nevertheless, from the historical point of view, our classification was justifiable, because the system of societal organisation appears as a most important classificational feature.

I suppose that the same method may be applied to choosing terms for the Fifth and the Sixth Phases. We did not call the Fifth Phase 'Early Medieval' (in parallel with 'Early Antiquity') but simply 'Medieval'. This corresponds to the European historiographic tradition according to which (at least as regards Europe) 'Early Medieval' means solely the period from the creation of the Germanic kingdoms to the end of the Crusades. To be consistent, we ought to have retained the term 'Middle Ages', 'Medieval' also for the Sixth Phase (just as we have retained the term 'Primitive' both for the First and the Second Phase, and the term 'Antiquity' for the Third and the Fourth Phase), but we should have added some new epithet to that term. This epithet should additionally characterise the system of the societies in question from the point of view of their typical organisation (cf. 'community', 'empire').

The new type of organisation of society in the Sixth Phase was a stable absolutist monarchy, which acquired the features of a national state. Should it be 'Absolutist Middle Ages'? The difficulty lies in the fact that the medieval states of the Fifth Phase also were, as often as not, absolutist; the difference is not in introducing absolutism (which actually already did exist), but in the stability of the absolutist state, and in its acquisition (at least in most if not in all cases) of the characteristics of a national state. But even if we add the epithet 'absolutist', it would be difficult to call e.g. Russia after Peter I, or Prussia under Frederic II 'medieval'. Therefore I have decided to call the new phase 'The Stable Absolutist Post-Medieval Phase'. This would exclude the properly medieval absolutist states (belonging to the Fifth, actually early medieval Phase), and the totalitarian states of the Seventh Phase. To be sure, the term 'post-medieval' smacks of a negative definition, which in itself might be regarded as undesirable, but anyway this is better than calling a long bygone stage of history 'modern', contrary to common sense – even if we use a delimiting attribute. Alternatively, this phase might be called 'Absolutist Pre-Capitalism'.

Typical of both the Fifth and the Sixth Phases was, first, the exploitation of cultivators of land and, secondly, the leading role of landowners in the state (although the forms of the state could vary); a substantial fact was the emergence of new classes: the bourgeoisie and the working class.

The more the striving of the governing class towards stability was satisfied, the stronger was the discomfort in the other groups of the population.

Women of all social conditions were living in a state of discomfort, and even hiding behind monastery walls did not guarantee full security, not to speak of the regimentation and the unnaturalness of monastic life.

The class of bourgeoisie which had emerged at the end of the Fifth Phase also felt very strong dissatisfaction, because it was not equal in rights with the ruling class of landowners, and was limited in its possibilities of enterprise and invention.

Of course, the class of hired workers were also dissatisfied. This class was formed out of ruined craftsmen, fugitive peasants (or peasants yielded to the employer by their landlords or the state), and even fugitive monks. But this was a mass too diverse for creating a common system of social impulses; a certain part would even be glad to lose connection with the traditional organisation of the tax-payers.

We already know that socio-psychological dissatisfaction may be removed by the appearance of a new socio-psychological impulse, a new ideology – but only in the case when this impulse has the possibility to be freely expressed. First, there must appear a feeling that 'one can also think otherwise'. Then new productive ideas may appear (including scientific ones), as well as new technologies.

For a change of Phases the creation of new technologies in arms production is also necessary. This may help to change the relations in production which are felt as a discomfort. However, new arms would still belong to the ruling class, and hence could not influence the situation of the lower class directly. The use of these arms might help to stabilise the centralised state and to destroy the persisting feudal vassalage system. But at the same time it should be noted that production of arms is the business of city dwellers, and this makes for their social advancement.

The most important conditions for the passage from the Medieval Phase to a Post-Medieval one are these: the creation of alternative ideas, of fundamentally new arms, and the emergence of stable states able to establish a certain equilibrium between the social classes – not only between 'andowners and the tillers of the soil, but also the emergent bourgeoisie and hire i workers. Their emergence was connected with the development of commodity–money relations, while their intrusion into agriculture weakened the formal and actual mutual interdependence of the landowners and the tillers of the soil, gradually replacing habitual exploitation by force with economic exploitation. The most onerous forms of dependence (as, e.g. serfdom) might be relaxed or even abolished.

These innovations were not all achieved at the same time, hence in the Sixth Phase we encounter societies 'completely' and 'incompletely' developed; e.g. there may exist new arms but no alternative ideology; or both may exist, but the state may remain unstable, etc.

As seen from the foregoing chapter, some of the main symptoms of the next, Post-Medieval Phase may gradually have appeared during the Fifth Phase, and, on the other hand, they may actually exist in the Sixth Phase, but also gradually, and not simultaneously in the different countries of Eurasia. During 1,000 years while the medieval society existed, dissatisfaction was located more and more in the different strata of this society. The main masses of the agricultural population, least of all, expected a comfortable life. Even for the ruling landowning class, the constant wars with changes of frontiers and overlords – which meant uncertainty for oneself and one's children – caused great discomfort. What was needed was stability of state structure and official ideology – a stability which could be supported by a positive and sufficiently strong social impulse towards it. Hence, now, instead of the unsteady feudal state formations not held together by a community of language and any traditional common culture appear stable absolutist states – so stable that they favour the creation, inside themselves, of a national self-consciousness, a historical factor most important for the further movement of the historical process. The task of the new, stable state was to guarantee a balance between the classes of the post-medieval society, of which there now were four.

By no means were all societies of the world able to reach the whole set of the diagnostic features characteristic of the Sixth Phase. Let us once more enumerate what is included in this set and is symptomatic of the Absolutist Post-Medieval Phase: these include the introduction of effective firearms, including artillery, which signifies the end of the existence of independent troops of armed landowners (troops of knights and similar structures); the emergence of new classes, beside the former ones who continue to be numerically dominant, namely the privileged landowners, and the agriculturists, more or less devoid of privileges. The new classes were the bourgeoisie and the hired workers; their appearance was connected with further improvement in the means of production, and especially in the technology of arms production. The social and ideological usages typical of the preceding stage caused growing dissatisfaction; this led, on the one hand, to peasant insurrections, and on the other, to the creation of numerous oppositional or alternative socio-psychological trends and ideologies, which grew in contrast to the former but still existing ideologies. Reformed religions were opposed to the official one, which, however, continued to influence the new ideologies. But a situation there emerged 'when one can also think otherwise'. This also liberated scientific thought; natural sciences were beginning to develop, although they had not yet become a productive force. Added to all this, for Europe (partly also for China) this was the discovery of new lands, and a colonial expansion. This led, first of all, to a considerable enrichment of the European trading bourgeoisie, and later also the industrial bourgeoisie, and, in Europe, finally to a new standard of life formerly unknown to the world.

Characteristic of this Phase was a special type of absolutism. Of course, absolutist states also existed in the former phases. However, typical of the Sixth Phase were stable absolutist states which had definite natural, religious and national frontiers. Inside such an absolutist state emerged one dominant religion, and one dominant self-conscious nationality. The absolutist monarchies of this phase still represented the old landowning class; but it is important that there had emerged a situation which saw, on the one side, a growing ideological fermentation, and on the other side, continuing attempts on the part of the formerly sovereign feudal nobility to retain power in their own apanage or principality – or if not in their own, then in some other. Under such conditions, only absolutism could safeguard, for the state and the official religion, a stability inside certain territorial limits; and for the bourgeoisie, a stable inner market. Absolutism was able to keep and to safeguard a balance between the four classes of the post-medieval society inside stable frontiers. It was able to withstand the development of alternative ideational and psychological tendencies, which potentially were to be destructive for the society structure of the Sixth Phase. The stable absolutist state reacted to the discomfort by creating stable frontiers, a stable inner market, by stabilisation of religious and national priorities. After stable absolutism had emerged, the uncertainties of life, even if it was a wretched one, were certainly diminished.

The creation of a stable absolutist state was an answer to the suffering typical of the Fifth Phase, which was due to the constant wars of everybody against everybody else, from which all suffered, including the citizens, the feudal lords themselves and most of all the peasants. But the emerging new, big, absolutist states had no new psychological base of their own. It was not immediately clear why one should serve the sovereign in the limits of just that geographical configuration, why one should sever certain habitual economical and religious ties.

To reach the new absolutist stability one had to have access to such arms as would make it possible to break the unruliness of the knights, and the stubborn rivalries of the minor sovereigns. These led an endless bloody struggle for power wherever you want, independent of territory on which the conflict began; hence they made a normal exchange of industrial goods impossible. Stability was therefore in the interests of the class of landowners, but also of the class of the bourgeoisie. This is why the production of effective firearms organised at the order of the kings by manufactories and handicraftsmen could be the condition and the prerequisite of a new Phase.

The stability of the state frontiers contributed to the development of a certain self-consciousness of those who lived inside those frontiers; more often than not, within them there existed a certain ethnic entity which appeared to be numerically prevalent, and could regard the emerging stable state as its own, and itself as the dominant nation. Alongside religious self-consciousness emerged a national self-consciousness.

The creation of a stable state could, at least partly, remove the contradictions inherent in the Fifth Phase in which two classes opposed each other: the landowners and the peasants. The emergence of the new type of state favoured the development of both new classes – the bourgeoisie and the hired workers – and of new alternative ideologies. However, these phenomena were not synchronous with the emergence of absolutism; therefore, those societies which displayed all the enumerated diagnostic features of the Sixth Phase, there also existed societies where the Phase transition had not been completed, due either to the weakness of the emerging industrial manufactures and the industrial bourgeoisie, or to the imperfect development of alternative ideologies.

At all events there are three circumstances which are fundamental for the Sixth Phase; namely, the emergence in any order of (1) effective firearms, (2) national self-consciousness as a socio-psychological factor, and (3) competing alternative socio-phychological trends. It is worth dwelling on these points in some detail.

Missile weapons (especially ballistas), sometimes rather intricate, but usually in the form of a giant bow (arcballista) had been known since Imperial Antiquity and were quite widely in use up to the thirteenth century. Different detonating and incendiary mixtures had been known since the same period. A smoking powder, a mixture of saltpetre, sulphur and charcoal, was invented in China during the tenth to eleventh centuries and was known (or invented anew) in Europe in the thirteenth century. The first mass use of firearms (pyroballistic arms) belongs to the fourteenth century. It became an export good; thus, Russia began to import cannons and gunpowder from the fourteenth to the early fifteenth century. Gunpowder was often mixed in the rear of the battle-lines or directly on the battlefield.

The first cannons were spherical or urn-like muzzle-loaded vessels. When ignited, the powder could throw out arrow-like objects, stones or stone balls and even wooden barrels containing an incendiary mixture. Soon cylindrical cannons appeared. They had no standard calibre but the calibre was usually very large. Until the fifteenth century cannons were mostly immovable, fixed on a wooden mounting. The apparatus was often not very solidly built and sometimes was more dangerous for the gunner than for the enemy; it always had a short range and was slow-firing. The powder-pulp got easily compressed and often did not explode at all, or exploded too late. Such cannons were not especially dangerous for cavalry, the riders being defended by chain mail or a coat of armour. Special tactics were used against cannon-fire: a continuous mounted formation was sent against the bombard with groups of mobile riders right and left, armed with pikes; after the first shot from the cannon, usually poorly aimed, the knights with pikes surrounded the cannon crew, cutting off a possible retreat; then the knights of the central group attacked it and destroyed the crew before it could reload the cannon.

Granulated gunpowder was invented at the beginning of the fifteenth century making the loading and shooting considerable easier.

Along with the primitive cannons, the first hand-guns were introduced, namely a primitive arquebus.[1] Tufang was the name in the Orient, arquebus in the Occident, but the terms, just as the terms bombard, couleuvrine, etc., could be applied both to the ancestors of the cannon, and to the ancestors of the rifle; gradually the term (h)arquebus was specifically allocated to the rifle to the last. Both a gun seven yards long with a charge of 200 pounds, and a gun one yard long with a bullet of a third of an ounce could be termed 'artillery'. An arquebus was originally a tube about a foot in length, with a hole drilled near the lower end. The gunpowder was stamped into the tube, then a lead ball was put into the muzzle, a wad was stamped over it, and the charge was set fire to by a lunt through the lower hole. A buff-stock for shooting from the shoulder took some time to be invented. Although a sort of arquebus was known in the Orient since the time of the Timurids, it did not help Oriental countries to reach the military technical level of the Sixth Phase.

Another feature which hampered the development of artillery battles, was, as mentioned, the lack of standardisation of the guns. Gunsmiths made arquebuses or cannons of any calibre they favoured. A gun could shoot so long as there were balls or bullets of the needed calibre, and that usually meant for a limited time only.

A special lock for the lunt of the arquebus was invented in the middle of the fifteenth century. In the middle of the sixteenth century the musket was invented – a construction heavier than the arquebus, in which the gun rested on a wooden support. The musketeer shot with heavy bullets which were loaded through the muzzle, eight or ten at a time. The musket gave a strong recoil, so that the shoulder had to be protected (for instance, by a special pillow). In the sixteenth century a flint-ignited fuse was introduced instead of the lunt. A gun barrel with straight rifling was introduced from the end of the fifteenth century; at the end of the seventeenth century and in the early nineteenth regular rifles were introduced, loaded from the breech end.

The heavy artillery gun also went through important changes. The first bombards and mortars were immovable, and could be used only for sieges (such as the

---

1. The most important weapon of the knights at the time of the Crusades was the arbalest (*arcbal-lista*, cf. above).

siege and capturing of Constantinople by the Turks in 1453). Later they were moved in carts, and from the end of the fifteenth century heavy guns were mounted on wheels. The transportation of artillery also underwent a development. At first artillery pieces were transported by oxen, later by horses driven tandem, the muzzles directed forward, and only from the middle of the sixteenth century, by special pairs of draught-horses, the muzzle backwards.

High-angle artillery fire (by mortars) was introduced only in the middle of the seventeenth century.

From the end of the fifteenth century through to the early sixteenth heavy guns were installed on ships. Attempts were made to standardise the calibres, but standardisation was fully achieved only in the eighteenth century.

The view that knights were superseded by artillery needs to be treated with caution: firearms did not gain the upper hand over the crossbow until the sixteenth to seventeenth centuries.

Innovations in firearms were quickly borrowed from one army by another, and often it is difficult to establish who was first responsible. From the point of view of military technology, the whole period from the sixteen to the seventeenth century can be regarded as a preparation for the consolidation of the Sixth Phase of the historical process.

Thus, in the Sixth Phase, society was furnished with firearms. But it was also armed with certain ideas. Here we must dwell upon a factor which we have already mentioned in passing, but which had become important in the Sixth Phase. It was to play a still more important role in the Seventh, and continues to be important today. This is national self-consciousness. It is based on the impulse 'to be as everybody is', but also 'to be among one's own' and therefore defended.

Ever since primitive man understood that there exists 'I', and there exists 'non-I', i.e. the external world, and that this world is, if not directly inimical, then at least bad and dangerous, man sought support in his 'fellows', 'his own'. (This was, of course, in the first place, the nuclear and the extended family, then one's clan, village, city.) But the wars during the Fifth and of the beginning Sixth Phase, as well as the state structure during that period, and the constant changes of the bellicose authorities, weakened or totally destroyed the extended family, the lineage; as for the continued existence of the city (which at that period was often a self-contained social unit), it was necessary to keep every city in touch with each other, to arrange their co-existence with each other, and their mutual relations.

Men and women always need a certain solidarity, and not only inside their own family, i.e. between man and wife and their children. Solidarity was created, first of all, by a common religion, but also by a common citizenship, and especially by a common stable state. When a Sixth Phase state received a more or less stable configuration, such a state also received a more or less stable population with a common language, religious traditions, and a certain type of mentality; even such peripheral groups which at first did not comply with this unity would now rather quickly be absorbed by the main population, because to these groups also the same state could guarantee a better existence than that which they had in the Fifth Phase.

One can detect the emergence of a feeling of cultural community (more seldom of linguistic community[2]) in some societies of the Third Phase (in the Egyptian, the Hellenic, the Roman, the Russian society), and then the feeling of a religious, and, to a lesser degree, of a linguistic community (in the Fifth Phase). But, for reasons stated above, only the formation of stable states in the Sixth Phase favoured the feeling of community of language and religion, and of cultural heritage, and of a statehood of one's own; all this we can term 'national self-consciousness' in the true sense of the phrase.

This does not mean that national self-consciousness is exclusively connected with the feeling of common statehood. On the contrary, once such self-consciousness has appeared in a population in possession of its own statehood, national self-consciousness begins to be perceived as a most important factor which allows any population to receive a stable niche in society, and hence as a most important value which becomes a necessity. It may happen that national self-consciousness may even appear as more forceful for peoples lacking statehood than for peoples that have it, because the absence of statehood in the presence of national self-consciousness is perceived as a powerful dissatisfaction which needs resolution as soon as possible.

But this process mainly is a feature of the Seventh Phase, and we shall discuss it below.[3]

In its primary form, national self-consciousness may be regarded as consisting of three components: religious self-consciousness, territorial and state unity, and linguistic mutual understanding.

The Jews are an exceptional case. According to their vernaculars, they were divided into three groups: the Eastern European Jews (the Ashkenazi, originally Polish Jews) whose vernacular was a language of the Germanic group – Yiddish; the Jews of Spain, Holland, Greece and Turkey (the Sephardi) whose vernacular was a dialect of Spanish, called Ladino or Judesmo; and the Jews of the Near and Middle East, who spoke Arabic, Persian or another Oriental language. However, they all had a common literary language, namely Hebrew (with some local variants). The religious dogma of Judaism required that every Jew should regularly – every day, if possible – read the Bible in Hebrew. Therefore all Jewish men (and some of the women) could always read and write in Hebrew, and many of them could speak

---

2. Note that in Ancient Mesopotamia there was a feeling of one common culture, but there were two languages in use (at first, Sumerian and Akkadian, and later Akkadian and Aramaic).

3. The recognition of the right of all nations to self-determination is a harbinger of a near transition to the Eighth Phase, in which this right is already one of the diagnostic features. National self-consciousness begins to be an important factor in international affairs between 1800 and 1900 (at first, mainly in Europe, a feature later important for the political reconstruction of the continent after World War I).

Hebrew. This was a heritage of the third and Fourth Phases in which literacy was typical.

In the epoch when proselytic religions were dominant – believers interested in broadening their religion's sphere of diffusion – the Jews followed a religion dissimilar in principle from that of their neighbours; proselytising, had been early forbidden. Therefore the Jews were united not only by their religion but also by the consciousness of their historical fate; which, as it happened, had made city-dwellers of practically all of them. Agriculture was nearly everywhere strictly forbidden to Jews by the state, which safeguarded the existing social relations between the landowners and the peasants. Since their religion required literacy of the whole community, all the Jews, wherever they lived, were united by a sacred language, which however was at the same time also much used in everyday life. For all Jews, it was not only a language of public worship but also of literature, and the means of cultural intercourse between men. Although their popular and religious self-consciousness was strong, they lacked the possibility and even the hope of creating a national state. Only in Poland did they have, for a time, a kind of self-government. It was not until the Seventh Phase that the Jews received (in some countries) equal rights with the local population. This led, on the one hand, to the absorption of a part of the Jewish intellectual élite in the local intelligentsia, and on the other, to a movement for the creation of a Jewish national state.

In their literacy (at least the men), the Jews differed from the rest of the medieval and post-medieval population which was almost totally illiterate. Only a minority, mainly the clergy – but later some of those belonging to the secular élite as well – could read and write in Latin, Church-Slavonic, literary Arabic, literary Chinese and Sanskrit: all of these were languages of cultural intercourse. None was national but each belonged to certain cultural and religious super-national regions.

National self-consciousness as a historical factor cannot be correctly understood without taking into account national mentality. National mentality is formed by the acquired traditional and cultural values (mainly religious) and the corresponding anti-values, created by the specific fate of the specific ethnic unit which constituted the base of the emerging nation. Note that the religion can be changed, and even be replaced by atheism, but the values and anti-values engendered by it can continue in existence (or, at least, may be traced) for centuries, until they be ousted by other powerful forces of historical fate. Any national mentality is always a part of national self-consciousness and is felt as a value; but the same traits of mentality may be perceived as anti-values by neighbouring nations which possess another religious and historical background. The whole of the Sixth and especially the Seventh Phase were full of bitter and often bloody national strife. However, it is important to take into consideration the following.

First, national mentality is not an eternal but a changing phenomenon: the modern peaceful Norwegian has different values from those of his ancestor, the pirate Viking; the Greek of the time of Pericles did not resemble the Byzantine

Greek, a typical dogmatic Christian, and the latter had little in common with a modern Greek. Secondly, the features of national mentality can be established only on average; that is, they do not necessarily appear in every individual of that nation. Thirdly, even if national features do appear in an individual, they do it only so long as he exists inside the national milieu in question. If a man enters another milieu, then his descendants in the second or the third generation will acquire the typical features of another national mentality – that of the adoptive nation. Therefore Kantemir is not a Rumanian but a Russian poet, Pushkin is not an Ethiopian (or, actually, Eritrean) but a Russian poet, Mandelstam is a Russian, not a Jewish poet, Victor Tsoi is not a Korean but a Russian singer. In the same way, Rousseau is a French, not a Swiss thinker, Anacharsis Kloots not a German but a French revolutionary, Modigliani not a Jewish, but a French painter, Handel not a German but an English composer, Bernard Shaw not an Irish but an English writer, Lord Beaconsfield not a Jewish but an English statesman, Beethoven not a Dutch but a German musician; Chamisso not a French but a German romanticist. And such lists can be continued *ad infinitum*.

As families are easily assimilated with a new nation so also are ethnic groups. We have already mentioned that we cannot identify men belonging to the Russian nation with the Slavs who spoke the Proto-Slavonic language of the Antae somewhere in modern Belorussia at the beginning of the Christian era. The Roman nation has also included Sarmatae, Venedi, Vod', Izhora (Ingrians), certain individuals descending from the Kumans, Mordva, Tatars, Poles, Jews, Germans, Dutch, Danes, Swedes, Zemaitians (or Zhmud'), as well as other Baltic peoples, etc. But from this heterogeneous melting-pot there emerged, by the beginning of the Sixth Phase and in the Seventh, the Russian nation with its specific national mentality, with their universally recognised merits and with the shortcomings which we well know ourselves. More or less the same can be said about any other nation which has a self-consciousness. Because of its composite origin, and the heterogeneous character of its traditions, which in certain circumstances can be regarded as values, and in other circumstances, as anti-values, no nation has the right to regard itself better than another: the English are not necessarily a nation of gentlemen, the Germans are no Herrenrasse, the Russians are not those who bear God in their hearts and who are destined to make the whole world happy; the Turks are not the zombies whom we observed in the janizaries' troops (the janizaries, moreover, were not born Turks). In general, national mentality is not stored in the genetic code but depends upon long enculturation. At the genetic level there are no nations, although at that level there can be certain abilities, talents, and also negative features of an individual mentality.[4]

---

4. The blood groups are distributed differently in different populations, but there is no such thing as racial blood; the blood groups have no connection with nationality; the distribution of blood groups, of languages, and of national characters do not coincide at all.

After making all these specifications, we must concede that, with the Sixth Phase, national self-consciousness becomes an important influence in the historical process, and we shall have to take this into account below.

Not all societies of Eurasia developed into the Sixth Phase during the seventeenth to eighteenth centuries: countries of Western Europe including France, Germany, Great Britain (and partly the Holy Roman Empire and Italy) belonged to the Stable Absolutist Post-Medieval Phase in its developed form; in the Far East, China was entering this Phase, and, with a certain delay, Japan also; the symptoms of the Sixth Phase were not so pronounced in Poland, in the Balkans, in Russia; it was just dawning in Turkey; as to Iran, Middle Asia, India and the Arab countries, they were still in the fifth Phase; during the nineteenth century, when national self-consciousness began to get the upper hand over religious self-consciousness, these nations had to catch up with the other nations which were already living in the Seventh, Capitalist Phase.

A quite particular path of development was that of America as we will see shortly.

Europe, in the Sixth Phase, left all its Eurasian neighbours far behind; it is here that the development of the Sixth Phase can be observed most clearly, so we will begin with Europe. It is important to note that by the fifteenth century national frontiers were still uncertain: the European intellectual élite which was responsible for preserving the old and creating the new intellectual movements had one common language of mutual understanding and cultural intercourse (namely Latin); therefore it would be difficult to divide our account according to the different countries or nations. A similar picture was also frequent in the other parts of the world.

Discussing the post-medieval epoch in Europe (sixteenth to eighteenth centuries), we may state that a capitalist social structure had been formed inside the society as a whole, but the capitalist class, although playing a steadily increasing role, did not come to power.

It is very important that during the post-medieval epoch began a trade in industrial produce between centres of capital placed at considerable distances from each other. Specialised industries designed for long-range trade were created. The leading role in Western Europe belonged to the fulling industry.

Until then, people wore homespun clothes made either at home, or even if in a manufactory, by the process of spinning and weaving by hand. Now, however, cloth was made in primitive fulling factories, and the production of fulled cloth was very profitable.

England during the sixteenth to eighteen centuries witnessed a process of enclosure – lands which formerly were regarded by the peasants as communal property (and also former monastery lands) became private property. On the enclosed land one could breed sheep for the fulling industry, and also cultivate grain, vegetables, etc. At the same time, the number of landless people grew; these were unconnected with production, and were ready to work in the factories for very low wages, with an unlimited working-day. This process had particularly grave results for the Scottish Highlands, where there still existed clans typical not of the Sixth or even the Fifth, but actually of the Third Phase.

Capitalist methods were used for the production of woollen cloth and the organisation of its trade, as well as in other wares; this practice needed a new ideology, different from that of the Middle Ages.

Similar phenomena development had taken place elsewhere and earlier: e.g. in the thirteenth to sixteenth centuries in Flanders, and in the fourteenth to fifteenth centuries in Florence. But these were but isolated foci of capitalist production inside a world dominated by medieval, feudal relations. In Flanders there was a struggle between handicraftsmen and patrician manufacturers; at first, the former won, but soon a feudal counter-revolution occurred, which hampered the development of manufactory production. In Florence, there was a plebeian insurrection of the 'Ciompi', but the scenario was similar to that in Flanders. Neither Flanders nor Florence was able to survive as a centre of capitalism because no viable formula was found for the balance in the conflict in interests of the wealthy capitalists on the one hand, and the mass of the indigent workers on the other.

This contradiction continued to be important even after the total triumph of the capitalists which became possible because of the massive accumulation of capital, and was accompanied by innovations in the socio-psychological and ideological fields, as well as by the introduction of new technologies, first of all in the production of arms.

During the seventeenth and eighteen centuries, capitalist relations spread over nearly the whole of Western Europe. The reason was that the capitalists did not turn the surplus value into 'pyramids and cathedrals', as a historian puts it, neither into sumptuous dresses and the upkeep of vast courts, but invested it in the expansion of capitalist production. In order to develop this tendency, what was needed was the creation of new ethics; the inherited medieval ideology hampered it: thus the compiler of the Latin Version of the Bible, St Jerome (fourth century), said that 'a rich man is either a thief, or the son of a thief'. The Reformation censured the riches of the pope, the bishops and the monasteries; but at the same time sanctioned the right of every man to the fruits of his labour and his abstemiousness, and hence to amassing wealth from production and credit. (In the Middle Ages, credit operations, i.e. usury were often discouraged by the Catholic Church and even legally forbidden to Christians, and were left to non-Christians.) No wonder that the capitalist economy grew first and foremost in countries that had accepted the Reformation: in England (where the rural character of the production of the fulling mills saved the capitalists from the fate of capitalism in Florence), in Holland, in Switzerland (particularly, in Geneva) and in some parts of Germany.

In France, the city bourgeoisie (as well as the poorer knights) joined the Reformed Christian sect of Huguenots. They did not manage to achieve political

ascendancy, although there was a civil war caused mainly by the Huguenot movement though partly by the rivalry between noble families that aspired to power
over the country (1562 to 1593). But the major part of the Huguenots exterminated
during the massacre of St Bartholomew's night (29 August 1572), and in 1593 their
leader Henry IV of Bourbon (originally king of Navarre) embraced Catholicism
('Paris vaut bien la messe'); according to the edict of Nantes (1598) the Huguenots
received only a limited religious liberty (later it was still more restricted). In 1685,
Louis XV abolished the Edict of Nantes completely, which led to a siphoning of
intellect through the emigration of Huguenots to England, Holland, Sweden and
partly to the New World. For the bourgeoisie staying in France dissatisfaction
increased, and later was to lead to the extremes and cruelties of the French
Revolution.

An important factor in the development of capitalist relations (especially in countries which remained Catholic) was the flow of precious metals from the New World,
and hence their comparative cheapness. At the same time, the growth of ground-rent
was less than the growth of prices (usually ground-rent was fixed a long time in
advance). Sometimes the landowners, in order to augment their income, would turn
to the capitalist system of exploitation (also by enclosure of common land). The
wages of the hired workers lagged further behind mounting prices. The incomes of
the manufacturers, the money-lenders and the merchants rose considerably, but they
were not allowed political power, this adding to their dissatisfaction.

For the development of capitalism, it was necessary to abolish the local customs
dues, to organise a stable money system, to promulgate laws which could protect
capitalist relations in production, to stop internecine strife, to defend the frontiers
of the national inner market, and to develop transportation by land and by sea.
None of this could be done by the private means of the bourgeoisie; what it needed
was a strong state, stable inside its national frontiers, even if the power in it did not
at that time immediately belong to the bourgeoisie.

Even before the French Revolution, individual representatives of the bourgeoisie occupied responsible positions in the state, but on the whole that part of the
bourgeoisie which grew more and more rich limited itself to attempts to mix with
the nobility and gentry through marriage, or through imitating the noblemen's
way of life or, at least, by adding the prefix 'de' to their surname – these are the
symptoms ridiculed by Molière in his 'Le bourgeois gentilhomme'.

The peasants rebelled[5] (without success), while the competition on commercial
markets caused wars. Their purpose was different from that of the medieval wars,
whose aim was prestige and glory accrued from grabbing tribute, and from the
submission of as many vassals as possible. If we discount the dominions of the
Holy Roman Empire which included small princedoms, actually or nominally subject to the emperor, we may observe that most of the different European states now

---

5. The 'Jacquerie' in France (1358), et al.

received more or less stable frontiers. The wars between them were caused by a desire to widen the inner market, or to capture new sources of raw materials; the motive of private military glory still existed, but the motive of national prestige also became significance.

The 1345–1349 pandemic of the plague had so ravaged Europe that one might have expected a slowing down of the historical process; this, however, did not occur. It was precisely the fourteenth century which saw the beginning of the Renaissance and of bourgeois development in Italy (Florence), in Flanders and to a certain degree in England. However the circumstance that marked the watershed between the Fifth and Sixth Phases, completely changing the fate of Europe, was the discovery of America in 1492. From this point of view it is important, that beginning with the sixteenth century, Europe acquired, in the American colonies, a source of riches which seemed inexhaustible. During half a century, the mass of silver and gold which was in circulation throughout the European countries increased, according to the estimate of some historians, sevenfold. Due to the growth of the money mass, the prices rose two- or threefold (i.e. there was inflation), so that both the incomes from agriculture and the workers' wages diminished. The growth of money circulation contributed to the development of capitalist relations in the economy.

The stable national states followed a policy of mercantilism: a state should accumulate silver and gold by creating a favourable balance between import and export. For this, the mercantilists required low wages and long working hours. This policy of mecantilism, in a situation when the mass of precious metals brought from the colonies was growing, led to a cumulative development of the economy. It was actually this cumulative effect that was decisive for the entrenchment of capitalist social relations in Western Europe. This effect has often been lacking in the developing countries of the twentieth century which reach not the Sixth Phase but only the Fifth; but even after reaching the Sixth Phase, the impulse which is necessary for the quick accumulation of money resources might not always have occurred.

This is one of the main reasons why the Sixth Phase of the historical process was best developed on the big peninsula of the Eurasian continent which is called Western Europe, and on the nearby island of Great Britain;[6] here the conditions were more favourable.

The change in the historical development of Europe did not diminish the dissatisfaction which existed there before, but actually augmented it. All those who were bypassed by the flow of the gold felt it: the peasants and the hired workers (whose condition deteriorated), and the gentry, who grew – relatively and sometimes

6. Later it was possible to abandon mercantilist practices, when Adam Smith made it evident 'how a state gets rich, and by what it lives, and why it does not need gold if it has simple produce' (quotation from Pushkin). The theory of Adam Smith was implemented when the capitalist structure of the economy became pre-eminent.

absolutely – poorer (because the growth of land-rent could not keep in step with the growth of prices). At the same time, the whole society suffered from military instability on the continent.

As for the bourgeoisie, it did get richer, but its activities were hampered by the frontiers which were drawn quite arbitrarily, and tended to change often. Moreover, its activities were also hampered by such negative factors of vital importance as the lack of a unified monetary system, lack of legal regulation of capitalist social relations, the dearth of qualified and disciplined labour power, the lack of a secure defence of a really stable territory which could form a national market, and the dearth of literate and qualified technicians for accountancy in the spheres of trade and credit. Taking part in governing the state was not a task that was urgent for the bourgeoisie at that period, but the bourgeoisie did require a strong state power. Thus, the bourgeoisie felt an important dissatisfaction, just as did most of the other parts of the population.

The dissatisfaction of the peasantry led to a number of insurrections (among them the Great Peasant war of 1524–1526); the dissatisfaction of other population groups led to wars which were the indirect result of the Reformation, on which more below.

The dissatisfaction of the different classes and strata of the society found expression, *inter alia*, in a negative attitude towards the Catholic clergy. And with good reason: by the richness of his household, his clothing and the extent of his secular power, an archbishop could compare himself favourably with a prince or a duke; some of the monasteries could vie with a duchy. The clergy was not notable for actual humility and self-restraint as preached once upon a time by Christ ('give away what you have to the poor, and seek salvation'). The church services were held in a language incomprehensible to the people, using manuscripts and rare books inaccessible to laymen. The ritual requirements from the believers became increasingly intricate and strict, and infringements were punished by severe ritual penalties. In 1477, the pope Sixtus IV permitted indulgences to be for money, i.e. documents which absolved the sinner from punishment for his sins by torments in purgatory (not in hell). All this was very unlike original Christianity.

Changes in the social structure, especially in the organisation of stable states, became possible, as mentioned above, because of the improvement in firearms. For the first time, and not very effectively, firearms were used at the end of the Hundred Years' War, and in the dynastic War of the Roses in England (1455–1487) which brought Henry VII of the new Tudor dynasty to power. After a long period of unrest, he managed to found a stable kingdom. But it was only later that artillery played a decisive role, as, for example, in the naval victory of England over the Spanish Great Armada in 1588, which brought about a final stabilisation of the state structure in England under Queen Elizabeth I (1558–1603); such was also the case in the Franco-Spanish wars for control over Italy (the battle of Pavia, 1525); in the Huguenot wars in France, which ended in a stable kingdom under Henri IV, etc. The knights gradually ceased to exist as a military force, a result of the growing effectiveness of firearms.

Growing dissatisfaction was characteristic of Western Europe in the sixteenth century, in spite of the fact that the stabilisation of the states continued. But in parallel with the growing discomfort, there also developed alternative socio-psychological tendencies.[7] Technically, their overall development was made possible by the invention of bookprinting (Gutenberg, about 1448), and the edition of books in numerous copies: the famous Italian publisher Aldus Manutius and his nearest descendants and successors printed more than 1,000 editions in 100 years (from 1495 to 1595); all in all, in the 100 years after Gutenberg's invention, tens of thousands of books were printed.[8]

At the beginning of the movement towards the realisation of the situation when 'one can also think otherwise' we meet three examples of late humanists, men who were modest, morally attractive and at the same time courageous. They were Johann Reuchlin (1455–1522), Erasmus of Rotterdam (1468–1546) and Sir Thomas More (1478–1535). It was their activities which allowed the scholars of the new generation to get acquainted both with the most important works of the ancient thinkers, and with the early works of the fathers of primitive Christianity which in recent times had seldom been copied. And it was they who created an impulse for the appearance of new independent thinkers.

Reuchlin, a brilliant Latinist and Hellenist from his youth, learned Hebrew and began reading the Biblical Old Testament in the original; his were the first vocabulary and first European grammar of Hebrew, based on the work of the Jewish grammatist David Kimchi and his school. When the emperor Maximilian issued a decree demanding the annihilation of all Jewish manuscripts, and especially of the

7. The first attempts to reform Catholicism were made by Wycliffe in England, and under his influence by Jan Hus (1370–1415) in Czechia. The needed reform was thought to consist of declaring the power of the pope non-obligatory, limiting the riches of the clerics and specifying some theological points. Hus was called to the Catholic ecumenical council in Konstanz and burnt at the stake as a heretic. However, Husites continued to exist in Czechia until the victory of counter-reformation in the seventeenth century. There is no trace of a connection between Hus and Luther.

8. The first attempts to introduce letter types seem to date to a period before Gutenberg, but it was only the latter who introduced a system of typesetting. In China typesetting had existed much earlier (from the eleventh century), but because of the tremendous number of types needed for Chinese texts the work of the typesetters was here much more difficult and time-consuming, so that the introduction of books printed in type happened slowly. In the Ukraine – in that part of the country which was controlled by Poland, typesetting in the Cyrillic alphabet was first introduced by Sz. Fiol in Cracow (1491). In Russia, Ivan Fedorov and Peter Mstislavets founded the first typography in 1564. However, unlike Western Europe, printed books were regarded in Russia as something perhaps not exactly devilish, but certainly not blessed by God. Therefore, Ivan Fedorov had to flee to the Polish-Lithuanian kingdom, where he continued to publish books in Church Slavonic for Belorussians and Ukrainians. Book printing was seriously started in Russia in the seventeenth century, but the tradition of producing chronicles in manuscript still continued under Tsar Alexei Mikhailovich (1645–1676).

Talmud,[9] in order to compel the Jews by force to embrace Christianity (as had already been done in Spain), Reuchlin intervened for the Jews, and was handed over to the Inquisition as a heretic; then his case was presented to Pope Leo X. Certain death awaited the scholar, but he was saved by the rivalry between the papal and the imperial power: the emperor, several of the Electors[10] and half a hundred cities in Southern Germany made declarations in Reuchlin's favour (but all universities which had been requested to state their opinion declared against him). Reuchlin's books, including his 'Book of Obscure Men', which had made great impression on the already rather numerous educated group of the population, were banned by the pope, but Reuchlin nevertheless gained a professorship of Greek and Hebrew in Austria, where he ended his life.

Erasmus was the illegitimate son of a priest, so he had only one choice in life – to become a monk. But taking into account his great proficiency in classical studies, the monastery authorities allowed him to lead a secular existence, and much of his life he spent teaching gentlemen ignoramuses (later he renounced his monastic vows, but, just as Reuchlin, remained a Catholic). Erasmus travelled much (from England to Italy); everywhere he contacted scholars and studied new manuscripts and rare books. In those times such travels did not involve much difficulty: the frontiers were, as a rule, perfunctorily guarded, and educated men, whether in England, in the Netherlands or in Switzerland, spoke one common language, namely Latin.[11] It can be said that Erasmus was the founder of the scientific criticism of manuscripts. Moreover, he achieved, for the study of the Greek original text of the New Testament, what Reuchlin had done for the Old Testament. The standard Latin version of the Bible, the Vulgate, did not retain the authority it had had in the Middle Ages (it had to be revised in 1592). Critical study of the text of the Bible and the Gospel became possible. What had been the prerogative of few clerics became accessible to the general public, as was noted by the eighteenth century

9. The *Talmud* (which means 'learning' in Hebrew) is the Post-Biblical Holy Writ of the Jews. The main parts of the Talmud are the *Mishna* (lit. 'Repetition' or 'Seconding', first to second centuries AD), which is a collection of very strict interpretations of the Law by the religious teachers of the time, in accordance with the needs of the new period; and the *Gemara* (lit. 'Completion', also called *Talmud* in the narrow sense of the word); this consists of alternating texts referring to law (the *Halakha*), and narrative texts (*Haggada*). Actually there are two *Gemaras*, the *Talmud of Jerusalem*, written (except for the Biblical quotations) in Western Aramaic, in the first to third centuries AD, and the *Talmud of Babylon*, written in Eastern Aramaic, in the third to fifth centuries AD. In the Talmud, there was evolved a complicated system of analogical and allegorical interpretations of the Biblican text, which allowed ancient dicta (which had the status of sacred law) to later changing conditions.

10. The seven most important vassals of the Holy Roman Empire, who were entitled to elect the successive emperors, were called *Electors* (*Kurfursten*).

11. This, no doubt, was a spoken but bookish Latin. Popular Latin had many local variants, and by this time had developed into Italian, Spanish, French and other languages, often not mutually understandable. But bookish Latin, although very different from the language of Cicero, continued to be a means of mutual understanding, not only for the clerics but also among educated laymen.

British poet, Alexander Pope, who said that Erasmus 'stemm'd the wild torrent of a barbarous age. And drove those holy Vandals off the stage.' Besides his scholarly works, Erasmus is famous for his satire *Praise of Folly* and other writings important in his time.

The Englishman Thomas More was a statesman, but he also had a great interest in new tendencies in what was then generally termed 'philosophy'. His friendship with Erasmus played an important role in his life. Inspired by reports of many newly discovered fantastic islands, he wrote, in his free time, a tale about the supposed discovery of still another unknown land, characterised by unusual customs, and a certain fairness of its mores, although preserving slavery. Thomas More did not ask whether such a country with such usages and customs can really be founded somewhere in this world; he regarded his work as a purely literary and philosophical one. It is not by chance that More's island was called 'Utopia', i.e. 'Nowhere', having no actual place in the real world. However, Thomas More's Utopia later inspired many dreamers about a happier future – and not only early 'Utopian' socialists, such as Fourier, Saint-Simon or Robert Owen, but also the so-called 'scientific' socialists. Thus More's Utopia found its place in the perennial dream of an eternal happy future for everybody. But More's contemporaries were not impressed to any serious degree.[12]

Like Reuchlin and Erasmus, Sir Thomas More was a devout Catholic (he even wore a hair-shirt); his undoing was that being Henry VIII's Lord Chancellor, he did not agree to the king's plan to marry a certain Anne Boleyn while his present wife was alive; so he was beheaded.

Although Reuchlin and Erasmus, studying the original Biblical texts and finding discrepancies with the Catholic tradition, still remained completely on Catholic ground, and did not urge any kind of alternative teachings, it was actually they (and their pupils) who supplied the stimulus for the activities of Martin Luther (1483–1546). In the beginning, Luther was a monk and a Catholic preacher. In 1517 he nailed to the door of a church in the city of Wittenberg his '95 theses', censuring the sale of indulgences and other abuses of the clergy. He refused to appear before a church court in Rome, and in 1520 he publicly burned a papal bull of excommunication. According to the laws of that time, he should have been burned at the stake, but he was taken under the protection of the Elector Frederic III of Saxony (Wittenberg was inside the borders of that country). The pope did not wish the election of the emperor to be contrary to his interests, and seems to have underestimated the danger of Luther, so he yielded to the influential Elector.

---

12. Here we should mention a man whose work later had an immense impact on the creation of an alternative ideology to Catholicism. This was the Polish monk Nicolaus Copernicus. His book proving that the Earth is not the centre of the universe, was published in 1543, the year of the author's death. Curiously enough, the first draft of the Copernican system met with the pope's approval, but the complete edition was withheld from publication in Nuremberg because of objections from Luther and the Lutherans.

During his Wittenberg confinement, Luther translated the Old and New Testaments into German. Before that, there had been attempts to translate the Bible into the new European languages, but these were merely word-for-word translations of the Latin Vulgate and were neither widely spread nor very influential. Luther's translation was made from the Hebrew and the Greek original.[13] Luther's German Bible, as well as his other manuscripts, were soon published in print and were very widely distributed. From the start, Luther found many adherents. When in 1518 the ecclesiastical powers published 'Antitheses' to his 95 theses, they were burnt by the students of Wittenberg.

Later a movement for the reform of Christianity (or, as the Protestants themselves thought, for the return to the unadulterated teachings of the Gospel) spread rapidly throughout Europe. The leading reformers were Zwingli in Southern Germany and Switzerland (1481–1531), Calvin (1509–1564) who fled from France and settled in Geneva, and King Henry VIII of England (reigned from 1509 to 1547).[14]

Luther denied the cult of the Madonna and the saints, monasticism, and, in general, all those elements of Catholic religion for which there is no authority either in the Old Testament or in the Gospel. Calvin, on the other hand, emphasised the doctrine of predestination: the sinfulness or righteousness of everybody is predestined by God at the beginning of time, and only those whom He has predestined for salvation can be saved, while those who have been predestined to destruction will perish. But in the hope that a man is predestined for salvation, he must try to prove it by a righteous life. Moreover, Calvin denied any church hierarchy. Calvin's teachings (with some modifications) were adopted by the Swiss and some German adherents of the Reformed Church, the French Huguenots, the English and the Scottish Presbyterians. The Puritans were not Lutherans.

Many city dwellers in Europe joined the Protestant or the Reformed Church, but this does not mean that the Reformation as such was a bourgeois movement. The moving force was the thinking part of the clerics, the literate part of the city population, and the poorer knights. Under the conditions dominant in the German-speaking countries, Protestantism could simply be a tool in the political struggle. Let us remember that the territory of Germany, as well as a good part of Italy, and the territories of present-day Austria, Hungary, the Czech Republic and Slovakia

13. Luther did not know Hebrew as well as Reuchlin did – but, of course, he made use of the latter's grammar and dictionary; the influence of the Vulgate on his text was very considerable.

14. As early as the 1520s–1530s, the Inquisition burned Protestants and Reformed Christians at the stake in France, in countries subject to the Holy Roman Empire and in other European countries. Especially abhorrent to both Catholics and to Protestants were the Anabaptists; they appeared in Luther's lifetime, being first mentioned in 1525. The Anabaptists thought that baptism, as implying adherence to Christianity, should be performed as a conscious act of a grown-up person, and only after a serious spiritual preparation; they rejected all oaths, practised community of goods in their joint settlements, and expected the end of the world. Mass executions of Anabaptists took place and they were totally exterminated in Germany, but they still survived elsewhere; their descendants are the Mennonites, still to be found in many countries, mostly in the USA but also in Germany.

were occupied by hundreds of small political bodies, both lay and clerical, and that they all recognised the superiority of the pope and of the Holy Roman Emperor[15] (who in theory was nominated by the Electors, but from the fifteenth century always belonged to the Habsburg family). The emperors had to be crowned by the pope. At the same time, there was always an opposition and a rivalry between the imperial power and the papal power (the latter maintaining the right of the clerics to secular landowning). The sovereign feudal lords who stood below the king, supported now the one, and now the other party and, striving for more independence, sometimes embraced Protestantism.[16]

Reformation took a particular form in England. The great power of the episcopate and the richness of the monasteries here also caused dissatisfaction among the populace. But the initiative in reformation belonged to the king, Henry VIII. He was worried over the fact that his wife, Catherine of Aragon, had not borne him sons. A divorce could legally be granted by the pope alone, but the pope did not grant it, although Henry had already chosen another lady, Anne Boleyn, whom he (his first wife being alive) married in 1533. Henry decided to declare that the king of England is – or ought to be – also the head of the country's church. To implement the reform, he selected Thomas Cromwell,[17] a lawyer from a bourgeois-artisan milieu. At first, no ecclesiastical innovations were intended, except for recognising the king as the head of the church rather than the pope (1534). Then the ecclesiastical courts were abolished, and first the smaller, then all monasteries were dissolved (1535–1540); in 1538 it was decreed that the service in all churches should be in English instead of Latin. However, in 1540 Thomas Cromwell angered the king and was beheaded; but the king repented at once and returned all the confiscated property to Cromwell's son. Anne Boleyn had been beheaded in 1536, and in 1542 the same fate befell a later queen. In such a discreditable form did reformation reach England. The foundation of the Church of England did not prevent the appearance of still other Christian doctrines, such as the Presbyterian or the Puritan; Presbyterianism became dominant in nearby Scotland from 1590, and later played an important role in the history of England.

The Reformation in its different forms was not only an ideological alternative to Catholicism; it opened the way to several alternative variants and it gave wide scope to the possibility of 'thinking otherwise'. It is true that the new Christian

---

15. As we had already mentioned, the title of 'King of Germany' was sometimes joined to that of 'Emperor of the Holy Roman Empire'.
16. In Spain, also ruled by the Habsburgs, attempts at introducing Protestant or Reformed teachings were completely quashed by the Inquisition. The latter was not so successful in the Netherlands which were dependent upon the Spanish Habsburgs. Its northern part (Holland) seceded, but a struggle of different Protestant denominations continued there. The southern part (Flanders) remained Catholic; part was seized by France and part continued to belong to the Habsburgs. In Italy no form of Protestantism had any adherence.
17. Not to be confused with Oliver Cromwell, active during the English Revolution, and a distant relative of Thomas Cromwell.

doctrines were also intolerant of the differently minded, but mostly they were more tolerant than Catholicism. Note however that the Reformation was unable to abolish totally all social dissatisfaction. Although it opened the way for many an outstanding public figure belonging to the third estate, it did not pave the way to power for the bourgeoisie, although it did extend its social possibilities.

The new attitude towards the accumulation of the good things of life ought to be especially stressed: for Christian Orthodoxy, a person living in abject poverty (like the Russian Vasily the Blessed) was a saint, while a rich man was a rascal just because he was rich; even Catholicism, although allowing the enrichment of its clergy, nevertheless taught that an odour of sanctity was connected with asceticism in everyday life (the mendicant Franciscan and Dominican friars played a great role). But for most of the Protestant doctrines secular wealth was a divine gift which one should treasure and multiply. Afterwards such a socio-psychological turn did much for the creation and entrenchment of European and North-American capitalism.

If for the city dwellers Protestantism was a viable alternative ideology, it did not alleviate the sense of suffering of the peasants. The peasant war of 1524–1526 in Germany did not develop within the bounds of the Protestant movement, but in parallel to it. Admittedly, Thomas Münzer, a radical follower of Luther, took part in the insurrection, but it is difficult to classify him as a leader of the mutiny. The peasants were defeated, their leaders were executed, and their own material and social conditions were not ameliorated. On the contrary, nearly complete serfdom was widely introduced.

The appearance of Protestantism and its manifold forms helped to further philosophical as well as religious thought, and later also natural history. Philosophers who should be mentioned in this connection are Francis Bacon (England, 1561–1626) whose opinion was that cognition should be based on observation and on experiments, and the great writer and thinker Montaigne (France, 1533–1592).

The seventeenth century saw the further development of philosophy (Descartes, 1596–1650; Spinoza, 1632–1677; Locke, 1622–1707), but now also of natural sciences, which was of the greatest importance for the further development of mankind: Galileo (1564–1642), Kepler (1576–1630), Huygens (1620–1695), and the greatest of them all, Newton (1642–1727).[18]

But the same pluralism of opinions allowed the movement of Catholic counter-reformation to begin.[19] Its epoch is mostly remembered in world history

18. In the seventeenth century, most of the European thinkers spoke or wrote Latin, which was natural for the educated part of the post-medieval society of Western Europe. The fact that Descartes was a Frenchman (but had lived twenty years in Holland), Locke an Englishman, Spinoza a Dutch (Sephardi) Jew, Galileo an Italian, Kepler a German, Huygens a Dutchman and Newton an Englishman, was of no importance. National self-consciousness at that period was not very much developed, if it existed at all.

19. It also made possible the cynical doctrine of political adaptability and time-serving, taught in Macchiavelli's clever book *Il Principe* ('The Sovereign', in Italian, 1532).

as that of unbridled bloody reprisals of heretics by the Inquisition courts, especially (but not only) in Spain. But the counter-reformation was not a wholly negative phenomenon. The Jesuits are usually remembered in history as an order of shameless hypocrites, whose every statement might have been false because their use of the rule of *reservatio mentalis*. But the Society of Jesus (i.e. the Jesuits) did much for enlightenment (of course, in a strictly Catholic spirit) both in Europe and in newly discovered countries, from China to Paraguay. The counter-reformation was a time in which the baroque style in art and architecture flourished; to this movement belonged such artists as Caravaggio, Guido Reni, Bernini, the Brueghel family and Rubens. Campanella (1568–1639), a Dominican monk, Catholic utopian and philosopher, and a friend of Galileo, also belonged to the counter-reformation; it is true that he was to endure much persecution. Perhaps the greatest and most humane genius among artists, Rembrandt (1608–1669) was a Reformed Christian.

At the end of the sixteenth century two great writers marked the extinction of the epoch of Knighthood: Miguel Cervantes Saavedra (1547–1616) – in the tragicomic figure of Don Quixote, and William Shakespeare (1564–1616) – in the comic figure of Falstaff and the tragic words of Hamlet, the student from Wittenberg: 'The time is out of joint.'

This age is, both in Western Europe (England, France, Portugal, and, with some reservation, Spain), and in Eastern (Poland, Russia), as well as Northern (Denmark-Norway,[20] Sweden), characterised by the emergence of absolutist national states.

France was the most typical absolutist kingdom: it was consolidated under the successors of Henry IV, but was actually ruled less by the kings (Louis XIII, 1610–1643; Louis XIV, 1643–1715; Louis XV, formally from 1715, practically from 1723–1774) than by their plenipotentiary ministers: Sully under Henri IV, the cardinal Richelieu under Louis XIII, the cardinal Mazarini and later Colbert under Louis XIV. These were gifted and vigorous statesmen who brought some order to the country's economy. Thus Colbert, himself of bourgeois origin, did what he could to encourage industry according to the principles of mercantilism. However, the state's incomes were mostly spent on the splendid royal court, on the royal mistresses, the building of palaces, etc. The bourgeoisie and the peasants, and especially the hired workers, were increasingly dissatisfied.

The centre of Europe – from Northern Germany to Southern Italy – was fragmented into tiny states, often in military conflict with one other. Most were vassals of the Holy Roman Empire, either actually or nominally. In these absolutist states, the power, nearly or completely unlimited, belonged to monarchs representing the

---

20. At that time, the Kingdom of Denmark united two kindred but different nations: the Danes and the Norwegians.

interests of the landowning nobility. Only in the Netherlands,[21] in mountainous Switzerland and (in the form of the rule of elected doges) in Venice did republican or semi-republican structures exist.

The most important events in seventeenth century Western Europe were the Thirty Years' War, and the English Revolution.

The 'Thirty Years' War' is the name given to military actions which developed mainly in what now is Germany and the Czech Republic between 1618 and 1648. But perhaps it would be more correct to speak of at least a dozen separate wars which took place between 1610 and 1660.

These wars, no doubt, appeared to be caused by the enmity between the adherents of Lutheranism, Calvinism and Catholicism, but this religious interpretation was more in the nature of propaganda, because actually Protestant rulers could ally themselves to Catholics, Lutherans were always inimical to Calvinists, and therefore now one group and another allied itself to the Catholics, etc. Only the rulers of the Holy Roman Empire were staunchly Catholic.

The main reason for the wars was rivalry between the Emperors who attempted to subdue the local rulers completely and to turn the Empire into a more unified absolutist state; the Electors, who wanted more independence and wanted the Emperor to be dependent on them; the lesser sovereigns who wanted independence both from the Electors and the Emperor; and the cities, centres of trade and handicraft, pursuing their own interests, often very different from that of the other participants in the war.

The Thirty Years' War spread to all of the territories actually or nominally part of the Holy Roman Empire of the German Nation. Since the emperors belonged to the Habsburg family, the events in Germany were similarly of importance for the Habsburg possessions in Spain. But in the middle of the lands belonging to the French king there were also certain possessions belonging either to the Spanish or to the Austrian Habsburgs. The Netherlands were also involved: here an anti-Habsburg war of liberation had been waged since 1568; likewise Denmark, because its king, being simultaneously the duke of Holstein, was, as regards his Holstein possessions, a vassal of the German emperor. The Electors of Brandenburg of the

---

21. In the Netherlands there emerged self-governing cities, but the country was, until the fifteenth century, mostly dependent upon the dukes of Burgundy (or on the Count of Holland, who served the Holy Roman Empire). After 1516, the Burgundian part of the Netherlands became a part of the dominions of Charles Habsburg, who in the same year became king of Spain as Charles V. The northern provinces, where capitalism was more developed, embraced Calvinism and, as the result of an insurrection of the so-called Gueux ('beggars'), seceded from the empire; some districts continued to recognise William I as Stadholder: he had joined the Gueux. In 1579 the northern Calvinist provinces joined the Union of Utrecht. The Spanish troops of King Philip II, headed by experienced generals, continued the war until the beginning of the seventeenth century; nevertheless, the unstable Dutch Republic, headed by the Estates-General and the Stadholder, and ruled by the assemblies of the individual provinces, retained its independence. The title of Stadholder was later inherited by the family of the dukes of Orange, who, in international relations, ranked as equal to kings.

Hohenzollern family were vassals of the Habsburgs in their capacity as Silesian rulers, and of the Polish kings as rulers of Prussia (which at that period meant only Eastern Prussia). Finally, Sweden, which felt itself strong enough under king Gustavus II Adolphus, aspired to control all the shores of the Baltic, including the German. Gustavus II Adolphus was militarily the strongest adherent to Protestantism. The result was that the French minister, Cardinal Richelieu, in his anti-Habsburg policy, allied himself with the Protestant princes in Germany while persecuting the Calvinists in France; and when in 1635 he declared war on Habsburg Spain, he was supported both by Catholic Catalonia and Portugal, and by Reformed England. The Habsburgs attempted to keep up a free trade route from Spain to the Netherlands through their own territory, since the sea route was no longer feasible after the failed attempt to conquer England in 1588 and the wreck of the Grand Armada: on sea, the English and the rebellious Netherlands were dominant.

The whole history of the Thirty Years' War consists of separate local wars between changing alliances. The armies taking part in it were mostly rather small, and the direct damage they caused was sometimes not very heavy (there were exceptions, for example the burning of the city of Magdeburg; the very important city of Leipzig was bombed and stormed five times, but this did not stop the yearly (!) Leipzig fair). Very heavy losses were caused by plundering, violence, hunger and epidemics which accompanied the war. In some regions the size of the population was reduced by nine-tenths. Some generals, such as Wallenstein, with the support of his loyal troops, turned into something like sovereign princes. The war brought about the end of the Hanseatic League, which was now in fact restricted to the territory of Holland; its decline began in the late sixteenth century, after the destruction of Novgorod by Ivan IV, and of Antwerp by the Spanish, and also as the result of the anti-Hanseatic policy of Queen Elizabeth I of England. Many rich banking houses, such as the Welsers, went bankrupt.

When more than a dozen different states take part at once in a bitter war, and each of them has entirely opposed and changing interests, achieving peace is a feat of tremendous diplomatic difficulty. Nevertheless, according to the Peace of Westphalia (1648) it proved possible to achieve conditions which satisfied nearly everybody.

The peace of Westphalia was concluded upon the following main principle: every state to maintain the religion of its sovereign as of 1624 (there was no longer any idea of suppressing the Lutheran and the Reformed Church). The religious dissenters were allowed to worship privately (except for the direct possessions of the Habsburg crown, where Catholicism was to have a monopoly); the Lutherans, the Calvinists and the Catholics were declared equal before the law. The northern Netherlands (The United Provinces) were acknowledged as a sovereign federation independent of the Empire and headed by a Stadholder belonging to the house of the dukes of Orange; the Netherlands concluded a peace with Spain. France achieved some territorial gains, and some special rights in Lorraine (Lotharingia) and in Alsace. Brandenburg gained a considerable part of Pomerania (on the Baltic coast) and a number of earlier Catholic bishoprics. The Swiss Confederation was declared independent of the Empire. The rest of Pomerania and other domains on the Baltic coast and in the estuaries of the Elbe, the Oder and the Weser were acquired by Sweden; moreover, it received considerable financial assistance. All German states were declared to have sovereign rights, with the only proviso that they should not be used 'against the Emperor and the Empire'.

The result was that there emerged a series of compact absolutist states with a tendency to develop into national states. (This tendency was countervailed by the fact that confessional division of the countries did not completely coincide with the frontiers of the emerging states.) However Brandenburg (Prussia) was clearly Lutheran, Bavaria was Catholic, etc. An Imperial Court was introduced, including twenty six Catholics and twenty four Protestants.

On the whole, it can be said that the Thirty Years' War contributed to the development of Germany, and of Central Europe in general, towards absolutism. The big landowners had made fortunes from supplying goods to the military forces; the bourgeoisie in some of the cities (e.g. Hamburg, Nürnberg) also grew stronger through vast credit operations, while the peasantry was being ruined; in Prussia (including Brandenburg and Pomerania) and in Mecklenburg a very onerous form of serfdom was introduced.

The war, however, continued after 1648; in 1648–1689 France and Spain were in conflict; the result was a correcting of the state frontier between the two countries; it more or less coincided with the national borders.[22] Moreover, in 1655–1661 there occurred the First Northern War between Austria, Poland, Prussia, Denmark and the Netherlands against Sweden (the individual states entered the war and dropped out one by one). The rivalry between these states was complicated by a new war of Russia first against Poland, and then against Sweden.

Let us now turn to the English Revolution.

Its development will be best understood if we start with the problem of enclosures. In the early Middle Ages each village community had a common pasture, which was used by both the peasants and the landowners; only a part of this land was tilled, and the plots of tillage were freely moved within the common. From the eighteenth century, the landowners and the richer peasants attempted to get a certain share of the common land for themselves, and to withdraw it from the rotation of the tilled parts. The rights of the lord of the manor prevailed over the right of the peasants, so that his part tended to diminish the common considerably. Eventually the tilled shares of the peasants were pushed aside, crop rotation became difficult, while the economy of the landlords prospered. Often enclosure was used for the pasture of sheep bred for wool; wool (and later cloth) became an important staple

---

22. However, a part of the territories inhabited by Basques and Catalonians was ceded to France.

of international trade. In some regions enclosures were used to improve the rotation of crops on the landlord's land in his interests.

In principle, enclosure of a part of common land required a compensation in land or money, but the landlords often abused their opportunities; and the result was a pauperisation of the peasants, and many of them fled from their land. At the same time, the landowners could make use of the market. This was the reason why during the Revolution a considerable part of the gentry which had started commodity production allied itself with the owners of the city factories and the richer craftsmen against the noble landlords, and were especially set against the existence of royal and monastic estates. The state attempted to hinder by legal means the process of enclosing land as early as the thirteenth century; protests against the use of common land for breeding sheep for wool were loud in the fifteenth, and especially in the sixteenth century, when the prices for bread rose too high. The authorities attempting to stop the rise of the prices, issued certain laws. However, by the end of the seventeenth century the peasants began to enclose common land; such enclosures became the norm, and only in some parts of the country was it still perceived as a calamity.

A new round of enclosures occurred from the second half of the eighteenth century, but now only after a formal consent of the majority of the inhabitants had been received, and according to an Act of Parliament.

Here we should dwell on the activities of the English Parliament. The Norman kings had gradually introduced the custom of calling together a council of the nobility (its members being at first appointed arbitrarily, but later evolving into a House of Lords, where all representatives of the titled nobility and the more outstanding of the untitled gentlemen had the right to participate). Until the sixteenth century, the lords were the main opponents of royal absolutism. Beside this House, and to a certain degree to counterbalance it, the kings convened representatives of the commons, and especially of the cities. The House of Commons was finally established under Elizabeth I, and became increasingly important for decisions upon matters of state; Elizabeth, however, maintained that questions of religion (the established religion being, since the days of her father Henry VIII, Anglican), and questions of war were prerogatives of the monarch. The House of Commons' demand to participate in ruling the state became insistent during the reign of James I (1603–1625), when members of the House declared their right to introduce taxes, etc. The secularisation of church and monastery lands at the end of the sixteenth century made the untitled gentry more influential.

At that time, the number of Puritans in Parliament increased – at first, the term Puritans was used to describe those adherents of the Church of England who insisted on its more complete purification from traces of Catholicism, and were often opposed to the clerical hierarchy. Among the Puritans, the party of Presbyterians was of the opinion that church administration should be entrusted to laymen (presbyters). Thus Calvinists were regarded as Puritans, as well as

Baptists, Quakers and other radical Christian sects, some of which constituted themselves only later.

King Charles I (reigned from 1625) sympathised with the Catholics but felt he could agree to Anglicanism with a church hierarchy; he also attempted to oppose the Parliament's wish to impose taxes.

From 1629 to 1640 he reigned autocratically (without a Parliament); this induced him to try and procure money by sequestration of land, obligatory loans, etc. A special title 'Baronet' was invented; like a knight, a baronet was addressed as 'Sir N. MM', and his wife was 'Lady MM'. But the title had to be bought from the king. In Scotland (which was united with England under James I, the son of Mary Queen of Scots who was executed by Elizabeth I), King Charles I tried to introduce the Anglican Book of Common Prayer, although Scotland at that time was decidedly Presbyterian. In 1638 the Scots introduced a religious Covenant, and in 1639 they abolished the episcopate. Finally, in the spring of 1640 King Charles I convened a Parliament (named the Short) to vote on taxes, but dissolved it very soon; in the autumn of the same year, however, he was compelled to convene the Parliament again (this was named the Long). The Parliament supported the Scots. In this difficult situation, Charles gave up his ministers to the Parliament, and also his right to collect taxes not approved of by Parliament ('ship-money'), as well as his supreme judicial prerogative. However, Parliament demanded more: it wanted changes in the structure of the Church, a right to install ministers and officials, and to control armaments. In 1641 there was an insurrection in Ireland, but Parliament did not finance the military expedition organised by Charles.

In 1642, after a failed attempt to arrest the parliamentary leaders, Charles I mustered his troops in the centre of England, and then started armed actions against Parliament. The country was divided into Roundheads (adherents of the Parliament), and Cavaliers (adherents of Charles). The gentry was divided, the navy supported the Parliament, and it was also the Parliament that was able to control the manufacture of artillery. Charles had a better cavalry, which, in the beginning, often helped to win his battles. But his financial means were inadequate, so he had to borrow money from his followers and from abroad.

The army of the Parliament was headed by generals belonging to the nobility: the Earl of Essex, Sir Thomas Fairfax, et al. From 1643, Oliver Cromwell became prominent. With the Scottish Puritans (Calvinists), the Parliament contracted the 'Solemn League and Covenant', and in 1644 a Scots army of 20,000 men entered England. Charles concluded an armistice in Ireland (where a war was more or less permanent), and ferried his armed forces over against the Scots; but Cromwell's new cavalry (the 'Ironsides'), the Parliamentary troops, and the Scottish troops inflicted a major defeat on Charles' army at Marston Moor; the royal forces suffered heavy casualties and many were taken prisoner.

In the beginning of 1645, the army of the Parliament was reorganised into the 'New Model Army'; a 'Self-Denying Ordinance' was introduced which meant the dismissing of most of the noble officers from the army; the influence of Cromwell was growing.

Meanwhile, in Scotland a royalist insurrection took place; Charles continued obstinately to refuse the demands of the parliamentarians, but was defeated in the battle of Naseby and retreated into Wales.

Then Charles fled to the royalists in Scotland, but the royalists did not succeed here, and the Scots extradited Charles to the English Parliament. At the same time, the general feeling in the Parliamentary army moved to the left; there appeared new factions – first the Independents, then the Levellers who did not recognise the Church of England, even in its new changed form, and demanded a new, one-house Parliament.

Charles I managed to flee, but his ship was stranded at the Isle of Wight which was in the hands of the Puritans, so the king again became a prisoner. Even from his captivity he attempted to dictate terms (he tried to come to an agreement with the Scots on the base of an official recognition of Puritanism).

The Civil War, having for a time subsided, was renewed: a section of the former Protestants who distrusted the Parliament joined the Royalists. But these opponents were crushingly defeated by Fairfax and Cromwell. Their army demanded a formal, public trial of the king; at the same time, it purged the Parliament not only of the adherents of the Church of England, but even of Presbyterians. In January 1649, King Charles I was sentenced to death and publicly executed. This did not end the Civil War which continued until 1651.

Although the parties at war for the most part did not harass the unarmed population (except in Ireland), the burden of civil war was felt by everybody. Piracy made overseas trade difficult, the taxes were heavy, and all parties wanted to pay off old scores. It was just at that period that England's hatred of a standing and garrisoned army has its origin. The population demanded complete freedom of religion, and this also became part of English culture.

At this period the Church of England divided into the High Church, which was practically Catholicism minus the worship of saints and the use of Latin in the service, and the Low Church which preserved more features of Protestantism; but from the point of view of organisation they are both one 'Church of England', and have a common hierarchy and administration.

The events in England between 1642 and 1651 brought about the creation of a 'low' variant of the Church of England, as well as a number of non-conformist religious denominations, such as the Quakers, the Baptists, et al.

When Fairfax refused to invade Scotland and to take part in the Civil War which was being waged there, the actual power in England passed to Cromwell.

From the end of 1651, Cromwell lived in the royal residence, taking possession of the royal property. The Parliament was curtailed to the Independents' 'Rump', but its members were accused of corruption, and in April 1653 Cromwell abolished it, introducing instead a Nominated Parliament. This Parliament, issuing a document called the Instrument of Government, made Cromwell Lord-Protector. Referring to a possibility of a Royalist insurrection, Cromwell introduced a new administrative system: the country was divided into eleven military districts headed by Major-Generals. There was some talk of crowning Cromwell and creating a new House of Lords recruited from his followers, but the army objected.

In May 1657 Cromwell declined the crown but accepted a new Constitution presented by the Parliament under the name of 'Humble Petition and Advice'. In 1658 he dissolved the Parliament.

Cromwell entered into advantageous trade agreements with the Netherlands (after a period of war), as well as Sweden, Denmark and Portugal. At this period there was a war between France and Spain, and Cromwell sided with France, because there, unlike in Spain, the Protestants were to a certain degree defeated by the Edict of Nantes. The English navy captured Spanish Jamaica in the Caribbean Sea, and France ceded to England two ports on the shore of the Channel.

It was Cromwell who introduced English into the courts of Common Law where French had hitherto been the official language. He established a 'freedom' of religion, but Catholic and Church of England services were allowed only privately.

Oliver Cromwell died in 1658. His son Richard Cromwell did not manage to remain in power. The troops of General Monk arrived from Scotland and occupied London. The Presbyterians decided that the only way to avoid complete anarchy was to reintroduce royal power, and Charles Stuart was called back from exile and crowned King of England in 1661. The new king declared a general amnesty; his policy was, on the whole, successful and rational. His wife, a Portuguese princess, brought him, as dowry, a Portuguese colony in India – the island of Bombay. This was the beginning of the British Empire in India.

In England, with Charles II, there began a period which may be likened to the period of absolutism in France. In Parliament, the upper stratum of the gentry was represented, and it was compliant until the question of the king's successor arose. Charles had fourteen children who all were born out of wedlock; his heir-apparent was his brother James who was, first in secret and later openly, a staunch Catholic. This induced the Catholics to become active and attracted harsh reprisals; James had temporarily to go abroad. When James II became king (1685–1689) he officially sought support from the Anglican High Church but made attempts to grant equal rights for the Catholics. A group of noble Anglicans appealed for help to the Stadtholder of five provinces of the Netherlands, William III Prince of Orange, who was married to James' sister Mary. James fled, and William and Mary were called to power. They ruled with the help of the Parliament, but since capitalism was still undeveloped in the country, the Parliament mainly represented the gentry.

Summing up the results of the English revolution, which we have described in more detail than many other periods of history, we would like to draw the reader's attention to the fact that this revolution developed according to a pattern which seems to be typical of all large-scale social revolutions. They are triggered off by less radical groups that gradually give way to groups more and more radical (Anglicans, Presbyterians, Independents, Levellers), and the revolution ends with a personal dictatorship.

In England, during the revolutionary years 1642–1649, the bourgeoisie had not managed to acquire full power, although it was not totally kept away from it; still less had it an occasion to come to power in France (in spite of the role played by such a representative of the bourgeoisie as Colbert); neither did it acquire power in other countries, except, perhaps, in the independent Netherlands.

The extent to which the medieval regime still prevailed in Europe can be illustrated by the War of Spanish Succession which began in 1701 and was caused by purely dynastic and medieval considerations.

The Spanish King Philip III (1598–1621) married one of his daughters to the French King Louis XIII, and another to the future Habsburg emperor Ferdinand III. Their heirs were Louis XIV of France, and Leopold I Habsburg; both were also married to Spanish princesses, daughters of Philip IV. The wife of Louis XIV declared that her descendants should not lay claim to the Spanish throne, but the wife of Leopold I did not make any similar declaration. The daughter of the latter married Maximilian, the Elector of Bavaria. Meanwhile, the Spanish King Carlos II, brother of Leopold's first wife (the spouse of Louis XIV was born by another wife of Philip IV), died without leaving sons. Leopold persuaded his daughter (the one who had married the Elector) to cede her rights to his children from his third marriage, in spite of the fact that she had a son of her own who had better claim to the Spanish crown. At the same time, Louis XIV, in spite of the fact that his wife had resigned her rights to the Spanish throne, laid claim to it for his grandsons.

Has the reader grasped the interesting situation? These family disagreements brought about a war in Europe which lasted from 1701 to 1713.

I am sure I am allowed to omit the events of this war, which involved the Netherlands, England and some Italian states, and the feats of the generals – the Duke of Marlborough, Prince Eugene of Savoy et al.; we shall only discuss its results for Europe as a whole, and how they were reflected in the Peace of Utrecht (1713) and in the further agreements of 1714 and 1715.[23]

France refrained from supporting the followers of the Catholic Stuart dynasty in England, but ceded to it a considerable part of its possessions in America (in present-day Canada). A trade agreement with England was signed; the French made certain concessions to the United Provinces of the Netherlands, also accompanied by a trade agreement; peace was concluded with Prussia, Savoy (on the border

---

23. A virtual continuation of the War of Spanish Succession was the Seven Years' War (1756–1763), which again involved France, Britain (and also Hanover in Germany, since it belonged to the British kings of the period), Austria, Prussia, and then also Russia, Spain, Portugal, and the British and French colonies in America. According to the peace treaties, a redistribution of colonies between Britain, Spain and France was arranged for, in America and partly in Africa, in Germany, the *status quo* was re-established.

between France and Italy), and with Portugal. Spain acknowledged the exclusive right of England to import black slaves to America, and ceded to it the rights to Gibraltar, to the island of Menorca, and to Santo-Domingo; still another trade agreement was made between Spain and England. The dynasty of Savoy received the island of Sicily. A peace was also concluded between Spain and the Netherlands, between Spain and Portugal. Of all the rulers the German emperor continued the war for the longest time, but finally he too concluded a peace with all his opponents. France received Alsace; the emperor received more: the Spanish possessions in Italy, the Catholic part of the Netherlands, and Sardinia. Philip V (Bourbon), the grandson of Louis XIV, was officially recognised as King of Spain after he had renounced his personal and hereditary rights to the French throne.

The period of prolonged military actions which agitated Europe was succeeded by trade agreements; this was to the advantage of the European bourgeoisie, at that period being definitely on the rise.

The scholars and the scientists of the eighteenth century – the so-called Age of Reason, or Enlightenment – laid the foundation for the development of sciences, which was not only characteristic of, but to a considerable degree decisive for, the next, Seventh (Bourgeois) Phase of the development of mankind. The most important scholarly and scientific works of this epoch were written in French. During that period French emerged as the common language of educated Europe.

Among the most important names of the Age of Enlightenment we should, perhaps first of all, name Montesquieu (1689–1755), the author of *De l'esprit de lois* (1748), a work which for the first time in history pointed out the necessity of a division of powers (the legislative, the executive, and the judicial). This principle was later to determine the entire state structure of the civilised societies of the Seventh and the Eighth Phase. Next we should mention Beccaria (1738–1794), the author of the treatise 'On crimes and punishments' (first published in Italian in 1764, translated into twenty two languages). He could prove that torture and secret investigation cannot lead to establishing the truth, and that social prevention of crime is more important than punishment; he decided that capital punishment was not an adequate method for combating crime. The materialist philosopher Diderot (1713–1784), and the mathematician, mechanician and philosopher D'Alembert (1717–1783) created the great French *Encyclopédie, ou Dictionnaire raisonné des sciences, des arts et des métiers*, in which many of the most brilliant men of France took part. The Encyclopedists thought positive knowledge and tolerance most important for society. For them, the mental activity was subdivided into memory, reason and imagination, leaving no place for faith. We should also mention Holbach (1723–1789), one of the main authors of the *Encyclopédie*, who was a convinced materialist and atheist: for him the cause-and-effect connections were mechanical, man is a mechanism, and soul does not exist, there is no God; man must recognise necessity and follow nature. Then Voltaire should be mentioned (1649–1778), author of fiction, historian, wit and thinker, courageous adversary of clerical reaction, the

Inquisition, serfdom and customs barriers, and an adherent of deism (i.e. an English philosophical trend of the late seventeenth–early eighteenth century, which recognised the existence of God, but thought it proper to honour God not by ritual, but by virtue). Voltaire corresponded with Catherine II of Russia,[24] and stayed for a time at the courts of Louis XV and Frederic II of Prussia. And finally, we have to mention Rousseau[25] (1712–1778), an author and a thinker of quite a different sort, less sceptical and more emotional, the author of the book *Du contrat social*, which left a very strong impression on intelligent mankind; he maintained that man is good by nature, that original sin does not exist, and that man's evil actions are conditioned by the unreasonable structure of society.

These men originated from quite different social strata. Both Montesquieu and Holbach were barons, Voltaire and d'Alembert were illegitimate children, and it took them some time to be recognised as gentlemen; Diderot and Rousseau were petty bourgeois. They created whole systems of socio-psychological orientation, which were different from the official Catholic ideology universally recognised by the people.

A society which had read the *Encyclopédie*, Voltaire and Rousseau, was ready not simply for a change of social and historical phases, but actually for revolution. That it occurred unexpectedly and violently, can to a certain degree be explained by the fact that in the seventeenth and eighteenth centuries France lacked that psychological safety-valve which in other European countries was created by the different currents of Protestantism. In France, the Huguenots were suppressed by the revocation of the Edict of Nantes in 1685. The majority of them fled the country; those who remained were few, persecuted and kept on the outskirts of society. The Calvinist religion did not open such vistas as did the teachings of the Encyclopedists, of Voltaire and Rousseau, who were very prestigious for all Europe.

In 1789 the Great French Revolution began. Along with the American Revolution of 1775 it led to a Phase transition which resulted in the termination of the Sixth (Post-Medieval) Phase of the historical process. The period from 1789 to 1848 cannot be considered to have been a separate Phase, but must be regarded as a transition from the Sixth to the Seventh Phase.

Before we pass on to the events of the Phase transition, let us briefly review what happened in North America, which had gradually begun to play a more and more important role in world history.

The colonisation of the Atlantic shore of North America began in the seventeenth century. In 1606 a London company and a Plymouth company each received a charter from King James I for settling two stretches of this shore. The first colony (1607) was Virginia, so called after the 'virgin' Queen Elizabeth I. In 1620, a group of sectaries ('The Pilgrim Fathers') founded a colony in Massachusetts. Then began a

24. On Russia during the Sixth Phase see below, pp. 186–7.
25. Rousseau's family were Calvinists of Geneva.

rapid settlement of the Atlantic coast, mainly by people dissatisfied with the religious policy of Charles I. In twenty years, about 20,000 people had settled in America. The colonists of 'New England' were practically self-governed, the governing body coinciding with the parish. A section of the colonies organised a military federation against the Indians, the French and the Dutch: the French had settled in what was later to be Canada, as well as in the estuary of the Mississippi, the Dutch – in 'New Amsterdam' (from 1621; in 1664 it was captured by the English and renamed New York, in honour of the Duke of York, the heir apparent, later King James II). The most successful of the colonies was Pennsylvania, founded by Quakers. The colony Maryland was founded by Catholics who had fled from persecutions by Protestants in England.

By the end of the seventeenth century each of England's North American colonies had its governor, council and assembly. In the northern colonies not only agriculture but also trade and manufactories were developing. In the southern ones, agricultural estates developed (mainly growing cotton), employing slave labour. Negroes, captured by pirates or sold by their own local chiefs, were being imported overseas in masses stored in the ship's hull, under quite inhuman conditions. The fact that production was based on slave-owning in the southern colonies did not impair the possibility of their union with the northern colonies, where capitalism was developing. We have already noted that slavery is possible in all phases of the historical process.

Import and export to the colonies were strictly regulated by England. The English government also attempted to hinder their industrial development. In the colonies, religious tolerance was the rule, in spite of the fact that some of the colonies did recognise a certain confession as a leading one. There was an influx of all kinds of religious dissenters, including Huguenots, Presbyterians, Quakers and even Jews. The ideological conditions were conducive to enlightenment: from 1636 to 1769 seven colleges and universities were founded. The French had to be kept back by military means; and so were the native inhabitants who were pushed further and further to the west during the eighteenth century and the first half of the nineteenth century.

From 1764, the English government began to assert its sovereignty in the colonies, both politically and militarily. The colonists responded by boycotting English commodities.

In March 1770 five Americans lost their lives during a scuffle in Boston (the 'Boston massacre'). In 1773 the so-called 'Boston Tea Party' took place, in which chests of tea on which English duty was to be paid were thrown into the sea.

In 1774 a Continental Congress was convened at Philadelphia to protest against the violation of the 'rights of man' by the British Parliament. In April 1775 British troops began a war against the colonies, but it was first in 1776 that the leader of the colonists, George Washington, raised the question of their total liberation from England. The Second Continental Congress approved a Declaration of Independence. Its preamble contained the following statement:

We hold these truths to be self-evident, that all men are created equal, that they are endowed by their Creator with certain unalienable Rights, that among these are Life, Liberty and the pursuit of Happiness. – That to secure these rights, Governments are instituted among Men, deriving their just powers from the consent of the governed, – That whenever any Form of Government becomes destructive to these ends, it is the Right of the People to alter or to abolish it, and to institute new Government ... Prudence, indeed, will dictate that Governments long established should not be changed for light and transient causes ... But when a long train of abuses and usurpations, pursuing invariably the same Object evinces a design to reduce them under absolute Despotism, it is their right, it is their duty, to throw off such Government for their future security.

It is well known that American colonies gained their independence, and in 1789 the Constitution of the United States was approved. It guaranteed a division of powers (according to Montesquieu), the individual rights, and the right of Congress to repeal such decrees of the President which did not agree with the Constitution. In 1791 the first ten Amendments were approved, which were formulated by James Madison and which are regarded as the Bill of Rights. It declared (1) freedom of religion, speech, the press, meetings and petitions; (2) the right of all citizens to bear arms;[26] (3) limitations on quartering soldiers in private houses; (4) prohibition of unreasonable searches and seizures and issue of warrants except upon probable cause, directed against specific persons and places; (5) necessity of a 'Grand Jury' indictment in prosecution for major crimes, and prohibition of double jeopardy for a single offence; no person shall be compelled to testify against himself; life, liberty or property shall not be taken without due process of law; private property is not to be taken for public use without just compensation; (6) an accused person is to have a speedy and open trial by jury in the state where the crime was committed; the accused is to be informed of the nature of the accusation, to be confronted with witnesses and to have assistance of counsel; (7) civil causes to be tried by jury; (8) excessive bail and cruel or unusual punishments are forbidden; (9) the enumerated rights are not to exclude additional legal rights; (10) powers not delegated to the United States are reserved to the states and the people. Subsequent Amendments to the Constitution established the rules for the election of the President, the abolition of slavery, rules of citizenship, and rules for the representation of citizens in Congress.

After the Second World War the Bill of Rights was to become the basis for the Charter of the United Nations. By no means do all the citizens of modern states enjoy all the rights formulated in the Bill, but certainly it is the world-wide ideological and socio-psychological base not so much for the societies of the Seventh

---

26. This made every citizen equal to a member of the gentry, cf. the comprehensive use of the term 'gentleman' in American and in British English.

Phase (which had for the most part not been able to reach the corresponding level of development), as for the Eighth, Post-Industrial Phase.

After 1789–1791, the United States of America entered upon the path of bourgeois development; here the Seventh Phase received its final form after the liberation of slaves in the Southern States after the Civil War of 1861–1865.

Note that all the advantages granted by the Constitution and the Bill of Rights did not accrue to the aboriginal population, which came into contact with the colonists at a time when it still belonged to the First and partly the Second Phase. The United States were nearly constantly at war with some of the aboriginal tribes, and waged it not only against men, but also against women and children, until the remnants of the aboriginal population were settled in reservations, especially (after 1830) on the barren lands of the Indian Territory in Oklahoma. Here the native people temporarily had a sort of self-government; but from the second half of the nineteenth century the Indian Teritory was opened to white settlers; at present the state of Oklahoma has less than 5 per cent native population.

Now let us return from the USA to its former metropolis.

The base for the capitalist structure which became the leading feature of society in the Seventh Phase was laid in the Post-Medieval Sixth Phase, during the so-called Industrial Revolution. It is important to note that the revolution occurred not only in general technology (and, at a later date, specifically in the technology of arms production), but also in social psychology: the former mentality had given way to a new one.

During the eighteenth century, mainly in England but to certain degree also in France, there were a number of technical discoveries and innovations. Among the most important were the mechanisation of the weaving loom ('the flying shuttle', 1739), of the spinning frame (1764–1769), the invention of puddle iron which revolutionised iron production (1767–1784), and the harnessing of water power (1769). During the eighteenth and the very beginning of the nineteenth century technical knowledge became a most important productive force, and this was the main substance and the most important result of the Industrial Revolution. The latter became possible because the knowledge of Nature had greatly increased: science began to influence Nature, and it was highly influential upon the processes of production. It is important to note that the inventors (such as J. Watt) were able to find capitalists who were ready to finance their experiments at a moment when these still did not yet yield any profits. This was the result of an accumulation of capital during the previous two centuries.

Adam Smith, in his book *Inquiry into the Nature and Cause of the Wealth of Nations* (1776), supplied a scientific and ideological basis for capitalism. He suggested that any kind of bureaucratic management of national economy should be abolished, and that the free play of a self-regulating market should be allowed to develop. He did not deceive himself by assuming inordinate moral qualities to capitalists, but he was sure that under the conditions of free competition they would not seriously harm society; through free competition private gain would be to the common good. In this he was somewhat too optimistic.

Developments in France were similar to those in England, but here industrial development was hampered by the absolutist state. Although Colbert's reforms helped to a certain degree to move the country towards the Capitalist Phase, there was much that stood in the way of such development. It suffices to point out that inner customs barriers had been first abolished only by the French Revolution.

Under the Hanover dynasty in England (from 1714)[27] royal power was limited by Parliament. The gentry were more strongly represented in Parliament than the bourgeoisie, but they too derived some profit from capitalist incomes.

The textile industry had a rural and domestic character, until mechanisation brought it into the cities. These were not the cities which had existed from times immemorial, but quite new industrial centres. The new cities, as often as not, were either not represented in the Parliament at all, or only quite inadequately.

An important factor which moved European society towards new ways was the growth of the population, which for those times was huge; this population could no longer be fed by medieval methods.

As we have seen above, the English Revolution of the seventeenth century did not bring the bourgeoisie to power as a class, but it had strengthened immensely its position in society. The first true bourgeois revolution was in France.

In 1787, Louis XVI, King of France, convened the Estates-General at Versailles. This body had not been assembled since 1614. The king hoped to mobilise resources for paying the public debts which had grown out of all proportion. Meanwhile, educated sections of French society was excited by the radical successes of the American revolution, and its representatives, having met at the Estates-General, began to feel themselves as a force which was able to insist on serious reform. In the beginning the Estates met separately (there were 300 deputies from the gentry and nobility, 300 from the clergy, and 600 from the 'third estate', comprising mainly the city bourgeoisie). The representatives of the third estate, meeting separately, declared the Estates-General to be a National Assembly. Some of the progressive representatives of the other estates joined it (thus the Marquis de Lafayette, the Abbé Sieyès and others). The National Assembly decided not to dissolve until a Constitution was introduced, and to form a sort of Parliament after the English pattern. This amounted to the seizing of the state power by the French bourgeoisie, and to the downfall of the so-called *ancien régime*. At the same time a popular uprising began in Paris. On 14 July 1789 it was symbolically celebrated by the storming and destruction of the state prison in Paris, the Bastille. In the provinces the peasants mutinied; the National Assembly abolished the feudal regime and the tithes. Then the Assembly introduced the *Declaration of the Rights of Man and the*

---

27. George I, elector of Hanover, was a son of the granddaughter of James I , who was the heir of Anne, Queen of England, the last of the Stuarts; thus George I inherited the right to the British throne.

Citizen, which declared freedom, equality, the inviolability of property, and the right to resist oppression. The declaration was based on the ideas of Rousseau and Locke. No mention of any special rights of the workers was made, and the slaves in the colonies were not liberated, but the Declaration was formulated in such a way that it could be applied not only to France but to all mankind. Louis XVI refused to sanction the decisions of the National Assembly, but people marched towards his residence at Versailles and brought the king to Paris, where he consented to agree to the Declaration.

The Assembly declared itself Constituent, i.e. empowered to grant the country a Constitution. First of all, equal rights in the election to state offices were declared, and ecclesiastical and monastic land ownership was abolished (the clergy were allotted salaries from the state); this lead to a general redistribution of land. The bourgeoisie and the richer peasants started buying up the land and sold it again. While the general economic situation deteriorated, the speculation in land and in corn helped certain parts of the population to get richer. The existing system of administrative segmentation of the country was changed; it was now divided into 'departments' approximately equal in size; the customs barriers were abolished, a system of elected judges was introduced. It was declared that the power of the monarchy would be limited by the legislative assembly elected by all citizens paying taxes not lower than a certain level. However Louis XVI did not agree to such a change in the state structure: he tried to flee but was apprehended and brought back to Paris.

The French Revolution called forth sympathy and many hopes in the neighbouring countries, which suffered from much the same problems.[28] In these countries revolutionary clubs now appeared in numbers, and the absolute monarchs, frightened by the events, began to introduce anti-revolutionary measures. Many French noblemen emigrated. Austria, Prussia and England were opposed to revolutionary France, and in April 1792 France declared war against Austria and Prussia. It lasted, off and on, during all the revolutionary years and also later, under Napoleon I. In the beginning, the allies were more or less successful. Fearing treason, the revolutionaries arrested the king in August 1792.

In September of the same year, after the French victory at Valmy, the new legislative – the Convention – started its work. Here, at first, the leading role was played by the Girondins, who attempted not only to establish a bourgeois republic in France, but also, if possible, to spread its ideas abroad. They were opposed by the Jacobins (or the Mountain), headed by Robespierre, who advocated the spread of the revolution not so much outwards, as in depth, with granting of all rights also to the indigent citizens, or *sans-culottes*. The Jacobins arranged a trial of the king, and obtained his condemnation and execution in January 1793. The Girondins were ousted from the Convention and many of them were also executed.

Meanwhile the food supply in the cities deteriorated. The Jacobins tried to limit

28. Serfdom had been abolished in Czechia already in 1784, and in Hungary in 1785.

prices, increased the taxes on the rich, declared the necessity of social protection of the poor and infirm, made education free of charge and universal, confiscated the property of the émigrés and of the executed persons (it was intended that the confiscated property was to be dealt out to the poor, but this measure was not carried out). The Jacobin reforms induced resistance and even insurrections, both in some of the cities (Lyon, Bordeaux) and in the countryside (Vendée, Normandy, Provence). The Jacobins responded by an enormous wave of Terror. The journalist Marat led an unbridled campaign of denunciations which immediately resulted in executions (he was killed by the young terrorist Charlotte Corday). Seventeen thousand persons were publicly beheaded, which created horror and anger in the general population; still more people were put to death in other ways (e.g., by drowning in barges) or died in prison. (Later the Bolsheviks were to take account of the mistakes of the Jacobins and shot their prisoners in secret.)

At the same time, inside the Convention there was an embittered struggle for power: the more radical deputies strove to arrest and execute their recent allies – even the leaders of the *sans-culottes*. Meanwhile, the situation of the French armies at the front improved.

The social and economic limitations and the Terror introduced by Robespierre, as well as also the shortage of food, induced the surviving part of the Convention to arrest Robespierre and to execute him (according to the revolutionary calendar, on Thermidor 9 of the year II of the Republic; i.e. 27 July 1794). The extreme economic measures of Robespierre were abolished. The Royalists made renewed attempts to retaliate, but they were suppressed by a young general, the Corsican Napoleon Bonaparte. The Convention voted for the introduction of a new Constitution and dissolved itself. The power was taken over by the Directory, an executive of five persons; a new bicameral Parliament was introduced; in both bodies a yearly rotation was contemplated, but actually the rule of the Directory was interrupted by its forcible reorganisations.

The advance of the French revolutionary armies continued. In 1795 Holland, Toscana, Prussia and Spain asked for peace. As the result of Bonaparte's Italian campaign in 1796, Sardinia and Austria did the same (Sardinia ceding to France Piedmont and Savoy in north-western Italy). In the conquered territories, republics after the French pattern were founded: the Batavian in Holland, the Cisalpine and the Ligurian in Northern Italy. The Directory continued the foreign policy of the Girondins – that of exporting the revolution to Europe – which made them respond to the appeals of the local Jacobins. In 1798–1799 the French conquered Switzerland (which became the Helvetian Republic), Rome and Naples (the Roman and the Parthenopean Republics). The Directory hoped to threaten England through her Indian dominions; to reach them, it organised a French military (and scientific!) expedition headed by Bonaparte, to Malta, Egypt and Palestine; but the French fleet was defeated by the British admiral Nelson near the Egyptian coast; Bonaparte had to leave Egypt and, with difficulty, to return to France.

The French threat led to the formation of a new coalition of powers in 1798–1799 (Austria, Russia, Turkey and England); the coalition began to advance on a wide front against the territories conquered by France. The French blamed the Directory for the defeats; Bonaparte, on the other hand, called forth enthusiasm by his victories. On 18 Brumaire of the year VIII (9 November 1799) the personal supreme power of the First Consul – General Bonaparte – was proclaimed; in 1804 he assumed the title 'Emperor of the French'.

Note that the authority of the First Consul (later, that of the First Consul for life) was acquired by Bonaparte by popular vote, with an overwhelming majority: the people were tired of *sans-culottes* in any form, and wanted strong power.

Napoleon was a 'man of the Revolution': it was only the Revolution which could raise a thirty-year old Corsican to supreme power in a mighty republic. But he did not believe in the sovereign right of the people in parliamentary debates. His attitude towards religion was that of Voltaire: he regarded as possible the existence of a Supreme Being, but he was sure that people needed a certain religion. He made an agreement with the Pope and received from him the imperial crown.

Somewhat earlier a code of law, which had been in preparation for some time, was promulgated; later it came to be known as the 'Code Napoleon'. It secured important achievements of the revolution such as personal freedom, freedom of conscience, freedom of labour, the secular character of the state, equality before the law, protection of private property (note that a considerable part of the land had already passed into the hands of the bourgeoisie and partly of the peasants); a greater freedom for the employers; but no special guarantees were introduced for the working class. This was a code needed for the bourgeoisie which at last was coming to power – and this was what Napoleon brought to the countries he was conquering. No wonder that his conquest was at first welcomed as a liberation, and that the main provisions of the Code Napoleon were introduced in many European countries. However, the title of Emperor presupposed the creation of an imperial court and of an imperial nobility; and the continuation of wars implied the keeping of a strict order in the country, which was enforced by Napoleon's ministers, especially by Fouché, the head of the police, and Talleyrand, the head of the diplomatic service.

Napoleon continued the wars of the French Revolution; however, just at the moment of his coming to power he was practically at peace with the Continental powers. Inside the country, he had his successes: inflation was brought under control, the Royalist opposition was suppressed; but Britain remained an inveterate enemy, and Napoleon was preparing a military invasion of the British Isles. At the same time, for England, the only way to resist France was by allying itself to Continental countries. France had no superiority at sea, and so made a military alliance with Spain, but the Franco-Spanish fleet was destroyed in 1805 in the battle of Trafalgar near the Mediterranean shore of Spain by admiral Nelson (who was himself killed in battle). Thus the anticipated French invasion of England became impossible.

England organised an anti-Napoleon coalition including Austria, Russia, Sweden and Naples (here a Bourbon kingdom had been resurrected). Napoleon quickly moved his forces into the centre of Europe and brought about a crushing defeat of Austria, and then, at Austerlitz, in December 1805, of Russia, capturing Vienna. Austria ceded Venice and the eastern shore of the Adriatic to France; some territories were ceded to German states which had allied themselves to Napoleon. The throne of the kingdom of Naples was given to Napoleon's brother Joseph. In 1806 the Confederation of the Rhine was established in Germany under Napoleon's protectorate. As the result of a deal with the Russian emperor Alexander I at Tilsit (in Eastern Prussia), there was signed an agreement about the division of spheres of influence between Russia and France. The Prussian part of Poland was made Duchy of Warsaw which was to be in vassalage to Napoleon, who received also other territorial and political concessions.

In 1807–1808 serfdom was abolished in Prussia and Bavaria.

Against Britain Napoleon introduced a Continental Blockade: all European ports (including the Russian) were closed to British trade. Napoleon hoped to induce a crisis of over-production in England. The only factor which disturbed the possibility of introducing total French domination in Europe was the continuing war in Spain and Portugal. Portugal became allied with England; in Spain the Bourbon dynasty[29] was deposed by Napoleon, but here he encountered a resolute popular resistance, which was supported by British troops.

When Austria again confronted Napoleon, it suffered a crushing defeat in the battle of Wagram, and a new peace was signed in Vienna; Napoleon married the daughter of the Austrian emperor, and in 1811 she bore him an heir. By 1810, Napoleon's empire included, apart from France, also Belgium, Holland and part of Italy; in a number of German, Spanish and Italian states (in Naples, in Lucca) there nominally reigned Napoleon's brothers and brothers-in-law. Also Switzerland, the Confederation of the Rhine and the Duchy of Warsaw were Napoleon's protectorates; Austria[30] was allied to Napoleon by marriage.

It is interesting and characteristic that Napoleon's troops carried all through Europe the revolutionary hymn 'Marseillaise'.

Meanwhile, amongst the thinking part of Europe's population, which had applauded the conceptions of the French Revolution and the fixing of its social achievements in the Code Napoleon, there began to develop ideas of national revival; the psychological base for the future creation of capitalist national states all over Europe was laid, although these ideas could actually be realised only at a later date. But the Spanish insurgents promulgated a Constitution in 1812 which united the ideas of the French Revolution with the principles of the British State system.

29. Louis XIV, king of France of the Bourbon dynasty, managed, during the war of Spanish Succession, to place his grandson Philip on the throne of Spain.
30. Actually, the state began to be called simply 'Austria' only after Napoleon's victory; before that, it still was termed the Holy Roman Empire of the German Nation.

Napoleon was dissatisfied with Russia because it did not keep strictly enough to the conditions of Continental Blockade (which actually was very disadvantageous for the Russian economy), and in the summer of 1812 his army of more than half a million men crossed the Neman which at that time was the frontier of the Russian empire. The following is well known from Russian history: the retreat of Barclay de Tolly, and later of Kutuzov to inner Russia along the Old Smolensk road, the battle of Borodino, Kutuzov's withdrawing to the flank, Napoleon capturing Moscow, its burning down, the disastrous retreat of the French, the catastrophic crossing of the Berezina, the final withdrawal of only ten thousand efficient French soldiers, the continuation of the war in Western Europe until the Russian, the Austrian, and the other allied troops entered Paris in 1814.

In Russia, Napoleon made a fatal blunder. Regarding Russia as an Asiatic power incapable of European forms of development, he made no attempt to win the population over to his side by giving it at least the same amount of liberty which he conceded to Germany and Italy – at least abolishing serfdom.

In 1813 Napoleon was able to restore his military power, but now those who waged war against him were not armies of hirelings or peasant serfs mobilised by force, but national forces fighting for the freedom of their own states. In the great 'Battle of Nations' at Leipzig in June 1813 Napoleon's 'Grande Armée' was routed. A collapse of Napoleon's armed forces began, and by the beginning of 1814 the allies reached the French frontiers. They declared that they were waging war not against the French nation but only against Napoleon. The French army consisted of young conscripts. The allies showed exemplary unanimity, and achieved successes all along. In April 1814 Napoleon abdicated. He was granted a 'state' of his own on the little island of Elba between France and Italy; King Louis XVIII of the Bourbon dynasty returned to France.

It is well known what followed: the 'Hundred days' in 1815, when Napoleon managed to recapture France, and the battle of Waterloo in Belgium, which he lost to the British General Wellington and the Prussian General Blücher; and then the exile to the distant islet of Saint Helena in the southern part of the Atlantic Ocean, where he died in 1821.

During 1804–1814 the general losses of France amounted to approximately 1,750,000 men.

The power in Europe passed now to the 'Holy Alliance' which included Russia, Austria and Prussia, and also Britain (later France as well); they decided the fate of the continent at their congresses of 1818, 1820, 1821 and 1822. Any movement of the nations towards their liberation (even from Turkey) was suppressed by the 'Holy Alliance', and all possible measures were taken in order to return Europe into the former Phase of development.[31]

---

31. This was difficult to achieve. The Code Napoléon was not repealed wherever it had been introduced. In 1820, serfdom was abolished in the last German state – in Mecklenburg; an unreserved return to the old Post-Medieval order it had not been possible to achieve anywhere.

The bourgeoisie began to return to power – this time finally introducing the Seventh, Capitalist Phase of the historical process – but only after the parliamentary reform of 1832 in England, after the 1830 and 1848 revolutions in France, in the German states, in Austria, in Hungary, after the abolition of serfdom in Russia in 1861, and of slavery in the USA in 1864. Thus the middle of the nineteenth century was the beginning of the next, Seventh Phase.

Hitherto we have followed the history of the Sixth Phase (and its passage into the Seventh) only in Western Europe and in America. Let us now turn to the same Phase in Eastern Europe.

There had been no real economic or political progress in Poland during the sixteenth–seventeenth centuries, in spite of the fact that it assumed politically the role of a great power. Poland was drawn into typically medieval wars: into a struggle with the Cossacks of Zaporozye,[32] into the rivalry between Moscow and the Khans of Crimea, and of the Habsburgs (in the Holy Roman Empire) with the Bourbons (in France). It had Frenchmen, Hungarians and Swedes as its kings, which drew the country into unnecessary wars; all this hindered the passage into a new historical Phase.

The peace of Andrusowo with Russia (1667) left Poland, territorially, still a very big state, but politically it was undermined by constant conflicts between the kings and the assemblies (*seims*) of the gentry. In 1652 right of *liberum veto* was introduced, according to which a single vote 'against' could kill any bill. A fierce struggle took place between the great noble families who together owned nearly half of Poland: the Czartoryski and the Potocki. The natural result of all this was the intervention

32. During the fifteenth and sixteenth centuries, in connection with the aggravation of the exploiting of peasants both in Russia and in those parts of Poland where the inhabitants belonged to the Orthodox Church (the Ukraine), groups of armed peasants began to wander southwards and eastwards, into the steppes, where they founded free self-governing communities of a military-republican type. They called themselves 'Cossacks' (a Turkish word denoting freemen); sometimes they were loosely dependent on Moscow. Thus a number of 'Cossack armies' became settled as the 'armies' of the Don, the Terek, the Hrebenskoye, the Ural, Siberia, etc. Every able-bodied Cossack was regarded as (and actually was) a soldier. The Cossacks regarded the Crimean Tatars, the Nogias, the Chechens, the Buriats and other neighbouring non-Orthodox peoples as natural enemies; they were intermittently at war and at peace with these neighbours.

A very special type of Cossacks were the Zaporozhye (Ukr. *Zaporizhzhe*, lit. 'Trans-Cataract') Cossacks; they had a fortified camp, the *Sich*, south of the Dnieper cataracts. They did not serve for life; in their old age they returned to their original villages north of the cataracts; these villages were mostly on territory paying tribute to Poland. A Zaporozhye Cossack wore a special set of clothes, a long forelock (*oselédets*) but shaved his head and, being introduced into 'cossackship', he had to swear on oath that he belonged to the Orthodox Church and was of sober behaviour. The Zaporozhye Cossacks made predatory raids against the Crimean and the Turkish dominions. In the eighteenth century (under Catherine II) a minority of the Zaporozhye Cossacks migrated to countries belonging to the Turks, but the majority was re-settled in the valley of the Kuban River; these received the same status as the Don Cossacks 'army' and the others; but they retained the Ukrainian language, while the other Cossacks spoke a Russian dialect. The Russian Tsars regarded the Cossacks as a barrier against armed attacks from the South and the East, and for a long time did not meddle in their internal affairs.

of foreign powers in Polish affairs, and then the division of Poland in 1772–1795 between Russia, Austria and Prussia.

The post-medieval society was in Russia still in a state of Phase transition under Peter I (1682–1725; ruling independently from 1689). Under Peter, the free cities which had once existed in Russia disappeared; there was practically no bourgeoisie, and the few manufactories in existence there were controlled by the state. After his first defeats, Peter I achieved a victory at Poltava over the troops of the Swedish king Charles XII who had attacked through Poland. Peter was somewhat less successful in his war against the Turks. He united the different social ranks of the boyars, the okolnichys, the gentlemen, etc. into one estate of the gentry (which also included the 'Ostsee', i.e. the German gentry of the conquered Baltic regions – Lifland and Kurland). He introduced some order into the bureaucratic system of state administration (introducing instead another system, also a bureaucratic one, but somewhat more effective). He preserved and strengthened serfdom, turning it practically into slavery. But before the 'Letter of Grace to the Nobility' of the empress Catherine II the peasants could be a nobleman's property only on condition of the latter being on State Service (however, gentlemen were freed from obligatory service in the army or the guards already by Peter III in 1762). Catherine II, moreover, extended serfdom to the Ukrainian peasants. The realm of Crimea was conquered during her reign.

Although Peter I used brutal and sometimes inhuman methods (for example, he ordered the execution of his own son for insubordination), he did much to make possible the introduction of Western European cultural and technical innovations into Russia (he even went to Holland to study shipbuilding, starting from scratch). In this respect he brought the country out of deadlock.

After Peter, Russia not only equalled the European powers in arms, but became open to European alternative thinking. Catherine II (1762–1796)[33] persecuted freethinkers among her subjects, and in 1773–1774 suppressed a great peasant insurrection headed by Yemelyan Pugachev.[34] At the same time, however, she made advances to the progressive thinkers of France – Voltaire and the Encyclopedists; and the more educated part of the Russian nobility was rising to the level of French Englightenment.

In the late eighteenth and the early nineteenth centuries French became the

---

33. She was the daughter of the owner of a tiny German princedom, Anhalt-Zerbst; her real name was Sophia-Frederica-Augusta; she was chosen by the empress Elizabeth as bride for her crazy German nephew and heir (the son of her sister), Peter III. But Catherine's outstanding wit and will, her tactful mastering of the Russian language and Russian customs and manners, as well as the unanimous support of the guard, made it possible for her, pregnant as she was (not by her own husband), on horseback and in a uniform of the guard, to head the coup which for 33 years made her a sovereign Russian empress and autocrat with the official title of Catherine the Great.

34. Catherine's officers hanged many of the rebels, but when the military operations were over, the brutal reprisals ceased, and some of the former followers of Pugachev were pardoned and returned home; some of them served as non-commissioned officers, small officials, etc.

vernacular language of the gentry all over Europe, including Russia, so that French literature and French culture became common property among educated Russians. They not only spoke but even thought in French. The war of liberation against Napoleon had brought the Russian army to France; this facilitated the adoption of the culture, which was common for Europe, by the Russian gentry, and made a liberation movement inside Russia possible. The so-called Decembrists came from the Russian nobility but were European in mentality, and this is why they could insist on reforms, which, if implemented, would lead to the introduction of the Seventh Phase of the historical process. The Decembrists are a good example of the fact that social movements cannot be reduced to the sphere of direct interests of the social group to which the public figures in question belong by birth.

A cultural upsurge was common in Europe during the nineteenth century; it led to a flourishing of the Russian language, Russian literature (created nearly exclusively by the gentry), and later of Russian science. At the same time, this upsurge should also be regarded as a response to the painful contradictions created by the backwardness of the social conditions in Russia; or rather, it was a negation of these, a symptom of the birth of an alternative social psychology. Nineteenth century literature had, in general, a liberating influence on human consciousness, and this is especially true of Russian literature.

In nineteenth century Russia we can already identify most of the diagnostic features of the Sixth Phase: modern firearms, including artillery, a national absolutist state, and alternative ideological and psychological currents. But the Russian bourgeoisie was quite undeveloped, and was constrained by unfavourable laws regarding the different level of rights of the social estates; as to the peasants, they were in servitude, as if still living in the Fifth Phase. The conditions of Phase transition required their liberation; this was a major historical task – capitalism had not begun to develop in Russia.

The giant space to the south and east of Russia: Turkey, Iran, Central Asia, Tibet, Mongolia, India, south-eastern Asia was, during the fifteenth to eighteenth centuries, still in the Fifth Phase, and we are not going to discuss it in this chapter. But China had reached the Sixth Phase even earlier than Europe; however, a number of circumstances hindered its passage into the next, Seventh Phase. And finally, Japan, although nearly unnoticed by the Western observers, was also in the Sixth Phase.

Now we shall turn to the history of China from the beginning of the Sixth Phase; its history during that period is instructive.

From the late ninth century the T'ang empire began to break up. Northern China was seized by nomadic Khitans of a Mongol-Hsien-pi origin, and later by another group of nomads, the Jurchens, who seem to have spoken a Tungus language. But in Central and Southern China the culture was not only preserved at a high level, but even developed further. Thus, literacy became more and more widely spread; xylograph books were printed (from engraved wooden planks);

later the books were printed using movable types (ninth century). All the more important Buddhist, Taoist and Confucian books were published in numerous copies.

In 960 General Chao K'uan-yin founded a new dynasty in the Yangtze valley, named Sung. The Sung empire was surrounded by hostile states on all sides: the Jurchens ruled the North, the Tangut states were in the West, and in the South were the Kingdoms Nan Chao and Annam. However, the Sung empire was a stable structure. This was a time when cities grew tremendously (Hangchow, for example, had more than a million inhabitants). Coins were circulating widely, and paper money was introduced in the twelfth century (which, however, led to inflation). Merchants, usurers and craftsmen flourished in the cities (among other things, chinaware was invented). The merchantry was no longer debarred from civil service; the power of the state bureaucrats grew together with the number of schools and the general level of literacy; while the loyalty of the civil servants was thought to be guaranteed by a strict examination system (a rank might be granted to one in a hundred aspirants); serious measures were taken against backstairs influence.

A regional division of handicraft labour appeared; there were factories in which up to a hundred workers might be employed (a phenomenon which could be observed in Europe first in the sixteenth to seventeenth centuries). With the help of irrigation, new agricultural lands were developed, new sorts of rice were introduced. Being cut off on land by inimical kingdoms, the Sung empire successfully developed navigation.

The system of education provided some limited opportunity for advancement to gifted men from the people, many well educated scholars, poets, historians, prose writers and artists appeared – and not only men but in a few cases also women (we may mention Li Ch'ing-chao, a woman poet and archaeologist). Private academies were also founded.

A great role in China's ideological life was played by the doctrine of Chu His (1130–1200), the most important representative of Neo-Confucianism. According to this doctrine, there are two world principles: that of order (*li*), and that of material force (*ch'i*). Both principles are united in a general 'Great Primary Principle'. Although Chu His wrote about the necessity of furthering knowledge and allowing freedom of study, these ideas were not developed further. Later China learned Confucianism basically in the form of Neo-Confucianism, and the Confucian books were mostly known in the form as edited and commented by Chu His: they were also the main subject of examination for the rank of civil servant.

Chinese self-consciousness developed in forms somewhat different from those of the European nations. It was to a certain degree formed by early Confucianism, and depended, on the one hand, upon a common culture of everyday life and ethics, which for every Chinese (even those who formally were Taoists or Buddhists) was based on Confucian principles; and on the other, upon the idea of

Chinese culture coinciding with the borders of the Chinese Empire which was thought to be unique: all other nations were regarded as Chinese subjects, either paying their tribute, or rebelliously abstaining from payment. Anyway, by the Sung period, Chinese self-consciousness was firmly in place.

In China the Mongol dominance (1280–1368) had a peculiar form. After the first devastating conquest, the Mongol dynasty Yüan adapted itself to the life of the conquered country. In effect, the Yüan period was actually a delayed continuation of the Sung dynasty. The network of canals and roads was widened, mail service stations were introduced, the Empire protected trade, including foreign overseas trade, a navy was organised, and the coasts of the neighbouring countries, from Korea to Burma and Java, were harassed.

In 1368 Chu Yüan-chang, the liberator of China from the Mongols, came to power, founding the new Ming dynasty (1368–1644). He was a cruel monarch, but managed to return the country to a more flourishing condition; his reign contributed to a new growth of national self-consciousness. Chinese seafaring during the Ming dynasty was, by its scope, comparable to the times of Vasco da Gama and Columbus in Europe – Chinese ships were visiting the South Sea, Ceylon and perhaps even Arabia and Africa. Trade with foreign countries and openness towards the outside world favoured the development of industries, and manufacturing was re-established. The energetic activities of the Jesuit Matteo Ricci (in China since 1583) helped Christianity gain some ground in China; it was something like a prematurely born embryo of an alternative ideology.[35] The European Catholic missionaries made China acquainted with new cultivated plants of American origin (Indian corn, sweet potatoes, peanuts, tobacco).

The Chinese already knew how to mix saltpetre, sulphur and coal for making an explosive mixture under the Sung dynasty; under Yüan there appeared grenades, and the first attempts to create firearms were made. In the fifteenth century, the Ming ships were already armed by arquebuses and artillery.

On the whole, one may state that under the Sung and especially under the Ming dynasty China reached a post-medieval level of technology and culture. However, if the Post-Medieval Phase were to be developed, changes were necessary in social psychology and ideology, and an independent bourgeois class had to emerge. But in China no preconditions existed for creating an ideology alternative to the ethics of Confucianism (although, alongside of Confucianism, adherents of the Buddhist, Taoist and even Christian beliefs existed, but the ethics were uniformly

35. The Jesuits were of the opinion that Confucian ethics and Confucian reverence for ancestors do not contradict the Christian doctrine, but the Dominicans and Franciscans opposed this opinion violently; after prolonged discussions, pope Clement XI issued in 1715 a bull against the Jesuit point of view, and thus practically destroyed all possibilities for introducing Christianity into China. Note that Matteo Ricci's writings in Chinese had a certain influence on Japanese non-Buddhist and non-Confucian thinking, since, in the eighteenth and nineteenth centuries, a new Shintoist ideology was being created on the base of archaic beliefs which had been preserved from the Third Phase of historical development.

Confucian). This contributed to the overwhelming domination of the Neo-Confucian bureaucratic state system, which furnished China with numerous literate but few independently thinking political figures.

All external achievements of the Ming dynasty were neutralised by the fact that the situation of the main mass of the population, namely peasants, did not become better but, on the contrary, grew worse. Very often peasants were driven from their land to make way for the plantation of some new kind of crops, or for other undertakings of the landowners. The seventeenth century was full of rebellions; one of the rebels, one Li Tzu-ch'eng, aided by the citizens, managed to capture the capital of the empire in 1644. The last Ming emperor committed suicide. Under these conditions, the noble landholders called in the Manchu for help (this was originally the name for one group of the Jurchens but was later used for them all).

Few mutinies bring the most enlightened forces to political power.

The Manchurian conquest (1644–1674) was no doubt an inhibiting factor in the development of China. The Jurchens, ancestors of the Manchu, were for a long time at the stage of primitive hunters; by the middle of the second millennium of the Christian era they had probably, in their mass, not developed beyond the chiefdom stage. They even preserved shamanism which was a far cry from the necessary alternative ideology of the Sixth Phase. And anyway they lagged far behind the Chinese economically.

K'ang-his (1681–1722), the second emperor of the Manchu dynasty (officially called Ching) has been compared to such outstanding monarchs of the Phase of Post-Medieval Absolutism as Akbar in Mongul India, Peter I in Russia and Louis XIV in France. However, the difference is obvious. For one thing, unlike the Mongol Yüan dynasty, the Manchu did not mix with the Chinese; they deliberately humiliated them, stressing their dependent condition: all Chinese were ordered to shave a part of their head and to wear a pigtail. Moreover, based upon the concept of the exclusiveness of the Chinese Empire, all other countries being regarded as its lawful tributaries, the Manchurians sealed off the Chinese frontiers; no sea voyages abroad were allowed, and no foreigners tolerated in China (an exception was made for the Jesuit mission; it is typical that it was actually the Jesuits who were responsible for the idealisation of 'chinoiserie' in Europe).

But it was not solely the Manchu conquest which was responsible for the inhibition of development in China, keeping it in the Sixth Phase. The reasons for the stagnation lay in the peculiarities characteristic of Ming society, and, moreover, in the very way in which the historical development had taken place in China. If in Western Europe the intelligentsia felt itself connected with the bourgeois enterprise, and the results of the thinking activities were employed in its interests, in China the intelligentsia was mainly concerned with preparing for examinations and aspiring to the rank of civil servants, and thus taking part in the advantages of the bureaucracy (or an intellectual might join a Buddhist monastery – the monasteries being the main Chinese centres of culture). The moving force of any bureaucratic society is the impulse 'to change nothing'. So enterprise was in China devoid of any ideological or socio-psychological base; the outer, decorative functions of power were given priority. Under these conditions, the coming of the Manchu to power not only discouraged Chinese enterprise, but deprived the society of any chance to move beyond the Sixth Phase, were it but for widening the sphere of foreign trade.

In the early period of the Manchu domination literature continued to develop. In spite of the fact that authors were mainly oriented toward the past, we must concede that there was no lack of fine writers. Well known in our country are the ironic and fantastic *Strange Stories from a Chinese Studio* (better known to Russian readers as *Foxes' Witchcraft*), by P'u Sung-ling (1640–1715). Noteworthy is the satirical masterpiece of Wu Ching-tzu (1701–1754), *Unofficial History of Officialdom*, and *The Dream of the Red Chamber* by Ts'ao Chan (Ts'ao Hseh Ch'in, 1715–1763). Drama also flourished. But the emperor Ch'en Lung, wishing to outdo all his predecessors by leaving behind him a monumental literary compilation, ordered collection at the capital of all rare books, even those in private hands (1772–1782). The whole of Chinese literature was to be 'unified'; more than 2,000 works were to be totally destroyed, and in others certain paragraphs were to be deleted; some scholars were executed.

With such a mental outlook, in a state of incompletely developed Post-Medieval absolutism, did China enter the nineteenth century.

Now let us turn to the easternmost civilisation of Eurasia – to Japan.

From the fourteenth century the number of trade and handicraft guilds (*za*) in Japan grew rapidly – a process similar to that occurring in Italy or Central Europe at the same time or somewhat later. The number of the cities grew, too – by the sixteenth century there were more than 150. Meanwhile, in the countryside, the minor and medium landowners (*shōen*) were gradually ousted by princedoms headed by hereditary nobles, the *daimyō*, who controlled not only the countryside but also the cities. The *samurai*, originally independent landowners, now served the *daimyō*. No Japanese felt any better because of these changes, and the socio-psychological discomfort grew appreciably.

During the entire period including the fifteenth and the sixteenth centuries, peasant rebellions were taking place.

In connection with the developing sea trade with Korea and China, the demand for metals (gold, silver and copper) was growing; the mining industry on land owned by the *daimyō* was on the rise, which not only led to the latter's enrichment, and a degree of liberation from the supremacy of the *shōguns*, but also to the accumulation, on the *daimyō's* territories, of a working (and dissatisfied) population.

In 1542 Portuguese sailors appeared in Japan, followed in 1584 by Spanish ones; they organised, as intermediaries, a trade not only with China, but also with the more distant countries of south-eastern Asia. Catholic missionaries started their activities, and initially had a considerable success.

The ruling class reacted to the dissatisfaction of the mass of the people by measures directed towards the creation of a strong unified Japanese state. Under the rulers acting as generals, especially Toyotomi Hideyoshi (1536–1598), not only was the peasant unrest cruelly suppressed, but the liberties of the cities were curtailed. In 1588 the disarmament of commoners (mostly peasants) was carried out, and in 1595 the peasants became bondsmen (actually serfs; this happened nearly at the same time as in Russia).

After the death of Hideyoshi, the power devolved to General Ieyasu Tokugawa. In 1603 he was declared *shōgun* and founded a new dynasty, the Tokugawa. The capital was moved from Kyoto to Edo (now Tokyo). Ieyasu succeeded in abolishing the *daimyō* princedoms, and create a centralised absolutist state.[36] The *daimyō*, from being princes, became territorial administrators, controlled by the *shōgun's* government. The entire population was divided into four estates: peasants, craftsmen, merchants and *samurai*; the latter were settled in the cities and received a rice allowance from the *daimyō*. Thus an independent knighthood was abolished. About this time Japan already had its own artillery, although of inferior quality.

Thus, by the end of the seventeenth century, certain symptoms of the Sixth Phase were to be observed: firearms, a 'national' absolutist state, the presence of a bourgeosie and of hired workers, although the traditional estates still existed. Thus, an incomplete passage to the Absolutist Post-Medieval Phase can be said to have begun. What was missing for complete transition was a clear alternative ideology; however, the monopoly of the inherited official ideology was already partly undermined by a Christian movement, and by certain reforms of the Confucian-cum-Shinto ethics: gradually, it began to be possible 'to think otherwise', although the government was fiercely against such changes. Only the transition to the Seventh Phase during the nineteenth century could finally remove the contradictions of the waning Sixth Phase.

36. Ieyasu relinquished the title of *shogun* for himself (but not for his successors) as early as 1605, but he continued to rule the country until his death in 1616. After him, *shoguns* of the Tokugawa dynasty stayed in power, and the whole period from 1603 until 1867 is termed 'the Tokugawa period'.

7   Seventh Phase (Capitalist)

The diagnostic features of the Seventh Phase are as follows: transformation of the natural sciences into a productive force (invention of the steam engine, the railway, the steamship, later the internal combustion engine, electric light, the telegraph, the telephone, etc.; introduction of science into industrial production and agriculture); rapid growth of armaments throughout the period (improved rifle firearms, smokeless powder, long-range artillery, ironclad battleships, at first powered by steam and later by diesel; the invention of the aeroplane, the tank, chemical warfare); the juxtaposition of the bourgeoisie and the hired workers as the two main social classes; the coming into being of an intelligentsia;[1] a tendency (although as yet not strongly felt) towards disintegration of the peasantry into the same two classes of entrepreneurs and hired workers; preservation, on the periphery of the society, of the former classes of the Sixth Phase; the growing importance of non-religious ideologies, both those accepting and vindicating the existing development of the historical progress (such as positivism), and those already alternative to them (such as Marxism); these ideologies grew and were strengthened at the same time as traditional religions were growing weaker; however, the latter did

---

1. In spite of its spuriously Latin form, the term *Intelligentsia* is of Russian nineteenth century origin; it denotes men and women involved not in production of material goods but in creative work, teaching, medicine and scientific cognition. Such persons had always existed in human populations, e.g. among the gentry, the clerics, etc. However, as a certain heritable social status of men served to disseminate morals and knowledge, it was formed (at least originally) in Russia. The Western counterpart of the intelligentsia – the *intellectuals* – do not usually constitute a specific social group; it is rather a social function which can be taken upon themselves by persons whose parents, brothers and children may not be intellectuals but, businessmen, farmers or anybody else. But the intellectuals fulfil the same social role as the Russian intelligentsia, and for simplicity's sake I shall use that Russian term in a comprehensive sense to denote those parts of society which create non-material values, at a point in history when creating such values is of paramount importance for production of material goods and for the economy.

    As a social force, the intelligentsia is a phenomenon of the Seventh, i.e. the Capitalist Phase. But its role is not limited to that Phase alone. Its role is very important for the transition to the Eighth Phase, when productive and necessary social activities have to be scientifically based. The intelligentsia is responsible for everything that makes life easier in the material sense. Moreover, the intelligentsia facilitates the process of turning the multitude into organised groups of socially conscious men and women. In the Eighth Phase, it is also the moral obligation of the intelligentsia to preserve mankind from an ecological catastrophe. It was also the main vehicle for introducing the alternative ideology which has brought about the change from the Seventh to the Eight Phase.

retain, in different degrees, their official status, and to a certain degree they were still determining factors in the formation of national character; creation of republican states, or of monarchies with the monarch's powers very limited by constitution; a complete parcelling, between the capitalist colonial powers, of the regions which had not yet reached the Seventh Phase; armed rivalry between the societies that had reached it; creation of colonial empires, or a struggle for their institution; wars on a vast scale with enormous destruction and loss of life.

The Phase of Capitalism can first be observed in Western Europe and North America. All other countries of the world, including Japan, had in the beginning and the middle of the nineteenth century not yet reached the Seventh Phase, and still stayed in the Sixth or even in the Fifth Phase. This does not mean that these societies were backward in an absolute sense, but only that there was some slowing down brought about by secondary causes, such as unfavourable natural conditions (in Africa, for example), or by inhibition through conquest by nomads; or through a belated development of alternative ideologies (in the Near and the Middle East, in China, to a certain degree in Russia before the reforms of the 1860s).

Even before the Industrial Revolution (i.e. the turning over from handicraft to industrial labour, which is the necessary prerequisite for the victory of the capitalist system), political revolutions occurred in the more highly developed countries, which prepared the conditions for a more rapid advent of the new Phase of the historical process. The first was the revolution in England (1642–1649) whose victory we have already described, but which resulted not in capitalists coming to power, but in the dominance of the Anglican Church, or the Church of England (i.e. of a slightly reformed Catholicism independent of the pope), and – for a short time – to more extreme forms of Protestantism. (Only in Scotland, another Reformed Christian religion, namely Presbyterianism, closely related to Calvinism, remained the national, since the seventeenth century.)

As noted above, a pattern of development characteristic of all social revolutions can be observed already in the English Revolution, just as in the French and particularly in the twentieth century Russian October Revolution: a radical change in the dominant ideology leads to a liberation of the stimulus to aggression which finds expression in an internecine extermination, with power passing to ever more radical, greater or smaller groups: a process which is apt to end in personal dictatorship.

The importance of the English Revolution consisted, first of all, in its making available alternative ideologies which indirectly favoured the development of natural sciences and philosophy. The monopoly of the Catholic Church organisation, with its rich monasteries, vast lands belonging to them and to the church, the absolute power of the ecclesiastical hierarchy – a monopoly which was one of the mainstays of the existing social system – broke down even before the English Revolution under the impact of Henry VIII's asserting his absolutist power in the first half of the sixteenth century. But the English bourgeoisie came finally to power only as a result of the Parliamentary Reform of 1832.

The war for the liberation of the English Northern American colonies and the foundation of the United States (1775–1791) was also a sort of revolution. In the United States, the main role was played not only by the bourgeoisie of the northern States, but also by the plutocracy of the southern States with their slave-owning economy. The Declaration of Independence (1776) and the Bill of Rights (1791) were the foundations of the Constitution of the United States; these documents declared the inalienable right of every man to 'Life, Liberty and the Pursuit of Happiness', which laid the basis for the slogans of the next, the French Revolution (1789–1799).

The stages of the French Revolution and of the Napoleonic Period have been described above.

Of all the social changes which owe their origin to the bourgeoisie, only the French Revolution can be described as a real revolution in the proper sense of the word – a social explosion which at once destroyed the traditional values and proclaimed new ones in their place. The brutal character of the revolution of 1789 I am inclined to explain by the fact that Roman Catholic ideological unanimity had in other countries already been undermined by the dissemination of alternative Reformation doctrines, while in France Revolution was carried out by those who in their youth were likely to have been involved in scholastic discussions (although sometimes leading to the death of some of the disputants) on the freedom of will and grace divine. As a result of Napoleon's conquests (although they proved to be short-lived), the ideas of the French Revolution spread all over Europe, event to places where the Sixth Phase was still underdeveloped, and the bourgeoisie was politically weak. Among other things, this shows that revolutionary ideas were not specifically bourgeois but were the expression of a general socio-psychological dissatisfaction.

However, this did not mean that mankind had finally reached the Capitalist Phase of the historical process. Europe was yet to go through the period of pre-capitalist absolutist reaction, when the 'Holy Alliance' of the monarchs of Russia, Austria[2] and Prussia, joined by the Bourbons of France and by Great Britain, was dominant in Europe, and all attempts at new revolutions were quashed.[3] Only after the Parliamentary Reform of 1832 in England, and the half-way revolution of 1848 in Germany and France; after the war of liberation and unification of Italy (ending

---

2. The Holy Roman Empire of the German Nation ceased to exist during the Napoleonic Wars (in 1806), and became the Austrian Empire, and from 1867 to 1918 it was the Austro-Hungarian Empire. The territories inhabited by Hungarians (a considerable part of these territories had formerly been held by the Turks), went over to the Habsburgs in the late eighteenth–early nineteenth centuries.

3. Inside Germany, minor duchies, princedoms and kingdoms were resurrected, but the lesser ones were 'mediatised', i.e. included into a nearby greater kingdom, preserving honours that had been due to the 'mediatised' prince. Finland, which had been won by Russia from Sweden, was granted to Russia but with the condition that it retain a certain degree of self-government; Sweden received sovereignty over Norway under a similar condition.

in victory in 1870), and after the reforms of Alexander II in Russia (1861–1864) did the capitalists get a certain freedom of action, and around the late 1860s they came to power in many European countries (but not in Russia, where the power began to pass to the capitalists only after the revolution of 1905 and the February Revolution of 1917). In the United States, the turning point was the war between the Northern (already capitalist) States and the Southern States of the planters (1861–1865).

Quite independently of Europe, Japan reached the Capitalist Phase as the result of the so-called 'Meiji Revolution' of 1868. The power of the *shōguns* was abolished, and the power of the *tennō* (emperor) was re-established. The revolution, which had begun as a traditional struggle between noble clans, quickly developed into a movement in favour of national unity and the mastery of Western technology (first of all, that of arms). The nascent bourgeoisie, the rank-and-file samurai and even peasants took part in this movement, and it soon acquired the features of a bourgeois revolution. 'Feudal' princedoms were abolished, private ownership in land was made possible, higher education on the European pattern was introduced. The possibility of introducing a parliamentary system was discussed; but the first parliament with rather limited rights did not meet until 1890.

Although traditional ideologies continued in existence, Buddhism lost official status; it was Shintoism which was declared the state religion. Originally, it was nothing more than the traditional cults characteristic of the Third Phase. However, existing in parallel to Confucianism and Buddhism (and later also to Christianity), Shintoism developed a religious-philosophical base of its own; along with the cult of the ancient supreme deity, the Sun goddess, a cult of *tennō* as the incarnation of the higher celestial powers was introduced. The fact that the highest deity had manifested itself, in the person of the emperor, only in Japan, was supposed to prove the superiority of the Japanese and their values over mankind in general.

The technology borrowed from Europe prospered and developed in Japan; by the beginning of the twentieth century it became a very powerful capitalist empire; it had a strong army and perhaps the world's best navy. The restructuring of the Japanese society was little noticed in Europe and especially in Russia, where it was judged by the traveller's notes of the writer I. A. Goncharov, *The Frigate Pallas* written in the late 1850s.

Thus the Seventh, Capitalist Phase of the historical process became in the middle of the nineteenth century dominant in a broad area from the Atlantic to the Pacific Ocean. Typical of the Phase was a rapid increase in the technological progress, and an optimistic belief in its unlimited possibilities; but it was also the shortest of the Phases. It was also marked by most devastating wars with ever-increasing numbers of casualties, and with devastating consequences.

The emerging dissatisfaction was no longer camouflaged by ethico-dogmatic religious ideas. The capitalists felt discomfort because they felt, again and again, the need for new sources of raw materials and new markets, and also because of growing competition with capitalists in other countries. The working class and the related part of the peasantry felt discomfort because capitalist exploitation was very hard to restrict; and the population in general felt discomfort because of the growing losses in the capitalist wars. Just as during the medieval epoch, there were no periods of peace; the only difference was that formerly the bloodshed was witnessed by everybody, while now it occurred in far away countries. In the home countries, a generation grew up which had never seen war and regarded it as an evil; the army, more than ever, became separated from the man in the street.

At the same time, capitalist production was much stimulated by the export of the produce to the colonies. We have already seen that the Dutch, Spanish and Portuguese colonies were formed as social entities not later than in the Sixth Phase; however, the complete annexation of the colonies (countries belonging to the Sixth, Fifth and earlier Phases) is a characteristic feature of the Seventh Phase, and the relations that arose between the main powers at that time depended largely on the urge of each individual capitalist state towards the division of the colonies in its own favour. Here a field for manifestation of the socio-psychological impulse of aggression was opened.

We have noted above that during the Capitalist Phase the natural sciences became a productive force, but now some of the humanities also attempted to influence the historical process. A philosophical incitement to socio-economic changes was attempted by Marxism, which originally was a theory of Capitalist relations in production. Marx's *Das Kapital* was a serious scholarly work, but the idea that it was 'not a dogma but a guide to action' was a delusion: for all the depth of Marx's analysis – and acknowledging that it did greatly influence not only the social processes of the capitalist epoch but also the development of learning – the book was still an 'exercise with the result given in advance'. The fact is that Marx wrote *Das Kapital* between 1867 and 1880, and the book, when finished, was to prove that the capitalist system was doomed, and that passing to a communist system was imminent; however, the conclusion that 'the ghost of communism' is 'wandering' all through capitalist Europe had been made *a priori* by Marx and Engels in their *Communist Manifesto* as early as in 1849, i.e. long before Marx started his scientific work (which was supposed to prove the inevitable victory of this ghost). The *Manifesto* had been published even before the Capitalist Phase had been firmly rooted in Europe.

After this general introduction to the history of the Capitalist Phase, we can turn to a more detailed description of the events during this Phase.

In England, the industrial revolution was more or less finished by 1800–1810. The bourgeoisie did not completely gain political power until parliamentary reform took place, but nevertheless life in the country was, by the beginning of the new century, mainly determined by capitalist production, with such typical characteristic features as unrestrained and inhuman exploitation of hired labour, periodic crises of over-production, etc.

The first actions of the working class occurred: riots of the so-called Luddites in 1811–1813 with destruction of machinery (Parliament reacted by introducing capital punishment for such destruction); the uprising in 1819 in Manchester, where the workers were suppressed by armed force (the Peterloo massacre). But the bourgeoisie felt itself politically hampered: although the country had a Parliament with two parties – the Whigs and the Tories – both parties reflected mainly the interests of the landowners (the Whigs, partly also the interests of the financial bourgeoisie).[4]

The structure of the Parliament (the House of Commons), had emerged during the sixteenth and seventeenth centuries, and did not now correspond to the real needs of economic and social life.

A number of members were elected from rural counties by the landowners; note that the comparatively sparsely populated and underdeveloped county of Cornwall had four times as many representatives as some of the densest populated and economically developed central counties. Some of the representatives were elected from boroughs. There were six different types of these; some had no longer any inhabitants at all but still had their members at Parliament; others were so negligible that the electors wholly depended upon the local landowner; at the same time, big industrial centres which had grown up during the seventeenth to eighteen centuries, like Birmingham or Manchester, had no representatives in Parliament. The question of parliamentary reform had been urgent ever since the 1780s.

Eventually, the Whigs presented to Parliament, and in 1832 got approved a Bill of reform, which actually meant that power in the country passed to the bourgeoisie. However, this Reform did not completely satisfy the population. Soon a movement emerged in the working class, called Chartism; its adherents demanded (in 1838) a charter, which was to include six points: equal electoral areas, universal suffrage, payment to members of Parliament, no property qualifications, vote by ballot, and annual parliaments. Chartism, with its popular petitions, manifestations, and the threat of a general strike, did not survive the year 1848; but in the course of history all Chartist demands were ultimately accepted.

The formation of capitalist economics led everywhere, but most of all in England, to colonial expansion. Capital needed new markets for the produce – if possible, with a monopoly right to selling it; a widening of the sources of raw material, and more possibilities for investment. The fact that Europe was technologically in a leading position facilitated the conquest of colonies in those parts of the world which had not reached the Seventh Phase.

---

4. One of the most important proponents of reforms from the late eighteenth century until 1832 was Jeremy Bentham, an outstanding economist and lawyer. He formulated the goal of any sensible legislation as warranting the 'greatest happiness for the greatest number'. He preached a total non-intervention of the state into the affairs of individuals, including their enterprises. Bentham was elected a citizen of honour in France (1792), but he never took part in any actual legislative activities.

The whole epoch of the Capitalist Phase shows a picture of a growing conversion of the non-industrial regions of the Earth into colonies, whose population was more or less lacking rights and was ruled by the colonisers – until finally, by the beginning of the twentieth century, all available territories had been conquered. No wonder that in the colonies a new social discomfort was developing, although it was not so acutely felt by the earlier generations.

In some cases the conquered territories were settled by emigrants from another country. The American countries, settled by colonists from Britain, gained their independence, constituting the United States of America; also Spain's and Portugal's colonies in Latin America (but not in Africa) gained independence. Later England began to anticipate the events, and ceded an increasing amount of independence to such colonies which were massively settled by the British. Finally Australia, Canada, New Zealand and South Africa became independent states inside the British Commonwealth of Nations.

Especially important for England was India.

The East India Company had been created by Queen Elizabeth I with the aim of furnishing England with pepper and other spices (formerly they were very important, because of the lack of refrigerators for meat). The first merchant factory was founded in Surat in 1613; others followed later. The island of Bombay which England received as part of the dowry of Charles I's queen, a Portuguese princess, was also ceded to the East India Company. By its efforts a city grew up there. A number of new English merchant factories grew up on both the western and eastern coasts of India; in 1690 the English founded Calcutta.

In 1702 a new United East India Company was organised; until 1858 it was sovereign over most Indian territories, including Bengal, Bihar, Orissa and other regions. At first the British possessions were nominally subordinate to the dynasty of the Great Moguls, but later this dependence was discontinued.

The possessions of the East India Company extended considerably during the nineteenth century. In 1828, on its territory, the Hindu custom of *suttee* (immolation of widows on their husband's funerary pyre) was prohibited, and in 1843 slavery was abolished; but on the whole, the British thought it necessary to keep to the order which was locally considered as legal, and to tax the population, without meddling in the existing social relations.

English expansion in the region of the Indian Ocean brought about conflict with China. In 1799 the Chinese government prohibited the growing of opium poppy and the import of opium. The British regarded this as an infringement on the freedom of trade, and in 1839–1842 the 'First Opium War' between England and China occurred. Also later China insisted on prohibition of opium, but had to retract its protests as the result of the 'Second Opium War' in 1858.

In 1857–1858 a great rebellion took place among the soldiers of the East India Company (the Sepoy Mutiny). It was directed against the (actually rather few) innovations which the Indians regarded as Europeanisation and a violation of Hindu values. The immediate reason was the introduction of a new English rifle; to load it, the lubricated cartridges had to have their ends bitten off by the sepoys, while the grease used for this purpose was a mixture of cow's fat and pig's lard. Cows were holy for the Hindus, and the pigs were taboo for the Muslims.

There followed a war which lasted for a year and a half; both sides committed atrocities. The result was, that the reign of the East India Company was discontinued, the last Great Mogul was deposed and exiled, and instead of the Empire of the Great Moguls there appeared the British Indian Empire, with Victoria, Queen of England, as the Empress of India. A part of the Indian territory was subjected to the British Crown, but there remained a number of big enclaves where local *rajahs* continued to reign guided by British 'counsellors'.

The British followed the rule: not to change anything in the local customs, if these customs did not infringe upon the *raj* (reign) of England. Thus, in Delhi, as long as this city was the capital of the Mogul empire, Hindu temples were not founded. This rule continued when Delhi became the capital of the British Indian Empire. Each *rajah* retained his income and honours, and the British did not get themselves involved in the complicated caste system.

Although, in their colonies, the British kept themselves apart from the local population and behaved rather haughtily, it cannot be said that their rule, both in India and in their other possessions (such as Nigeria, Kenya or Ghana in Africa) amounted solely to oppression of the local population and gaining an income from it. When, in the middle of the twentieth century, the British abandoned their colonies, they left behind them railway networks, telegraph and postal services, industries, and an infrastructure which the states of the Medieval and Post-Medieval Phases could by no means have independently created. Most of the former colonies preferred to remain in the British Commonwealth of Nations.

France turned decidedly to capitalism as a result of the July Revolution of 1830. Now the Tricolour flag of the revolution was re-introduced (instead of the white flag with the Bourbon lilies). Although the moving force of the revolt were the workers and the petty bourgeoisie, it was the financial bourgeoisie which actually made use of the situation. The Chamber of Deputies was somewhat democratised, but a republic was not declared, and the throne was offered to the Duke of Orleans, Louis Philippe, a representative of the junior line of the Bourbon family. The 'Holy Alliance' did not react (because of a disagreement between the Great Powers), and starting from this point one can say that the Alliance ceased to exist.

The revolution of 1830 caused unrest in other European countries. The Russian part of Poland rebelled in 1830–1831, but the insurrection was put down; Poland lost the constitution which had been granted by Alexander I in 1815, and a policy of forced Russification of Polish lands was started.

In Russia, the revolution of 1830 made a great impression on Nicholas I; politically, he veered strongly to the right; preparations for the relaxation or abolition of servitude of the peasants ceased.

Meanwhile, in France serious events were again in the offing. The greater part of the bourgeoisie was not satisfied by the results of the 1830 revolution; in the 1840s there were bad harvests, and in 1847 a crisis of overproduction occurred; as for the proletariat, it got nothing from the preceding revolution. A new revolution broke out in 1848. A temporary republican government was proclaimed, based on a broad coalition; universal suffrage for men was introduced, the working day was shortened to ten or eleven hours, taxes on landowners (including peasants) were raised. But the elected Constituent Assembly moved strongly to the right; popular demonstrations led to governmental reprisals; an insurrection of the proletariat was suppressed. The Constitution voted for by the Constituent Assembly gave nearly absolute power to the president. Louis Napoleon Bonaparte, a nephew of Napoleon I, was elected and in 1851 declared himself emperor Napoleon III.

In parallel to these events, French colonial expansion continued. Thus, between 1830 and 1847 Algeria was conquered.

The 1848 revolution called forth more response in Europe than did that of 1830.

In Austria, revolutionary actions brought about the retirement of Metternich, who since 1815 had been the soul of the 'Holy Alliance'. At first, the Austrian government proclaimed a constitution, introducing a diet with strict electoral qualifications, but later it was compelled to call together a Constituent Assembly and to promulgate a new law which introduced universal suffrage for men. The labour movement was held in check as much as possible, but the peasants were liberated from servitude.

At the same time a democratic revolution was going on in Hungary; here the peasantry played an important role, as did the national movements, especially among the Slavic population. At the beginning of 1849, the Austrian government sent troops into Hungary, but the newly formed revolutionary detachments managed to oppose them fairly well. Still the Hungarian nobility supported the Habsburg cause, and the Habsburgs appealed to Nicholas I, asking him for Russian troops to suppress the revolution, and so they did. Nevertheless, the status of the bourgeoisie was also strengthened in this country.

In 1848 a revolution started in Germany, but here the local rulers, through concessions to the liberal bourgeoisie, managed to suppress the revolutionary forces. The same happened in Italy. The Italians faced the problem of creating a national state: the country was divided into different domains, a considerable part of it belonging either to Austria, or to the Bourbons. The revolutionary leaders, Garibaldi and Mazzini, hoped to create a democratic republic embracing the whole of Italy. But the revolutionary movement was suppressed by Austria, France, Spain and the Bourbon dynasty of the Two Sicilies (which included Naples). However, in Piedmont (in the Italian north-west) a constitutional monarchy emerged. In Northern Italy an industrial revolution started.

In Germany, an industrial revolution, after having lagged for a while, also developed, and a national unification of the country was on the agenda. The role of unifier was taken up by Prussia's King William I, or rather by his very gifted statesman Bismarck. As the result of a war with Denmark in 1864, and especially of the *Blitzkrieg* of 1866 with Austria, Prussia had become the incontestable leader of the movement for German unification. Some of the smaller German states were absorbed into Prussia. According to the Constitution of the North German Federation established in 1867, the responsibility of the Federation extended to military affairs, international relations, the money system, the postal service and railways. A Federation government headed by Bismarck as chancellor was established; the latter was responsible solely to the president of the Federation, i.e. to the king of Prussia, who was also the commander-in-chief in wartime. A Federation parliament, the *Reichstag*, was founded; it had the right to vote on the budget, and was elected by universal male suffrage, exclusive of rank-and-file soldiers and household servants.

The lesser German monarchs kept their honours and their civil lists, but had little influence on the state policies of united Germany; we can regard 1867 as the beginning of the new Capitalist Phase in Germany.

Of great importance for European politics from the middle of the nineteenth century, was the so-called Eastern Question, i.e. the question about the fate of the Ottoman (Turkish) empire, which was being torn asunder by internal contradictions and by separatist movements, especially in the Christian regions of the Balkans. For France and England, this was mainly a question of military and trade ascendancy over the Mediterranean; for Austria and Russia, this was a question of possible territorial expansion. Austria had a common frontier with the Balkan provinces of Turkey, and Russia, regarding itself as 'The Third Rome', hoped for the resuscitation of a new Christian Orthodox and Slavonic Byzantian Empire in the Balkans. Rumanians, Bulgarians, Serbs, Montenegrins, Macedonians and Greeks were all Orthodox Christians; an important part of the population of the Asia Minor Peninsula consisted of Armenians who were Monophysite Christians.[5]

But most of all, Russia, which had long applied pressure to Turkey, dreamed of capturing the Straits between the Black Sea and the Mediterranean, and of getting free access to the Mediterranean.

In 1774 Russia secured for itself a number of fortresses on the Black Sea, declared the independence of the Khanate of Crimea, and asserted the right to protection of Christian subjects of Turkey; in 1783 it annexed Crimea, in 1801–1802 it took possession of the Orthodox Christian Georgia, in 1812 it annexed Bessarabia and acquired the right to guarantee the autonomy of Serbia (at about the same time, Persia ceded to Russia its lands north of the river Araxes, as well as the Khanate of Talysh). All this made Austria apprehensive of the creation of a strong Slavic (actually Russian) force in the Balkans, and during the nineteenth century preferred to support Turkey.

---

5. In the Balkans there were also Catholic Christians, viz. the Slovenians and the Croats, including the Dalmatians; but most of the Bosnians were converted to Islam.

In 1822 Greece arose in insurrection. The Greeks declared their independence, but the Great Powers wanted Greece to remain in a vassal dependence of Turkey.

In the Balkans there existed not only anti-Turk but also anti-Greek feelings: in Walachia, Moldavia and Croatia, there was a group of Greeks, called Phanariots, who formed part of the Turkish administration. Therefore, when in 1821 Alexander Ypsilanti, a Phanariot, attempted, basing himself on Russia, to organise an anti-Turkish insurrection in the Balkan region, he was unsuccessful. The Turks hanged an Orthodox Patriarch in Istanbul. Russia severed diplomatic relations with Turkey.

In 1826 Nicholas I of Russia gave an ultimatum to Turkey, demanding autonomy for the Danubian principalities (Moldavia and Walachia), and for Serbia. In 1827 the Turko-Egyptian fleet was defeated by the Anglo-Franco-Russian fleet at Navarino, and in the next year the Russians, having defeated the Persians in Transcaucasia, occupied Yerevan and Nakhichevan, whereby the conquest of Transcaucasia was brought to an end. In 1828–32 the independence of Greece was finally established (with the help of French troops); the Russo-Turkish war of 1828–1829 ended favourably for the Russians by the compromise of Adrianople: the reason was that Nicholas I thought that a weak Ottoman Empire was better than a strengthening of England and France or even Egypt in the Balkans.

In 1831 Muhammad Ali, the pasha of Egypt, having received nothing for his pro-Turkish efforts in the Balkans, declared the sultan heretic, and started a conquest of Palestine and Syria. In this case Russia backed Turkey; the Russian troops evacuated the Danubian principalities.

The apple of discord between the great powers was the question of the Straits of the Bosphorus and the Dardanelles. Nicholas I thought that either the Straits should be open to Russia, or closed for all powers; France and England demanded their opening for themselves. There were also other points on which the powers differed, but it seems to have been decisive that, under Napoleon III, France stood in need of spectacular victories, while England feared that Russia, demanding the right to defend the interests of Orthodox Christians in Turkey, was actually planning the establishment of its own protectorate over Turkey. All this led in 1854–1856 to a war of France, England, Turkey and the Italian state of Piedmont-Sardinia[6] against Russia. The allies decided that it was necessary to curtail the Russian dominion over the sea, and besieged the Russian Black Sea naval base of Sevastopol. After a heroic defence lasting for eleven months, Sevastopol was captured.

According to the Paris peace treaty of 1856, Russia ceded to Turkey the part of Bessarabia near the Danube and lost the right to defend the Orthodox Christian interests in Turkey (all Christian interests were submitted to international supervi-

---

6.   The official name of this state was 'The Sardinian Kingdom'. It included the island of Sardinia, Piedmont, Nice, Savoy, Genoa and the duchies of Aosta and Montferrat.

sion); the autonomy of the principalities on the Danube was guaranteed, and the Russian Black Sea navy was to be reduced.

But the main result of the Crimean War for Russia was that the complete unfitness of its army structure became apparent, based as it was on the conscription of recruits for a term of 25 years; and – even more importantly – the complete inadequacy of Russia's social structure was revealed. Nicholas I died before the war was ended, and the new emperor, Alexander II, started a series of reforms; the most important was the abolition of serfdom – although it is true that the peasants had to pay a certain ransom. A law of trial by jury was introduced.[7] The requisite conditions for capitalist development were created (but no actual power passed to the class of capitalists immediately). The abolition of serfdom made a labour force more readily available; the railway network was quickly growing, industry was developing. And, of course, the colonial wars usual for this Phase started.

For Russia's later history, it was very important that Russia's colonies (only Russia's!) were contiguous to its own territory: Transcaucasia was conquered between 1801 and 1827 (but finally secured for Russia only after the victory over the Caucasian mountaineers in their war of liberation of 1820–1859).[8] Kazakhstan (then called the Kirghiz Steppe) was conquered in the reigns of Catherine II, Alexander I and Nicholas I, and the so-called (Western) Turkistan, i.e. what now is Uzbekistan, Tajikistan and Turkmenia, was conquered only in 1865–1885. The forward movement of the Russian troops was stopped at the Amu-Darya, beyond which British influence prevailed. Inside Persia the limits of interests of both powers were defined.

There was a steady Russian immigration to colonial territories.

The comparative liberalism of the early years of Alexander II was followed by a new period of political reaction during his reign, at least in the 'western provinces', i.e. in the Polish Kingdom (officially, the 'Polish Tsardom' for the Russian authorities), and also in parts of Lithuania, Ukraine and Belorussia. A new Polish liberation movement emerged.

It contacted Russian democrats, Hertzen and Ogarev who published the journal *Kolokol* ('The Bell') in London, and the Central Committee of the underground organisation 'Land and Freedom' in Russia itself. The Polish insurrection was

---

7. This was an important step towards the modern concept of the necessity of a division between independent powers (according to Montesquieu): the legislative power, the executive power, and the judicial power. In Russia, the three powers have never been independent; the judicial power is still not independent today.

8. The war against the Russian conquerors was waged under the leadership of Islamic *imams*: Ghazi Muhammed, Hamzat-bek and Shamil. The mountaineers of the Caucasus lived at that period in a state of transition from the Third Phase, as were the mountaineers of Pamir and Afghanistan. The British made three attempts at conquering Afghanistan (1838–1843, 1878–1880, 1919–1921), but had every time to retreat. Nevertheless, they managed to incorporate into their Indian Empire a considerable part of the territory inhabited by the most important people of Afghanistan, the Pathans, with the city of Peshawar (now in Pakistan).

directed not against the Russians but against Tsarism. In January 1863, the insurgents attacked the Tsar's garrisons in several places inside Poland. They organised a temporary government almost immediately, and published a Manifesto, promising land to the peasants, and a compensation by the State to the landowners.

However, soon the so-called 'Whites' gained ascendancy among the insurgents. The 'Whites' refused to introduce agrarian reforms, did not create a central military High Command, dropped the contacts with Russian revolutionaries, and hoped in vain for external help. The Polish insurrection had little success in Belorussia and in right-bank Ukraine (west of the Dnieper), because here the peasants regarded the Poles as landed gentlemen.

In May 1863, the new governor-general of Lithuania and Belorussia, Muraviev ('the Hangman'), and the governor-general of the Kingdom of Poland, Berg, started a mass Terror against the Poles; at the same time they introduced agrarian reform in Lithuania, Belorussia and in right-bank Ukraine, and retained the social reforms of the Polish insurgent government in the Kingdom. By May 1864, the insurrection was crushed. A great number of insurgents were hanged or banished to Siberia, a still greater number of Poles were settled in the eastern European provinces of Russia, where they were gradually Russianised.

Later the Poles were given 'equal rights' with the Russians but only on condition that they adopted the Russian language. Polish was banished from the schools and the courts, Polish newspapers were prohibited, the Kingdom Poland was to be called 'Tsardom', and a process of its administrative Russification was started. At the same time, the abolition of customs barriers between Poland and Russia was favourable for the development of industry in Poland.

For the Poles, the situation in Austria-Hungary was somewhat better. From 1815, Cracow was a republic under the guardianship of Russia, Austria and Prussia; when in 1846 it was included in Austro-Hungarian Galicia, the Poles allied themselves in Parliament with the Austrians against the Ukrainian and Slovak members who were oriented towards Russia.

In the United States, during the time after the War of Independence, the capitalist mode of production took root in the Northern States. The so-called 'frontier' – the movement of the American settlers westward over the territory of the USA – expanded ever further to the West; the native people were pushed aside or annihilated. In the 1840s Texas, formerly belonging to Mexico, was annexed and following a war with Mexico, so were the territories which later constituted the States of New Mexico, Arizona, Colorado, Utah, Nevada and California. The discovery of gold in California produced a stream of immigrants in 1849. Still earlier, Britain ceded to the United States its rights to Oregon, another territory on the Pacific coast.

The industrial and agrarian revolution went on in the USA as actively as in Europe, if not more so: we may mention the introduction of the sewing machine, the electric telegraph, the all-metal plough, the mechanical harvester, the building of railroads, the introduction of hire-purchase on an instalment plan, trade advertisement; all this led to a flourishing both of capitalist industry and of capitalist agriculture. The United States started to export wheat from the new States.

But this technological progress was barely felt in the Southern States with their patriarchal planters' grain- and cotton-growing economy, based on slave labour. The life and mores of the southern planters were reminiscent of the mores of the Roman free citizens, or those of the medieval nobility with their duels and their notion of personal honour. The free population of the Southern States was uneasy about the creation of new States in the West, because they feared that a strong anti-slavery coalition may be consolidated in Congress and in the government; the flight of the Negroes to the Northern States, where they gained freedom, began to acquire a mass character and threatened the Southern economy. The opposition between the Southern and the Northern States brought about in 1861 a declaration of independence made by the Southern States (which formed a 'Confederation of States'); and this led to a civil war, which the Northerners won, and slavery was abolished in 1865. Shortly before that, the leader of the Northerners, President Lincoln, was shot by a terrorist.

The victory of the Northerners was not an unconditional boon. The economy of the Southern States was destroyed, the former slaves proved to be unsuited for a free labour market, the South was invaded by an army of occupation. The camps organised for the prisoners of war by the Northerners were not very much better than those later organised by Hitler. The reconstruction of the economy in the United States required considerable time.

In Europe and in America the growth of capitalist production engendered a pauperisation of a considerable part of the population, and an unrestrained exploitation of the working class. A 14-hour working day was standard; no mechanism for social protection and security existed; any attempt of the workers to create trade unions was suppressed. Under such conditions, a growth of revolutionary movements was imminent.

Revolutionary movements were not the only socio-psychological alternative to the grim capitalist reality; there was also literature, first the romantic, and later the realistic. European literature formulated the necessary new ideas of Man, of his dignity when facing the historical ordeals; it showed Good and Evil not in dogmatic half-religious forms, but as they really appear, coexisting in man's actual life.

It is not our task to relate and analyse the literary production of the nineteenth century. We shall only mention the names of writers who were important for the historical process itself. It is their creative work, much more than any religious or philosophical trends, which provided an alternative to the ideology of capitalism. These were Goethe (1749–1832), Schiller (1754–1805), Hoffman (1776–1822), Heine (1797–1856) in Germany; Stendhal (1783–1842), Balzac (1799–1850), Hugo (1802–1885), Merimée (1803–1853), Zola (1840–1902) in France; Scott (1771–1832), Wordsworth (1770–1850), Coleridge (1772–1834), Shelley (1792–1822), Byron

(1780–1824), Dickens (1812–1870), Thackeray (1811–1863) in Great Britain; Mickiewicz (1798–1855) in Poland; Pushkin (1799–1837), Lermontov (1814–1841), Gogol (1809–1852), Turgenev (1818–1883), Dostoyevski (1821–1881), L. Tolstoi (1828–1910), Chekhov (1860–1904) in Russia; H. Melville (1819–1891), Mark Twain (1835–1910) in the USA.

In Russia, the works of publicists Hertzen (1812–1870), Belinski (1811–1848) and Chernyshevski (1828–1889) had a great influence on the formation of the Russian liberation movement.

The great writers of the nineteenth century helped to understand their contemporaries: they showed what tormented them, what was their discomfort, and what was their strength and greatness.

Although the capitalist class, after its accession to power, attempted to base itself on the existing church, nevertheless, to justify the capitalist order in daily life and in the minds of men and women, something more than unreasoning faith was needed: namely, facts, and the knowledge of what at that period of development in knowledge could be regarded as indisputably, mathematically and physically proved truths. In science and philosophy the dominant trend was that of the positivists, who believed in capitalist progress as much as in the Bible. They identified capitalist progress as progress in general, that is, as what they believed to be as aspiration for the infinite common good. Their philosophy attempted to justify technological and social development, which they regarded as unquestionably progressive.

However, one should not regard the positivists simply as apologists for capitalism: some of them thought capitalism to be an evil, but an evil that will, of itself, develop into a better society.

But there was also a clear alternative to the capitalist ideology, namely, the revolutionary movement.

Extreme groups which were revolutionary and anti-capitalist in their outlook had appeared in France in 1789–1799; in England at the beginning of the nineteenth century; in Germany during the 1848 revolution. Here several tendencies can be traced: first, a Utopian (Count de Saint-Simon,[9] 1710–1825; Fourier, 1772–1837; Owen, 1771–1858); secondly, a conspiratorial, developing towards terrorism (A. Blanqui in France, 1805–1881, the People's Will in Russia, beginning in the 1870s); thirdly, an anarchist (Bakunin, 1814–1876); and lastly, the tendency of those who sought a scientific understanding of capitalism, and methods for liberating oneself from it (F. Lassalle, 1825–1867; K. Marx 1818–1883; F. Engels, 1820–1895).

Since in practice capitalism was becoming more and more international, it seemed reasonable to internationalise resistance to it.

9. Saint-Simon is traditionally regarded as a Utopian Socialist; however, he regarded his doctrine as a scientific theory; it is characteristic that (alongside of Hegelianism) it was Saint-Simonism that had the greatest influence on Karl Marx.

In 1864 an 'International Working Men's Association' (The First International) was founded in London. It was not organised by Marx, but it was Marx who headed it. The members were a rather mixed lot. The Marxists were not in the majority, it also included adherents of Blanqui, of Lassalle, of Bakunin, of Proudhon;[10] and it did not survive beyond 1875. But the Second International, founded in 1889 – although at first only including Marxists but also adherents of Lassalle, and anarchists, by the middle of 1890s turned completely Marxist. At the same time, inside the Second International, both a revolutionary wing (the two Liebknechts, father and son, Rosa Luxembourg, G. V. Plekhanov), and a reformist wing (E. Bernstein) were established. K. Kautsky, a pupil of F. Engels, kept to a centrist position. The history of the twentieth century finally proved that the reformists were right.

The British movement of the Trade Unionists was not involved with the Second International. These waged not so much a political as an economic struggle for the improvement of the conditions of the proletariat. Neither was the movement of the Fabian society connected with it. The Fabians represented left-wing intellectuals (Sidney and Beatrice Webb, Bernard Shaw, and others). In 1900 the Trade Unionists and the Fabians joined in founding the Labour Party which was soon to become one of the deciding political factors in the life of Great Britain.

The revolutionary movement in Russia developed, at first, practically without connection with the International (and without any connection with the Decembrist movement in Russia suppressed in 1825, but whose ideas were being developed by Hertzen who had emigrated to England). The Russian revolutionaries started with conspiratorial activities, then they turned to the policy of 'going into the people' (populist revolutionaries disguised as peasants tried to make propaganda to the peasant masses); and when this venture proved futile, the populists were divided into the terroristic 'People's Will', and the reformist 'Black Re-Allotment', which later merged with the Marxist movement.

A number of acts of terrorism culminated in the murder of Alexander II, on the day when the first timid project of a Russian constitution prepared by Minister Loris-Melikov was laid on the emperor's desk. On the advice of the influential reactionary Pobedonostsev, this project was not accepted by the son of the late emperor, Alexander III; and the introduction of a constitution was postponed until 1917, when it was thwarted by the Bolsheviks coming to power.

It is very characteristic that the bomb which mortally wounded Alexander II also killed a little boy who chanced to be passing by. Such boys perished regularly as the result of terrorist and other revolutionary acts.

The execution of Sofia Perovskaya, a young lady belonging to the nobility, of Zhelyabove, a peasant-born intellectual, and the other organisers of this murder

---

10. Proudhon (1809–1865), who coined the aphorism 'property is theft', did not actually profess an abolition of private property; he protested against the suppression of small-scale private property by large-scale capital.

did not stop the Russian revolutionaries from continuing terrorist actions; in the twentieth century they developed into a party which aimed at organising a peasant revolution in Russia, viz. the Socialist-Revolutionary Party, or the SR. The Marxists, or Social Democrats (at least their Bolshevik wing) did not approve of terrorism directed against individuals; they advocated mass terrorism based on the support of the working class. The aim of the Marxists in Russia was a proletarian revolution, with a shift of power from the minority to the majority. There was an internal contradiction in this attitude: the peasants constituted the majority of the Russian population, but the Social Democrats regarded the peasants only as fellow-travellers, and even among the peasants they planned to base their policy only on the poor peasants, i.e. those whose economy was least productive. As for the city proletariat in Russia, it constituted a small minority of the population which merged with *déclassé* groups.

It is easiest to account for the later history of capitalism by describing, as its landmarks, the most important wars of the epoch. It is usual to regard these wars as the result of political struggle for export markets and sources of raw materials, and of competition in this struggle. It certainly is true that the clash of interests between different national groups within the bourgeoisie played a most important role. What is startling is the triviality of the immediate causes of the wars of the nineteenth and early twentieth centuries.

The main warmonger in the 1850s–1870s was the French emperor Napoleon III. He envied the laurels won by his uncle, the great Napoleon, and he believed, mistakenly, that the most important attainment of the Napoleonic epoch was the augmentation of glory for French arms. The success of the Crimean campaign in 1854–1856 inspired him, and he started a new war in Italy.

Here capitalist production had gained ground only in the north-west, in Piedmont which was a part of the Sardinian Kingdom, alongside Sicily, Savoy and Liguria. Nominally, the Sardinian Kingdom was ruled by King Victor Emmanuel II (married to an Austrian princess), a man of little merit; but actually the power was in the hands of his energetic and gifted prime minister Cavour. The latter's idea was to create a united Italy, but not as a republican state (as envisaged by Mazzini who used conspiratorial tactics), but rather a conservative one with a moderate parliamentary monarchy. It was obvious that only Piedmont could be the core of such a state. Here, together with capitalism, a bourgeois national self-consciousness emerged, Literary Italian (the Tuscan dialect) had become vernacular, ousting local dialects and French from general usage.

Sardinia-Piedmont had taken part, as an ally of France, in the Crimean war, and Cavour encouraged Napoleon III to start a war against Austria; he planned to unite at least Lombardy, Tuscany and Venetia into a single Italian state. Napoleon III was easily persuaded: he wanted to reduce Austrian influence over the smaller Italian states, and thus to weaken the Austrian empire. The allies began to provoke Austria, and finally succeeded in making it declare war on the Sardinian Kingdom and France in 1859. But Napoleon III did not want Piedmont which was ready to conquer Tuscany, Umbria and the papal lands, to become too strong, he therefore concluded an armistice with Austria. Meanwhile, in Italy, a strong liberation movement emerged, organised mainly by Garibaldi, a veteran of the Italian freedom movement. Cavour gained Napoleon III's agreement to the liberation of further territories in Italy – in exchange for the Piedmontese territories of Savoy and Nice which were ceded to France. In 1860 the new state of Italy was founded, including Piedmont, Lombardy, Liguria, Tuscany and Romagna, and also Sardinia.

In the same year, Garibaldi, another conspirator, Crispi, Mazzini who had allied himself with them, and a number of adherents invaded Sicily, and entered the Kingdom of Naples. Francis II, the Bourbon king of Naples, fled. In 1861, Cavour occupied the papal territory, and his army entered the territory of the Neapolitan kingdom, including Sicily. Here the result of a plebiscite was unfavourable to Garibaldi, who, like Mazzini, did not support the process of creation of an Italian bourgeois state. Meanwhile, Italy allied itself with Prussia in a war against Austria, and was able to acquire Venice. For some time, the city of Rome continued in its status of an independent papal territory, and the troops of Napoleon III defended it from Garibaldi's attempt to capture it.

However, in 1870, when the Franco-Prussian war began, Napoleon III removed his garrison from Rome. The Pope retained, as his own state, only the territory of the Vatican and Lateran palaces; the government and parliament of unified Italy were transferred to Rome. Amid the venerable ruins of ancient Rome, a hideous giant marble construction was erected, as a memorial for Victor Emmanuel.

The Italian events did not bring much glory to Napoleon III, and he started a new hazardous adventure. In 1863 he persuaded a group of Mexicans, exiled from their country which was being ruled dictatorially by President Juárez, to suggest to Archduke Maximilian, a brother of the Austrian emperor Francis Joseph I, that he assume the title of Emperor of Mexico. It was represented to Maximilian as if the Mexican people had 'voted' for him. Accompanied by French troops, Maximilian arrived in Mexico, was crowned there, and started a series of liberal reforms which, however, were not supported by the Mexican landowners. The USA declared that the presence of French troops on the American continent violated 'the Monroe Doctrine';[11] Napoleon had to evacuate his troops; Maximilian was arrested by Juárez and shot.

France's next war was with Prussia. To be sure, Prussia had an interest in the industry of Alsace (a region adjoining the Prussian frontier and speaking a German dialect), and the German bourgeoisie was more and more competing with the French on different markets. But the immediate reason for the conflict was something else: it actually was again a War of Spanish Succession! The Spanish Queen

---

11. The Monroe Doctrine, formulated by President Monroe in 1824, and always subsequently adhered to by the United States, consisted in the following dictum: any attempt of a European power to control any part of the American continent is to be regarded as an action inimical to the United States.

Isabella II was deposed in 1868, and the Spanish government was looking for a suitable candidate to the throne among the reigning houses of Europe. William I, King of Prussia, suggested a distant relative of his, Prince Leopold of Hohenzollern-Siegmaringen. This caused the wrath of Napoleon III, especially since, after the war with Austria, Prussia had been greatly strengthened, and thus violated 'the balance of power'. William was ready to give in, but his minister Bismarck edited his telegram in such a way that Napoleon regarded it as a personal insult; on 14 July 1870 he declared war on Prussia, which was exactly what Bismarck wanted.

Prussia and the whole Northern German Union, with its allies, Bavaria, Baden and Würtemberg, were well prepared for the war; they quickly mobilised their forces and had a superiority in artillery. The French army had certain advantages, but it was badly organised behind the lines, and its high command committed tactical mistakes. On 31 August, barely six weeks after the war had begun, the French army suffered a complete defeat at Sedan, its main force with Marshal MacMahon and the Emperor Napoleon III at its head were taken prisoners. The French, led by Léon Gambetta, continued a resistance, mainly with the help of soldiers newly called up for military service. The Germans laid siege to Paris, and the war continued; however, the roads were blocked by thousands of prisoners of war, and the German troops required rest and re-formation. On 1 March 1871 a republican National Assembly convened in Bordeaux signed a peace. But on 18 March an insurrection broke out in Paris.

It was started by revolutionary workers, made desperate by the siege, who were expecting reactionary measures from the National Assembly in Bordeaux (and from the new government of Thiers which was sitting in Versailles); the workers were supported by the National Guards (militia) whom the government had failed to pay. Among the insurgents there were a number of foreigners. The insurgents elected a Central Committee.

An election to the Paris Commune was launched; the moderates did not take part. All over the country Communes were organised on the Paris model, but they were quickly suppressed by the government of Thiers. The Paris Commune administration consisted of seventeen members of the First International, eight adherents of Blanqui, eight members of the Central Committee which organised the military resistance, and thirty adherents of the traditions of the Great Revolution of 1789, mostly university students, salaried employees, journalists and *déclassé* elements. The Commune had not the time to introduce any radical reforms; it contained conflicting political trends, but it managed to arm 30,000 militiamen. Thiers sent against Paris an army of 130,000 men headed by Marshal MacMahon who had been released by the Germans. The battle for Paris lasted for seven days, and on 21 May 1871 the last armed defendants of the Commune were shot at the Père Lachaise cemetery, where now a monument stands to their memory.

During the battle for Paris the communards executed about sixty hostages, including an archbishop. In battle, more than 20,000 lost their lives; after the insurrection was suppressed, 38,000 were arrested and many of them were shot. About half of the prisoners were sentenced to penal servitude or to prison. Some of the working districts of Paris were half empty – more than 50 per cent of the house-painters, shoemakers, construction workers and joiners had disappeared from the city.

Karl Marx regarded the Paris Commune as the prototype of the future proletarian dictatorship which he foresaw for the entire world.

According to the peace treaty, France ceded to Germany Alsace and most of Lorraine. While they were on French territory, the German military did not conceal their disdain towards the vanquished, and earned a lasting hatred which was still felt half a century later.

After the war, all the German states except Austria entered the German union which was now declared to be an Empire, and William I of Prussia was in January 1871 crowned its emperor – in the palace of the French Kings at Versailles. Bismarck became his chancellor.

The next major war in Europe was the Russian–Turkish war of 1877–1878. Once again it was connected with the Balkan question. The Ottoman empire was on the verge of disintegration: the nations of the Balkans strove for independence and hoped for the support of Russia. A small number of Rumanians and Bulgarians served in the Russian army. On the Caucasian front, the Russian troops captured Kars and Ardahan with the surrounding territory, at that time inhabited by Armenians. On the Balkan front the battles were initially unsuccessful, partly because of difference of opinion among the military leaders (both fronts were headed not by experienced generals but by Grand Dukes). Eventually the Russian troops utterly defeated the Turkish army at Plevna and captured a very considerable number of prisoners. The Russians were very near to Istanbul. Then Britain introduced its warships into the Dardanelles, and Russia opted for peace. It retained its conquests in Transcaucasia. In the Balkans, the princedoms of Moldavia and Walachia which had been dependent on Turkey, were replaced by the big kingdom of Rumania (minus Bessarabia, which remained Russian, and Siebenbürgen, or Transylvania, which had Rumanians, Hungarians and Germans among its population, and which remained Hungarian). But the first attempt to create a strong Bulgarian state in the Balkans failed: the preliminary peace treaty of San Stefano between Russia and Turkey was invalidated by the Berlin Congress of the European Powers. According to its decisions, the southern part of the Bulgarian princedom was separated and became an autonomous district of Turkey, under the name of Eastern Rumelia; its governor was to be a Christian. The German Prince Alexander of Battenberg, a relation of Alexander II of Russia, was appointed to rule Bulgaria, and in Rumania, its ruler Alexander Cuza was replaced by the German Prince Karl of Hohenzollern-Siegmaringen.

The *fin-de-siècle* was full of colonial acquisitions and colonial wars. We shall dwell on the Anglo-Egyptian, the Spanish–American, the Anglo-Boer wars, and on the events in China.

During the entire nineteenth century, Egypt was nominally subject to Turkey, but actually its viceroy ruled the country as an independent sovereign. The importance of Egypt for Europe increased considerably after the French engineer de Lesseps and his collaborators had built the Suez Canal between the Mediterranean and the Red Sea (1859–1869); this drastically reduced the distance between Europe and Southern and Eastern Asia. As in all countries which were still in the Fifth to Sixth Phase of the historical process, certain attempts were made in Egypt to acquire European achievements in technology (including military technology) and in enlightenment, and at the same time a liberation movement developed against the European countries pursuing colonial policy. The rulers of Egypt could not do without European technical, financial and political counsellors, which gradually led first to an actual and later to a formal British protectorate over Egypt. In 1882 the revolt of Arabi Pasha took place in Egypt, impelled by nationalist, Islamic and liberationist rhetoric. The revolt was suppressed by the British, who from then on became the actual bosses of Egypt. Meanwhile, the building of the Suez Canal attracted the attention of all European powers to Egypt – but, of course, Turkey continued to regard Egypt as its vassal state.

Beginning with Muhammad Ali (1805–1849), the rulers of Egypt extended their military power up the Nile (to Sudan) to the borders of Ethiopia and the Saharan princedoms of Darfur and Kordofan. In 1884 a revolution started in Sudan; it was headed by an impostor calling himself the Mahdi, i.e. a Muslim Messiah, who according to popular Muslim (non-canonical) beliefs was to appear at the end of times. The Mahdi amassed considerable forces and captured the capital of Sudan, Khartoum, which had been defended by a military force headed by a British general. The whole garrison and a certain part of the city's population were massacred, but the following year the Mahdi died of typhoid fever, and the Mahdists were unable to resist the British onslaught.

An Anglo-Egyptian condominium over Sudan was established; but in fact, both Sudan and Egypt itself became territories dependent on Britain.

The Spanish–American war began with riots among the local population of Cuba in the Caribbean Sea; the island belonged to Spain. American public opinion regarded the cruel repressive measures taken by Spain against the insurgents as a violation of the Monroe Doctrine and the rights of man; the United States sent the battleship *Maine* to Cuba, but it was sunk in a Cuban harbour as a result of an explosion, either accidental or deliberate. This was the pretext for the Spanish–American war. The Americans not only established the independence of Cuba from Spain (actually under the protectorate of the USA), but annexed the island of Puerto Rico situated near the southern shore of the USA,[12] and landed

---

12. Later Puerto Rico received the status of a 'commonwealth associated with the USA', which meant, among other things, that Puerto Ricans were free to migrate to the USA. The island is grossly over-populated, and at present more Puerto Ricans live in the USA than on the island.

their troops in the city of Manila in the Philippine Islands, an Asiatic possession of Spain. The landing of the Americans in the Philippines was agreed to by the Filipino leader Aguinaldo, who had led a war of liberation against the Spanish government but at that moment was abroad; he had promised his help to the USA in their war against Spain. After the Americans had landed, Aguinaldo voiced his wish to acquire independence for the islands; but the insurgents had neither the arms nor the unity necessary for withstanding the Americans. The whole matter was made more complicated because the Philippines were inhabited not by one nation but by several tribal groups which spoke different languages and lived at different levels of development. The Americans needed three years to break down the resistance of the Filipinos, and to make Aguinaldo surrender. Simultaneously, the Americans deposed the last queen of the Hawaiian islands, Liliuokalani (1893), and then included these islands in the USA as a territory (1900; a state from 1959).[13] In 1899 Samoa, another island group in the Pacific, was divided between the United States and Germany. Thus United States became one more colonial power.

In South Africa, near the Cape of Good Hope, there is a fine harbour, a closed bay which from the sixteenth century was used by British and Dutch sailing ships as a resting place en route from Europe to India.

This harbour was appropriated by the Dutch East India Company. Here, in 1652, a small permanent Dutch colony was founded. The territory of South Africa south of the Orange river was at that time inhabited by stray wandering tribes of Hottentots (and, deeper inland, of Bushmen) who still lived at the first stage of historical development. The colonists organised barter with them. Black slaves had also been brought to the colony. At the beginning of the eighteenth century the population of the Cape Town colony numbered about 3,000; nearly half of them were slaves. The others, who were of European extraction, called themselves 'Boers' (lit. 'Peasants'). Later the term 'Boer' was applied to the Dutch population outside the Cape Town fortifications, and only later did it become a national self-designation. By the end of the century the Boers (including also a small number of French Huguenots, etc.) numbered about 15,000; they spoke Afrikaans, a local dialect of Dutch (the latter in its literary form was for a long time the official language; only in the twentieth century did Afrikaans receive that status). The number of slaves by the end of the eighteenth century was about 17,000. Two special categories of the population also emerged – the 'Coloureds' and the Griqua: descendants from liaisons between whites and Negro or Hottentot women. The local population was gradually ousted and often exterminated; some of the locals had to work for the whites; not a few died from new diseases imported by the colonists.

---

13. During the period of independence, Japanese, Chinese, Americans, Filipinos and Europeans begin to settle on Hawaii. At present, no more than 10 per cent of the island's population is of Hawaiian origin; only a minority of these have retained their native language. The same situation can be observed on many other islands of Polynesia that were (or still are) subject to France, the USA, New Zealand and Australia.

From 1779 a series of wars with the Bantu tribes began. These tribes had moved from the North. The main role, then and later, was played by the tribal groups Nguni (including Xhosa, Swazi and Zulu) and Soto (including Soto proper, or Suto, and Tswana). The Bantu tribes were on the level of early chiefdoms.

In 1795 the Cape Colony in South Africa was captured for a short time by the British, who nominally acted on behalf of the Prince of Orange (of the Netherlands) who had fled to England from the Republicans. In 1806 the Cape Colony was again occupied by the British, and this time they arrived to stay.

From the late seventeenth to the early nineteenth century a portion of the Boers, mainly those who were engaged in cattle-breeding, began to move (*treken*) to the inner regions of the country; they received the name of Trekboers.

As early as the beginning of the nineteenth century conflicts developed, with indiscriminate shooting between the British administration and the Trekboers, sometimes because the latter were accused of mistreating their Hottentot servants and the 'Coloureds'. In 1835 12,000 Boers left the colony together with their cattle and their coloured servants (slaves) and moved northwards to the steppes which were outside the limits of British authority (the so-called 'Great Trek'). As the Boers formulated it, the British had placed the slaves 'on an equal footing with Christians, contrary to the laws of God and the natural distinctions of race and religion, so that it was intolerable for any decent Christian to bow down beneath such a yoke; wherefore we withdrew in order thus to preserve our doctrines in purity'. The next decades were spent in partly armed, partly political struggle between the British, the Trekboers, the Nguni and the Soto. The two latter groups created rather strong militarised kingdoms. In 1852–1854 the Trekboers organised two republics of their own: the Orange Free State and Transvaal. However, more than three quarters of the Boers remained in the British Cape Colony, which received a representative government; the right of voting was here limited not by race but by economic status, which made little difference, because the blacks and the coloureds, as a rule, were anyway disfranchised by the property qualification. There were attempts to create schools for the blacks as well, but for a long time such attempts met with little success. In the Boer republics only whites had the right to vote.

By the end of the nineteenth century the population of the Cape Colony and the neighbouring colony of Natal reached the half million level; most of the population was of British descent.

During the nineteenth century the British authorities of the Cape Colony and of Natal had their hands full combating the strong militarised chiefdom of the Zulu tribe (of the Nguni group) headed by the kings Shaka, Dingaane and Cetchwayo in north-eastern Natal. The Zulus were finally conquered only in 1889.

The whole picture changed drastically when diamonds were found in 1867 in the valleys of the Orange and Vaal rivers, and abundant gold deposits in Witwatersrand in Transvaal (1870). In the next quarter of a century the population grew nearly fourfold; railroads were built, cities grew quickly. Mining for diamonds and gold was soon taken over by monopolistic Anglo-Boer companies.

At this stage, an important role in the history of South Africa was played by Cecil Rhodes, a prominent British millionaire and confirmed imperialist. Rhodes' political idea was that of creating a continuous zone of British possessions from the Mediterranean to Cape Town united by a single railway (later we shall observe on several occasions, that the building of railways had a great political importance). The implementation of Rhodes' idea was hindered by the existence of German and Portuguese colonies in Eastern Africa (these are at present the independent countries Tanzania and Mozambique) – and, of course, by the Boer republics. Britain endeavoured to surround the latter. For this, it made Bechuanaland (modern Botswana) its protectorate, and made it a subject of the British crown; the same happened with Rhodesia (now Zambia and Zimbabwe). The independence of the Boer republics was also threatened by the large influx of *uitlanders* ('foreigners', chiefly British) who were the main source of taxation in the republics. Kruger, the President of Transvaal, and the parliament of Transvaal, introduced laws which practically deprived the uitlanders of the right to vote (actually, the age and settlement qualifications were raised). Rhodes (who at that time was the prime minister of the Cape Colony), supported in secret by Joseph Chamberlain (the elder), the British Secretary of State for the colonies, organised an armed intrusion into Transvaal in 1895. However, the British authorities denied responsibility. Nevertheless, the conflict deepened. Britain demanded control over the foreign policy of Transvaal, and then began transferring troops to South Africa; in 1899 the Boers and the British, almost simultaneously, stated their ultimatums. The Anglo-Boer war had begun. The Boers had some initial successes, but the British brought new forces into action (partly from Australia, New Zealand, and Canada). By the autumn of 1900 Transvaal was conquered, Kruger escaped, but guerrilla warfare continued until 1902.

Two factors first introduced by the British (by General Kitchener) were later important during the World Wars. The first was the scorched-earth tactics used by the British in retreat, and secondly, concentration camps for women and children of the guerrillas.[14]

The Boers expected support from Germany – the declarations made by William II gave them a hope. Moreover, aggression of the huge British Empire against the tiny Boer republics produced public sympathy for the Boers – in Russia as well. The fact that the Boers were actually slave-owners did not register with public opinion.

The main point in the peace treaty was the Boers acknowledgement of British sovereign power; otherwise the conditions were comparatively favourable for

14. Two more inventions from the period of the Anglo-Boer War have been adopted by all armies of the world: khaki uniforms (they were introduced because the British soldiers clad in their traditional red uniforms incurred too many casualties from the Boers' sniper fire); and trench warfare tactics.

them: there were no severe trials of the leaders, no indemnities to be paid; the concentration camps were abolished. Britain even paid a sum of £3,000,000, and issued state loans on favourable conditions for the rehabilitation of the country for a total sum exceeding ten millions. Transvaal and the Orange River province received self-governing status (just as the Cape Colony and Natal), and Boer generals headed them. In 1910 all four colonies were constituted as the Union of South Africa; as its state languages both English and Dutch (after 1925, Afrikaans) were introduced; the Boers insisted that the coloured and black population should be disfranchised.[15]

Now let us turn to the Far East.

Under the Manchu dynasty China not only did not develop but in some respects it even went backwards in comparison with the Ming epoch. The tight closing of the Chinese frontiers was most harmful for the country – for one thing, because it cut Chinese society off from all the technical and social achievements of the outer world, and also because it made it impossible for the Chinese merchants to invest in other countries, which was of great importance for bourgeois development at the end of the Sixth and all through the Seventh Phase both in Europe and in America. Even the bourgeois class itself did not develop independently in China: the leading role still belonged, as before, to the bureaucrats who were selected by an examination system. Their big idea was not to change anything at all. In technology, including armaments, China lagged behind in an early stage of the Sixth Phase. There was no stimulus to any development of alternative ideologies.

Under such conditions, it is no wonder that China became an easy prey for Western capitalists. In 1839–1844, and again in 1856–1860 the Western Powers imposed on China, by military force, treaties that were to their sole advantage, while the Chinese stubbornly rejected the very idea of regarding foreigners as their equals. Pieces of Chinese territory were occupied by Europeans. Between 1851 and 1864, China was additionally weakened by an insurrection of the secret, half-Taoist, half-Christian T'ai P'ing Society. It won mass support, and they communicated independently with Western Powers; they also created something like a state organisation of their own, and declared their leader to be 'the younger brother of

15. In the Cape Colony a 'colour-blind' electoral system was introduced: there was no law debarring the Coloureds and the Blacks from voting, but, in fact, they were debarred from it by an economic and educational census. Later, inside the South African Union (since renamed the South African Republic) were founded autonomous territories, and in some cases, independent states, of the Bantu. These are Zululand (a part of the South African Republic), the kingdoms Swaziland and Lesoto, and the Republic of Botswana; the latter participates in the United Nations Organisation. The most numerous people, the Xhosa, have no specific territory of their own, and are the mainstay of the Africa National Congress party in the South African Republic, while the Zulus mainly support another party. As to the Hottentots, they have been preserved (under the name of Nama) only in Namibia; the Bushmen still exist in Namibia, in Botswana, and small groups of them also continue to exist in Zambia. As to the so-called Coloureds, a portion of them speak English, and another portion speaks Afrikaans. There are also numerous Indian and Pakistani immigrants.

Jesus Christ'. In their attempt to capture Peking, the T'ai P'ing were defeated. This period contributed to a further weakening of the country. The result was that representatives of one capitalist state after another received concessions to build railways, preferential rights to inspect Chinese habours, the possibility of concluding inequitable commercial agreements; opium was imported as before.

Chinese territory was divided into 'spheres of interest' of the different Western Powers.

In 1894–1895 there was a war between China and Japan, because China pretended to certain supremacy rights in Korea. The Chinese allegedly 'modernised' army was quickly defeated by the actually modernised Japanese army, which occupied the Liaotung peninsula, several harbours, and important points on the road to Peking. According to the peace treaty of Shimonoseki, China recognised the independence of Korea and ceded Liaotung, the Pescadore Islands and Taiwan to Japan, and had to pay a considerable indemnity. However, on the insistence of Russia, France and Germany, Japan withdrew from Liaotung.

The European powers imposed upon China a so-called 'capitulation regime'; China was forced to cede a number of harbours: Germany seized Tsingtao and the Kiaochow bay, Britain got Wei-hai-wei and, in addition to the island of Hong Kong which it already held, the Kowloon peninsula; France received Kwang-chou Wan on the Kwangtung peninsula, and Russia occupied Lü-Shun (Port Arthur) and Ta-lien (Dal'ny, Dairen) on the Liaotung peninsula. Nominally, all this was leased for 25–99 years. Russia also received the right to build a railway line across Manchuria, thus shortening its approach to Vladivostok and Port Arthur. In the zone of the railway the actual power belonged to Russia.

Inside China itself – as usual inside any state of the Fifth–Sixth Phase influenced by foreign capital – there existed two contradictory political forces. Those adhering to the one thought it necessary to introduce European knowledge and technology, if possible, immediately, and the necessary social and political reforms; those supporting the other trend viewed the foreigners solely as predators and barbarians; the way forward lay in getting them out of the country, and in strengthening traditional Confucian values. Of course, the first line of reasoning represented bourgeois and partly intellectual groups, while the second won response, on the one hand, among the Manchu and Chinese bureaucracy, and on the other, at the grass roots, because the mass of the people saw in the intrusion of foreign capital only greater oppression, proletarisation and lumpenisation. The conservative bureaucracy was headed by the cruel, unprincipled and domineering dowager empress Tz'u His, who ruled China from 1861 to 1908. She executed a portion of her reform-minded opponents, but the movement for reform continued.

In 1900 a popular insurrection of the I Ho T'uan (or 'Boxers') broke out. It was partly a peasant movement, but it also included declassed persons and the lower classes, e.g. in the cities. The 'Boxers' required the complete expulsion of Europeans, and generally all Christians, from China. These requirements were solicited with violence on their part, and by outright murders. Britain, France and Russia sent troops who temporarily occupied Peking (and looted its treasures).

Of great historical importance was the Russo-Japanese war 1904–1905.

The advance of the Russians to the Far East through Siberia had begun under Ivan the Terrible in the sixteenth century, when the Siberian Kingdom, a fragment of the Golden Horde, was conquered. At that time, a considerable part of the Siberian taiga zone was inhabited by tribes still remaining in the First or the Second Phase of historical development.[16] Therefore, the conquest of Eastern Siberia and the Chukotka peninsula, with a general direction towards the Pacific Ocean, resembled the movement of the North American 'Frontier' towards the Far West. It was mainly groups of Cossacks who infiltrated the tribal territories, exacting a *yasaq* (tribute) from the local population (mostly in the form of highly valued furs); then a movement eastward of Russian immigrants followed. In contradistinction from the European part of Russia, there was no serfdom in Russian Siberia, and even deported convicts (like my great-great-grandfather) could secure a plot of land of any size and achieve considerable success in agriculture.

During the nineteenth century, the Russians settled in the Amur valley, which nominally, according to the Russo-Chinese treaty of Nerchinsk (1689) was a tributary to China, but the latter was not in a condition to withstand the Russian forward movement headed by the governor of Siberia, N. N. Muraviev (Amursky). According to the treaty of Aigun (1858), Russia acquired most of the territories along the Amur and the land beyond the Ussuri river, with a fine natural harbour, where the important city of Vladivostok was built. Still earlier, in 1853, the Russians occupied Northern Sakhalin. This island was inhabited by tribes of the First Phase, the Ainu,[17] and at its southernmost end there were Japanese settlements. In 1861 Russia attempted to create a military base on the island of Tsushima between Korea and Japan, but owing to British pressure this doubtful enterprise had to be abandoned. In 1875 Russia occupied all of Sakhalin but ceded to Japan all claims to the Kuril Islands. In 1896, as already mentioned above, a treaty was concluded with China giving Russia the right to build a railway from Vladivostok across Manchuria, with a branch-line from Kharbin (Ha-erh-pin) to Mukden and further to Ta-lien on the Liaotung peninsula (see above). A strip along the railway was to be guarded by Russian troops. There were 80,000 Russian soldiers stationed in Manchuria and in Port Arthur on the Liaotung; here the Russians kept a strong squadron of warships (a smaller one was stationed at Vladivostok).

The *casus belli* for the Russo-Japanese war was the fact that certain Russian businessmen with contacts in the government acquired forest concessions in the valley

---

16. The Buryats – Mongol-speaking Buddhists of Lake Baikal area – belonged to a higher Phase of the historical process.

17. A tiny group of the Ainu, having practically lost their native language, still remains on the Japanese island Hokkaido. The Amu do not belong to the Mongolian race, and may be akin to the aborigines of Papua and/or Australia.

of the Yalu river – on Korean territory, which was emphatically regarded by Japan as within the sphere of its interests. Japan had more than half a million soldiers (including those just called up for military service), but of course Russia could eventually send twice as many soldiers to the front. Therefore, it was important for the Japanese to win the war as quickly as possible. In the night between 8 and 9 February 1904 the main Japanese fleet attacked Port Arthur; the Japanese managed to sink several warships, and arranged for a close blockade of its harbour. Simultaneously, they sunk or captured some Russian warships in Chinese and Korean harbours. The Russian command, both of the army and the navy, proved rather ineffectual (the best naval commander, Vice-Admiral Makarov, perished when trying to run the blockade: his flag-ship was blown up by a mine at the entrance to Port Arthur bay). On land, in spite of sending 30,000 soldiers every month to Manchuria, the Russians were defeated in the battles of Liaotung and Mukden.

The Japanese forces were already very tired, but the Russian fleet remaining in the Far East was incomparably weaker than the Japanese navy. Russian journalists of patriotic conviction persuaded the government to send a number of the best remaining ships in the Baltic to the Far East, and later also the Black Sea fleet (in October 1904). The movement of this 'Rozhdestvensky Squadron' was very slow, because it had to stop intermittently to load coal and food on its way while the British colonial ports were closed for the Russians, since Britain had declared a 'friendly neutrality' towards Japan. The movements of the Russian fleet were made public by the world press, and were no secret for the Japanese. While the squadron was on its way, the news came that the Japanese had unexpectedly captured Port Arthur in January 1905; thus the ships had to continue moving to Vladivostok, which meant through the Tsushima Straits, where Admiral Togo's Japanese fleet was dominant. Togo's ships had an advantage in speed, as well as in the armour-piercing force and the range of their artillery. Nearly the entire Russian fleet was destroyed – only a few high-speed ships were able to come out safe from the general slaughter; most of them retired to neutral ports. Taking into account the dissatisfaction rising in the country, the Tsarist government was forced to sue for peace with the United States as mediator. According to the Treaty of Portsmouth (1905), Russia ceded to Japan the Liaotung peninsula and Southern Sakhalin; it renounced claims to Korea and evacuated the troops from Manchuria. The Russian ships which had been sunk in Port Arthur harbour and the Korean ports (including the famous cruiser *Varyag* which was sunk by its crew in preference to yielding it to the Japanese) were salvaged by the victors and included in the Japanese navy.

The shameful defeat in the Russo-Japanese war and the great and useless losses induced a revolutionary situation in Russia. But already in 1900–1904 there were symptoms of unrest. Discomfort was felt by the peasants who had suffered the greatest losses in a war that had no sense for them, who carried the heaviest burden of taxation, and were dissatisfied with the landowners (whose number was small, but they owned at least half of the land, and after 1864 they still continued to require certain payments from the peasants who had formerly been serfs). Discomfort was felt by the bourgeoisie which still had not come to power in the country; discomfort was felt by the intelligentsia – first of all, because of the censorship of books and the press; discomfort was felt by the labourers because conditions of work were hard, and the labouring time long (10–11 hours); discomfort was felt by the conquered nations on the outskirts of the empire – the peoples of the Baltic regions, the Poles, and also the Ukrainians, the peoples of Transcaucasia and Central Asia. The war brought hardship, losses and bitter resentment to all strata of society.

On 22 January[18] 1905, a huge public demonstration involving more than 100,000 men and women brandishing placards approached the Tsar's palace at St Petersburg; it demanded sundry liberties. It was met by gunfire,[19] and about 1,000 people died. Strikes started in St Petersburg, and in some places streets were barricaded. All over the country there was a wave of strikes; nearly half of the proletariat took part in them. The movement was directed against the autocratic Tsar and the military; in the outlying territories it was also boosted by local national feelings.

It seemed that a revolution was in the offing. In this connection, everybody looked back to the Great French Revolution of 1789. But both the intelligentsia and the liberal bourgeoisie were afraid of anything reminiscent of the Jacobin dictatorship and its atrocities; as to the Marxist social democracy, which already had considerable influence among the working class, it, on the contrary, wanted a Jacobin-type dictatorship, but not a 'petty bourgeois' one (as the actual Jacobin revolution was regarded) but proletarian. There were disagreements among the Marxists as to the role of the peasantry or the bourgeoisie, and whether the introduction of a dictatorship of the proletariat was feasible or not.

Meanwhile, the strikes multiplied and more and more acquired a political character. From May to July the textile-workers of Ivanov-Voznesensk went on strike and organised a 'Soviet (=Council) of Workers' Deputies' (later this form of political power was adopted by the Bolshevik revolution of 1917); insurrections and rebellions occurred in Poland, in Georgia, and in the navy – in the Baltic and the Black Sea fleet (notable was the rebellion of the battleship *Potemkin*). The soldiers returning from Manchuria were ready to support the revolutionary movement. On

18. The dates are quoted according to the 'New Style' (i.e. the Gregorian calendar). In Russia, up to 1917, the official calendar was the Julian, which in the twentieth century was thirteen days behind the Gregorian. So in the Russian historiography, this demonstration bears the name of 'The 9th of January events'.

19. The procession was organised by a priest, Gapon; he had persuaded the workers that the Tsar was bound to understand their complaints. Afterwards, Emperor Nicholas II made Tsarkoye Selo near St Petersburg his residency, and appeared in the capital no more. The connection of Gapon with the police is certain, but he may have sincerely believed that he would be able to make use of the police for his 'revolutionary' purpose. Later he was murdered by Social Revolutionaries.

6 August 1905, the Tsarist government summoned a 'consultative Duma (parliament)', but the revolutionary movement did not abate, the strikes extended to ever new factories and to the railways. In October an All-Russian political strike began.

Finland had been annexed to Russia after the Napoleonic wars but enjoyed a certain autonomy during most of the nineteenth century, which it had recently lost. Now it demanded its reinstitution (and the demand was granted).

In the end of October, Nicholas II issued a manifesto which introduced a 'legislative State Duma'; the electorate was slightly expanded. Also, there was an amnesty for political convicts. Exaction of redemption money which had been paid by the peasants since 1864, was discontinued; censorship of books and of the press was abolished.

Non-revolutionary political parties emerged; the most important of those represented in the Duma were the Constitutional Democrats (the *Kadets*), and the right-wing Octobrists. The revolutionary parties were not admitted to the Duma, and they continued to agitate outside it. The workers organised trade unions all over the country; an eight-hour working day became common. Unrest increased. The social democrats (including the Bolsheviks) and the populist 'socialist revolutionaries' (SR) began to prepare a general uprising. In order to finance the revolutionary parties, banks and private persons were robbed (this was called 'expropriation'). A Soviet of St Petersburg was organised, dominated by the social democrats and the SR; it urged the people not to pay taxes, to withdrawn their deposits from the savings-banks, and to demand payments in gold.

The government answered with a counter-offensive. Reprisals were made against peasants in Russia, Poland and Transcaucasia; revolutionary leaders were arrested. In answer to the first reprisals, a rebellion began in Moscow in December 1906; then uprisings also occurred in some other cities. These were unsuccessful and quickly suppressed. By spring 1906 the number of executions exceeded 15,000.

The revolution began to lose force. In 1905 more than two million labourers had been on strike (60 per cent of the city proletariat, which constituted just above 3 per cent of the entire population), but in 1906 no more than one million were on strike; mass redundancies began, unemployment was growing. At the same time, navy personnel became involved in the revolutionary movement.

The First State Duma, assembled in April 1906, had but limited rights, and was dissolved by July. Courts martial were introduced all over the country; Stolypin was appointed prime minister. Early in 1907 there were elections to the Second Duma, which was more leftist than the First. It was likewise dissolved by the Tsarist government.

The Russian people remembered Stolypin for breaking up the Duma and especially for mass hangings and the obdurate policy of Russification in the frontier (non-Russian) regions. With public opinion thus set against Stolypin, the importance of his agrarian reforms went unappreciated. These reforms consisted of releasing the peasantry from ransom payments to their former owners, from being obliged to partake in a rural community (called *mir*), which bore a collective responsibility to the administration for its members, and in stimulating market-oriented farmers. Nicholas II did not approve of Stolypin's agrarian politics. In September 1911 Stolypin was killed by a terrorist under circumstances which were never clearly explained: either the murderer was a member of an SR terrorist organisation, or he belonged to the Tsarist police spy system.

By the 1910s the whole of Eurasia and Africa had been subdivided among the great powers. This was the result not only of those wars already described: on the scale which we use to describe world history, we have had to omit a number of 'minor' wars and other examples of mass bloodshed and mass human suffering.

In Asia six states still retained their independence: China,[20] Siam (now Thailand), Nepal, Afghanistan, Persia (now Iran) and Najd (in central Arabia); in Africa only Ethiopia. China (pieces of which had been torn out by Britain, France, Germany, Russia and Japan)[21] was in a semi-colonial state, being the object of foreign capitalist exploitation; Nepal was actually dependent on the British Indian Empire. Persia was semi-officially divided between Russia and Britain into 'zones of interest'.

Colonial possessions of Britain were the islands Cyprus and Malta in the Mediterranean, the port of Aden near the entrance to the Red Sea (also some Arab principalities along the coasts and on the islands of the Indian Ocean and the Persian Gulf were dependent on Britain); also among its colonies were India, Ceylon (now Sri Lanka), Burma, Malaya (with Singapore), Northern Borneo (Kalimantan) and the protectorate of Brunei, many of the Pacific Islands; in Africa, British Somalia, Kenya, Tanganyika, the island of Zanzibar, Uganda, Nyasaland, North and South Rhodesia, Bechuanaland (now Botswana), Nigeria, Gold Coast (now Ghana), Sierra Leone, Gambia; Egypt was a British protectorate, Sudan was an Anglo-Egyptian condominium. Britain also owned the island of St Helena in the Atlantic Ocean, and in the region of America its possessions were the islands of Trinidad, Tobago, Jamaica, the Falklands, the Bahamas, and Bermudas and, on the continent, British Guiana (now Guyana) and British Honduras.

Some of the former British colonies where the number of inhabitants originating from Britain substantially exceeded the number of the surviving aboriginals received the status of Dominions in the British Commonwealth of Nations and the right to independent international relations. These were Canada, Newfoundland (later joined to Canada), South Africa,[22] Australia and New Zealand.

Colonial possessions of France were located in Asia: French Indo-China (now Vietnam, Laos, Cambodia), the port Pondichéry in India; in Africa: Tunisia, Algeria

20. Although the Great Powers recognised China's sovereign power over Tibet and Mongolia, these territories were practically independent.
21. After the Russian–Japanese war, Russia retained her rights to the railways in Northern Manchuria.
22. In 1946, Newfoundland became a part of Canada; in 1961, South Africa left the Commonwealth.

and (with the nominal preservation of the sovereignty of the Turkish sultan) Morocco, French Western Africa (now Mauritania, Senegal, Guinea, Mali, Burkina Faso, Côte d'Ivoire, Togo, Dahomey and Niger), French Equatorial Africa (now Cameroon, Gabon, Congo-Brazzaville, Central African Republic); in the Indian Ocean: the island of Madagascar and other islands; in the Pacific: the islands New Caledonia, Tahiti, Tuamotu and others; in South America: French Guiana.

Note that the political attitudes of England and of France towards their colonies were different. The British attempted to make use of traditional structures: chiefdoms, princedoms, etc. When its colonial empire fell asunder, many of the former colonies, though achieving independence, expressed their wish to remain in the British Commonwealth of Nations. France ruled its colonies directly through French bureaucrats – and in the middle of the twentieth century lost all its colonies.

The United States owned the Philippines, the island of Guam and part of the Samoa archipelago in the Pacific, and the island of Puerto Rico in the Caribbean, as well as the Panama Canal Zone.

In Western Africa former black slaves from the USA founded the republic of Liberia.

It is difficult to decide the extent of the Russian colonial empire, because conquered land bordered on land which either was Russian from olden times, or had long ago been nearly completely Russified, as, e.g. Siberia. Doubtless non-Russian were the part of Poland which not so very long ago had been occupied by Russia (and not by Prussia or Austria-Hungary), autonomous Finland, all Transcaucasia and Daghestan, and the regions then known as 'Turkestan', i.e. modern Kazakhstan, Kirghizia, Tajikistan, Uzbekistan and Turkmenia. Other non-Russian possessions of the empire were the Baltic districts which had been acquired by Russia partly from Poland, and partly from Sweden; but the prevailing literary language in most of the Baltic territories was not Russian nor the local languages but German. The Ukrainians also considered their land as non-Russian; however, the territory of the Ukrainian language did not coincide with the present-day frontiers of the Ukraine: the Black Sea coastal strip (Novorossia) was mainly Russian-speaking but with considerable Jewish, Greek and German minorities; the eastern regions (the Donbass coal basin) were settled mostly by Russians (including Cossacks). Both Poland and the Ukraine had a considerable Jewish minority. The Crimea was gratuitously presented to the Ukraine by Khrushchev, but is now officially regarded as originally Ukrainian land; the Turkic-speaking Crimean Tatars had been deported to Siberia by Stalin; now their survivors attempted to return to Crimea against the wishes of the authorities.

Italy's colonial possessions were Tripolitania, Cyrenaica, and Fezzan (=Libya), Eritrea and Italian Somali in Africa, the islands of Rhodes and the Dodecanese islands in the Aegean Sea.[23]

---

23. These colonies emerged as a result of Italian armed incursions into certain regions of Africa, and also of the war between Italy and Turkey in 1912.

The colonial possessions of Portugal were the Azores islands (the population now speaking only Portuguese), the Cape Verde Islands, Portuguese Guinea, Angola, Mozambique in Africa, the port Goa in India, Eastern Timor in Indonesia.

Of Spain's former colonial dominions, all that remained were the Canary Islands (now Spanish speaking) and an unimportant territory in Western Africa.

The Netherlands owned the rich Netherlands East Indies (now Indonesia), and the Dutch part of Papua New Guinea.

The colonies of Denmark were Iceland and the Faeroe Islands (both with self-government), and a few islands in the Caribbean.

An exceptional case was the Belgian Congo. From 1876 to 1908 this huge colony belonged not to Belgium, but personally to the Belgian king Leopold II, who had organised an 'International Organisation of the Congo for its Exploration and Civilisation'. As the result of the civilising mission, the colonised territory was devastated, and its population exploited as slaves; in thirty years their number was reduced to a half of what it had been before Leopold.

The colonial acquisitions of Germany were limited to South-Western Africa (now Namibia), to the small colony of Togo, to Cameroon, to German Eastern Africa (which included Rwanda-Burundi, later ceded to Belgian Congo), to Tanganyika (which now constitutes the major part of Tanzania), to a part of New Guinea and some Pacific islands, of which the islands in the north-eastern part of the Ocean and a part of the Samoan archipelago were the most important. From the point of view of German capitalism, whose level of development was behind only Britain and the USA, these colonies were quite insufficient. It was Germany first of all which needed a redistribution of colonies. The slogan of German politics became *Weltpolitik*, i.e. 'politics on a world scale'; in order to implement it, a 'Battle Fleet of the Open Sea' was built, which England regarded as a direct threat to itself.

It is not so easy to decide which part of Austria-Hungary should be regarded as colonial. On Austro-Hungarian territory lived Czechs, Slovaks, Ruthenians (who later identified themselves as Western Ukrainians), Poles, Germans, Rumanians, Slovenes, Croatians, a few Serbs, and also Jews who inhabited both Austria and Hungary in considerable numbers. These ethnic groups were represented in the Austro-Hungarian parliament, but of course they were always in the minority. All of them, during the second half of the nineteenth century and in the twentieth developed national liberation movements.

Since 1878, Austria-Hungary had had under its protectorate the region of Bosnia and Herzegovina, which previously belonged to Turkey, and was inhabited by Serbs (Orthodox Christians), Croatians (Catholics) and Bosniaks (Muslims).[24] In 1908 the Austro-Hungarian government annexed Bosnia and Herzegovina, causing great indignation in Serbia and, to a certain extent, in Russia as well.

---

24. The Serbs, the Croatians, the Muslim Bosniaks and the Montenegrins speak dialects of practically the same language.

In spite of Austria-Hungary's claims in the Balkans, Turkey kept to the alliance with Germany, and hence also with Austria-Hungary. German military experts made serious efforts to modernise the Turkish army, German engineers made plans for constructing a railway track from Berlin to Baghdad.

Turkey, although lagging behind the other powers, also had an empire of its own: it included Iraq, Syria, Palestine, Trans-Jordan, and, in Arabia, Hijaz (with the sacred Muslim cities Medina and Mecca), and Yemen. Egypt, together with Sudan, was actually lost for the Turkish (Ottoman) Empire. The Balkans and Northern Africa were also completely lost for Turkey from the nineteenth century into the early twentieth.

Now we are approaching the fateful events of World War I (1914–1918), and we must characterise the main actors in the ensuing drama. These were Germany, Austria-Hungary, Italy, Turkey, Britain, France and Russia. (Serbia and Belgium were more acted against than acting themselves.) What did each of them need?

Germany, with its strong and quickly developing industry, needed sources of raw material and readily available markets. Since the coming to power of Emperor William II, the relations between Germany and Russia, in spite of short-lived spells of 'friendship', had in general been deteriorating. It seems that William regarded friendship with Russia as incompatible with the alliance between Germany and Austria-Hungary, and with German interests in Turkey.

For Austria-Hungary it was necessary to strengthen its position in a milieu of awakening Slavic national movements, which made a stormy political situation both inside and outside the empire; these movements were to a considerable extent instigated by Russia. Austria-Hungary also regarded it as desirable to extend its territory.

Italy hoped to round out its frontiers by annexing the Italian-speaking districts of Austria-Hungary, and to play a greater role than before in acquiring colonies. It had already seized from Turkey the island of Rhodes (inhabited by Greeks), and Libya.

Turkey wanted to preserve its empire, which included a part of the Balkans and most of the Arabic-speaking countries in Asia. Its integrity was threatened by internal national movements, as well as by European powers. For instance, Russia dreamed, at the very least, of acquiring Constantinople (Istanbul) and the Straits. With Russia's help, several independent Slavonic states had arisen in the Balkans – Bulgaria, Serbia, Montenegro.

Britain claimed the regions around the Suez Canal (which at that time was, to all intents and purposes, owned by the British); they wished to retain their worldwide empire, and to keep up the communications with all its parts. Britain feared industrial and naval competition with both France and Germany, and therefore hoped to extend its Indian Empire all the way to Palestine and Suez. Cecil Rhodes bequeathed to Great Britain the idea of the Port Said–Cairo–Cape Town railway which was made impossible by the existence of German East Africa. Moreover, the very maintenance of so huge an empire as the British was a great problem in itself, and Germany was, in this respect, a major threat.

The relations between Germany and the other powers were anything but simple. Germany, on the one hand, of course wanted to continue modernisation – but was mainly modernising the army and the navy; on the other hand, William II's idea of building a railway from Berlin to Baghdad might have resulted in a German protectorate over Turkey, which was dangerous not only for Britain but also for France and for other powers.

We have already remarked that in the first half of the twentieth century the building of railways was regarded as a measure of the greatest economic and strategic importance. And no wonder, since as yet there was no transportation either by motorcar or by air; there were not even asphalted roads. Who owned a railroad controlled exports and imports.

At the end of the 70s and the beginning of the 80s of the nineteenth century Europe was dominated by the 'Dreikaiserbund' (Alliance of the Three Emperors – those of Russia, Austria-Hungary and Germany); this Alliance was a survival of the 'Holy Alliance' of the early nineteenth century. But after the beginning of the reign of William II in Germany, and his dismissal of Bismarck – whose main anxiety was not to let Germany wage war on two fronts – and also after the war between Serbia and Bulgaria in 1886, which showed the incompatibility of the interests of Russia with those of Austria-Hungary, Germany decided to rely solely on the latter. The Dreikaiserbund, for some time, remained in existence, but rather nominally. Russia, losing the support of Austria-Hungary and Germany, decided to turn to France – not without misgivings, since France had a republican government. In 1891–1894 Alexander III and the French president worked out a mutually helpful treaty and confirmed it officially. (If Germany, or Italy allied with Germany, attacked France, Russia was to be on France's side; if Germany, or Austria-Hungary allied with Germany, attacked Russia, France was to be on Russia's side.) During the following decade France advanced considerable loans to Russia, and therefore was interested in keeping up the Franco-Russian alliance.

The march of events was to some degree shaped by the personality of the German emperor William II. Narrow-minded, cruel and conceited, he regarded world politics as the affair of a few interrelated families (he was himself grandson to the British Queen Victoria, a cousin of Nicholas II; many Russian Grand Dukes were married to German princesses, German princes sat on the thrones of Rumania and Bulgaria). At the same time, William's mentality was limited by certain strange ethnic (or, rather, racial) idiosyncrasies: Slavs and Gauls (read Russia and France), foreign to the Germanic blood and spirit, were eternal enemies of the Germanic principles, which also embraced the Anglo-Saxons who were by origin a Germanic tribe; they must join the Germans against the Gauls and the Slavs.

All this was a vaguely misunderstood perception of some ideas originating in late German romanticism, and of a pseudo-scientific theory of the superiority of the

Germanic race (which was thought to include the Germans, the Austrians, the British and the Scandinavians) over all other races. (The term 'race' was in this case conceived not in the scientific sense, i.e. as a stable combination of certain observable biological traits, e.g. the colour of the hair, the skin and the eyes, form of the skull, etc., but as including language and even some other changeable features, not readily formulated, nor clearly observable, such as 'mentality' and 'culture', which depend not on race but solely on a common historical fate.) These ideas were propagated in the nineteenth century by the Comte de Gobineau, the composer Richard Wagner, and especially by his son-in-law H. S. Chamberlain, and in more rationalised forms by F. Nietzsche, O. Spengler, etc. This pseudo-philosophical mish-mash, connected with arbitrary mental constructions regarding some vague national traits supposedly inherited from Antiquity and the Middle Ages, was quite seriously absorbed by William and his associates, without taking into any account the inevitable intermixture of the peoples during the centuries and millennia of their existence.

It should also be taken into consideration that from the middle of the nineteenth century Germany developed a strong and many-sided militarisation of mass consciousness. Even in a collection of folk songs in the popular edition of *Reclam Universum*, we encounter, alongside of a few real masterpieces, quite a lot of rhymed militaristic rubbish, something like 'Let us go, let us go, let us murder, let us murder the French.'

Egypt was one of the main points where the interests of Britain and France clashed in the Near East. Nominally, it belonged to the Ottoman Empire, but it had an autonomous status, and moreover was actually dependent on Britain. The political struggle between France and Britain for Egypt, made it one of the hot spots in politics before World War I.

Like Germany, France also regarded its colonial empire as insufficient.[25] It hoped to regain Alsace and Lorraine from Germany, and to pay for the defeat of 1871 in such a way that it never could happen again. Moreover, Germany was a threat to France's African colonies.[26]

And finally Russia was interested, first of all, in disintegration of the Ottoman Empire and the possibility of becoming a Mediterranean power. Russia still hoped (quite seriously) to create a Great Slavonic Empire which would engulf the Czechs, the Slovaks, the Slovenes, the Serbs, the Croatians and the Bulgarians. Although this was not publicly announced, the example of the Poles clearly showed that Russia regarded all Slavs simply as material for their complete Russification.

It is evident that Russia was a threat to Austria-Hungary.

25. Sometimes French interests could also be in conflict with the British ones: an example was the Fashoda crisis in 1898, when an armed French detachment, moving from Central Africa, captured the fortress Fashoda on the Upper Nile (in Sudan), creating the possibility of war with Great Britain.
26. This was apparent from the Agadir incident in 1911, when a German gun-boat entered the Moroccan port Agadir, in violation of a French–German agreement.

The Balkan war of 1912–1913 began when Bulgaria allied itself to Serbia against Turkey, at a moment when the Turks were engaged in a war with Italy for dominion over Libya. But later Bulgaria and Serbia quarrelled over Macedonia: the Serbs regarded the Macedonians as Serbs, and the Bulgarians regarded them as Bulgarians. Actually, they are a separate Slavonic-speaking group,[27] whose dialect is related to the Bulgarian language, but is not identical with it. Serbia was supported by Greece and Rumania. Being dissatisfied with the outcome of the war, Bulgaria decided to enter into a bloc with Austria-Hungary (and even with Turkey). One result of the war was the creation of an independent Albania. Greece acquired some new land, particularly some islands in the Aegean. Serbia acquired a part of Macedonia and a common frontier with Montenegro. Its relations with Turkey and Austria-Hungary deteriorated, and Serbia sealed its future with Russia.

As mentioned above, by 1878 Austria-Hungary already occupied a former Turkish region – Bosnia and Herzegovina. Other Slavonic regions also belonged to Austria-Hungary: Polish Cracow, Czechia, Slovakia, Ruthenia,[28] Ukrainian-speaking Galicia, Croatia (with its Dalmatian coast of the Adriatic) and Slovenia. The mountaineers of Austria are, by a majority, Germanised Slavs.

It is but natural that under these conditions the Slavonic nationalists in the Austro-Hungarian dominions became oriented towards kindred and independent Serbia, and later towards Russia.

Italy was nominally a member of the Triple Alliance together with Germany and Austria-Hungary, but in actual fact their common interests were not important, and from 1902 Italy was bound by a secret treaty with France; according to this treaty, if Germany attacked France, Italy would remain friendly to the latter.

The Young Turk government of the Ottoman Empire was concerned with modernisation of the Turkish society and the armed forces. The Young Turks wanted to stop the disintegration of the Turkish empire, and they feared nationalist movements inside it: these had already led to the loss of the Balkans; in Asiatic Turkey a great many Arabs, Armenians, Kurds and Greeks lived beside the Turks; the seizure of the Turkish Straits was constantly desired by European powers, most of all by Russia, which also claimed the right to protect the interests of all Christian subjects of Turkey (including the Armenians), and also the sites in Palestine sacred to the Christians. Therefore, the Young Turks favoured the German *Drang nach Osten*. The German General Liman von Sanders was appointed Chief Inspector of the Turkish army, and a number of German economic, engineering, and military counsellors were sent to Turkey. It regarded Russia as its main potential enemy.

---

27. Of course, the modern Macedonians are Slavs, and have nothing whatever in common with the ancient Macedonians, who were akin to Greeks and Thracians, and became world-famous in the fourth century BC under Alexander.

28. This is now the Uzhgorod oblast of the Ukraine. The population of northern Bukovina occupied by Austria-Hungary was also Ruthenian (Rusinian); the southern part of that country had a Rumanian population.

By the end of 1913 all the multiplying tensions in Europe came together in a war of proportions unheard of in the history of the Earth. No 'movement for peace', like the one frequently mentioned in our generation, existed – perhaps with the exception of a few socialists. Thus, in France, Jean Jaurès warned against the threat of a war, but he was killed by a right-wing nationalist terrorist. At the fatal moment, the social democrats (parties of the Second International) voted for war credits in their respective parliaments, for 'the defence of the fatherland'. But the awful fact was, that the coming war was planned, by everybody concerned, not as a defensive, but as an offensive war. Even the nationalist liberation movements – those of the Czechs, the Slovaks, the Croatians, later the Arabs – pinned their hopes with an offensive war.

The Russian government regarded itself as prepared for war: between 1905 and 1913 very much had been done for the modernisation of the army, including artillery and rifles; but it is true that not all of the new modernised navy was ready in the Baltic – and neither was it quite ready in the Black Sea. The Russian railway network was of course inadequate for the needs of contemporary troop-transportation, and any mobilisation in Russia was doomed to delays.

But if the technological lessons of the Russo-Japanese war were being taken into consideration, the same cannot be said either of the probable economic consequence, or of the moral and psychological state of the population. Both in Germany and in Russia, the leaders of the country were thinking in purely military terms; they did not at all care for the economic and political events which would necessarily result from entering a war much more formidable than the one which only nine years ago had been lost to a certain newfangled Oriental political marvel. One might have remembered that even this 'small' war had led to a major shock to the whole social and state structure of Russia.

In June 1914, when the heir to the Austro-Hungarian throne, the archduke Francis Ferdinand, inspector general of the Austro-Hungarian army, arrived in Sarajevo, the capital of Bosnia, for taking part in military exercises, two attempts were made on his life. They were organised by a Serbian secret agent, but without the knowledge and permission of the Serbian authorities, who even tried to avert the incident. The first attempt, on 28 June, when a grenade was thrown at the archduke, was unsuccessful; but after three quarters of an hour, Francis Ferdinand and his wife, when passing through the streets in a car, were shot dead by a Bosnian high school student, Gavrilo Princip. The outburst of rather bellicose public sentiments in Austria-Hungary was even more strongly supported by William II in Germany.

In Vienna the opinions on what measures should be taken differed. But from the outset, the German emperor William II insisted that Serbia should be punished. After only a month of deliberations, on 23 July 1914 Austria-Hungary presented an ultimatum to Serbia which, nevertheless, was to be answered in less than 48 hours. On 24 July all Powers were informed of the ultimatum through diplomatic channels. It was deliberately couched in such terms that no independent government could agree to implement it: its aim was to involve Austria-Hungary deeply into all internal affairs of Serbia. Actually, what was meant by the ultimatum was the annihilation of Serbia as an independent state. Germany took upon itself the task to 'localise' Russia, and to prevent its interference. Russia, on the other hand, declared that it was not going to allow the suppression of Serbia by Austria-Hungary.

The Serbian prime minister Pašić delivered his answer to the ultimatum strictly on time. Serbia accepted all terms required by Austria-Hungary, except two: the right of the latter to remove Serbian officials, and the right of Austro-Hungarian officials to act on Serbian territory in order to investigate the activities of possible subversive organisations on Serbian soil, and to take part in court proceedings against such.

Austria-Hungary mobilised for war. Britain suggested a mediation of four Powers: Britain, France, Germany and Russia. At first, William II regarded the Serbian reaction to the ultimatum as a victory, and suggested only a temporary occupation of Belgrade. But then the Austrian government, instigated by the German Ministry of Foreign Affairs, and the German General Staff, declared war on Serbia on 28 July; on 29 July Belgrade was bombed, and thus began the mass murder of men and women who were in no way personally involved in the conflict.

Although Russia had no direct treaty of mutual aid with Serbia, they had common interests, and were bound by oral agreements. Therefore, on 30 July it mobilised for war against Austria-Hungary. The latter took counter-measures. In Germany a 'state of war danger' was proclaimed; on 31 July Germany presented two ultimatums: one to France – to keep neutral; the other to Russia – to stop mobilisation. It is characteristic that all parties thought in purely military, not political terms.

On 1 August 1914, Germany declared war on Russia. France began to mobilise. On 2 August 1914 German troops violated the neutrality of Belgium and began advancing towards Paris. On 9 August Germany declared war on France.

At the same time, the Kaiser applied his favourite nationalist racial rhetoric, trying to convince the British king George V (his own cousin) of the need for Anglo-Saxons to support their blood-brothers against the racially alien Gauls (Celts) and Slavs.

Britain was connected with France (and through France with Russia) not by a defensive alliance but only an 'Entente cordiale', and in the first days it doubted the wisdom of being involved in a European war. But when the Germans started to conquer neighbouring Belgium,[29] which had received a guarantee of its neutrality from Britain, the threat of German troops reaching the coast of the European

---

29. Also Luxembourg, but this evoked less repugnance, perhaps because it was partly German speaking. Its population speaks three different languages – French, German and Letzeburgesch, a Germanic dialect.

continent became real, and Britain declared war on Germany on 4 August. Sometime later, on 5 September Britain, France and Russia ('The Entente') signed a treaty agreeing that no signatory would make a separate peace with the Central Powers. (This proved most unfavourable for the future of Russia.)

The strategic plan of the late General Schlieffen, which had been prepared inside the German General Staff for securing a quick and unavoidable victory over France, proved to be one of the steps towards the downfall of the German Empire.

As usual, the German strategists were thinking only within the limits of the military situation, and did not take into consideration either the political aspects of the action they were planning or the difficulties presented to their yellowing plan by their adversary's technological progress; thus, they did not consider the importance of the French *rocade* railways (i.e. directed parallel to the front-line), which enabled troops to be moved quickly from one section of the front to another.

According to Schlieffen's plan, five German armies were to make a fan-shaped advance along five directions into Belgium, and from there, turning westwards and southwards, to make a movement surrounding Paris, and thus also the main forces defending the capital. Such forces were to be pressed back towards the south-west, to Lorraine (Lothringen), where two more German armies would be awaiting them. The German strategists did not consider the possibility of the French moving their troops quickly across the front, and – no less important – the outcry of world public opinion at the occupation of neutral Belgium, which of course involved atrocities against the peaceful population, and – this was especially important – deprived all states of the confidence that neutral frontiers were inviolable.

The German army did not succeed in surrounding Paris; the French (together with the British expeditionary force based themselves in the strong fortress of Verdun placed where the Northern and the Western fronts joined), managed to stop the German advance in the valleys of the Marne and the Moselle. From the middle of September both armies were entrenched and there began (between September and October in the different sections of the front) a protracted and exhausting positional war – something the strategists of the time had not foreseen but which became typical of World War I generally.

In October 1914 the German army occupied the main Belgian port of Antwerp.

On the Russo-German front the Russian High Command's wish was to cut off Eastern Prussia, which encroached on the frontiers of Russian Poland. The Russians had double the forces, but the Germans had easier access to reinforcements. Moreover, the advantages of the Russians were nullified by the bungling actions of the Chief of the General Staff, Zhilinski, and the generals Samsonov and Rennenkampf (who were mortal enemies ever since 1905 when they had boxed each other's ears on a railway platform in Mukden); also by the lack of attention to the specific peculiar features of the swampy terrain, by the irregularity of supplies, and the lack of discipline among the officers who transmitted secret messages by wireless without cipher. The resolute and intelligent actions of the German generals (Hoffmann, later Ludendorff and Hindenburg) led to a complete defeat of the Russian troops. They lost a quarter of a million soldiers and a great amount of military equipment.

The southern Russian armies had more success: thus the city Lwow (Lemberg) in Galicia was conquered. However, irregularities in the flow of supplies, and the destruction of the weak Polish railway network by the retreating Austrians made advance difficult. Here trench warfare also began. Note that the Germans had to transfer some troops from the Western front both to Eastern Prussia and to Poland, thus somewhat relieving the stress on the French.

On the Balkan front, the Serbs lost Belgrade, but to the south they successfully withstood the Austrians, in spite of heavy losses. A new front was opened by Turkey. At that time the moderately modernising but in actual fact rather chauvinistic Young Turk party had come to power; it was headed by Enver, Talaat and Jemal. The policy of the party was to have maximal contact with Germany, since Russian traditional policy presupposed a gradual dismemberment of the Turkish Empire, and the British desired to acquire the Turkish Straits (no less than did Russia), as well as the Turkish Near East, which was a threat to the Suez Canal and the British road to India.

On 2 August 1914, Turkey and Germany concluded a secret treaty of alliance. The Turks wished to create a modern navy of their own, and had ordered two new battleships from England; but they were informed that the battleships would be incorporated into the British Navy. Then the Germans sent their battle-cruiser *Goeben* to Turkey as well as the light cruiser *Breslau*. These ships managed to cross the Mediterranean in the very first days of August just managing to evade the British squadron on patrol service there;[30] reaching Istanbul (without changing officers and crew), they hoisted the Turkish flag. At that moment, the Russian Black Sea fleet consisted only of old battleships with an outdated range of artillery fire and outdated speed; they could not vie with the *Goeben*,[31] so she was able to shell the Russian ships from a safe distance.

On 29–30 October 1914, the *Goeben* and the *Breslau* shelled the port of Odessa and

---

30. England declared war on Germany on 4 August 1914, and on Turkey only on 12 November, and before that, the *Goeben* and the *Breslau* could act as if they were in neutral waters until reaching the Bosporus straits.
31. The best Russian warships were sunk in Tsushima. The new battle-ship *Empress Maria*, built specially for the Black Sea taking into account the lessons of the Japanese war, overturned and sank in the harbour shortly before the World War. Swindlers from the commissariat furnished the seamen with footwear with soles unfit for use; therefore sailors went to the powder-magazine to cut soles for themselves out of sheeted gunpowder; such soles wore excellently. But once a sailor entered the magazine with a lighted candle. (This story I have from Professor – and Admiral – A. N. Krylov, an outstanding specialist in shipbuilding.) For the Baltic, where also the experiences of the Russo-Japanese war were taken into account, a complete new modern fleet was being built by Russia: battleships, battle and light cruisers, destroyers and submarines. But by 1944 this fleet was still not ready for service.

other points on the Russian coast, without Turkey declaring war on Russia. At the same time, military action began on the Transcaucasian front. On November 1914, Russia declared war on Turkey.

In autumn 1914 the German navy made cruiser raids against merchant vessels *en route* to England and France. The Cruiser *Emden* in the Indian Ocean became famous for its raids; she not only managed to sink fifteen British ships but once dared to enter the British Indian harbour of Madras (adding a fourth funnel to her original three, which made her look like a British cruiser), and open fire upon oil reservoirs there. Subsequently, the *Emden* was confronted by British warships and sunk.

If the *Emden* acted independently, the rest of the German high sea squadron acted together as a unit. It managed to inflict a major defeat on a British squadron near the Pacific coast of Chile. After entering the Atlantic Ocean, the German admiral decided to attack the Falkland Islands – a British possession near the coast of Argentina[32] but here he encountered the British fleet. This time the German squadron was almost completely annihilated, while the British suffered only few losses. Later, there were some German defeats nearer home, in the North Sea.

From that moment, Germany turned to submarine war. Its submarines already had had considerable success: on 22 September 1914, a German submarine sunk no less than three British cruisers in harbour; the submarines could freely enter Scottish bays, and they compelled the British not only to transfer their main naval base to the Orkney Islands, to the faraway bay of Scapa Flow, but also to arrange strong defences of that base from submarine attacks. The British battle fleet hardly ever left Scapa Flow.

From the very beginning Germany suffered strongly from the dominance of light British warships on the seas; they blocked the supplies to the country. Germany decided to reverse using submarines to disrupt British sea-trade. Originally, the crews of the ships to be sunk were allowed to get away in boats, but soon the Germans began to sink the ships without advance notice. From February 1915, the waters surrounding the British Isles were declared a 'war zone', where any ship was a legitimate target.

However, the British naval blockade of the German harbours by surface ships proved to be more effective than the German submarine blockade of the British waters: during the first three months of the German blockade 12,000–13,000 merchant ships entered British harbours, while only fifty-one ships were sunk. The British used anti-submarine nets and deep-sea bombs. The German submarines sank not only British merchant ships carrying military cargo but also passenger and even neutral ships (they had the colours of their flag painted large on the ships'

---

32. The Falkland Islands, which originally were uninhabited, are now populated by immigrants mainly from Scotland and partly from Scandinavia, no permanent Spanish speaking population ever existed there; nevertheless they are still claimed by Argentina.

sides). The most striking case occurred in the Atlantic Ocean. The American passenger liner *Lusitania* was sunk on 7 May 1915, and 1,200 passengers and members of the crew perished.

Anti-German public opinion was very strong (especially in the neutral United States), and with each new merchant ship sunk by the Germans, resentment grew more. In the military sense, German submarine warfare was a success. In the political sense it boded defeat. However, the time for the USA's entrance into the war had not yet arrived, and meanwhile the Americans sent protest notes not only to the Germans for sinking American ships and for the loss of American passengers, but also to the British for blockading German harbours.

Meanwhile, the Germans were gradually losing their colonies to South African, British or French occupying forces. In German East Africa, however, Colonel von Lettow-Vorbeck organised guerrilla warfare, and kept fighting until the end of the war. In China, the German enclave of Kiaochow with the port Tsingtao was captured by Japan; this was the reason for Japan declaring war on Germany (from August 1914).

By 1915 both sides in the war had realised that trench warfare which used rapid-firing field artillery, machine-guns and modern rifles had created a stalemate everywhere. In order to change the situation, new means had to be found: the Germans employed poison gas (January–May 1915), the British introduced tanks (in the summer of 1916). Neither gas nor the tanks brought decisive victories. So the British launched the idea of circumventing the whole theatre of war, and striking the Central Powers 'from the belly'. For this, it was decided to try to take the Dardanelles by force through a landing operation by British, Australian, New Zealand and French troops, in order to reach the Black Sea. This was also very important because all supplies to Russia from the Allies were sent via the Dardanelles which actually belonged to the enemy. Supplying Russia through the Arctic regions was at that period more than difficult. (Nevertheless, the Murmansk harbour was being built as quickly as possible, and a railway was constructed from Petersburg to Kola.) As to supplying the Russian army from Vladivostok through Siberia along the insecure thread of a single railway line, this also was by no means an easy matter.

The Dardanelles operation ended in failure. But the Allies occupied the harbour town of Salonika which belonged to Greece, at that time still neutral.

The Entente lost nearly 250,000 men, but a breakthrough 'from under the belly' was not to happen. Moreover, two attempts to advance against the Germans on the Western Front in April and in September 1915 brought no success.

In May 1915 Germany and Austria-Hungary started a decisive offensive against the Russian army on the Eastern Front. According to the reckoning of the German High Command, one German division was stronger than one Russian, but one Russian division was stronger than one Austro-Hungarian. Therefore von Mackensen, the German Front Commander, moved some German troops over to the Austrian sections of the front. But again, as in 1914, some forces had to be taken from the Western Front to reinforce the Eastern. The Russians, stubbornly resisting, retreated. Now the front-line extended from the river of Dvina (Lielupe) near Riga, to the west of Dvinsk (now Daugavpils), and further in a nearly straight line to the Rumanian frontier in Bukovina. Galicia, Poland and a part of Latvia (Kurland) were abandoned by the Russians. But they still were able to maintain the new front-line, in spite of millions killed, wounded and taken prisoners.

In Western Europe the front remained immovable, but both sides sustained heavy losses.

Beginning with the autumn of 1914, Turkey regrouped its troops towards the East (mainly on foot – there were not enough railway lines); the final goal was that of capturing Baku with its oil. As a secondary movement, the Turks invaded Iranian Azerbaijan (i.e. North-Western Persia with a Turki population). They seem to have expected help from the Azerbaijani Turks, not only from Iranian but also from Russian Azerbaijan. Although, in contradistinction from the Anatolian Turks, the Azerbaijani Turks were not Sunnites but Shïites, the Turkish government hoped that community of language and culture would be a guarantee of success. The High Command apparently reckoned that the troops would provide for themselves by marauding, because it did not have available railways or even dirt roads in the necessary direction to provide supplies. At the beginning of 1915 the Turks experienced a severe defeat at Ardahan.

The Christian Armenians (and partly also the Christian Assyrians – also called Syrians, or Aramaeans) were clearly ready to help the Russians; guerrillas appeared here and there. On 11 June 1915, the Turkish government ordered the wholesale deportation of the Christian (i.e. mainly Armenian) population into the deserts of Northern Mesopotamia. This became genocide of more than 1 million Armenians of both sexes and all ages.[33] The surviving Armenians started a guerrilla warfare, and they certainly did not spare the lives of the Turkish village population.

In September 1915 the Grand Duke Nicholas Nikolayevich, who commanded the Russian troops on the German front, passed his command to the emperor himself, and headed an offensive against Turkey in Eastern Anatolia. (The actual commander, however, was General Yudenich.) The Russian troops occupied Erzurum, and later Erzincan, and reached the Van Sea and the city of Bitlis. On the southern shore of the Black Sea the Russians occupied Trabzon (Trapezus). The Armenian front was stabilised until the spring of 1917.

In Persia – although in 1914 it had declared its neutrality – the British–Russian agreement of 1907 on mutual interests continued to be valid. Here there were random military actions by Russian,[34] British and Turkish forces, and by groups of sympathisers.

---

33. A small number of Christian Assyrians (actually Aramaeans) reached Russian Transcaucasia and settled in different Russian cities. Most of them later fell victims of Stalin's purges.
34. Thus, the Russians landed some troops at Enzeli on the southern shore of the Caspian Sea.

The fate of the very important Turkish positions west of Persia, namely in Mesopotamia (Iraq), was still undecided, when the Temporary Government called Nicholas Nikolayevich back to Russia in March 1917.

In the Indian Ocean zone, Great Britain had important aims: to guarantee access to Iraqi oil, and to organise a rising of Arabs against Turkey. Employing Indian armed forces, the British secured the oil fields and refinery at Abadan in 1914, and then a small group of British forces occupied southern Iraq; but until the spring of 1916 this campaign had little success.

Meanwhile, after the failure at the Dardanelles, the British drew their troops (about 250,000) back to Egypt (which had completely severed ties with its Turkish suzerain). Pressure was exerted on the British from the Turks both to the east of Suez, and from the belligerent Muslim sect of the Senussi dominating in Libya, from the west.

In July 1916 the royal Arab family of the Hashemites instigated an anti-Turk rebellion in Hijaz. The actual leader of the Arab liberation movement was the brilliant English intelligence officer T. E. Lawrence 'of Arabia', and the commander of the British troops in Near East, General E. H. H. Allenby. In the North, shortly before the end of the war, the British created several Hashemite Kingdoms, including Syria which the British, French, and partly Arab forces had wrested from Turkey (the Turks had hoped to achieve a breakthrough towards Suez), Iraq, Trans-Jordan and Hijaz. Palestine was taken over by the British as a protectorate of their own. Along the Southern and Eastern coasts of the Arabian peninsula were situated the sultanates of Asir, Yemen, Oman and others; all of them had stopped paying Turkey the former symbolic tribute. All of Arabia was at that time at the Fifth Phase of historical development; due to the preponderance of nomadic camel-breeders, its society had a specific character.

The reconstruction of Arabia according to British muster did not fully succeed. After the war, continental Najd took over Hijaz (with Mecca and Medina), creating the Kingdom of Saudi Arabia; in Syria, the French authorities did not recognise the Hashemites.

Nevertheless, from the second half of World War I, the British had been building the Hijaz railway, fortifying the harbour Aden near the entrance to the Red Sea (on its other end they firmly held Suez), and laying pipelines for oil.

Meanwhile, on 23 May 1915, Italy declared war on Austria-Hungary. Its aim was to annex the Italian-speaking valleys near the frontier, in the districts of Trieste and Trento, and also the Istrian peninsula and Dalmatia, which had prevalently a Slavonic population but had in the past belonged to the Doges of Venice. At Isonzo, from June 1915 to the autumn of 1916, there were constant battles; on 28 August 1916, Italy also declared war against Germany. In the operations, the Italians lost about half a million soldiers, the Austrians about 250,000, but there was little change in the military situation.

In the summer of 1915, both fighting coalitions tried to influence Bulgaria in their favour. Three attacks by the Austro-Hungarians against Serbia did not solve the problems of the very existence of this state, and that of its possession of Macedonia. In September 1915 Bulgaria concluded a treaty with Austria-Hungary; in October Russian troops tried to invade Bulgaria but without much success, in spite of the promise of Greek aid. The Serbs procrastinated, awaiting help from Salonika,[35] which, however, did not materialise. Under the pressure of Bulgarian troops, the Serbian army retreated to Albania, and was from there transferred to the island of Korfu, and into the region of Salonika. The territory of Serbia was divided between Austria-Hungary and Bulgaria. In December 1915, the Allies considered the possibility of leaving Salonika, but kept on there as long as possible, hoping in this way to exercise pressure on Rumania. The losses of the British, the French, the Italians, the Russians, and the Serbs were very considerable.

In December 1915 a consultation of the Allied commanding officers took place in France. It was decided to begin a co-ordinated offensive against Germany and Austria-Hungary in the summer of 1916. In January 1916 Great Britain, like the other powers, introduced a system of military conscription (instead of voluntary service).

At the same time, the German Commander-in-Chief, Falkenhayn, presented a plan of operations for 1916. In his opinion, the key to the Anglo-French positions was the fortress of Verdun, which was a salient protruding from the general front-line, and hampering the German initiative. On 21 February 1916, a bombardment of Verdun was undertaken, from the land positions and from the air. On 1 July 1916, the Allies began their own great counter-offensive from the valley of the Somme. Tanks were for the first time employed, but the troops had insufficient artillery cover, and so experienced heavy losses. The total losses for the 1916 campaign were 650,000 French and British, and 440,000 Germans. But the latter did not manage to capture Verdun.

With the war on the Western front continuing for three years without any success, and with losses of more than a million, the Allied command hoped for better results on the Eastern Front.

Here the Russians were periodically in retreat, and tired to the point of exhaustion. Irregular supplies of food and ammunition were a constant problem. However, Falkenhayn decided to concentrate on Verdun and not on the East, and there was a hope that a Russian effort might save the Allies. In March 1916, the Russians, attempting to divert some enemy troops from France, started an offensive at Lake Naroch east of Vilna (Vilnius).

The plan of the Russian command was to launch their offensive in three directions: towards the North (General Kuropatkin), in the Centre (General Ewert), and to the South and South-East (General Brusilov). It was thought that this last direction

---

35. Salonika (Thessaloniki) belonged to Greece, which at that time was neutral, but the region was occupied by the Allies under a specious pretext.

was the least important, because Brusilov's troops had become stuck in a swampy region. But the general himself thought that this fact might be an asset, because his offensive would be unexpected. Brusilov had no more troops than his adversary, but the surprise offensive – there was even no artillery at the ready – overwhelmed the enemy. And although even Ewert did not begin his offensive at the appointed time, the quick advance of Brusilov broke the Austro-German defence, and by the end of the summer his troops had captured Lwow (Lemberg) and entered Bukovina, taking a great number of prisoners.

Brusilov's victory aroused hopes among the Russian command, the bourgeoisie, and the intelligentsia, but in no way did it revive the spirits of the peasantry which was losing skilled hands, and for whom the war meant only mass deaths of their near ones, with hunger following; nor the working class, who had to work under pressure, and who also experienced losses in every family. At the same time, prices for food and other necessities were steadily rising.

Of course, there were heavy losses also among the officers, the intelligentsia, and even among the bourgeoisie, but in their case there was an impulse of glory for some, and of super-profits for others.

The gravest situation menaced the entire country – and the entire world.

Until the summer of 1916, Rumania had remained neutral, but the result of the war was by no means of indifference to the Rumanian government: a lot of ethnic Rumanians lived in Austro-Hungarian Transylvania (Siebenbürgen) and in Southern Bukovina, and the territory of Rumania proper was squeezed between pro-German Bulgaria and pro-German Austria-Hungary. On 27 August 1916, Rumania declared war on Austria-Hungary; and within five days saw itself at war with all the Central Powers. The fact that Rumania entered the war at so late a date, had two consequences: on the one hand, Rumania had the time to mobilise a big army, but on the other hand, its military experience was zero. Russia could not help the Rumanians to any important degree; the latter began a rather leisurely offensive in Transylvania. After an unfortunate battle at Tîrgu Jiu the Rumanians were forced, on 6 December, to surrender Bucharest, and the Central Powers got access to new rich reserves of oil and grain. Walachia was occupied; only Moldavia still remained.

The year 1916 was the turning point as regards the war in the air. The light plywood biplanes and monoplanes were from the very beginning used for reconnaissance, and when the pilots met with enemy' reconnaissance planes they drew out their pistols. But 1915 saw the appearance of fighter aeroplanes armed with machine guns. When trench warfare began, the aeroplanes received a new mission: to drop bombs on enemy positions. The German aircraft started bombing raids against the enemy's rear at an early date, and as early as 1914 began the bombardments of British harbours and cities – at first, using bomber aircraft, and later also the spectacular floating airships, the dirigibles, or Zeppelins, which created panic among the peaceful population. However, the Zeppelins were too vulnerable, and the Germans had to discontinue their operations. As to the activities of the reconnaissance, fighter and bomber planes, although they never reached the scale typical of World War II, their presence was increasingly felt on all fronts from 1915–1916.

The spring of 1916, after a lull, witnessed the greatest naval battle in world history. It took place in the North Sea between the coasts of Britain and the Danish Jutland Peninsula.

The Grand Fleet of Britain and the High Sea Fleet of Germany had avoided confrontation for a long time. According to the British naval doctrine, the sea should be held free for commerce and for supplies to the mother country. The German fleet was blockaded in its harbours to the south-west of Jutland; the German command was confident that the actions of their submarines would not only harm the British navy and sea trade, but also prevent danger to the German 'High Sea Fleet' of Admiral Scheer in its moorage sites. The German command counted on their own forces gradually becoming equal with the British navy, which would make it possible to defeat the British in open battle. But since no apparent successes in the war between the German submarines and the British Grand Fleet could be registered, it was decided to engage with isolated British warships or small groups of ships, at moments when, for some reason, these would be separated from the Grand Fleet. Thus, on 25 April 1916, German light cruisers shelled the British harbours of Lowestoft and Yarmouth. And, as expected, a squadron of battle cruisers under Admiral Beatty, which was keeping to the east of these ports, was at once sent against the German ships. But at the same time, unexpectedly for the German command, Admiral Jellicoe, the commander-in-chief of the British navy, moved his battleships out from Scapa Flow, supported by light cruisers. The British and the German fleet met by chance: at 2.30 pm on 31 May, light cruisers from both fleets had sighted a small Danish merchant ship, and started to come near it for inspection. At 3.20 pm the squadrons of the battle cruisers of Beatty and Hipper met; Beatty lost two battle cruisers. A British patrol cruiser noticed the squadron of Jellicoe, and signalled it to draw nearer to Beatty, who had meanwhile joined another squadron of British battle cruisers, that of Admiral Hood. For some time mist and smoke made the visibility poor, but it became clearer about 6.15 pm, and then it was apparent that the German fleet was moving into a trap, exposing itself to the fire of the squadrons of Hood, Beatty and (sideways) that of Jellicoe. Although the British had numerical superiority, the Germans nevertheless managed to sink Hood's flagship; and the German fleet, in spite of the damage it was receiving on all sides, preserved its fighting capability. At 6.36 pm Scheer ordered a 180° turn for all ships, and began to escape the trap. Smoke and mist continued to cover the sea, and Jellicoe did not notice that his squadron was still preventing Scheer from entering any coastal harbour. But Scheer knew it, and a little past 7 pm he ordered his battle cruisers and destroyers to attack Jellicoe's column. If at that moment the British admiral had sent his battleships against the Germans, they would have suffered total defeat. But Jellicoe was anticipating a torpedo attack from German submarines (which actually did not take part in the action). Also, he had not received Scheer's radiogram (although it had been intercepted by the British) which could point to the actual direction of the Germans' movement. At 3.00 am Scheer's fleet hid behind minefields defending the entrance to the German naval base.

On the British side, in the Jutland battle, were 28 battleships, 9 modern battle cruisers (3 were sunk), 8 old type battle cruisers (3 were sunk), 26 light cruisers and 79 destroyers (8 were sunk). On the German side there were 22 battleships (1 was sunk), 5 battle cruisers (1 was sunk), 11 light cruisers (4 were sunk), and 62 destroyers (6 were sunk). The losses in personnel, not counting those wounded and those taken prisoner, were 6,100 men on the British side, and 2,500 on the German.

Never before in the history of naval wars was there a more terrible sight. Out of the clouds of powder smoke appeared giant ships, some of them in flames, others going down vertically into the water – into a narrowing funnel of the sea. Through the roar of artillery one could hear the pitiful cries of thousands of men dying or drowning in the cold water. Four huge British battle cruisers moved in a line ahead; then one of them was blown up because an enemy shell hit it right amidships – and when the next ship in the line, minutes later, reached the place, nothing was afloat: no ship, no men – only a huge whirlpool. And in the screening line of light cruisers, one of them had experienced such a fire (it seems its depot of fuel and shells blew up), that it continued in its place in the line with the same speed, but all red-hot, with a crew of dead men. Only in World War II could anything more terrible be witnessed.

The horror engendered by the Battle of Jutland was perhaps not less important for the development of further sea battles than the mere statistics of losses on both sides. Another sea battle occurred on 18–19 August 1916. But here the main role was played by sumbarines; the British lost a cruiser, and a battleship was heavily damaged on the German side. This time the battle also ended in a draw.

A consequence of the Battle of Jutland was the conclusion that big battles involving big squadrons of more or less equal strength cannot lead to decisive results; also, that they cannot influence submarine operations, which until the end of the war were the main military factor at sea.

The great powers did not build more battle cruisers: their armour had proved inadequate for combating battleships, and their speed was insufficient for quick manoeuvres in cruiser operations. Battleships continued to be built for a long time; that they were worthless was found out only after the heavy air raids of World War II.

The air force during World War I was still very deficient. There were no aircraft carriers or regular airfield services; it was only some decades later that effective heavy bombers were produced by Igor Sikorski in the USA, and by a number of European engineers. During World War I, deep bombing raids against enemy industry, and cities generally, were made by the Germans, using heavy aeroplanes and especially Zeppelins, as mentioned above. But their speed was slow, their altitude of flight was low, and they were too big a target for fire. The new important elements of warfare – tanks and gases – were barely out of the trial stage during World War I.

In a situation which had involved the entire planet in war for three years – because America also suffered – and neither side could achieve a decisive victory, thoughts turned to the possibility of ending the war by compromise – or even by revolutionary measures.

Throughout the war, the social democrats (mainly those of the neutral countries) sought peace. At the beginning of 1915 there was a conference in Copenhagen for social democrats from neutral countries only (because the social democrats of the countries at war, except the extreme left, had voted for war credits to their respective governments). In February 1915 there was a conference for social democrats of the Entente in London, and in April a conference for the social democrats of the Central Powers in Vienna. In both cases it appeared that the majority of socialists (except Lenin and Martov from Russia) supported their respective governments, and no agreement could be reached. In September 1915, a new conference was convened in Zimmerwald, Switzerland, where socialists from eleven countries were represented – both from countries at war and from neutral ones. Here Lenin, for the first time, formulated his idea of 'turning the imperialist war into a civil war', but did not win majority support. The majority signed Trotsky's declaration 'To the Proletariat of Europe', with the appeal not to support the bourgeois governments, and to demand an armistice. A similar situation arose at the conference in Kienthal (Switzerland, April 1916), which introduced the slogan: 'Peace without annexations and indemnities'.

Thoughts about peace were not only in the minds of the extreme left opposition. In Germany, in December 1916, the chancellor Bethmann Hollweg, addressing the Reichstag, set out conditions of possible peace; but alas, they were based on the presumption that Germany would keep most of what it had been able to annex. At the same time, President Wilson of the USA demanded an official statement of the 'goals of the war' from all combatant countries. In January 1917, the Allies declared that their goal was the 'liberation of Italians, Rumanians, Slav, and Czechoslovaks from foreign domination' – a declaration which, of course, could not satisfy anyone.

Meanwhile, resources on both sides were dwindling. The British and the French had c. 4 million soldiers including colonial troops; but their commander-in-chief, Joffre, declared that the French forces would be sufficient for only one more decisive battle, after which they would not have enough men to call up for military service. Germany had 2,500,000 soldiers (not counting those of its allies – Austrians, Hungarians, Turks and Bulgarians), but as to reinforcements by conscription, the situation was even worse than that in the Entente countries. Industry on both sides of the front-line still functioned but with increasing difficulty. The air force as it existed at that time could not damage industry seriously, and the supply of raw materials was not completely arrested. But food supplies were deteriorating with every month, especially in Germany; ration cards had to be introduced.

The situation in Russia was worst of all. Social democrats were not admitted to the Duma, which, on the whole, took up a position they regarded as 'patriotic'. However, the government enjoyed no political confidence. At the imperial court, a religious swindler and confidence-man, Rasputin, was the boss. He promised to cure the boy heir-apparent who had an incurable disease (haemophilia); meanwhile, Rasputin appointed and removed ministers and high officials, arranged orgies with ladies of the court, etc. Public opinion accused some ministers and even the empress Alexandra (who was by birth a German) of treason. Many outstanding right-wing members of the Duma and leaders of the intelligentsia attempted to arrange 'masonic' and other plots against Rasputin and the Tsarist government.

Russian industry was incapable of supplying the army with the munitions and new arms it needed. Agriculture was bled white from the mobilisation of men, and was in no condition adequately to supply the army and the cities with bread, and food generally. In the cities, people queued up for bread. At the same time, a civil organisation ('Zemgor') grew up with nothing in particular to achieve – it was not apparent whether it was a charitable, or a profiteering, a civil or home front organisation. The stock exchange was lively, especially because of the buying up of the military industry shares *en masse*.

When the very young and the elderly men called up for military service arrived in the army, they told sorry tales about the destruction and desolation in the villages, about the hard life of working women in the centres of the proletariat. Note that the situation was, no doubt, very bad indeed compared to what it had been, but considerably better than it was going to be for years and years to come.

In March 1917 (February according to the then current Russian Julian calendar), in the workers' districts of Petrograd (thus was St Petersburg renamed in 1914), disturbances among women standing in lines for bread broke out. It seems that the reason was not that bread was actually unavailable at the wholesale stores, but that the administration was negligent. A military detachment staying at that time in Petrograd to replace casualties and to reform, was sent to bring the women to reason. The soldiers supported the mutinous women, and, with red placards, moved towards the Duma. A wave of strikes started in Petrograd, growing into an uprising. The Tsarist government resigned, and on 13 March 1917, was arrested. The Duma created a new, provisional government. Disturbances took place all over the country and in the army. The Duma passed a law on election to a Constituent Assembly: by general, equal, secret and direct ballot.

The army remained in its trenches but hoped to discontinue war operations. The soldiers, after countless losses and defeats, badly clad, badly trained, led by worthless and quarrelling generals, including members of the Imperial family (and Nicholas II himself), who knew more about parades than scientific strategy and tactics – these soldiers listened with joy to the SR and Bolshevik propagandists: 'Peace to the huts, war against the palaces', etc.

Actually, while Russia's allies and adversaries were to wage war for a further eighteen months, the Russians were destined to continue war for nearly five years more, and a war, at that, where there was no great difference between the actual front and the home front. But all this was hidden in the future; meanwhile, achieving peace quickly by revolutionary means seemed both possible and desirable.

That the Russian army actually fell out of the war was perceived by her allies in the Entente as a catastrophe which required a total rethinking of military policy, and by Germany and Austria-Hungary as the long-awaited breakthrough for victory in the World War. Both sides were wrong in their reactions, as we shall be able to show below.

Instead of the parliamentary regime expected in Russia, a dictatorship of left extremists, the Bolsheviks, emerged.

From the point of view of world history, the events of the Russian Bolshevist, and later of the German Nazi revolution were more important than the events of the on-going World War. But we have to dwell on the latter before we can discuss the October Revolution in Russia and all its world-wide consequences and reverberations.

During 1916 and 1917 the main front of the World War was still the Western front.[36] The battles here were severe and debilitating; they made it apparent that co-ordinating the activities of the commanding officers in the Allied armies was difficult, and that they could be misled by the enemy (thus, a change of some German troops to better positions was taken for flight). In July 1916, the British general Haig (on French instigation) attempted in vain to break the front along the Somme, with a plan to free the Flemish ports; ignoring intelligence data and the meteorologists, he sent his troops across swampy land; the Anglo-French troops lost 250,000 men. But this neither advanced nor retarded the historical process which we are discussing. By 1917, the general attitude of the soldiers on both sides of the front could be formulated as follows: 'we shall defend the trenches, but we are not going to advance'.

On the Western front, during 1916, the line of the trenches, stretching from the Channel to the frontiers of Switzerland, and the analogous line on the Austro-Hungarian front, became a very strong thousand-mile permanent fortified double rampart, which could not be broken through at any point.[37] One could perish from stray bullets or machine-gun fire, or because of a random artillery bombardment. The few primitive tanks were considered as not very dangerous toys, and using chlorine or mustard gas on certain sections of the front required due regard for the

36. From April 1916, the German troops were under the command of Hindenburg (Falkenhayn took over the command in Turkey), the French troops were (after Joffre) under the command of Nivelle; the latter, suffering serious reversals, was replaced by Pétain.
37. No tanks were employed. At that time, the first models of tanks were still under construction.

meteorological situation (so that one's own soldiers should not suffer); gas contaminated the territory, and was not favourable for a following advance by one's own forces.

The situation on the Eastern (Russian) front was more or less similar; but the difference was that the line of trenches was not always so strong and impenetrable, the soldiers' supplies were much, much worse, the squabbles in the staffs were unmatched, and the scope of thefts in the commissariat would be unthinkable by Western front standards.

In the ensuing situation, different avenues were contemplated. The Germans relied mainly on the submarine blockade. The result, however, offered little consolation to the German authorities: the British surface blockade inflicted more losses on Germany in foodstuffs and expenditure than the German submarine blockade inflicted on Britain.

England and France hoped that the United States would enter the war on their side because the German submarine blockade of Europe and the general confusion of world economies spelled important losses to the Americans.

There was also one specific point in which the United States played an important role world-wide. In 1879–1889 the famed French engineer de Lesseps decided to join the Atlantic Ocean with the Pacific in the same way as in his younger years he had joined the Mediterranean Sea with the Indian Ocean by the Suez Canal. However, it appeared that it was considerably more difficult to arrange matters with Latin American landowner factions than with the Arabs. The Company of the Panama Canal, after having received much credit, declared itself insolvent – and at a tremendous scale! The word 'Panama' became a byword for 'monstrous swindle and monstrous ruination'. The building of an Atlantic–Pacific canal was taken over by Americans; American statesmen knew how to deal better with Latin American presidents. 'Suddenly' it so happened that, as luck would have it, for some reason a strong and by no means poor separatist movement appeared on the isthmus of Panama (which had belonged to Columbia); a new republic emerged, Panama; across it was a neutral zone, rented for so many years by the United States of America. And finally, in 1914, through this zone the famous Panama shipping canal was built; there began a new epoch in world navigation, in merchant and political contacts between the Far East, the countries of the Pacific, the Caribbean Sea, and the entire Atlantic Ocean, and, of course, Europe.

If we add the high level of technical development and the huge money and manpower resources of the United States, it stands to reason that the Russo-Franco-British coalition could not dream of a better ally; however, the Americans were in no hurry to join the war.

Meanwhile, the scale of the war meant that it was no longer possible to wage it according to medieval ideas of chivalry and soldierly honour. On both sides, the press created a highly negative image of the enemy: the Germans were 'bloodthirsty Huns', killers of children and destroyers of temples (the last accusation was not untrue), on the other side, the reputation of the British, the French and especially the 'wild Slavs' was no better. This propaganda had three goals: to strengthen the warlike spirit of one's own troops, to create hatred towards the enemy, and to influence the public opinion in the neutral countries towards one's own side. Often the limit between propaganda measures and military actions was unclear: there were attempts to destroy the telegraph cable in the ocean between the USA and Germany, to depose objectionable ministers in neutral countries, etc. Strict military censorship was introduced; in England and in France the censors were civilians, in Germany and Austria-Hungary they were military.

The situation changed drastically when the United States entered the war.

For a long time, President Wilson urged reconciliation; later he took up a position of friendly neutrality towards the Entente. As early as May 1916, he formulated his idea of a post-war League of Nations, which was to resolve peacefully all emerging conflicts. But about the same time the United States began to prepare for war. In December 1916, Wilson addressed the belligerents and demanded strict formulation of their military goals. Both Britain and France were most dissatisfied with this, because the outcome of the war could not be prognosticated (one could only hope for the best). Wilson's Secretary of State, Lancing, secretly suggested to the British and the French governments that they should declare such goals which obviously could not be achieved without complete victory in the war. He judged rightly that half measures would not result in a durable peace. However, as late as January 1917 Wilson continued secret talks both with Great Britain, and with Germany. But the damage inflicted by the submarine war on the United States was too great in both material and moral terms; partaking in a victorious war promised important gains in the post-war period.

The chancellor Bethmann Hollweg sent a note to Wilson, stating Germany's peace conditions and appealing to the President to continue his peace-making efforts; but at the same time there arrived the news that Germany had begun 'an unlimited submarine war', i.e. it declared its 'right' to sink any ships which attempted to run the blockade of the Entente states. On 3 February 1917, the United States broke off diplomatic relations with Germany, and on 4–6 April a declaration of war against Germany was passed through Congress. A new system of conscription was introduced, and by the end of the war the Americans had called up for service 4,800,000 soldiers. All the workers, socialist, radical and pacifist press was silenced, the railroads were militarised and important measures were taken for financing the war.

On 18 January 1918, President Wilson stated in Congress his Fourteen Points, containing the demands presented by the USA: (1) Diplomacy only in public view. (2) Absolute freedom of navigation. (3) Removal, as far as possible, of customs barriers in international trade. (4) Guarantee of a general reduction of national armaments to the lowest point consistent with domestic safety. (5) An impartial adjustment of colonial claims, also in the interests of the population concerned. (6) Evacuation of all the territory of Russia, and her independent determination of her own political development. (7) The restoration of Belgium and her independence. (8) The restoration of France to her frontiers before 1871. (9) The adjustment of the frontiers of Italy along recognisable lines of nationality. (10) The peoples of Austria-Hungary were to be accorded the opportunity of free development. (11) German occupation should be abolished in Rumania, Serbia and Montenegro; Serbia accorded access to the sea. (12) Non-Turkish nationalities under Ottoman rule to be secured an internationally guaranteed opportunity for autonomous development; the Dardanelles should be permanently opened for all nations. (13) An independent Polish state should be founded. (14) A League of Nations should be formed.

By March 1918, 85,000 Americans had taken part in battles on the Western Front; by September, the number had grown to 1,200,000.

Following the USA, Panama, Cuba and Haiti declared war on Germany; other Latin American republics at first limited themselves to breaking off diplomatic relations, but then Brazil declared war (in October 1917), afterwards Guatemala (in April 1918), Nicaragua and Costa Rica (in May), and Honduras (in July). Moreover, Liberia and China also entered the war during 1917.

This book is devoted to the theory of the historical process; therefore we cannot dwell in detail on all the events of the First and Second World Wars. If up to now our narrative has been comparatively detailed, it has been in order to show how the entire globe was involved in the First World War.

During February through July, Wilson twice made important political moves. These concerned the 'four principles': peace should be concluded on just principles and according to just demands in every particular case; nations and regions should not be made objects of trade and barter at the negotiations; each decision in territorial questions should take into consideration the interests of the territory's population; all clearly formulated national wishes must be satisfied in so far they did not affect peace. Then there were the 'four goals': destruction or weakening of any arbitrary power which can threaten peace; solution of territorial, legal, political and economic questions, first and foremost, in the interest of the nation involved; keeping to civilised moral norms in international relations; the creation of a 'certain tribunal of opinions' to ensure the rights and equity through 'united efforts of free nations'. Finally, there were specifications: peace negotiations to be impartial; common interests should have preference over individual interests; members of the League of Nations were to abstain from specific agreements with its individual members, and not only in political but also in economic questions; international treaties should be published openly and fully.

Wilson's statements had a tremendous significance for the creation of a sociopsychological atmosphere which later made it possible for mankind to pass into the Eighth Phase.

Of course, in part Wilson's speeches proved to be no more than well meaning, but most of his recommendations were, at least nominally, adopted by the members of the League of Nations; the decision on its foundation was a part of the Peace Treaty of Versailles; the League was actually founded in 1920.

Let us dwell, very shortly, on the events following the withdrawal of Russia from the war in November 1917–March 1918, and the joining of the war by the USA in April 1917.

On the Western Front, to which the Germans moved their forces which were being released in the East, the French maintained a heroic defence at Verdun; losses in shipping began to diminish owing to the improvement of defences against submarines. Development in the air made the role of bombardments somewhat more important, but not very much so. Mutinies continued in the German navy. In July 1917, the German Reichstag discussed the possibility of a peace agreement. However, this was not a direct proposal of peace, and was not regarded as such by the Entente. Secret peace negotiations had been started by Austria-Hungary in the spring of 1917; but they were discontinued after the Austrian forces inflicted a crushing defeat upon the Italians at Caporetto.

The situation on the Eastern Front allowed Germany to begin a new, unexpected offensive in the West headed by Ludendorf. He depended on poison, and underestimated the importance of tanks. The offensive (the Second Battle of the Somme) involved 62 divisions on a 35-mile front from 21 March 1918; by the end of March the Allied armies were in speedy retreat; a considerable salient was cut into the Franco-British positions. The British alone had lost 300,000 men. But early in August 1918 the Anglo-Canadian and the French troops started a counter-offensive. By 8 August Ludendorf wrote: 'The war has to be brought to an end.' As the introduction of new and well-fed American forces gathered momentum, the question could finally be decided.

On the Eastern Front, Bolshevik Russia arranged for an armistice in December 1917. Election of officers was introduced in the Russian army: Communist party committees were established in the military units; fraternisation with German soldiers was organised; the number of deserters grew vastly. On 28 December peace negotiations were broken off by the Germans. The demoralised Russian troops put up little resistance. The Germans advanced rather quickly along the whole of the Eastern Front, occupying Riga and most of Belorussia. If the Bolsheviks procrastinated with peace negotiations, it was because they regarded their own revolution (in Russia) only as a first act in a World Revolution. Finally the peace treaty was signed on 3 March 1918, at Brest-Litovsk (see in more detail below); Russia lost the Baltic countries and the Ukraine. (The Germans had already signed a peace treaty with the leftist nationalistic government of Ukraine, called the 'Central Council', or the 'Rada'.)

But by September 1918 it was the Germans who were in retreat all along the Western Front; they were pursued by American, British, French, Canadian and Belgian troops. On 14 September Austria-Hungary sued for peace; about the same time there was a breakthrough on the Turkish front in Palestine. On 19 September

Bulgaria capitulated. On 3 October Prince Max of Baden was appointed chancellor of Germany; he was supported by a majority in the Reichstag which wished for peace. But on 1 October 1918 Ludendorf and Hindenburg also demanded peace without delay, and in the night of 3–4 October a note was sent to Wilson through Switzerland, with a request to open negotiations on the basis of his 14 points. This was the beginning of a series of notes (although fighting did continue in France). On 26 October Ludendorf resigned. (Note that he ended his life an ardent Nazi.) On 30 October, an armistice was agreed to with Turkey (but, as will be seen below, the war between Turkey and Greece was soon resumed). On 3 November, peace was concluded between the Entente and Austria-Hungary, and allied troops were admitted to that country.

To Wilson's original 14 points was added the demand that Germany recognise its full financial responsibility for damages to the civilian population and their property, incurred because of Germany's aggression on land, on sea, and in the air.

On 8 November in a railway coach in the forest of Compiegne near Paris, German representatives signed the offered terms of armistice.

Meanwhile, just as in Russia a year before, some revolutionary events took place in Germany. After disturbances in Hamburg, Bremen and some other cities, a 'Democratic and Social Republic of Bavaria' was declared on 7–8 November, and at different places, following the Russian model, there arose 'Councils (Soviets) of Soldiers' and Workers' Deputies'. In the Reichstag, Max of Baden was losing the support of the Social Democrats, and while William was deliberating on whether he should renounce the title of Emperor, and keep only the title of King of Prussia, on 9 November, Max declared that William II had abdicated his rights both to the German and the Prussian throne. Germany was declared a republic, and a social-democratic government, headed by Ebert, was created under the name of a 'Council of the People's Representatives'. Early on 10 November, William fled to the neutral Netherlands. Revolutionary actions were put down with the collaboration of the Ebert government.

Could Germany have continued the war and won it, if the United States had not joined the Allies? Could it have improved its economic and political situation by plundering the occupied territories in the East? The answer to both questions is no. Had the USA not taken part in the war, Germany would have lasted for a year or so, paying the price in streams of German and foreign blood, but she could not achieve a decisive victory, and reasonable men had understood that for some time. In the East, contacts with Bolsheviks both on the armistice line and beyond it were helping to break up the German army; the country was ruined, transportation was semi-paralysed, so that there were no hope of a quick solution to the problem of food-supply at the expense of Russia and the Ukraine.

The data published by the *Encyclopaedia Britannica* on the number of mobilised men (and in brackets the number of losses) during World War I (in millions of men) are instructive.

All in all, 67 million men had been mobilised, or about 9 per cent of the adult male population of the globe. The losses were 36 million, or about 5 per cent of it. The losses should have included those who died from epidemics, and the percentage of non-born as compared to the statistical expectations, but these are not included in the following table:

	Mobilised (in millions)	Losses		Mobilised (in millions)	Losses
Russia	12	(9 before the peace of Brest)	Greece	2.3	(0.03)
Germany	11	(7.2)	Bulgaria	1.2	(0.27)
Great Britain and the British Empire	9	(3.2)			
France	8.4	(6.2)	Serbia	0.75	(0.5)
Austria-Hungary	7.8	(5.8)	Belgium	0.25	(0.09)
Italy	5.5	(2.2)	Portugal	0.1	(0.033)
USA	4.4	(0.3)	Montenegro	0.05	(0.02)
Turkey	3	(1)			

Let us now turn to the revolution in Russia, and return to 1916.

Of all the armies involved in the war, the Russian was probably in the worst condition: not only did it sustain tremendous losses, but the local food supply situation kept it on the verge of hunger; 90 per cent of the soldiers were peasants, and it was obvious to them that at home their households were in complete disorder, and that real hunger had set in.

The rightist and the centrist deputies in the Duma were worried about how the war was developing. A conspiracy of some Duma representatives and some members of the nobility brought about the murder of Rasputin (late in 1916), but nevertheless the administration continued to be in a deplorable state.

In March 1917, as already mentioned above, disturbances in Petrograd broke out among the working women, who were joined by soldiers. Power was taken over by the Duma itself; however, it had been elected according to a complicated and non-democratic system, so it hardly could legitimately represent the Russian people. Meanwhile, in Petrograd and in some other cities, there spontaneously emerged Soviets (=Councils) of Workers' and Soldiers' Deputies, who claimed to offer a more equitable representation of popular interests. On 15 March the Petrograd Soviet issued 'Order No 1 for the Army', which invited the soldiers to elect their committees; these should delegate some of their members to the Soviets. Political leadership in the army was to be ceded to the committees, while the officers were to have only purely military functions, and even arms should be dealt out to them only as far as immediately necessary. The committees were headed by elected or simply nominated commissars. The new Petrograd Soviet declared that Russia was to conclude a peace 'without annexations and indemnities'. In the Duma, as well as in the Provisional Government formed by it, mainly right-wing and centrist forces were represented, while to the left of them only A. F. Kerenski of the Labour (Trudovik) party was important. The comparative liberalism or even quasi-socialism of Kerenski soon earned for him great popularity among the liberal intelligentsia and those officers and soldiers who wanted a left-wing government but not Soviets.

There was decidedly a difficulty in recognising the legitimacy of the Duma's actions because of the parallel existence of the Soviets which had already assumed governmental power. In the Soviets, which were something of a self-appointed socialist parliament, Socialist-Revolutionaries (SR) and the Social Democrats, both Mensheviks and Bolsheviks, were represented. The slogan of the Soviets was: 'stick the bayonets in the mud and demand immediate peace'.

From the point of view of international law, there was the problem of convincing the Allies of the legitimacy of the Provisional Government formed by the Duma. Note that all treaty agreements with East and West had been signed by the abolished Tsarist government. The wartime union between Russia on one side, and England and France on the other, had been agreed by a no longer existing government. But immediate peace with Germany on the whole Eastern Front would nearly double the numbers of German soldiers on the Western Front, and hence probably mean defeat for the Allies. A group of the left-wingers, the centrists and the right-wingers regarded this as direct treason which could lead to unpredictable results for Russia.

Let us attempt to view the events of World War I in the light of our theoretical premises.

World wars are the unavoidable outcome of the natural development of capitalist production in the Seventh Phase. The goal of capitalist production is accumulation of profit; the use of this profit for further development of productive forces, culture, etc. has but a secondary importance; it is just a side effect that a part of the profit is spent on the development of technical sciences – and thus indirectly for a rise in the general standard of living (by applying the achievements of science to production). However, it should be stressed that science was introduced into military production in the most liberal terms which, of course, was conducive to widening the sources of raw stuffs, and to the development of the markets so necessary for capitalism.

This widening is an inalienable part of development of a society based on a maximal increase of profit, and it inevitably led to an increase in colonialisation, until finally the whole surface of the Earth was grasped by the different powers; there inevitably had to follow a redistribution of the entire surface of the Globe by force. What was especially wrong with classical capitalism was the fact that it did not and could not create a mechanism of holding in check the destructive results of the production development; this meant that world wars were inescapable, and this was not simply a socio-psychological discomfort, but discomfort multiplied by discomfort.

The experience of the Phases of human history shows that a general, mass discomfort can be relieved, so that new conditions for production may emerge, only by the creation of an alternative social psychology, with the necessary condition that a new system of superior arms is also introduced which then can guarantee the introduction of the new social order. But at the moment when the world was going to be redistributed by the Great Powers, neither a new social psychology, nor really superior arms were available; however, it was apparent that something had to be done.

It is but natural that under such conditions there had to emerge alternative ideologies, and more than one at that. One of them was Communism.

The conditions which made it possible for the revolutionary parties in Russia to act was the débâcle of the Russian empire at the height of World War I, and the diffidence, the inclination towards half measures, of the parliamentary parties coming to power (inside the Provisional Government): they still could not offer the people what it urgently needed at that moment – ending the senseless war which was ruining peasant Russia, and transferring ownership of land to the peasants.[38] The SR, who in the preceding period pinned their hopes on individual terror, now preferred parliamentary methods in the new situation. Their programme agreed with the interests of the peasants, and they had a good chance to win the elections to the Constituent Assembly, planned for the winter 1917–1918, and which were to be general, equal and according to secret ballot. The same tactics were also planned by the right wing of the Social Democrats (the Mensheviks). However, the leftist Social Democrats, the Bolsheviks, proceeding from the theory of Marx and headed by Lenin, chose, as we know, another way.

Marx had created a sufficiently convincing theory of capitalist production (the drawbacks of his theory, especially the erroneousness of the assertion of an absolute pauperisation of the proletariat as imminent under capitalism, became obvious at a much later date). He was right when he postulated that capitalism is a transitory phenomenon. He foresaw the advent of a new Phase of the historical process which was to succeed capitalism, but he still imagined this Phase as Communism, i.e. as an absolute harmonious future. He clearly understood that the relations in production can be changed only when all possibilities of capitalism are exhausted, but according to his hypothesis, a more or less forcible upheaval would be needed. Note that the Marxists, in their evalua-

---

38. To be exact, members of the democratically elected Constituent Assembly planned to achieve peace, and to launch a land reform; at least that was the plan of the Social-Revolutionaries, who were in the majority. But the process of elections and of convening the Assembly dragged on until the beginning of 1918, when the Bolsheviks had already seized power, and could dissolve it, and even shoot some of the deputies.

tion of the historical process, were proceeding only from the experience of Europe (and partly of the USA), and more than anything, they regarded the development of the French Revolution as having a world-wide application and relevance.

In the capitalist Phase, as pointed out above, natural sciences had become a productive force. The Marxists, however, attempted to use a humanitarian science (an economic theory) for intervention in the historical process. Of course, this meant that Marxist scientific theory must gain a mass international support. (Marx was perfectly aware of the fact that capitalist production was transnational.) In order to gain such support, the International Working Association (The First International) was founded, which, however, had little influence. After Marx's death, the Second International was organised, and this already included mass European Social Democratic parties, most of them represented in national parliaments.

But masses are unfit for scholarly work, they are only able to learn by rote particular suggested theses which thus become demagogic. A scientific theory which ceases to be perfected and is reduced to dogmatism ceases to be a science. Under conditions of mass propagation, such a theory is checked neither by experiment nor even by sheer logic, and must perforce become a religion. The cases of early Buddhism and of Confucianism show that a religion may exist without a supreme deity. Such transformation of the theory led to faulty prognoses.

In the early twentieth century, no exhaustion in the possibilities of capitalism could be detected, and the social democrats of Western Europe took practical roles in parliamentary activities. But this was not the case in Russia.

For Lenin, the leading Russian Marxist of the twentieth century, the World War, waged for redistribution of colonies, was symptomatic of the emergence of 'Imperialism as the Last Stage of Capitalism', and of an 'Epoch of World Wars and Revolutions' (in this he was guided by the experience of the Russo-Japanese war and the subsequent failed Russian revolution of 1905). He suggested a scientifically quite unfounded hypothesis of the 'weak link'. According to this hypothesis, the revolution from capitalism to communism is to happen not in a country where capitalism had exhausted its possibilities, as the classical Marxist theory had it, but on the contrary, where capitalism had not appreciably developed, and hence was weak. However, with respect to Russia, we must appreciate the fact that not only was capitalism here weak but so too was the proletariat, to whom the role of the 'grave-digger of capitalism' was assigned: it constituted but a very small percentage of the population (in 1910 it was 2–3 per cent, not counting the farm-hands).[39] In the seven years since 1910 this percentage could not have grown much. Thus, the

---

39. The percentage quoted is from the *'Granat' Encyclopaedia*, 7th edn [1932?], vol. 36-II ('Russia IV'), table III, the summing up. The percentage quoted by Lenin in his *Razvitie kapitalizma v Rossii* [Development of Capitalism in Russia], viz. 10 per cent, includes non-working dependents and 'half-proletarian strata', but even so this is not a 'majority'.

1917 revolution in Russia, if it wanted to transfer power from the minority to the majority, had to be a peasant, not a proletarian revolution.[40]

But according to Lenin's hypothesis, after a revolutionary 'breakthrough' in the 'weak link', the Communist revolution was to take place not only in Russia but also in other countries, where capitalism certainly was not only strong but where the proletariat constituted the majority of the population. It was with a view to this orientation that the revolution in Russia was planned as a 'proletarian revolution'. When Lenin finally came to power, he established the 'Staff of World Revolution' – the Comintern. In 1917 Lenin subscribed (temporarily) to the slogan of the SR: 'land to the peasants', and hence could (in November of that year) achieve a revolutionary upheaval which won over to his side not only the rather unpopulous working class of Russia but, what was more important, the army consisting of peasants. The promise to found a federal republic, and the obvious internationalism of the communists also won support from the oppressed national minorities of Russia.

On 16 April 1917, Lenin, Martov and about 200 Social Democrats arrived in Petrograd. This was unexpected, because they could get to Russia only through Germany. That was actually the case: after an intercession by neutral leftists, the Germans let through a railway train with sealed carriages, to Sweden, and from there it was easy to get to Finland and to Petrograd. It has not been proved that Lenin gave any secret promises to the German government, but the latter obviously thought that an implantation of a big group of alleged 'pacifists' in Russia would be useful to Germany.

In the square beside the Finland Railway Station in Petrograd Lenin and the others were met by a big crowd of workers and soldiers. Lenin got up on an armoured car and made his famous speech, which was the basis of the Bolshevik policy for 1917 (but it seemed forever). He demanded immediate peace with Germany, immediate distribution of landowners' land among peasants, and assignation of 'all power to the Soviets'; in other words, he urged the population to nonrecognition of the Duma and the Provisional Government.

Until that moment, all Social Democrats of Russia, Bolsheviks as well as Mensheviks, were following the well-known doctrine of Marx, that the pre-capitalist order has to be destroyed by a revolution of the French 1789 type, under the leadership of the bourgeoisie; and only when the inner contradictions of the capi-

---

40. Lenin's government had a right to regard itself as representing the majority of the nation, and regard the Temporary Government as representing a minority, only so long as they kept to their slogan 'Land to the peasants', from which also followed the slogan 'A union between the working class and the peasantry'. But these slogans became empty words after the Bolsheviks, in 1919, introduced a system of confiscating grain from the peasantry (the so-called 'surplus-appropriation system', *prodrazverstka*); then, after a short period when the peasants actually owned the land (1922–1929), a mass extermination of the entire commodity-producing peasantry started, under the false slogan of 'liquidation of the *kulaks* as a class'; the term *kulak*, originally meaning a rich peasant exploiting his neighbours, was given an inconceivably broad interpretation; and the *kulaks* were 'liquidated' (or at least exiled) not 'as a class', but as persons.

talist society ripened, would the numbers of the proletariat, its inner organisation and 'class-consciousness' (i.e. devotion to Marxism) grow appreciably – only then might power be seized by the proletariat, thus laying the foundation for the new, socialist relations in production. But Lenin thought that the 1905 revolution had shown the weakness of the Russian bourgeoisie, and its incapability of seizing power. Therefore, the bourgeois stage of the revolution should be put into practice by a proletarian vanguard. Lenin recognised the necessity of help from Western workers, but he believed that an alliance between the workers and the poorest peasantry in Russia would suffice to maintain the first stage of the revolution until the inescapable proletarian revolution occurred in Western Europe. In other words, if we apply the terminology suggested in this book, Lenin hoped to skip from the border between the Sixth and the Seventh Phase (which was where Russia was actually situated) directly to the Eighth Phase. But historical experience teaches us that a spontaneous passing to a Phase C from a Phase A across Phase B is only possible if that higher Phase had already been dominant someplace, and there had been prolonged and fruitful contacts between the societies belonging to the different Phases (B and A, and the emerging C in our example).

Another point of view was that of the Social Democrats of the so-called 'Between-District' group, headed by Trotski; first he supported the Mensheviks but later, and finally, went over to the Bolsheviks. Trotski did not agree with the possibility of a survival of capitalist social conditions after the victory of the proletariat; he insisted that the revolution which was beginning in Russia, should be a 'permanent' revolution, i.e. that it should be followed by similar upheavals throughout Europe and all over the world. But at this particular stage he had no serious quarrel with Lenin. He entered the Bolshevik party, and was to play an important role in it.

For Lenin, taking part in a parliamentary political system was unthinkable because any parliamentary procedure requires compromise, and, moreover, the Bolsheviks could not hope for a majority, or even for an important opposition in an elected parliament, and hence, would have no hope of coming even partially into power. Quite another thing were the Soviets: these loosely arranged bodies could easily be dominated by Bolsheviks. Hence the famous slogan: 'All power to the Soviets.'

Meanwhile, on 5 April 1917, the new foreign minister, P. N. Milyukov (as if answering President Wilson) declared that the Russian military goals were annexation of Austro-Hungarian Galicia (inhabited mainly by Ukrainians and Poles), as well as of Constantinople and the Dardanelles. Four days later, the Petrograd Soviet passed a resolution demanding the conclusion of an immediate peace 'without annexations and indemnities'. As to the Duma, it voted for 'securing a stable peace on the base of self-determination of nations'. This resolution was delivered to the Allies on 1 May, and at the same time they were informed that Russia would continue fighting until victory. In answer to this, there were major public demonstrations in Petrograd; Milyukov and the minister of defence, Guchkov, resigned; the new coalition government included representatives of the SR and the Mensheviks (there were no representatives of rightist groups).

The net result of all these events was the break-down of discipline in the army. Nevertheless, Kerenski, as the new minister of defence, decided to persuade the soldiers' committees to continue military operations; he even managed to begin a new attempt of an offensive in Galicia. Nothing came of it; many units simply refused to fight.

On 1 July the Congress of Workers' and Soldiers' Deputies met in Petrograd; the Bolsheviks' representatives accounted for some 12 per cent of the Congress members. But when the leaders of the Congress attempted to organise a mass public demonstration in defence of 'revolutionary democracy', the Bolsheviks staged a counter-demonstration, demanding an immediate interruption of the war. On 16 July, the Bolshevik demonstration was resumed, involving the participation *en masse* of workers, soldiers, and the sailors of the naval base Kronstadt. It looked as if the demonstration could end in a new *coup d'état*. It resulted in soldiers firing on the demonstrators and dispersing them. The Provisional Government attempted to arrest the leading Bolsheviks. A rumour was launched that Lenin was a paid agent of the Germans, and he had to hide in the vicinity of Petrograd and then in Finland. On 21 July the Provisional Government was reorganised, and Kerenski became prime minister. Although this meant a certain reorientation of the government to the left, it also meant the continuation of war.

Meanwhile, on the outskirts of the empire there began a movement for the liberation of non-Russian nationalities. On 17 May, Kiev saw the organisation of a Provisional Government of the Ukraine – the Central Rada (=Council), headed by the well-known historian Hrushevski. The Provisional Government in Petrograd refused to recognise the Rada on the grounds that it was not elected by a general popular ballot (as if the rump of the Duma had been democratically elected!). Certain concessions were made to Finland, but the question of Finland's independence was left to be decided by the Constituent Assembly. Local governments also emerged in the Baltic regions; this was more dangerous, because until 1940 these regions had had rich and influential German minorities.[41] Armenia and Georgia waited until the Constituent Assembly should meet. In May, a Congress of the Muslims of Russia was convened in Moscow. But the Provisional Government made no promises to anybody.

In August, a 'Democratic Conference' met in Moscow. Representatives of certain groups of the population, chosen rather at random, were present, as were members of former Dumas. The Bolsheviks did not participate, and no perceptible results were achieved. The demands of the different public and national bodies were declared acceptable as a matter of principle, but the main problem remained the

---

41. In 1940, after having lived in the Baltic region for seven hundred years, they were re-settled to Germany according to an agreement between Hitler and Stalin.

continuation of military operations, which showed little understanding of the needs of the soldiers, and of their attitudes of mind.

On 3 September, the Germans captured Riga, and Petrograd was now in danger. This led to a rightest insurrection against Kerenski, led by General Kornilov. Kerenski asked the Soviets for help. Their representatives had no difficulty in demoralising Kornilov's troops through propaganda; Kornilov himself was arrested. On 15 September Kerenski declared Russia a republic; this decision was preceded by secret talks with Nicholas II (who was keeping to the rear of the Russo-German front), and his abdication in favour of his brother, who also abdicated immediately. But the September events brought no new power to Kerenski, nor any glory: it was the Bolsheviks who were actually successful. During the Sixth Congress of the Bolshevik party (held in Petrograd during July and August) the idea of taking power independent of the position of the Soviets had already been aired. Among the Bolshevik leaders Zinoviev and Kamenev suggested waiting a little, but Trotski and Lenin (the latter still in hiding) suggested that power should be seized immediately.

International public opinion vacillated between support for the rightists (Kornilov) and the leftists (Kerenski). The activities of Bolsheviks were completely ignored. As for the Bolsheviks, Kornilov's failure was a signal that power could be seized. Trotski, as president of the Petrograd Soviet, formed a secret 'Provisional Revolutionary Committee'. Kerenski's feeble attempts at securing more power came to naught: the Bolshevist agents and commissars had already been introduced into the military units, and into the main industrial factories. In the night between 6 and 7 November (24–25 October according to the old Julian calendar) the Bolsheviks were able to mount a *coup d'état* in Petrograd. The members of the government were staying at the former residence of the emperors – the Winter Palace. Kerenski had fled on the eve of the revolution, and, as the rumours had it, in changed clothes – one rumour even implied that he fled clad as a woman. The palace was guarded by a battalion of women volunteers, ranged behind huge stacks of firewood piled before the palace for its heating. But when armed insurgents began to appear on the approaches to the Palace Square, one sergeant-major sent the women home.

The Winter Palace was not stormed, despite what has since been depicted in films and big paintings in oil-colours. The insurgents came up the square to the left palace entrance, and discovered that it was not defended. They went up the stair-case to the 'Malachite Drawing-room' and the 'White Dining Hall', and arrested the members of the Provisional Government who were there. There were no excesses when the Palace was entered; only a portrait of Nicholas II was pierced by a bayo-net. The sculpture, the paintings, the furniture were all left intact. But after a while, since the Palace was not guarded, stray criminals and drunkards put in an appearance; mainly, however, they were interested in the rich wine-vaults.

On 8 November was the first sitting of the Petrograd Soviet, with only Bolsheviks and the SR taking part. The most important decrees were approved. The first decree advised all the countries at war immediately to conclude a peace without annexations and indemnities; the Soviet government agreed to discuss any peace proposals. It was also declared, that all secret treaties and agreements made by the former government were going to be published. The second decree was about land. It declared the confiscation of all landlords', imperial and monasteries' estates, which were to be divided between the peasants according to rules which were to be introduced by a future Constituent Assembly (which never met). Then an eight-hour working day was introduced. Some industrial enterprises and all banks were nationalised (the whole industry was nationalised during the summer of 1918). An All-Russian Committee of National Economy was instituted to administrate industry as a whole.

In the middle of November the Bolsheviks appointed a new Commander-in-Chief of the Western Front, namely ensign Krylenko.[42]

Lenin had years earlier declared that 'national entities have the right of self-determination and even of secession' but the great problem concerned, who the Bolsheviks regarded as legal representatives of the nationalities. Thus, they recognised the right of the Ukraine to secession as a matter of principle, but they regarded the existing Central Rada as non-democratic, because the industrial Russian speaking districts (who favoured the Bolsheviks) were not adequately represented, and also because the Rada did not hinder the Tsarist officers to travel to the Don, where a Volunteer Army was being formed (it was 'White', i.e. anti-Bolshevik): but it did hold back the Bolshevik troops ready to pursue the Whites. So the Bolsheviks set up a Ukrainian government of their own in Kharkov, headed by one Christian Rakovski.[43] From here a campaign against the Central Rada was launched. Members of the Rada attempted to address the Allies, but the Allies did not recognise the independence of the Ukraine; in February 1918, the Central Rada signed a peace with Germany at Brest-Litovsk; but for German tastes the Rada was too democratic, and instead they set up the self-appointed headman Skoropadski to head Ukraine.

In Transcaucasia was created a Transcaucasian Commissariat which overtook power pending the decisions of the Constituent Assembly.

Inside the Soviet Government, Lenin created a commissariat (=ministry) for national affairs, headed by Djugashvili (Stalin); the Bolsheviks had little skilled personnel; ever since the period of underground work, they were not well acquainted with each other, and Stalin's very dubious past was not commonly known – especially since afterwards he ruthlessly exterminated everybody who knew anything at all about his history, whether good or bad. The undertakings of this commissariat were actively supported by the Volga Tatars, among whom there was a considerable percentage of industrial workers. In Kazakhstan, a local

---

42. Later he frequently acted as prosecutor in the phony trials staged by Stalin, but he himself did not survive the fatal year 1938.   43. Later he was shot.

nationalistic organisation, the *Orda* ('Horde'), emerged, and there was an attempt to found a 'Muslim Council' in Central Asia, but the Russian-speaking proletariat of Tashkent (mainly railwaymen) not only did not recognise it, but even prohibited Muslims from occupying administrative jobs. The Muslims created a Council of their own in Kokand, and for several months they dominated the countryside, while the cities were mainly held by the Bolsheviks. Guerrilla warfare was waged in Central Asia for decades.

During the second half of 1917, preparations for convening the Constituent Assembly were in progress. In the beginning, the elections were planned for early autumn, and were to be general, equal and by secret and direct ballot. But in so backward a country as Russia, and under the conditions of acute political struggle both inside the army and in the cities, the elections could be held, without Lenin raising an objection, only in November 1917. The results of the ballot were as follows: the SR (Russian and Ukrainian) won 419 seats, the Bolsheviks 168, the Mensheviks 18, the Constitutional Democrats (Kadets) and the rightists 17, and others 81. The left SR and many of the 'others' voted with the Bolsheviks, who thus had more than 200 deputies voting for them, and nearly 400 against them (however, the rightists and the Kadets did not form an alliance with the Mensheviks). The Bolsheviks declared that it was the Soviets of Workers' Deputies who should rule the country, since the Constituent Assembly was a bourgeois institution, and that it anyway did not reflect the current opinion of the people but belonged to the past.

By 18 January 1918 – the day when the Constituent Assembly was to be convened – only about half of the elected members were able to reach Petrograd. The Bolsheviks and the left SR moved for recognising the rights of the Soviets above those of the Constituent Assembly. When this motion was turned down by a vote of 230:136, the Bolsheviks and the left SR walked out. In the night between 18 and 19 January, the sailors who were guarding the Tauride Palace, where the Assembly was convened, declared that 'the guard is tired', and suggested that everybody should go home. When in the morning there appeared a manifestation of protest, it was dispersed by gunfire.

For some time anarchy reigned in Petrograd: unknown persons were arresting or shooting people whom they did not like. The banks went on strike, but they were taken over by commissars with Mauser hand-guns. Formally, a 'people's commissar' was equivalent to a minister in the new Bolsheviks and left SR government, but actually commissars, whether nominated or self-appointed, appeared also in the factories and workshops, in the offices, in the house-managing offices, etc. They were all armed with hand-guns, and, without a twinge of conscience, shot anybody who they regarded as 'bourgeois', or 'countric' (i.e. counter-revolutionary).

By the use of extraordinary measures, the Bolsheviks managed to sustain a semblance of order, but the food situation kept deteriorating, and continued to be most grave during the whole of the Civil War.

Immediately after the seizure of power by the Bolsheviks, all newspapers, except official Communist ones, were suspended. For some time, it is true, one independent newspaper, rather critical of the Soviets, continued to appear; it was published by Maxim Gorki, the well-known writer who at that time had not yet gone over to the Bolsheviks. As for the latter, they established an 'Extraordinary Commission to Combat Counter-Revolution and Sabotage', better known as the Cheka, which had only one form of penalty, namely immediate shooting. The Cheka was headed by Dzierziński, a descendant of Polish nobles; but it employed a lot of ignorant, shady and unscrupulous men. The Cheka had tens of thousands of men and women executed without any legal inquiry. People were shot for former political or anti-Bolshevist activities (in the broadest sense, and without the shadow of legal proof), for having been an officer in the Tsarist army, for having been a big (or not so big) landowner or merchant, etc.

On 15 December 1917, the Bolshevik government signed a provisional armistice with Germany at Brest-Litovsk. The fact that there had been numerous strikes in several German cities strengthened the Bolsheviks' belief in the proximity of a World Revolution. Hence, instead of responsible authorised representatives, they delegated agitators with the goal of demoralising the German soldiers at the front, and to direct their aspirations towards a revolution. On their side, the German representatives insisted that the negotiations not concern Latvia, Lithuania and Poland which had become part of the German Empire. Trotski, who headed the Soviet delegation, clung to his preposterous formula: 'neither war, nor peace'. By February 1918, Germany had already concluded a peace with the Ukrainian Central Rada, but the Soviet delegation had even earlier (at the end of 1917) left Brest-Litovsk; so Germany and Austria-Hungary resumed their offensive. After prolonged debates, and having gained but a precarious majority, Lenin got the Central Committee of the Bolshevik Party to agree to a peace with Germany, which was signed on 3 March, 1918, at Brest-Litovsk. However, not being sure that the Germans would keep to the peace agreement, the Bolsheviks shifted the seat of the government, 12 March 1918, from Petrograd to Moscow.[44]

According to the treaty of Brest-Litovsk, Russia lost Estonia, Latvia, Lithuania, Poland and part of Belorussia. Ukraine had been dominated by the Central Rada, but was soon to come under what amounted to actual rule by Germany. Soviet Russia had already earlier granted full independence to Finland without anywhere officially encroaching on its territory; however, certain guerrilla and putschist activities continued there for years. Soviet Russia ceded to Turkey the port Batumi on the Black Sea, and the cities Kars and Ardahan with their districts, at that time still inhabited by Armenians.

---

44. In May 1918, Rumania concluded a peace with the Central Powers. By the end of the year the Germans and Austro-Hungarians left Rumania; at the same time Bessarabia, which was Russian for more than 200 years, became a part of Rumania. The central part of Bessarabia is inhabited by Moldavians, the latter, along with the Vlachs, constitute the Rumanian people; they speak practically the same language.

Transcaucasia was in the years 1918–1922 occupied by foreign troops (Turkish, then British, then again Turkish); a bloody internal strife was also continuing. For a certain period, there existed independent republics – Georgia, Armenia, Azerbaijan (on which more below). Sometimes these republics were democratic.

At their Seventh Party Congress in March 1918, the Bolsheviks gave a new name to their party: now it was called the 'Russian Communist Party (Bolsheviks)', or RCP(B). The treaty of Brest was ratified by the Congress of the Soviets immediately after the SR left the Congress (for quite other reasons). Shortly after that, the Communists provoked an SR mutiny, and all the leading Socialist Revolutionaries were arrested. For some unknown reason, some of the SR leaders, including their most outstanding figure, Maria Spiridonova, were imprisoned but not shot for a very long time: not until the German army was approaching Moscow in the autumn of 1941; then Spiridonova was shot in a prison near Moscow together with a number of other former political figures.

By the middle of 1918, the country was clearly divided into two counter-balancing political camps: the 'Reds', and the 'Whites'. The Bolsheviks and their sympathisers were 'Reds', whereas all who did not sympathise with them for a number of different reasons, but who wanted a united non-Bolshevist Russia, were 'Whites'. The 'Reds' had a large but poorly disciplined army, and up to 1920 they were supported by most of the peasants, while the 'Whites' had a well-organised small nucleus of an army, partly using the rather meagre supplies furnished by the Allies; it was first headed by General Kornilov, and later by General Denikin in the valley of the Kuban river in Northern Caucasus.

A new war, considerably more bloody than the German, was in the offing.

The next German offensive on the Western Front in 1918 induced the countries of the Entente to make an effort and create at least the similitude of an Eastern Front. A small troop of British and American soldiers landed in Murmansk (by agreement with the local Soviet) in March 1918. At that time a squadron of Russian warships was stationed in Murmansk.[45] The British captured them, and later (in the early 1920s) dismantled them for metal. The Japanese occupied Vladivostok and the Amur region in April, and the Turks occupied Batumi (by agreement with Russia, but not even informing the Georgian authorities, whom Moscow did not recognise). In August the British occupied Arkhangelsk; here a puppet government was installed, headed by the extremely aged Populist Chaikovski.

On Russian territory, there had been in the former years organised an armed Czechoslovak Legion, which included Czechs and Slovaks who had either been taken prisoner, or had deserted from the Austro-Hungarian army. The Soviet government suggested that the Czechoslovaks should go by train to the Far East, in order to be evacuated from there by sea. But the Czechoslovaks felt themselves

---

45. These were warships which had been captured by the Japanese in 1905; among them was the famous 'Varyag'.

trapped, and armed conflicts began between them and the local authorities. Trotski, as Commissar for the Army and Navy, ordered the Czechoslovaks to disarm. They declined to follow the order, and captured the Trans-Siberian railway line. Partially in connection with these events, partly spontaneously, there emerged an embryo of an alternative government (mostly organised by the SR). Then the Bolsheviks excluded all the SR and the remaining Mensheviks from all Soviets, and introduced for them a prohibition of any political activities. In July 1918, a group of left SR killed the German ambassador in Moscow, Graf von Mirbach-Harff. This was not all. On 30 August, Uritski, the chief of the Petrograd Cheka, was killed, and in Moscow, a woman SR named Kaplan seriously wounded Lenin.[46] For a short time, the SR seized the residence of the Moscow Cheka, but were ousted from there. Soon also SR insurrections in Yaroslavl, in Vologda and other places were suppressed.

The quelling of the SR rebellion made Soviet Russia a one-party state. From now on, all important decisions were made not in the Soviets but in the Central Committee (CC) of the Communist party, a body not elected by the people.

Regarding the Cheka, it is worth explaining the character of its activities. In 1919, a group of anarchists attempted to blow up a former private residence in Moscow where members of the Bolshevik CC were to have met for a conference. The conspiracy was discovered, all anarchists involved were shot, but while they were about it, the Cheka rounded up a number of persons from different groups of the population, having nothing whatever to do with anarchists, but who might be thought to disapprove of Soviet authorities. Several hundred persons were shot. This is just one case; all over the country there were hundreds if not thousands of cases of this sort.[47]

In September 1918, some members of the Constituent Assembly which had been

---

46. Kaplan was not tried; she was placed in a motor-car, and shot.
47. Among the victims of the revolutionary terrorism was the family of Nicholas II. First the ex-emperor and his family were exiled to Tobolsk, then they were removed to Yekaterinburg where they occupied a strictly guarded detached house where they lived with some servants, a governess, a doctor, etc. In the night of 16–17 July 1918 all these persons, including the chronically diseased boy, the heir of Nicholas II, were led into the house's underground vault and shot; the corpses were removed to the suburbs and there burned, rather perfunctorily. It was officially declared that this was done by the local Soviet and not sanctioned from above, but it was later proved that the shooting of the victims was ordered by Lenin and his henchman Sverdlov. In the 1990s this episode has been used for large-scale monarchist propaganda. But let us remember how many families had been exterminated by the Bolsheviks just as brutally; why should the fate of this particular family induce any special emotions? Nicholas II was a poor sovereign, a worthless military leader; he was among those most responsible for the bloody reprisals of 1905–1906, and for the launching of the First World War, as well as for all its sequences; there is a suspicion that he was involved in the murder of Stolypin, at a moment when the latter stopped the mass hangings and started the land reform so much needed by Russia. As a personality, Nicholas II was insignificant. Nevertheless, the publicity made for the massacre at Yekaterinburg focuses the popular attention on the general character of the 'Red Terror' started by the Bolsheviks from the middle of 1918.

dissolved a year before (of course, mostly SR) met in Ufa, Bashkiria; another Committee of the Constituent Assembly existed in Samara, on the Volga. The Assembly in Ufa appointed an All-Russian Directory as a provisional governing body pending the convening of the legal Constituent Assembly in full session. However, the Red Army, organised by Trotski and his collaborators, could by the autumn of 1918 occupy not only most of the western, but also the eastern part of Russia. The Directory was transferred to Omsk in Siberia, where a new 'White' army was quickly being organised, headed by Admiral Kolchak. British and American military missions were accredited to the Directory.

The participation of the Western Powers in the events of the Russian Civil War was very limited and largely symbolic, but it gave the occasion for the Communists to launch a grand propaganda campaign not only about an Allied 'intervention' but even about a 'campaign of the Entente against the RSFSR'; but the Entente would, they insisted, experience a defeat as the result of the World Revolution. The advent of such a Revolution was an article of faith for the early Communists. Meanwhile, the Entente had much to think about elsewhere.

Kolchak thought the SR to be just as Red as the Bolsheviks. In November 1918 he organised a coup which made him sole dictator – until the awaited moment of the restoration of the Empire in Russia.

The Civil War in the Ukraine had a more complicated and many-sided form. The Skoropadski regime, supported by the Germans did not survive their withdrawal; part of the Ukrainian territory was now dominated by Ukrainian nationalists headed by Petlyura, who was inclined to general bloody massacres, and to pogroms of the Jews. In another part of the Ukraine, including the Donets coal basin and Kharkov, mostly inhabited by Russians, the power belonged to Communists who also massacred unwanted groups, but mostly not openly, in secret. Moreover, a part of Ukrainian territory was occupied by anarchists headed by Nestor Makhyno; this one was no more sentimental in his activities, but flirted with everybody else, except the Whites.

The emissaries of the Whites in the countries of the Entente tried to explain that they never had failed the Entente's cause, and that the real Russian army headed by Denikin actually exist on the Kuban river. They pointed out that communism was a threat to the entire world, since revolutionary events were occurring not only in Russia but also in the countries which had lost the war – in Germany and in Hungary, where there were attempts to found Soviet republics; therefore, the Entente ought to aid the enemies of the Communists. The governments of the Entente countries regarded these ideas without enthusiasm: of course, the introduction of a full-scale army into Russian territory could not seriously be envisaged; such a measure would result in the failure of any government to win the next elections. Their economic aid to Kolchak and Denikin was on rather a small scale. Their armed help was negligible. The French, who had landed in Odessa, could not fully understand whom they were supposed to aid, and called their troops back in

March–April 1919; the British and Americans left Murmansk and Arkhangelsk by September–October 1919. Only the Japanese continued to occupy the Far East somewhat longer.

But the main events of the Russian Civil War occurred exactly during the years 1919 and 1920. Early in 1919, Kolchak started an energetic offensive from Siberia across the Urals, although Red guerrillas were troubling the rear of his army; but by the end of the summer his offensive petered out, and a hurried flight to the East began. The provisional government which Kolchak had established at Irkutsk was captured by the SR, who delivered Kolchak to the Reds; the Admiral and persons of his retinue were shot early in 1920; shootings of real and supposed followers of Kolchak came next.

Late in the summer of 1920 Denikin began a powerful advance from the Kuban towards Central Russia. In August he occupied all the Ukraine. In October 1919 he captured Orel – no great distance from Moscow. At the same time, General Yudenich, having organised an armed force in Estonia, began an offensive aimed at Petrograd; there, as usual, mass arrests and shootings started. But by that time the Red Army had already reached quite a good fighting efficiency, its officers (officially they were called 'commanders') had sufficient experience, and both Yudenich and Denikin were defeated with heavy losses. Yudenich's army returned to Estonia, and there fell apart, while the dwindling forces of Denikin fled as far south as Novorossisk, where they embarked on board Entente ships in March 1920.

However, a strong centre of resistance still existed under the leadership of General Wrangel in the Crimea. Soon after the October coup, the Bolsheviks had attempted to occupy the Crimea, but all their leaders were captured and shot. In April 1918 the Germans, in violation of the peace of Brest, attempted to occupy the peninsula; but then, with some assistance from the Entente, it was occupied by the Whites. By the end of 1920, the Crimea became an asylum for the very numerous refugees fleeing from the Communists. The Perekop isthmus, which joins the peninsula with the mainland, was heavily fortified. In June 1920, when a Polish offensive against the then already Communist Ukraine began, Wrangel's troops moved out of the Crimea into the Ukraine and towards the Kuban. But the Reds were by that time so much stronger, that the only thing Wrangel's troops could do was to secure a speedy evacuation of the civil population from the Crimea, from the Kuban, and from Odessa. From the Crimea alone 150,000 men and women were evacuated. The Red Army, headed by Frunze, broke through the White positions at Perekop and occupied the peninsula. After that, Bolshevik authorities, headed by Rosalie Zemlyachka, the Hungarian Communist Bela Kun, and Lenin's own brother Dmitri Ulyanov, organised an unreported massacre of Wrangel's officers and soldiers who had surrendered to the Reds, and of 'bourgeois elements' including the intelligentsia – mostly summer residents who had failed to flee in time.

One might have thought that the Civil War was now over; however, the SR had organised a peasant insurrection around Tambov in Southern Russia; it lasted for nearly a year, and was suppressed by élite troops of the Red Army, headed by Tukhachevski. According to Moscow's order, in every peasant family who had failed to deliver the amount of grain tax due from it, one man was to be shot. In the villages of the Cossacks on the Don and the Kuban, a considerable part of the population had supported the Whites, and there a mass campaign of dispossessing and murdering of Cossacks was launched; hundreds of thousands perished.

For a long time there was no stable peace in the Muslim regions of Central Asia, and guerrilla raids of the so-called Basmachi based on Afghanistan (and indirectly – on the British Empire) continued to 1930.

In the Ukraine also the problems had no easy solution. Petlyura had a treaty with the Polish President Pilsudski, and hoped for a future Polish–Ukrainian federation. The Poles wanted their frontiers of 1772 restored, which meant the occupation of all Belorussia and the part of the Ukraine to the west of the Dneiper. But the Ukrainian population did not want them. This period is remembered for terrible Jewish pogroms committed both by Petlyura's men, and by Poles. The number of victims is unknown, but it was probably in the hundreds of thousands. The Red Army dislodged the Poles from Kiev and swiftly moved westwards in two columns.

1920 was the year of the Communist attempts to start a revolution in Germany; and the Kremlin, which still hoped for a World Revolution (without which a Communist revolution in peasant Russia lost its significance for world history), decided to defeat the Poles and to enter into revolutionary Silesia. The northern army group, led by Tukhachevski who had been taught at a Tsarist military school, had considerable success. In occupied Bialystok a provisional Communist government of Poland was installed, and by August the Reds were approaching the Vistula. But the southern group led by Budenny, a former cavalry sergeant-major, and recruited by poorly organised and undisciplined privates, instead of moving in support of Tukhachevski, advanced deep into Galicia following the military operations with outright plundering. Meanwhile, the revolutionary movement in Germany was suppressed.

In August 1920, the Poles launched a counter-offensive. The fighting spirit of the Reds was falling because of bad news from home (food was being requisitioned from peasants by Communist authorities without payment), and in October 1920 the RSFSR signed an armistice with Poland. According to the final treaty of Riga (18 March 1921), Poland acquired a considerable part of Belorussian and Ukrainian territories (especially important was Galacia, formerly Austro-Hungarian, where the peasants felt themselves to be Ukrainian, but the cities were decidedly Polish).

In the Baltic regions, after the failure of the Yudenich offensive, the Communists attempted to gain power; they held Riga until May 1919 (we may note that the Latvian rifle-men were from the start considered as the most reliable – and probably the cruellest – part of the Red Army). But by 1920, the Red Army was too exhausted, and the British brought their warships into the Baltic. In February RSFSR concluded a peace treaty with Estonia, and in July with Lithuania (but

Pilsudski soon occupied Wilno, or Vilnius, Lithuania's Polish-speaking historical capital, and the district around the city); in August a treaty was signed with Latvia. The Communists did not attempt to conquer Bessarabia, although they did not recognise Rumania's rights to it.

In 1920 Georgia, Armenia, and Azerbaijan were recognised by the Entente *de facto* (and, theoretically, Armenia was to include the former Armenian regions of Turkey which had lost their Armenian population as a result of the Turkish genocide in 1915). Mustafa Kemal-pasha (later receiving the surname 'Atatürk' – Father of the Turks) restored the former Turkish frontiers in Armenia, including Kars and Ardahan. However, the Armenian Nationalist ('Dashnak') government managed to inflict a serious defeat on the Turks, and to force them back across the Araxes river. In Georgia the Menshevik government had a rather solid popular support.

In Azerbaijan[48] the problem was, that the nationalist Musavat party had the support of the Turki (now called Azerbaijani) village population, and of the small towns; but Baku, a big industrial centre with a Russian, Armenian, and Jewish proletarian population, did not want the Musavists.

Threatened by an insurrection in Baku and by an offensive of the Red Army, the Musavist government resigned in April 1920. In December of the same year, RSFSR concluded a peace with Kemalist Turkey; according to the agreement, the Araxes was designed to be the frontier between Turkey and Russia; most of Russian Armenia and the region of Batumi were recognised as Russian. In May 1920, the Russian Soviet Government concluded a peace with Georgia, but this did not withhold the Soviet troops from occupying that country. In December 1922, a Transcaucasian Soviet Federation was founded, which later became an integral part of the USSR. At a still later date, Transcaucasia was divided into Georgia (with the Abkhazian, South Ossetian,[49] and Adjarian autonomies), Armenia, and Azerbaijan.

In the Far East, a buffer socialist state was created, the Far Eastern Republic. The Japanese seem to have been satisfied with this solution, but they continued to fight

---

48. See n. 36 to chapter 5 (the Fifth Phase). Note that in the early nineteenth century the population of Tbilisi was mainly Armenian (not Georgian), that of Yerevan was Turkic (not Armenian), and that of Baku was mixed, including Russians, Armenians, Jews – of all Azerbaijani Turks. The present day situation, when Tbilisi is completely Georgian, Yerevan completely Armenian, and Baku completely Azerbaijani, is the result of later developments.

49. It is difficult to explain why two separate Ossetian autonomies exist: Southern Ossetia south of the Caucasus, and Northern Ossetia to the north of it. Presumably, Stalin, who was commissioned to solve the Caucasian national problems, did not want to create a resentment among the Georgians who regard Southern Ossetia as an integral part of Georgia. However, the allegation that Southern Ossetia was formerly inhabited by Georgians is not proven; and anyway, since the Ossetians have certainly lived there for centuries, there is no reason why they should not regard this land as their own.

The Adjarians, who have an autonomous region of their own in Southern Georgia, are a group of formerly Islamised Georgians with a specific dialect (those of them who have retained the Islamic religion, are called Meskheti Turks; they were exiled by Stalin to Central Asia).

the guerrillas; although leaving the Baikal region, they did not want to leave Vladivostok, and the region between Vladivostok and the Amur. Such a strengthening of Japan was contrary to the interests of the United States, and in autumn 1922 the Japanese government informed Washington that it was going to evacuate its armed forces from former Russian territory. The Far Eastern Republic was immediately included in the RSFSR.

Lenin's unfounded hypothesis – which was the basis of all the revolutionary activities (and that led to the great bloodshed during the Civil War and to the most brutal reprisals) – resulted in the emergence of new relations in the territories of the somewhat diminished former Russian Empire; from 1922 it was declared to be a Union of Soviet Socialist Republics (USSR). Besides the Russian Federation (the RSFSR), it also included the Belorussian SSR, the Ukrainian SSR, the Transcaucasian SFSR and the Soviet republics of Central Asia which were composed of several republics, in different ways at different times.

The USSR retained its imperial character because the different degrees of autonomy granted to the non-Russian nationalities were nominal in all cases.

Although the state was called the Russian Socialist Federative *Soviet* Republic, and later the Union of *Soviet* Socialist Republics, in practice the Soviets played only a decorative role, because all political, economic and even cultural decisions were made by the Central Committee of the RCP(B), and by its regional and district committees.

The second man in the Republic after Lenin was certainly Trotski. As the People's Commissar (=Minister) of the Army and Navy, he converted the Red Army from a mass of untrained rabble, of re-enlisted servicemen, and of workers who had spent the time of the First World War in the factories, never having smelled gunpowder, into a disciplined and very efficient army. This was achieved in spite of the fact (or even because of it) that officers ate together with the soldiers, and did not differ from soldiers in outfit; 'comrade' was the only mutual form of address without regard to rank. It was also Trotski who obtained the permission to include loyal experienced officers of the Tsarist army into the cadres of the Red Army (another outstanding communist leader, Zinoviev, was more inclined to shoot them; Stalin who was more or less of the same opinion, had at that time still no particular importance). The army discipline was strict, and the party discipline was strict. By the end of the Civil War the Red Army was far more efficient than the White formations. That victory was achieved by the Reds, was also partly due to the fact that the Bolsheviks firmly held the centre and the central communications, while the Whites were on different and not communicating peripheries.

As we have pointed out above Lenin and the Communists came to power in 1917 because they adopted the SR slogan 'land to the peasants'. But being Social Democrats, the Bolsheviks were always of the opinion that the agriculture should be nationalised, and the peasants should be proletarianised; this conviction was deeply rooted in Bolshevik mentality, in spite of the fact that in 1917 Lenin had declared that land should be given to peasants. Moreover, the war itself required that not only the army but also the country as a whole should be supplied at least with a minimum of food. To continue the war, one had to mobilise able-bodied peasants (and hence also those who were most efficient for labour on the land), and to requisition food. This was nicknamed 'military communism', with the understanding that these conditions would not continue after war was over. However, even the notion 'peasantry' somehow disappeared from Communist vocabulary. It was officially held, that there exist 'kulaks' producing for the market and using hired labour, and therefore to be regarded as class enemies; neutral 'middle peasants'; and 'poor peasants', who were regarded as a sort of rural proletariat, but who actually – unless they were ill or crippled – were simply ne'er-do-wells, drunkards or loafers.

The relations between the peasants and the Communists deteriorated from 1920, when the earlier introduced 'surplus-appropriation system' (*prodrazverstka*) was rampant; it amounted to a complete confiscation of all food resources of the peasants over and above what the commissar in question thought to be strictly necessary for the peasants' survival.

The working class had been greatly depleted, because its most active and capable representatives had been recruited into the army or into the ranks of the 'commissars'. Industrial production was in a state of complete disorder. It was under these particular conditions that it occurred to Trotski and his friends that 'military communism' should continue until the World Revolution (which, of course, was to occur shortly), and that 'military communism' might even be regarded as a model for the future Socialist industrial production.

Early 1920 saw mass strikes in Petrograd for political as well as economic reasons. The workers demanded the liberation of the non-Bolshevik socialists who had been arrested. In March, sailors of the Baltic naval base Kronstadt mutinied; they demanded that power be shifted from the Communist party committees to the Soviets, as had been announced in November 1917, and an end to the exorbitant extortions from the peasantry.[50] On 17 March 1921, the bay being still under ice, considerable military forces were assembled against Kronstadt, and its shelling began. The sailors answered with artillery fire, but on 18 March the city was stormed, and a massacre started. A few men fled in boats to Finland; some sailors were left alive, because the ships could not be left entirely without crews; but it seems that most of the garrison was slaughtered.

In the same month (March 1921), the Tenth Congress of the RCP(B) took place. Here a group of the so-called 'Workers' Opposition' required the repression only of actual class enemies, but in addition to this a freedom of thought for working

---

50. Note that a large number of military seamen had moved (often – as commanding figures) into the Red Army, and by 1921 the fortress and port of Kronstadt were to a considerable extent manned by recruited peasants.

people, and a shift in political centre from the party committees to the trade unions. The somewhat similar 'Democratic Centralism' group agreed to keep to the one-party system, but with a certain freedom of view for the members of the party. Lenin attacked the opposition, and it lost against an overwhelming majority vote in favour of Lenin. Note that by that time very few of the original Bolshevik Social Democrats were still alive, and the majority of deputies at the Congress had had an experience of participating in the Cheka and in military reprisals.

The Congress prohibited any factions inside the party. 'Fractional activity' was regarded as any address to the directing bodies of the party stating an opinion shared by more than one individual.

The most important decision of the Congress was the renunciation of the 'surplus-appropriation system' and the introduction of a 'goods tax'. Moreover, Lenin seems to have become aware of the fact that no 'World Communist Revolution' was to be expected. The revolution in Russia had been planned just as a slow-match to set fire to other revolutions in other countries; but the capitalist forces had easily put an end even to the half-hearted attempts to start a socialist revolution in Hungary and Bavaria. Therefore, Lenin went back to Marx's original idea of a slow ripening of communist relations in production, which were to be victorious only when all positive possibilities of the capitalist production system were exhausted. So, Lenin declared the introduction of the 'New Economic Policy' (NEP); controlled private enterprises were allowed (even in book-publishing) for an indeterminate but sufficiently long period. Many Communists, and Stalin among them, disagreed, but Lenin's authority brought them to silence. Thus the peasants, at long last, did receive the land which was promised to them in 1917.

Lenin's personal authority had been growing ever since the proclamation of the absolute and indisputable power of the Communist party. A Communist 'cell' had to follow the decisions of the higher party bodies, and these had to obey the Politbureau with its auxiliary bodies – the secretariat headed by the Secretary General, and the Organisational Bureau. Lenin was at the top of the pyramid. Until now, such dictatorial power was unheard of in the twentieth century.

For Lenin, this was still not the last word. One had to find out how the monopolistic power of the party could be preserved under conditions of returning to the capitalist (though controlled) economy. But Lenin had not long to live. As a result of intrigues and manipulations inside the party, one of the most obscure and unprincipled (but not one of the nearest) disciples of Lenin, namely Stalin, came to power. And thus a new and perhaps the most tragic period in the history of mankind was to begin.

The number of losses during the Civil War is difficult to access.[51] In one of his

---

51. According to the data of the emigrated statistician I. Kurganov, which seem trustworthy, Russia's population between 1917 and 1959 was less than expected to the extent of 110.5 million persons, including the expected number of births that did not occur.

verse opuscula, the poet Mayakovski addresses his audience by the words: 'Silence, comrades! Comrade Mauser has the floor!' But the unfettered activities of a hand-gun culture cannot be subordinated to statistics; organised shooting very often went on in secret, in cellars, in dark ravines. The Whites, it is true, sometimes hanged their victims in public, but not always. We should also take into considera-tion the violent epidemics of typhoid fever and other illnesses, which were the indirect result of total war. Between the influenza pandemic of 1918–1919 which carried away millions of lives, and the loss of a million Russian soldiers in World War I before the Brest peace, the direct losses during the Civil War came to not much less than 20 to 30 million. But the main losses of the population in our coun-try were still to come.

Since there was no change in the productive forces and in the technology of the production of arms, no post-capitalist society did or could arise. Instead of that, the period soon after Lenin's death in 1924 saw the revival of capitalism in its most primitive and rude form, later on also including production by slaves. This kind of capitalism, which at first called itself 'communism', later 'socialism as the first stage of communism', or even 'developed', or 'real socialism', was, of course, a society where the productive forces belonged to the state, and the new ruling class was construed as a huge bureaucratic *apparat*. At first it consisted of the most active of the Bolsheviks (i.e. Communists of Lenin's persuasion). Then began a period of ruthless struggle for power between Lenin's heirs: between Trotski and Stalin,[52] between Bukharin and Stalin. The one who could gain the upper hand (in the final reckoning, this was Stalin) was also able to organise exe-cutions on a mass scale and other atrocities, which were justified by the state-ment that 'violence is the midwife of history'. In addition Communists whom Stalin deemed to be insufficiently devoted to him were shot or sent to concentra-tion camps.

The new governing class emerged from those best able to survive and rise to power under these uncanny conditions, i.e. usually the most unprincipled

---

52. Djugashvili (party pseudonym Stalin) appeared as a notable figure during the revolution of 1905, when both the SR and the Bolsheviks, in order to finance their growing political activities, began to resort to so-called 'expropriation', that is, to robbery on a large scale. Naturally, the Bolshevist party incorporated, at that period, a number of *déclassé* criminal persons. One of these was Stalin; he seems to have been recommended by Lenin as a member of the Central Committee of the party (after the 'Russian Bureau' of the Central Committee had been arrested in 1912) by Malinowski, one of the outstanding figures among the Bolsheviks, later unmasked as an *agent provocateur*. A strong will and a com-plete, paranoid unscrupulousness allowed Stalin to climb higher and higher inside the party hierarchy. However, it would be wrong to suppose that it would be better if the upper hand had been gained by Trotski with his ideas of a total militarisation of the populace (being under the jurisdiction of the law of the handgun), or by Bukharin, who argued in favour of an extermination of all 'alien elements'. The history would not be quite the same, but the scale of the murderous reprisals was inherent in the Communist idea itself.

who felt at home in the most bloody situation. Protected by an impregnable, painstakingly guarded state secrecy, they lived in comfort such as might gain the envy of many a Western capitalist. The class was euphemistically called the *nomenclatura*. A member of the *nomenclatura*, like any other Soviet citizen, was liable to be arrested at any moment and thrown into a concentration camp or shot, on the ground of any fantastic and entirely unfounded accusation without any legally valid evidence; and it was regarded as necessary that the person politically accused – as was also the case with any Soviet prisoner – should unfailingly admit his guilt: for this, he was exposed to the most inhuman tortures, to threats to 'take' the prisoner's children, etc. But if a member of the *nomenclatura* was lucky enough to evade the 'meat chopper', he stayed in the *nomenclatura* forever; if he inadequately fulfilled his political or economic responsibilities, the most he risked was, to be demoted to another post in the *nomenclatura*, perhaps with somewhat diminished material privileges.[53]

Among others, an important drawback of Lenin's theory was that he, as well as his followers, did not appreciate the historical role of the intelligentsia (the intellectuals) for the development both of the Capitalist, and more especially of the Post-Capitalist Phase. (For more on this, see below, this chapter.) The Leninists regarded the intellectuals not as an independent factor in the development of the historical process, responsible for the socio-psychological impulse to social change, but as a part of the bourgeois class; it went without saying that the bourgeoisie, if anything, had certainly to be physically exterminated in the course of revolution – so a great part of the Russian intelligentsia was also exterminated. If a certain part of it, usually the most conformist part, did survive, this was only because the social and state mechanism could not be put into action without intellectuals. However, although some bright intellects, some well-trained specialists, were preserved in Russia, and although atomic and space[54] technologies were developed, the technical and scientific revolution necessary for the passage of the Russian society into the Post-Capitalist Phase was not fully attainable.

In spite of the great differences in the ideological orientation between Communism and, say, Nazism, the Soviet Union, functionally, played the historical role of a totalitarian state. Typical are, first, the merging of the party with the state machinery, and, secondly, the fact that all important decisions were made at the party rather than the 'Soviet' level, and, practically, by the dictator personally (as head of the party).

53. It is important to remember that the bloody 'reprisals' were by no means just a form of struggle between Communists of different shades of opinion. They were used much more widely as a form of conscious class struggle.
54. Thus, e.g. aircraft and space technology in the USSR was to a great extent created by the work of concentration camp prisoners (Tupolev, Korolev, Petlyakov and others).

Victims of the 'reprisals', if they had not been shot,[55] were sent to far-off, strictly secret concentration camps in the taiga or the tundra for slave work and slow death. The vastness of the non-developed waste lands of the country made it possible to keep in secret the very existence of concentration camps; the general population did not know about them. The number of slave-convicts was different from time to time, but it probably vacillated between 5 and 20 million.[56]

The majority of the population did not know anything, positively, either about the luxury enjoyed by the *nomenclatura*, or about the torments of the imprisoned (the 'zeks'); and that because of the all-embracing regime of secrecy: any smallest breach of these secrets could be fatal for the offender (and for his family). One did not know about these things, but the more intelligent did surmise. However, even a private talk with a friend of family member might cost one's life; hence everybody kept silent, usually even at home. Stalin hoped that he could have one informer for every five persons in the population. Therefore, everybody acted in the way they did act not only out of Communist enthusiasm (only strengthened by fear) but also out of sheer animal terror; at the same time, people grew indifferent in regard to their duties: individual welfare did not depend on the results and character of the work done, neither did the possibility to be 'repressed' depend on them. A powerful propaganda machinery was persuading the population (and the regime itself), that the cruel 'reprisals' and the 'policy of economy' (which meant a general tendency to the lowering of the standard of living), were due to an impregnable blockade of the country by the forces of the capitalist countries, armed to the teeth, and firmly united in their hate of the Soviets (but actually there was no unity among them).

---

55. That millions of people did perish can to a certain degree be explained by two circumstances: first of all, in a usual war men who shoot at each other are armed in more or less the same way; after a battle, the fallen are buried, and the prisoners are led away, but not forever. In a civil war, however, the class enemy is to be totally exterminated (who is a class enemy is decided by rough approximation). The law of 'comrade handgun' involved the shooting of prisoners and of persons of 'alien class' on the occupied territory; this was included in the duties of the 'red commanders' (Communist officers), and especially of the commissars, just as was the duty of shooting at the enemy in battle. In the second place, if one did not get a confession from an arrested (and hence automatically guilty) person, this was regarded as a serious defect in the interrogator's work, or as his direct sabotage, and ever new groups of the Chekamen (GPU, NKVD-men) were themselves shot. Note that the Whites did not show much humanity towards their enemies either, but the executions they organised had a greater terroristic effect because they were performed publicly. As for the Communists, they shot and buried their victims with the greatest secrecy, and the relatives were not informed of the death of a son, husband or wife. This was certainly the case since 1938. The desire to see loved ones again prevented protest, which anyway was fatal. Later the secret police supplied the relatives with sham certificates of death from illnesses which supposedly occurred at different dates between 1939 and 1945, while actually the person in question had been shot immediately after the verdict.

56. According to Solzhenitsyn's computations, between 1918 and 1956, as a result of Bolshevist 'reprisals', about 60 million people died; according to Kurganov the number of killed up to 1959 was 66.7 million. Note that the official statisticians who arranged the general census of the population in 1938, were shot by Stalin as 'saboteurs'.

If anything was really inherent in the mentality of every 'Homo Sovieticus', it was the idea of living inside an enemy 'blockade' (restrained only by the solidarity of the revolutionary forces abroad); and also the vital necessity of silence in regard of any political problems (more especially of political 'reprisals'), even among one's own nearest friends and relations. All such problems were especially to be kept secret from children and juveniles, who nearly all were included in special Communist organisations ('Pioneers' for children, 'Komsomol' for youths).

By way of 'class struggle' the Communists had exterminated (or exiled to the Far North) those peasants who produced for the market (they were nicknamed 'kulaks'); the result was the catastrophic hunger of 1932–1933. The surviving peasantry can be said to have become a part of the working class, and just as mercilessly exploited; the ruling *apparat* took away not only the surplus produce, but also a part of the necessary produce. The peasants were in a state of serfdom in their kolkhozes. Market exchange had practically ceased to exist, and was substituted by a distribution through the same *apparat*; this was regarded as achieving socialist principles in economics; in the USSR, and by many people in Europe, this was regarded as a liberation from the discomfort of capitalism. In actual fact, however, the redistribution system only led to a catastrophic bureaucratisation of the state structures. As always in history (cf., e.g. Ancient Egypt), the dominance of the bureaucracy led finally to more or less prolonged chaos, and to the beginning of a dissolution of the empire.

However, before this became apparent, the Communists had managed to seize power in China, as well as in some other comparatively underdeveloped countries (Cuba, Vietnam, Cambodia, et al.), with similar or worse results. But, on the whole, the Communist religion proved to be very durable; it lasted in the Soviet Union and abroad for more than half a century.

After the end of World War I, the discomfort created by capitalism as such became evident, especially because a universal war was its destructive consequence. The problem of liberation from this discomfort (although this was not thus formulated), became urgent not only for Russia but also for the highly developed capitalist countries of Western Europe and America. Even before the end of the war, ways of breaking the impasse it produced were under consideration.

Understandably for a person fostered by a legally minded capitalist society, the US president Woodrow Wilson approached the problem as an ethical one. Of course, Wilson and his colleagues in the USA and the Allied states treated ethics in their own way, because they were professional politicians, reared on classical capitalist economics. Such an interpretation of ethical problems could not save mankind, and this it was to learn by its own bitter experience. However, the general discomfort was so obvious, that serious politicians could not simply reject Wilson's proposals as empty propaganda, and started to introduce them into *Realpolitik* – of course, 'improving' them according to ideas imbibed from their childhood, and in accordance with the inherited political situation. A general decision was to be made on the creation of a universal League of Nations. It was to be based on the idea that an aggressive war was a crime, not only against the victim of aggression but against the entire human community (only an aggressive war! But how easy it is to declare a war to be actually defensive!). Putting a stop to an aggressive war should be the right and the duty of all nation-states, and if they all act in accordance with this principle, new aggression would be if not entirely impossible then at least much less probable. In connection with this, the idea of collective security was first introduced into political practice. This idea made away with the formerly current notion that unlimited sovereignty was the undisputed supreme right of any independent state.

From the conferences at the Hague in 1899 and 1907 emerged the idea of international arbitration between two disagreeing countries; but all actual treaties invariably contained a stipulation which rendered an international court helpless in all except the most trivial conflicts. However, notwithstanding all such tricky contrivances of the politicians, the idea of introducing a legal conciliatory mechanism (mediation) to solve international disputes was gaining ground in the scholarly literature. Moreover, there were some precedents of creating internationally valid agreements, and even international organisations, such as the Lloyd's Register of Shipping, the Universal Postal Union and the Red Cross.

The following idea was launched: war is caused, in the first place by 'unlimited armament of the states';[57] and, in the second place, by 'secret diplomacy'.

From spring 1915, the politicians of the Entente started discussing projects of a future community of victorious nations. By January 1918, not only did Wilson insist that all the countries presently at war should state their military goals but he also launched the idea of a universal association of nations, which would warrant the political independence, and the territorial integrity, of all states, both great and minor.

After the end of the war, the problem of establishing a League of Nations acquired some urgency. In February 1919, the Paris Peace Conference was acquainted with the project of a 'Covenant of the League of Nations'; on 28 April 1919, it was adopted unanimously. What remained was to ratify it. The Covenant provided for the creation of an Assembly of representatives from all nations participating in the League, and of a Council consisting of five permanent members (from the USA, Great Britain, France, Italy and Japan), and of four changing members elected for a certain term from different groups of states. All members of the League were to agree a commitment to reduce their armaments 'to the lowest point consistent with domestic (or national) safety'; to prohibit private production of arms; and regularly to exchange information on armaments.

---

57. The only result of the attempt to restrain the armaments drive was an international agreement reached during the Washington Conference of 1921–1922 to limit the number and the tonnage of battleships belonging to the different great powers. Later history showed that, ultimately, battleships were of no use.

The original members of the League of Nations were the victor states, and also those states that were created by the Versailles Treaty itself, as well as by a similar treaty dictated by the Entente to Austria and Hungary.

The latter treaty declared Austria-Hungary non-existence; it was divided into German-speaking Austria, Magyar-speaking Hungary, Czechia and Slovakia, whose inhabitants spoke different Slavic languages (later united in Czechoslovakia; it also included Ruthenia speaking a dialect of Ukrainian); the Slavic speaking regions of southern Austria-Hungary were given to Serbia, first renamed 'Kingdom of the Serbs, Croats, and Slovenians' and later 'Yugoslavia'; Transylvania (Siebenbürgen) was ceded to Rumania; Polish-speaking territories (and a part of the Ukrainian and Belorussian speaking ones) were ceded to Poland, a new independent state which included regions formerly belonging to what used to be Russia and Austria-Hungary, and a part of Germany, inhabited not only by Germans, but also by Poles. Poland also received a 'corridor' between Western and Eastern Prussia, with an outlet to the sea. The former German cities of Danzig (Gdańsk), with a Polish minority, and Memel (Klaipeda) with a Lithuanian majority among the rural population, were separated into self-governing units.

All members of the League of Nations pledged themselves to respect the inviolability and the independence of the other members in every way, in order to prevent any possible aggression. All imminent conflicts were to be submitted to the League of Nations, and the conflicting parties were to abstain from war for three months pending an agreement reached through the mediation of the League. If an aggression should nevertheless take place, all members of the League would apply economic sanctions against the aggressor, and should any state fail to implement the sanctions, to that state, too, such sanctions should also be applied. If all other measures should prove ineffective, members of the League of Nations were obliged to declare war on the aggressor. Any diplomatic agreement was to be valid only after being sumitted to the Secretariat of League of Nations; any treaty not in accordance with the Covenant of the League was automatically to be declared invalid.

A special chapter was devoted to mandated territories. The former colonies of the Central Powers (and, in some cases, also others) were assigned to a mandatory, which was one of the victorious Great Powers, until such time as the population of the colony reached a level of civilisation sufficient for acquiring independence. Who was to make such decisions, and in what way, remained undetermined.

Different international organisations were founded; we may mention the International Labour Organisation, which was created in order to provide for the general introduction and encouraging of humane conditions of labour: this was an important victory for the workers' economic movement.

The Covenant of the League of Nations did not satisfy the more extreme pacifists. History has since shown that they were right. In the light of our later experience, many provisions of the Covenant can certainly be stated to have been naïve and ineffective. Two of its drawbacks were most serious: first, the League of

Nations lacked its own forces which could provide for putting its decisions into practice against an aggressor, who of course would have been armed; secondly, all decisions of the League were to be unanimous[58] (except decisions on questions of procedure). In other words, the members of the League had a 'Liberum Veto', and hence the League of Nations was destined to share the fate of the defunct Polish Republic of the seventeenth century. When discussing a dispute, the votes of the conflicting parties were not taken into consideration. According to the adopted usage, nations whose proposal did not get a majority of votes in the League's committees, abstained from voting at the Assembly. The officials of the League's secretariat were exempted from the jurisdiction of their own countries. The Budget of the League amounted to the trifling sum of $5 million.

A catastrophe happened as early as 1920, when the United States Congress refused to ratify the Covenant of the League of Nations because it was regarded as infringing on the constitutional prerogatives of the USA. Without the participation of the USA – or the USSR – no important decision (such as introducing sanctions against an aggressor) could be made. Nevertheless, the League of Nations managed to introduce some humane legislation which played a certain role in the Planet's life.

A fatal mistake of the victorious Powers – which, however, was historically understandable – was exacting from the defeated Powers, namely from Germany,[59] excessive reparations calculated to be paid for decades; this led to a sharp fall in the German living standard, and to a corresponding rise in the level of discomfort.

In the 1920s and the beginning of the 1930s all nations who were members of the victorious coalition, except the USA, became members of the League of Nations; its headquarters was in Geneva. Most of the states which had been at war with the Entente, also gradually entered the League: Austria and Bulgaria late in 1920, Hungary in 1922, Germany in 1926, Turkey[60] in 1932. Some neutral states, as well as

---

58. In the United Nations Organisation – the successor of the League of Nations – the rule of unanimity is applied only in the Security Council.

59. As already mentioned, Austria-Hungary fell asunder. Turkey actually did continue the war with Greece.

60. According to the original treaty, huge pieces were cut out of Turkey – mostly land inhabited by non-Turkic peoples. She was deprived of all islands, including Cyprus; in Eastern Anatolia there was founded an Armenian Republic. Nearly all these innovations were done away with by Kemal Pasha (Atatürk), who did not recognise the Peace of Versailles and continued war – first of all, against Greece. Most of the Armenians had already been massacred during the reign of the Sultan, in 1915–1916; Kemal attempted to continue the genocide of Armenians in Transcaucasia, and of Greeks on the coast of the Aegean. Especially heartrending and horribly bloody was the genocide of the Greeks in Smyrna (Turkish Izmir), where they had lived since the tenth century BC. After Turkey had concluded a peace treaty with Greece, both countries were admitted to the League of Nations. By this time, Turkey had been deprived of all land inhabited by Arabs: Syria and Lebanon were mandated to France (actually becoming French colonies), Palestine and Iraq were mandated to Britain (but there emerged an 'independent' Hashemite kingdom in Iraq); Hijaz and Asir were declared independent, and so were a number of princedoms along the Persian Gulf, including Kuwait and Oman, and also Hadhramaut and Yemen; these may

pacifists all over the world, insisted on accepting Germany, and later the USSR, into the League. The idea was, that membership in the League would act as a counterbalance to the activities of German nationalists and revanchists.[61]

Among the positive achievements of the League of Nations mention may be made of the following: establishing the Polish–German frontier; saving Austria from a financial catastrophe; providing collective aid to Hungary, Bulgaria and Greece; solving the Ruhr problem (the Ruhr iron-producing basin in Germany was for several years occupied by the French army);[62] keeping Italy (where the Fascist Mussolini had meanwhile come to power) from occupying the Greek island of Corfu.

By 1924 a project of organising universal security on a world scale had been prepared, but it was declined by three of the four[63] Great Powers in the League of Nations' Council (except France). A definition of aggression was agreed upon: the side in a conflict refusing arbitration by the League of Nations was to be regarded as an aggressor. Provisions for general rules concerning arbitration between nations were made (but they were not included in the Covenant of the League!); projects of how to organise mutual security and disarmament were discussed, but objections to them were raised, especially by Great Britain.

In 1925 the states of the Entente and Germany concluded certain agreements at Locarno. In one of them, Germany acknowledged the provisions of the Versailles Treaty, which until then it had been fulfilling under compulsion, the Allies being able to dictate their terms, since they kept troops in the Ruhr, the Rhineland and in Saar. In the same year Germany was included in the Council of the League as its fifth

probably be regarded as belonging to an earlier (Third?) Phase of the historical process. The harbour of Aden and the island of Soqotra belonged to the British. In 1921, from the mandate territory of Palestine, the emirate of Transjordan, also under British mandate, was separated.

The first state to acknowledge the government of Kemal, was RSFSR (the Russian Soviet Federated Socialist Republic), which at that moment was in need of any possible international contact.

61. In 1922, RSFSR concluded a treaty with Germany in Rapallo and, in accordance with its secret clauses, produced, for Germany, submarines, tanks, chemical arms, etc., which were forbidden for it by the Versailles treaty. Russia also trained German military pilots, etc. Note that Russia was not the only country to rearm Germany: Sweden furnished it with artillery, and Switzerland with machine-guns. In 1935, Britain waived her objections to German naval armaments (but only within the quota of 35 per cent of the British navy).

62. According to the plan of Stresemann, the German Minister of foreign affairs, the French troops evacuated the Ruhr in 1925; the Ruhr was demilitarised, and the French–German frontier was guaranteed by the League of Nations. A 50-kilometre frontier zone along the Rhine was demilitarised, and the Saar coal basin was occupied by French troops for a considerable period. It is interesting that Stresemann, while being trusted by Briand, Austin Chamberlain, and other leaders of the Entente, at the same time published, under a pseudonym, a booklet where he called the 'Versailles Diktat policy' a crime against Germany, and suggested the necessity of depriving Poland of the 'Polish Corridor' (the entrance to the sea between Western and Eastern Prussia) and of some other territories, and to return Danzig (Polish Gdańsk) and Memel (Lithuanian Klaipeda) to Germany. All this was soon adopted by the Nazi propaganda.

63. Let us remind the reader that the supposed fifth Great Power – the USA – did not join the League of Nations.

permanent member.[64] Those who had the say at the League were now Briand (from France), Austin Chamberlain (from Britain) and Stresemann (from Germany). In the same year 1925, the project of a Protocol on General Disarmament was compiled, and there began a preparation for a Disarmament Conference; the USA and the USSR promised to send their representatives. According to the Versailles Treaty, all defeated countries had taken upon themselves the obligation to limit their armaments, but Stresemann pleaded that it should be repealed for Germany. Meanwhile, the Germans were allowed to build battleships only of a restricted size (so-called 'pocket battleships'; however, they were no less effective than the 'real' ones).

The League of Nations functioned more or less satisfactorily until 1929, which was the year of a new Great Economic Depression, typical of capitalism; this time it was very destructive indeed.

In 1927 and 1933, two universal economic conferences were convoked under the auspices of the League of Nations. They were devoted to the problem of a more exhaustive and organised international exchange; but the beginning catastrophe in the world economic structure made the discussions pointless. Among other things, the Polish–German, Iranian–Turkish, Greek–Bulgarian relations were deteriorating considerably.

In 1932 a Disarmament Conference was convened; but it was meeting at a time when the Economic crisis was rampant. The discussions stuck in the committees; the main problem of 'disarmament' actually amounted to the question of Germany's additional armament. The German delegation even left the conference for a time; it returned only when it was assured by the other participants that Germany would regain a parity in armaments.

Let us now turn to the events in the East, and especially in China. Here the thinker and reformer Sun Yat-sen was the most influential political figure. His revolutionary activities began as early as 1894. His program was formulated as 'The Three Popular Principles': *nationalism* (which meant the dislodgement of the Manchu dynasty, and returning sovereign power to the Chinese, or the Han, nation); *democracy*, i.e. sovereignty of the people; and *welfare* (which was understood as equality of rights to landownership, and uniform taxation according to the ideas of the American economic utopist, Henry George). In 1911, the millennial empire was abolished, and China was declared a republic, with Sun Yat-sen as president; but soon he had to resign; Yüan Shi-k'ai became the new president – and dictator. However Sun Yat-sen continued, first in emigration, and later in China itself, to head a 'national' party, the Kuomintang (at that time this was a revolutionary party). After the October Revolution of 1917 in Russia, Sun Yat-sen managed to contact Lenin; the Soviet government sent to China some prominent military leaders and a political counsellor (Borodin). The

---

64. This induced Poland and Brazil to demand a similar status. It is interesting to note that the Netherlands, although owning a considerable empire in Indonesia, did not claim to be a Great Power.

Kuomintang party became the focus of all leftist forces in China. Sun Yat-sen himself did experience a strong influence of Communist ideology. He died in 1925, and the leadership in the Kuomintang passed to Chiang Kai-shek.

During the 1920s and later, China was torn asunder by civil war between different militaristic leaders. The union of left-wing Radicals and Communists in the Kuomintang was of a short duration: the former allies became armed enemies, with specific territories of their own. Chiang Kai-shek never controlled the whole Chinese territory, and his capital was not Peking, not even Nanking, but Chungking in the Southwest. However, most countries of the world recognised Chiang Kai-shek's China.

In September 1931 Japanese troops invaded Chinese Manchuria on an absurd pretext.[65] In order not to be classified as an aggressor by the League of Nations, the Japanese government described its occupation as 'liberation' of the Manchu Empire (Manchou-Kuo in Chinese). A certain P'u Yi, the last descendant of the Ch'ing dynasty,[66] was made a puppet emperor.

The conquest of Manchou-Kuo was a beginning of the realisation of the 'Tanaka Plan'. Japan was to attempt to implement this plan more thoroughly during World War II.

It is interesting that the plan of Tanaka was very similar to Cecil Rhodes' plan, which was calculated to secure for Great Britain not only all of Eastern Africa from Cairo to Cape Town, but also Cyprus, Crete, and the whole of the Near East, including Palestine.

Some members of the League of Nations demanded, according to its Covenant, a boycott of Japan as an aggressor, but for several reasons this was unacceptable for the Great Powers. Thus, the USA and the USSR were against boycotting Japan. Instead, in 1933 a resolution was carried that Manchuria, as a matter of principle, should be returned to China. Japan reacted by leaving the League of Nations.

In October 1933, the Nazis, headed by Hitler, came to power in Germany as a result of a nation-wide vote in their favour.[67]

---

65. The Japanese alleged that the Chinese had dismantled the railway before a Japanese train, and only an intervention of a supernatural force (which seemingly was thought to be vested in the divine Person of the Emperor) saved the train from perdition.

66. P'u Yi was a grandson of the Chinese dowager empress T'zu His, and by her testament was declared Emperor of China at the age of one year. This intensified the internal disagreements in the country. China, where the comparatively liberal Kuomintang party was in power, was involved in a civil war which lasted for many years – against a number of generals with dictatorial pretences, against Japan, and later against a Communist Red Army. In 1945, P'u Yi was delivered up to Soviet troops which had entered Manchuria; they, again, delivered him up to the Chinese government (this meant, at that time, to the Kuomintang). During the period of Mao Tsu-tung's Communist dictatorship, P'u Yi was imprisoned but survived, and wrote a book of memoirs in his old age.

67. Like Stalin, Hitler belonged originally to a declassed milieu (which, under the conditions of Germany in that time, meant the most embittered stratum of the population); for a time, he worked as a house-painter; during the First World War he served as a private (*Gefreiter*).

In 1934 the USSR entered the League of Nations. An able representative of the Soviets, Litvinov, made eloquent speeches on the necessity of general disarmament; meanwhile, all Powers were solely preoccupied with the problem of how legally to achieve more effective armament.

During the 1930s, the League of Nations made some useful decisions; thus, with partial support from the USA, it succeeded in enlisting Mexico, Ecuador, Afghanistan – and also Iraq, nominally liberated from the status of a British protectorate. The League of Nations helped to quiet down the emotions aroused by the assassination by a Croatian terrorist of Alexander I, king of Yugoslavia, and the French Foreign Minister Barthou in 1934. In 1935 a plebiscite was held in the Saar region which hitherto had been occupied by France, and Saar was returned to Germany. The League was also able to settle a conflict between Columbia and Peru, but not that between Bolivia and Paraguay.

In 1938 Germany left the League of Nations. In the beginning of 1936, Hitler denounced the agreements of Locarno, and declared the terms of the Versailles Treaty not binding for Germany. The USSR, being since 1939 a *de facto* ally of Germany was expelled from the League of Nations. After that, the League supposedly continued to exist until 1941, when it declared itself dissolved.

By the end of the 1930s, mankind faced the Second World War.

Here is the occasion to dwell upon the phenomenon of Nazism (also Fascism, etc.), not only in the light of politics, but also in the light of social psychology.

Communism was not the only attempt to jump out of the normal process of capitalist development. Other such attempts were the creation of Fascism in Italy, and of Nazism (National Socialist) in Germany.

The Nazis were and are, in the common parlance of this country, Fascists; however, the latter term, strictly speaking, pertains only to the monopolistic party of the Italian totalitarian state. The Italian Fascists did not plan any genocide of Jews, or victimising of anybody else for racial reasons (at least not before they were compelled to do so by their German allies in the middle of World War II). Racial persecution was advocated only by Hitler's Nazis (and now also by our own Russian 'National Patriots'). The Fascists regarded it as their right to create a world empire on the strength of their being the descendants of the Romans; they identified the state with the party, and organised the party (and the Italian society as a whole) on half-militarised lines. They persecuted all kinds of workers' unions and parties – and, no doubt, they served their own Italian capitalism. While the militarised troops of the Nazis, the SA, wore brown shirts and had as their symbol the swastika (stolen from the Indians), the Italian Fascists wore black shirts, and their symbol was the Roman lictors' fasces: an axe surrounded by rods for flogging. On the whole, the Nazis were more or less the same as the Fascists only more so. It was just the Italian Fascists who were the model imitated by Spanish Falangists (who wore green shirts), the Portuguese, the Greek Fascist-type parties and many others.

Just as was the case with Communism, the reason for the blossoming of Nazism was the crass lowering of the population's standard of living, which was a sequence of the First World War. The goal of Nazism was a redistribution of material wealth in favour of Nazi Germany, and the projected means were mass murders (genocide) of certain national groups. According to the plan which was half-officially published, the first to be subjected to the 'final decision' (i.e. genocide) were Jews and also, for some reason, the Gypsies.[68] Then, after a time, would come the turn of the Poles. As for the Russians, it was planned to exterminate the élite, including the intelligentsia (that ill-fated intelligentsia again!), while others were to be prohibited from all schooling except learning the alphabet and arithmetic, and the only future to be left for them was slaving for the good of the German nation.

After the lost war, the economic situation in Germany was bad, the living standard of the population was low, and with the beginning of the Big Crisis in 1929, it was very low. Fearing a victory for the Communists who gained considerable strength at the elections of 1932, the leading German representatives of monopolistic capital (who had their own National Party) decided to make a compact with the 'Führer' of the Nazis, Hitler. He obtained the possibility to organise a 'socialist' upheaval and to 'nationalise' the industry, under the condition that the former owners would be left as 'führers' of the enterprises. (The principle of 'führertum' was consistently put into practice by the Nazis in administration and in industrial management; the regional units were directly subordinated to party functionaries, the *Gauleiters*.)

Note that the German Communist party had the highest membership among the Communist parties of the West, and was very influential both among the working class and the intellectuals. In the USSR, there were great hopes that a revolution in Germany could prove to be the next step to the world-wide victory of

---

68. According to Nazi doctrine, the Germans belong to 'the Aryan Race'. 'Aryan' is an antiquated designation of people of the Nordic blood anthropological race, which includes Scandinavians, Baltic nationals, Finns and a part of Germans and Slavs. In modern scholarship, the term 'Aryan' is applied only in a linguistic sense, implying people who originally used the term *Arya* as a self-designation, i.e. Ancient Indians and Iranians. Their descendants are the present-day Iranians (Persians, Tajiks, etc.), Pakistani and Indians, and also Gypsies. According to the Nazi ideology, 'Aryans' are a master nation (*Herrenvolk*) *par excellence*. Note that when the disappearance of capitalists in the USSR made it impossible to explain the failures of the 'Real Socialism' by activities of the Russian bourgeoisie, these failures were explained in terms of underhand plotting of the capitalists abroad (who, of course, were to say the least, not much interested in the strengthening of the Soviet regime); but moreover, Stalin also borrowed from the Nazis the idea and the practice of genocide. It is true that the peoples who were subject to persecution in the USSR, were not immediately murdered in gas chambers; they were just arrested and sent to places not adapted for human survival, and either died in the trains, or in the camps, where they were subjected to some form of slave labour. In countries which were occupied by the USSR according to the agreement with Hitler, those sent to die in distant parts of Siberia consisted not of the entire population, but about 10 per cent of it (this practice did continue also after World War II). Russians from the 'old' territories of the USSR were encouraged to settle in the newly acquired countries where the living conditions still were better than in Russia proper. Some peoples destined to be transported to the tundra regions of Siberia (as, e.g. Jews), did not actually experience the fate prepared for them, because Stalin died.

Communism. However, Stalin, who now totally dominated the world Communist movement, gave instructions that German Communists were not to form a block with non-Bolshevist Social Democrats. Meanwhile the Nazis were allied with Nationalists (afterwards the two parties merged), and won a stunning victory at the elections, receiving three times as many votes as the Communists. The industrial enterprises were 'nationalised', the workers' trade unions were dissolved – and replaced by Nazi trade unions, which were able to give much more to the employees (sanatoria, pleasure cruises abroad, etc.). The peasantry also received an organisation of their own: each spring an inventory was taken of each farm, and after harvest a part of the income (during the war, corresponding to an industrial worker's ration card for each member of the family) was left at the peasant's disposal; the rest was delivered to the state through shops for a price fixed at the level of 1932 (in Austria, of 1939). In the thirties, the German economics entered a period of prosperity. All would have been well were it not for the fact that the whole economy flourished on credit, i.e. on the expectation of plundering other countries. This meant that war was close at hand.

We are now entering an epoch which we ourselves, or at least our parents, have witnessed personally.[69] Digressing from the chronological outline of our story, we shall dwell shortly on the fate of Nazism as an experiment of creating an alternative ideology necessary for getting out of the Seventh (Capitalist) Phase. It can be stated very briefly that Nazism as a political, economic and socio-psychological system did not justify itself; and, as a result of the Second World War – far more bloody than the First – ceased to exist. An important role was played by the policy of the victorious powers, but this we shall discuss below in detail.

After having shortly reviewed a way of development which, in the Seventh Phase, reached an impasse, we may turn to the events which were induced by World War II, and discuss the war itself, these events being also the preconditions of the Eighth, Post-Capitalist Phase of the historical process.

Nobody was satisfied by the Versailles Treaty. The 1920s and 1930s saw the development of situations that just had to bring about conflicts. It was obviously impossible to cut out new independent states without making some part of certain national groups subject to a state created for another nationality. Throughout this period antagonisms were aggravated, to be followed by reconciliations and fresh aggravation; unstable alliances and coalitions were being created inside the League of Nations itself; such alliances would be declared definitive and then fall apart in a year or two.[70] Perhaps more stable than the other alliances was that of the Little Entente, including Czechoslovakia, Rumania and Yugoslavia, and directed mainly

69. Some of the facts quoted by me and referring to Nazism and the Second World War, are not taken from published sources but became known to me when I served in the Soviet Army as an intelligence officer or officer of the staff department for propaganda to the enemy troops.

70. Note that in 1932 the USSR had assured Poland that it would not aid any state which committed aggression acts against that country.

against Hungary. The latter had survived a short-lived Communist revolution (which was conceived as a part of a World Revolution), and at the same time felt itself particularly unfairly treated: big slices of its former territory, with a very considerable number of Hungarian (and German) nationals, had been taken away from it and given to its neighbours. Numerically, the population of the Hungarian state had diminished considerably, the living standard was extremely low. For a long time, all through Eastern Europe, the problems of state structures had been unsettled and unsatisfactory. Here the League of Nations proved to be a body of diminishing effectiveness.

In 1929, a major economic crash occurred at the American stock exchange. Gross national product fell to the half of the former amount, the level of production was 48 per cent lower than formerly. Shares fell in value; the after-effect was tremendous, and was painfully felt in all capitalist countries; unemployment rose everywhere to the level of twice to four times the formerly existing; in the USA, the number of unemployed reached 13 million. The crisis affected Germany in particular: to pay the sums demanded for reparation, the Germans had to get investments and credits from the victorious Powers. According to the treaty concluded in 1932 in Lausanne, Germany was freed from further reparations, and part of her war debts was annulled. Although usually the capitalist world quickly recovered after a crisis, this time the critical situation continued for several years – mainly because of a dramatic decrease in the buying capacity of the population.

At the same time, industrial development began in the USSR on a major scale. 'The First Five-Year Plan'. Later it appeared that the achieved high speed of construction activities was to a great extent due to the use of slave labour, and to a considerable lowering of the living standard of the free workers; the constructed objects left much to be desired as to their quality; but at that time the Five-Year Plan raised a wave of enthusiasm both in the Soviet Union and among the workers and the left intelligentsia in the West; they regarded it as a positive response to the crisis of Western capitalism. A number of Western experts came to the USSR to take part in the construction of socialism. If they had not fled in good time, their way lay directly to the slave camps, because in Stalin's mentality everyone who was a foreigner, was *eo ipso* a potential agent of the imperialistic secret services. But the number of Soviet nationals among the 'builders of socialism' who landed in the concentration camps was, of course, incomparably greater.[71]

Note that by this time, Stalin's power had become so immense that he was either personally responsible for any political action of importance, or was commonly believed to be. From here on, whenever we state that 'Stalin did', or 'Stalin planned' this or that, the situation must be judged in accordance with this statement. In

---

71. Stalin organised excursion parties for writers to concentration camps along the White Sea Canal and Moskva–Volga Canal; here was staged a picture of a heroic and manly life of the 'reoriented' prisoners. This staging deceived some of the writers, but not all of them.

how far it might be actually some of Stalin's collaborators who were responsible for the action or decision in question, can at present not be decided. Anyway, for the nation and for the world in general, this was always personally Stalin's decision, and Stalin's personal action.

As mentioned above, the Nazis had great success at the elections to the Reichstag in 1932. In January 1933, the aged Field Marshal Hindenburg, then President of Germany, offered Hitler the chancellorship, although the Nazis still had no parliamentary majority.

In February 1933, the Nazis set fire to the Reichstag, hoping that a great criminal trial would ensue, discrediting the Communists (the Bulgarian Communists Dimitrov, Popov and Tanev were put on trial, together with a lumpen-proletarian of Dutch origin, Van der Lübbe).[72] The trial was a failure, but owing to Nazis propaganda, the prestige of the Communists did fall appreciably. At the elections in March 1933, the Nazis won 288 seats in the Reichstag (together with the Nationalists and Centrists – as many as 441 seats); the Communists got barely 81 seats, but actually they were not allowed to partake at all in the sittings; 94 Social Democrats voted against this decision.

In October 1933, Hitler's Germany left the disarmament conference, and also the League of Nations. By that time, the German army (the Reichswehr) had only 21 regiments, but as many as 40 generals and 8,000 officers, so it was an easy matter to develop a major army – which was exactly what Hitler did; at the same time he renamed the Reichswehr ('the Imperial Defence'), calling it the Wehrmacht ('Defensive Force'). In January 1934, the federal structure of Germany was abolished; and in July 1934 the Nazi party was declared the only legal party in the country. The Nationalists were engulfed by the National Socialist party. A number of Germany's international agreements were annulled, among them the treaty signed with the USSR at Locarno, including its secret paragraphs; thus, Germany no longer received any military aid from the USSR.

In May 1933, under the conditions of growing nationalism and militarism, Japan violated the frontiers of China. Japan demanded that China drop the practice of inviting foreign military advisers (except Japanese), prohibit anti-Japanese activities, and prohibit the foreign troops on Chinese territory (again except the Japanese). The situation in China was complicated by the constant armed conflicts between the not completely incorruptible Kuomintang government, several single generals who were the actual dictators in different parts of the country, and the Communists, who also had their own armed forces. For some time, the Communists supported the Kuomintang government of Chiang Kai-shek, but later they were persecuted by the Kuomintang, and an offensive was launched

---

72. The court, taking into consideration world public opinion, sentenced to death only Van der Lübbe. Popov and Tanev were later arrested in the USSR and disappeared, but Dimitrov became one of the leaders of the Comintern.

against the districts in Southern China controlled by them. The Communists, headed by their political leader, Mao Tse-tung, and their military leader, Chu The, later organised the so-called Great March from the South of the country to a more or less isolated territory in the north-western part of China proper, where they organised a practically independent militarised region; here Communism was the official doctrine, and here they were able to stay until 1945. For some time, the Chinese Communists employed Soviet military advisers.

In spite of Japanese protests, there were quite a number of foreign military detachments in China. Thus, in 1937 Japanese aeroplanes sunk the American gunboat *Panay* on the Chinese river Yangtze, and Japanese–American relations began to deteriorate.

On 9 July 1933, one more convention was signed in London; among the participants were the USSR, the Baltic states, Turkey, Iran (Persia) and Afghanistan. This time the term 'aggressor' was defined. The subject of the conference was timely: Hitler did not conceal his intention to put into practice the ideas already stated by him in the 1920s, in his pamphlet *Mein Kampf* when he served a term in prison together with his confederate R. Hess, for attempting a *putsch* in Munich. Hitler declared that the frontiers of 1914 and even 1871 were not adequate to the needs of the German people, because they did not include German-speaking Austria and, to put it short, limited the possibilities to create a broader area for settlement of Aryans, whom he erroneously identified with the Germanic-speaking peoples. Hitler's first big idea (not original but borrowed from certain other German authors) was to annihilate Poland: Germany, he decided, had not enough *Lebensraum* ('living-space'), which should include all regions that were or could be inhabited by Germans. He meant, in the first place, Austria, but also Poland,[73] the Baltic regions and Russia; here the local population was either to be expelled or used as farm-hands, or something like serfs.

In June 1934, a conflict broke out between Hitler and his assistant Roehm, the head of the brown-shirt troops (the SA). Roehm insisted that the SA should be incorporated in the army, which caused the resentment of the generals, whose support was very important for Hitler at that juncture. Moreover, Roehm had begun to show a spirit of independence. On 30 June, Hitler ordered a massacre of the brown-shirts (but also of other unwanted persons). Gradually, the SA troops, except for a few detachments, were replaced by the SS (black-shirts), who were subordinate to Himmler, the head of the newly established Nazi Secret Police (Gestapo).[74]

In August 1934, a plebiscite was held; the Nazis got 88 per cent votes. Hitler's party busily started creating an 'image of the enemy'; the Jews were chosen for the

---

73. However, in May 1933 Hitler had declared that the frontiers of Poland were inviolable.
74. During the war, a portion of the SS was reorganised into military units (the Waffen-SS); they were placed under the Wehrmacht command, but often carried out special assignments, as, e.g. actions against guerrillas, or shooting Jews, including children.

role of the enemy-in-chief.[75] From 1 April 1933, the SA troops organised a boycott of Jewish shops. From 7 April it was prohibited for non-Aryans (i.e. the Jews) to be employed by the state; later the prohibition was extended to all scientific, scholarly, cultural, medical, or teaching activities; any person who had at least one Jewish grandparent was declared non-Aryan. Jewish artists, actors and musicians were forbidden to appear before Aryan audiences, and also to engage in journalism.

According to the racist Nürnberg laws, enacted between 15 September and 14 November 1935, in the 'Reich' (i.e. 'Empire'; that was now the official name of the German state) the only persons entitled to citizenship were those 'of German or kindred blood, and who had proved by their behaviour that they both wish and are able to faithfully serve the German nation and the Reich'; a Jew was not a citizen of the Reich, and was not entitled to vote. Not only were marriages between Aryans and Jews prohibited, but even extramarital relations. Jews were forbidden to hire 'female persons of German or kindred blood[76] aged below 45 years'. The passports of Jews carried a special stamp; all Jews bearing atypically Jewish personal names had to change them, to obviously Jewish ones.

In November 1938 the Nazis organised systematic pogroms of Jewish lodgings and shops, homes for the aged and orphanages; tens of thousands of Jews were imprisoned in concentration camps; synagogues were burned, the Holy Scriptures of the Jews were desecrated. According to the decrees of 12 and 23 November 1938, the Jews were totally excluded from German economic life, and a fine of a thousand million German marks was imposed upon them collectively.

Beginning in 1941, the Nazis started that they called 'the final solution', which meant that every Jew without exception was to be killed off (by burning in specially constructed incinerators). Actually by the end of the war in 1945, about 85 per cent of the Jews originally inhabiting territories accessible to the Nazis had been annihilated. We may note that certain Christian organisations attempted to resist anti-Semitism.

Meanwhile, no less – perhaps even more – bloody events were happening in the USSR. Arrests and shooting of politically unwanted persons went on all the time, although the Soviet secret police changed its names (the Cheka, VChK, GPU, OGPU, NKVD); the surviving prisoners were used as slaves in the Five-Year Plans' Great Construction Enterprises. But late in 1936, by Stalin's special order, a giant

---

75. It was thought that eliminating Jews could be achieved with impunity, since the Jews were not representing any actual state, a conflict with which might have been untimely.

76. The notion of 'German(ic)' (or 'Russian', or any such) 'blood' being a decisive indication of race or nation, is absurd: there do exist blood groups, but they do not correspond to biological races (in a few cases a certain group may be frequent or rare in the race in question, but it never is symptomatic of a biological race); and, of course, genetic physiological features have no connection with any specific culture or language. Moreover, many Indo-Europeans ('Aryans' in the Nazi parlance) are dark-haired and dark-complexioned, while a number of, e.g., Fenno-Ugrian ('non-Aryan') peoples are blond and light-coloured.

campaign was started to arrest and exterminate 'enemies of the people' throughout the country. Among those exterminated were workers who were Party members of too long standing, everybody who ever had voted for Stalin's rivals, children
of the gentry and tsarist officers, persons who had served abroad, a lot of intellectuals, and simply people not clearly defined in official Soviet terms. In 1991, a newspaper published the reminiscences of an executioner who adopted some of the
children orphaned by his activities. According to his evidence, he alone (not counting the rest of the team) executed, by a shot in the back of the head, up to fifty persons every night; this was physically exhausting, so that a special doctor had
periodically to massage his hand. Poor Hippocrates!

The more blood Stalin shed, the more he feared hate for himself.[77] In the late
1930s he carried out one of his maddest actions, shooting about 80 per cent of the
marshals, generals and higher officers of the Red Army and Navy. He hoped that
while Hitler was making short work of France and Britain he would have the time
to organise a new officers' corps of persons really devoted to him. Such notions as
qualification and talent did not exist for Stalin; he considered all persons as
replaceable 'little screws'; one had only to order a person, on pain of death, to fulfil
the task formerly entrusted to somebody else, and he would carry out the same
duties as well: nobody is indispensable, he declared.

The result was that at the beginning of the new World War intelligence departments of armies and fronts could be headed by officers who formerly were in
charge of companies or battalions of frontier troops of the NKVD, but now had
received high staff ranks; field units of the army were as often as not headed by
former sergeants who had been speedily elevated to the rank of officer. For the
same reason, the army's battle formations contained few modern tanks, the infantry was not defended by modern aircraft – the necessary tanks and aircraft existed
only far back in the rear, and the most important constructors were under arrest
while working. The inventor of the multi-rail rocket projectors (the 'Katyusha'),
which were to play a most important role during the war, had been shot, together
with a number of other military experts.

In an instruction booklet handed out by the German intelligence service in
December 1940 to officers ranked company commanders and above, it was stated
that although the Russian soldier was the best in the world, the Red Army was destined to defeat, because its higher officers had but poor military education, and
hence the divisions, the army corps and the armies were unable to co-ordinate their
actions.

Soviet foreign policy also changed with Stalin's bloody domestic policy. First
Stalin attempted to bridge over the gap between his country and the former Powers

---

77. It is important to note that, as the result of a total propaganda of 'Leninist' ideas about social-
    ism, Stalin, as leader of the Communists, not only did not become a hate figure but, on the con-
    trary, was beloved by the masses. This is characteristic of all totalitarian societies.

of the Entente. In 1935, the USSR negotiated a mutual assistance treaty with France and a similar one with Czechoslovakia; the latter treaty, however, had a proviso that it would come into effect only if Czechoslovakia received similar help from France.

In 1935, Italy a member of the Council of the League of Nations, attacked a member of the League of Nations, Ethiopia. Mussolini explained that 'proletarian Italy brings civilisation and liberation [to Ethiopia] replacing a front of corruption and hypocrisy'. (It seems Mussolini was also a proletarian.) The armed forces of Italy were sent to Africa through the Suez Canal controlled by Britain. The League of Nations declared Italy an aggressor, but no important sanctions were introduced. The USSR and Rumania proposed to stop the export of oil to Italy, but this initiative was frustrated by the conservative representatives of Britain and France, Hoare, and Laval. Instead, they suggested a scheme of dividing Ethiopia. This scheme was not adopted, but all of Ethiopia was conquered and turned into an Italian colony.

Then the attention of the newspaper readers was directed towards Spain.

During World War I, Spain's position was moderately pro-German and, like all neutral countries, it made certain profit out of the European war. However, the standard of living was low, and Spain had other troubles as well: a war with the Moroccan (Berber) leader Abd al-Krim dragged on, while inside the country, an Anarchist terroristic movement was developing. Officially, Spain was regarded as a parliamentary monarchy, but its governments were very unstable: in the space of twenty years more than thirty of them had come to power and resigned. In 1923, the king Alfonso XIII invited General Primo de Rivera to head a government, and gave him dictatorial powers. With help from the French, a victory over Abd al-Krim was achieved, and a part of Morocco was annexed by Spain (the rest became a French protectorate). The Spanish opposition, formerly parliamentary, went underground, which, of course, led to its crass radicalisation. Early in 1930, the king dismissed Primo de Rivera. At the 1931 elections, the Republicans won, and Alfonso XIII fled the country. There was, however, little concord among the Republicans: on the contrary, there developed serious political conflicts.

In 1936 a Popular Front government was established. It was conceived as an imitation of the Popular Front government (of Léon Blum) which existed in France; but there the coalition consisted of Socialists and Radicals, and was only indirectly supported by the Communists. In Spain the Popular Front was a broader and looser coalition.

The new government began with reprisals against the parties of the right wing, but in July 1936 a rebellion was started by some army officers; by September they were headed by General Franco. Popular opinion in Europe, in America, and in the USSR (especially among the intellectuals) regarded the Popular Front government as pro-democracy, and the adherents of Franco as Fascists. There was a strong sense that what happened in Spain was a rehearsal of the long-awaited conflict between the powers of democracy (including – as it was thought – Communists), and the powers of Fascism. Actually, however, the organisation known as the Spanish Falangists, who might have been regarded as Fascists, was by no means the only group that supported Franco. On the side of the Popular Front there were Liberals, Radicals, Socialists, Anarchists, Communists oriented towards Stalin and Communists oriented towards Trotski, Catalan and Basque separatists. On the side of Franco there were, beside the Falangists, conservative bourgeois and landowners, monarchists of two different persuasions, most of the clergy, and most of the army officers. Franco had Spanish troops of the regular army at his disposal as well as Moroccan troops and the 'Tercio', i.e. volunteers having taken part in the war against Abd al-Krim. The core of the army was the 'Falange' reinforced by a monarchist militia.

The military formations of the Republicans were weaker; these were mainly volunteers from the Socialist and Anarchist parties; regular military cadres were scarce. The Republicans would have been easily defeated, were it not for the arrival of International Brigades consisting of high-principled (and therefore better disciplined) volunteers from Europe and America. The USSR did not send rank-and-file soldiers, but did send military advisers, staff officers and instructors, as well as tanks, aircraft and artillery. In October 1936, the Republican government transferred its gold reserves (5.5 thousand million golden pesetas) to Moscow. The French government of Léon Blum permitted 100 aircraft with volunteer pilots to aid the Republicans. Italy sent 100,000 legionnaires to Spain, and its aircraft helped to transfer Franco's troops from Morocco. Moreover, 10,000 Portuguese volunteers joined Franco. Against world public opinion which largely favoured the Republicans, Franco's troops advanced, slowly but irrepressibly; they isolated proletarian Asturia on the shore of the Bay of Biscay, and began advancing on Madrid, but at the near approaches to the capital they met opposition mainly from men of the International Brigades. The discipline in the Republican army was unsatisfactory, the Anarchists and the Trotskyists did not obey the orders of the Communists (and *vice versa*); all parties used measures of reprisal. In general, during the civil war, human life was worth little, not only at the front but also in the rear.

The government of Franco was recognised by Germany and Italy. Mussolini boasted that he had introduced the Fascist spirit into Spain. France declared a policy of non-intervention, and was seconded by the Conservative government of Britain. A Non-intervention Committee was organised with representatives from both Italy and Germany and also the USSR. From the summer of 1937, constant acts of piracy were conducted in the Mediterranean, their purpose being to block the import of arms to the warring parties. The Committee attempted to put an end to the piracy, but in practice it mainly impeded the import to the Republicans. In March 1938, the army of Franco reached the Mediterranean coast, cutting off Catalonia from Valencia (whence the Republican government had moved from Madrid). Meanwhile, in Madrid, those who were prepared to conclude a peace with Franco collaborated in a *coup d'état*, and by March 1939 all Republican regions of Spain were brought under the control of his followers.

The totalitarian regime of Franco is usually regarded as Fascist. Like the Fascists and the Nazis, this regime was based on militarised groups, and used terror methods against its enemies. However, unlike Italian Fascism and German Nazism, it lacked social demagoguery; it kept to the slogan 'For God, the King, and the Fatherland!' In 1939, Franco, following the example of Italy, and at nearly the same time as Hungary and Manchou Kuo, signed the Anti-Comintern Pact concluded in 1936 between Germany and Japan.

The peoples of Europe followed with suspense the events of the Spanish Civil War, since it was commonly perceived as a rehearsal of a great war for which Hitler was quite openly preparing. In 1938 meeting virtually no resistance, he organised the 'Anschluss' of Austria (i.e. its annexation to the German Reich). From 1933, Hitler had constantly provoked minor conflicts with Czechoslovakia, which he called 'a Soviet aircraft-carrier aimed at Germany'. Both London and Paris thought (and suggested through diplomatic channels) that peace could be preserved if the Sudeten borderland (inhabited by Germans) was ceded (on the basis of the 'Right of Nations to Self-Determination') to Germany. (This meant, however, that the frontiers of Germany would pass beyond the Czechoslovakian defence lines.) Without allies, Czechoslovakia nevertheless declared a mobilisation. On 24 September 1938, Neville Chamberlain, the prime minister of Britain, delivered to Prague Hitler's ultimatum requiring immediate cession of Sudetenland to Germany. On 29 September, Chamberlain again asked for another (actually the third) meeting with Hitler and Mussolini to discuss the problem of Czechoslovakia. Czech representatives were not invited personally to the discussion, and its result was announced to them only after midnight: Sudetenland was to be ceded to Germany immediately. Chamberlain returned to London rejoicing; he had brought back peace with honour. But Churchill, later to become prime minister, described it as 'a complete and unmitigated defeat'.

Meanwhile, Hungary and Poland also demanded their share of Czechoslovakia; and the Slovak separatists formed their own government at Bratislava. In March 1938, Hitler turned Czechia into a German protectorate called 'Bohemia and Moravia'. Moreover, he presented an ultimatum to Lithuania, and it submissively ceded Klaipeda (Memel) to Germany.

In April 1939, Italy occupied the kingdom of Albania.

For a few years, Hitler flirted with Poland, attempting to persuade its leaders that Germany and Poland had a common enemy in Soviet Bolshevism. But after the occupation of Sudetenland, Czechia and Klaipeda, Hitler passed from flirting to threatening.

The reason for this sharp turn was not the fate of Sudetenland or Klaipeda. During the summer of 1939, representatives of Britain and France had arrived in Moscow to negotiate an agreement on mutual help, which was also to include minor European states. No agreement was reached. An important reason for this, it seems, was that Poland (rather naturally) did not want a form of help which presupposed that

Communist armed forces could be introduced into the country in peacetime. But the main reason was that Stalin had decided to change his policy; this appeared, among other things, in the fact that the Jewish Litvinov was substituted as foreign minister by the Russian Molotov, a favourite retainer of Stalin, and that the negotiations with the British and French delegations were entrusted not to the Foreign Office, but to Marshal Voroshilov. Molotov and Stalin did not waste much time before reaching an agreement with Hitler's foreign minister Ribbentrop, and by August 1939 a Soviet–German treaty of non-aggression was already signed, with secret paragraphs and a map defining future spheres of influence. The Soviet Union was to acquire Bessarabia (Moldova, which during the Civil war had been re-united with Rumania), the northern (Ukrainian-speaking) part of Bukovina, and the eastern part of Poland (i.e. Western Ukraine and Western Belorussia), Lithuania,[78] Latvia, Estonia and Finland; Germany was to have a free hand in the other countries of Europe.

On the night of 1 September 1939, a group of SS-men in Polish uniforms staged a violation of the German frontier by Poles. At 5 o'clock in the morning, the German offensive against Poland began. The Polish army had excellent soldiers but – as usually is the case – the organisation and the strategy were conceived in accordance with the conditions of the preceding war (that between the Soviets and Poland in 1920). The Polish army was oriented towards offensive actions, but these were to be implemented by cavalry. Meanwhile, the German army applied a quite new strategy, and new tactics. Its troops of attack were autonomous mechanised divisions and tank corps, which were calculated to move speedily into the territory of the enemy, dispersing its infantry and cavalry.

On 3 September, France and Britain declared war on Germany, although the French and British forces were not ready for immediate action. On 10 September, the Commander-in-Chief of the Polish army, Marshal Rydzl-Smigly, ordered the evacuation of Central Poland, and a general retreat towards the East. Warsaw fell on 28 September but isolated groups of the Polish army continued resistance until 5 October. Meanwhile, on 17 September, the Soviet troops crossed the Polish frontier in the East under the pretext of defending the Belorussians and the Ukrainians who constituted the majority of the population in what was then Eastern Poland. Of course, the Germans were not threatening the Belorussians and the Ukrainians, since the Polish territory had already been divided by a secret agreement between Hitler and Stalin. But at the same time, thousands of refugees from Central Poland arrived in the same territory, as also did the retreating units of the Polish army. They were taken prisoners by Red Army units and sent to nearby concentration camps. Later all Polish officers (mostly reservists) and most of the soldiers were shot – a fact which the Russian authorities acknowledged only fifty years later.

78. According to the original variant of the agreements, Lithuania was to be annexed by Germany.

On 10 October, again on the pretext of defending the frontiers, the Soviets presented a demand, in the form of an ultimatum, to Lithuania, Latvia and Estonia, requiring the introduction of Soviet troops into the territories of these countries.[79]

On 12 October the USSR, again under the pretext of security, proposed to Finland that the territory of the Karelian isthmus (between the Gulf of Finland and Ladoga Lake) be exchanged for a vast but sparsely populated part of Soviet Karelia which was rich only in swamp cranberry and dense forest; of these resources Finland already had more than enough and would not agree to such an exchange. On 30 November the Soviet troops crossed the Finnish frontier from Beloostrov to Lake Ladoga, and Soviet aircraft bombed Helsinki. The so-called 'Winter War' had begun along the whole frontier from the Gulf of Finland to the Barents Sea.

Like the Poles, the Soviet military had been preparing for a war similar to the Civil War of 1918–1921. The strategy of quickly moving tank armies (which was being planned and elaborated, in parallel to the German General Staff, by Tukhachevski and his collaborators) had been defined by Stalin as subversive; all of the generals in question, as was usual at that time, were shot. Against the Finns, a mass of infantry was thrown into battle; but the soldiers had no winter outfit – they were clad in standard mantles and high boots, and they had no idea of such things as snipe-shooting, trench-mortars or minefields. The pretext for beginning the war was the so-called 'Mannerheim Line'[80] built by the Finns across the Karelian Isthmus; it was declared to be a threat to Leningrad which allegedly could be attained from there by artillery fire. The pretext was absolutely false, because the distance from the 'Mannerheim Line' to the frontier town of Beloostrov, not to mention the city of Leningrad, was well beyond the range of artillery. The 'Line' was a very strong defensive construction buried deep within the earth's surface and a serious obstacle for any Soviet offensive.

Soviet troops crossed the boundary of Finland and occupied the frontier town of Terioki (now Zelenogorsk). A meeting was immediately held in this town for what was to become the puppet Communist government of Finland headed by the aged Comintern leader, Kuusinen. Official information about the capturing of Terioki was withheld for a short period in order to create the impression that the tidings about the emergence of a Communist Finnish government had been received through a radio intercept. An agreement with the Kuusinen government was made immediately, to be ratified after the occupation of the Finnish capital Helsinki by the Red Army.

---

79. After that, in 1940, there were staged 'plebiscites' in the Baltic countries, after which they were included in the USSR. Immediately, Baltic statesmen and tens of thousands of other persons were deported to Siberian camps; such actions were repeated again after the war.
80. Finland's independence was acknowledged by Lenin as early as 1918, but this did not hinder Finnish Communists from waging guerrilla warfare; the remaining Communist guerrillas retreated to Soviet Karelia. Mannerheim, who had formerly been a general in Tsarist Russia, became President of Finland, and its commander-in-chief. It was his idea to build a line of fortifications across the Karelian Isthmus as defence against the USSR.

The French and British authorities, regarding the USSR as Germany's ally, deliberated upon supplying food, equipment and perhaps troops to Finland, but such help did not materialise, because neutral Norway and Sweden refused access through their territory, and Finland's only port on the Barents Sea was already occupied by the Russians. The British leaders, more particularly Churchill (who had not yet replaced Neville Chamberlain as prime minister) considered plans of bringing Allied troops to Norway, partly to help the Finns, partly to stop the import of iron by the Germans from the Swedish town Gällivare through Norwegian Narvik, and partly in order to improve the supply of the British naval forces acting against Germany in the North Sea.

The Finnish war, which had been begun by the forces solely of the Leningrad military district, began to involve other military districts as well. The losses of the Red Army were enormous – according to British information, about half a million; according to Soviet estimates, about a quarter of a million. In February 1940, a breakthrough of the Mannerheim Line was achieved, and the Finnish troops began retreating. A landing was made to the west of Viipuri; on 7 March the Finns sued for peace, and by 12 May the war was over. There was no more talk about Kuusinen's government and an occupation of Helsinki. But the Soviet Union could annex a big slice of the most fertile part of Finland, including the second biggest Finnish city Viipuri (Vyborg).

Hitler knew about British plans concerning Norway, and decided to forestall them through the German occupation of Norway – and likewise Denmark, in order to facilitate the liaison with German troops in Norway. On this question there were negotiations with Quisling, the leader of the Norwegian Nazis (most unpopular in their own country), and on 9 April 1940 German naval forces entered all the more important Norwegian harbours from Narvik in the north, to Oslo in the south. The occupying forces were somewhat delayed near Oslo when two missiles launched from an antiquated fortress at the entrance to the Oslo fjord sank a German cruiser. However, German parachutists seized Oslo airport and, in military formation, paraded through the city streets the same evening; after that the Norwegian government recognised the fact of the occupation of Norway. Denmark had been occupied without bloodshed some time before.

The Germans soon put up a government of their own choosing in Norway, headed by Quisling; but in Denmark, King Christian X[81] and his government remained nominally in power.

Although the Norwegian government had capitulated, resistance headed by King Haakon VII continued within the country. On 14 April 1940, a small formation of British and other Allied troops occupied a beach-head at Narvik in northern

---

81. Denmark, being 'racially akin' to the Germans, was allowed by Hitler to retain its pre-war constitution and its king. When Jews began to be persecuted in Denmark as well, King Christian X started wearing the yellow badge obligatory for Jews in Nazi Germany; he also aided nearly every Jew to flee to Sweden. Christian was brother of Haakon VII, king of Norway.

Norway. Together with the small residue of Norwegian armed forces (which were not numerous at the best of times), there were about 20,000 men at Narvik. But since a very dangerous situation had developed in France, the Allied troops were evacuated by 7 June.

Meanwhile, according to the plan agreed with Hitler, Stalin presented an ultimatum to Rumania and took away from it Bessarabia and the northern part of Bukovina (this part was mostly inhabited by Ukrainians).

Hitler's military doctrine, as Commander-in-Chief, was Blitzkrieg ('lightning war') which involved using tanks to penetrate enemy territory while saboteurs parachuted behind enemy lines, and at the same time bombing the militarily more important sites, bridges, etc.

In Western Europe, the so-called 'phony war' persisted for more than six months. But on 10 May 1940, the Germans started their advance. They, as it were, repeated Schlieffen's plan in an extended form, based on a new strategy of swiftly moving tank corps, and destroying enemy communications by diversions. The offensive was directed simultaneously through the Netherlands, Belgium and Luxembourg. The aim was not only to crush France but also to make it impossible for the British to enter any of the continental ports. Two-thirds of the German armed forces were deployed in the offensive against France; (the remaining third was placed against the French-fortified 'Maginot Line'). The Germans moved swiftly in all directions along the front. The world was appalled by the strategically senseless bombing of peaceful Rotterdam (when the Dutch resistance had already collapsed), although this bombing did not amount to much if compared to the later bombings of German cities: the German bomber planes 'Junkers-88', and the dive-bombers 'Junkers-89', usually carried four half-ton bombs, and flew in small groups. Towards the end of the war, the British and American aircraft appeared over Germany in whole fleets, aiming at covering the entire territory destined for bombing, each plane carrying a bomb load of five or even ten tons. But that happened much later.

On 10 May the Germans occupied Luxembourg. On that day Churchill headed the British government. On 13 May Holland's Queen Wilhelmina fled to England together with her government. On 12 May passing through Belgium, the Germans invaded France. Using tanks to accelerate the offensive through the supposedly impassable hilly region of the Ardennes in Belgium, they entered France near Sedan, countered only by infantry and cavalry. Their plan was to reach the sea near the French port of Dunkerque, cutting off the French and Belgian troops, and also the British expeditionary force, and then to move westwards. After a half hearted attempt at a counter-offensive (by infantry troops with tank support), it became apparent to the British headquarters, that the Germans were planning to encircle both the expeditionary force, and a great mass of French and Belgian troops. It was decided to organise a mass evacuation through Dunkerque. Luckily, on 24 May the German offensive was held up by Hitler's order, because he overrated the danger of a flanking counter-stroke by the actually not numerous British tanks. German Headquarters decided that it would be a good idea to spare their own tanks for future battles, and Hermann Göring, Marshall of the Reich, declared that his planes were sufficient to frustrate the British attempts at evacuation. Nevertheless, the evacuation began on 26 May and continued until 3 June; many different kinds of vessels were amassed at Dunkerque, even yachts and other small craft. The evacuation went on under a steady bombardment from German aircraft. But even when the Germans started a direct offensive, it was held back by heroic rearguard action by the British. In all, it proved possible to evacuate about 200,000 British and 150,000 French soldiers. During the three weeks of the battle of Dunkerque, the Germans took about a million prisoners, while 60,000 of their own soldiers were killed or taken prisoner. Two British divisions which were too far from Dunkerque had to be left in France.

The Germans began a new offensive on 5 June employing ten tank divisions. The resistance continued for two days; the German forces broke into central France and fell upon the rear of the French divisions defending the Maginot Line along the French–German frontier.

On the basis of such an unprecedented defeat of the British and French forces, Mussolini decided that this was just the time for Italy to enter the war. It was declared by Italy on 10 June, but no important results were achieved by the 'Duce'.

On the Northern Front, what remained of the French army was disintegrating; the French government headed by Reynaud, changing its residence again and again, finally settled at Bordeaux on the Atlantic coast. On 14 June the Germans occupied Paris; Reynaud resigned. A new government was formed by the hero of the defence of Verdun, General Petain, who signed an armistice with Hitler and Mussolini on 25 June 1940.

France was divided into two zones – the one 'independent' (in the centre) with the virtually pro-German government of Petain, and its seat at Vichy, and the other actually occupied by the Germans; this included Paris and the northern coast. The British found themselves face to face with Germany, and the Battle of Britain began.

All that the British had for this battle were about 700 'Hurricane' and 'Spitfire' fighter planes (the first not very satisfactory); they were largely manned by volunteers. The Germans had an air force of *c.* 12,000 bombers and nearly 1,000 fighter planes. The German bombers were unable to strike uninterruptedly and with overwhelming force, and the British radar managed to counter the element of surprise. The 'Messerschmitt-110' fighter planes were better than the 'Hurricanes' but could not match the 'Spitfires'; the range of the 'Messerschmitt-109s' was less than that of the 110s, and they were used mainly to cover the bombers which had insufficient fire capacity. In August 1940, the Battle of Britain reached its highest point with about 1,500 sorties a day on each side. German losses were about double those of the British. Aerial photographs made it clear to the German Headquarters that daytime bombardments were too imprecise given their own high casualty rate. As a result, beginning in the autumn of 1940 and all through the following year, the Germans attacked whole cities at night but did not aim at individual targets. However, they did not abandon the idea of conquering Britain.

In the Balkans, the occupation of Bessarabia and Northern Bukovina by the Soviet Union seems not to have been regarded locally as an action agreed with Germany. Indeed, pro-German feelings were strong. The fear was for aggressive action coordinated between the Soviet Union and Italy. Although, as a result of German arbitration, two-thirds of Transylvania were returned to Hungary (under the dictatorship of Admiral Horthy) from Rumania (while Bulgaria received Southern Dobrudja from Rumania), General Antonescu, who had come to power in Rumania as 'leader [*führer*] of the nation' and was supported by the local Fascist-type 'Iron Guard',[82] adopted a pro-German policy. In this there was nothing new: by May Rumania had already concluded a treaty with Germany; it was agreed that Rumania should supply Germany with oil and arms. The concessions to Hungary were attributed to King Carol, who was dethroned and replaced by his son Mihai. In October 1940, a German military mission arrived in Rumania to prepare the Rumanians for a war against the Soviet Union – because, although Stalin did not want to believe it, the decision to begin such a war had been made in Germany when it lost the Battle of Britain.

In the end of October 1940, Italy attacked Greece through Albania. A war with Yugoslavia was also contemplated, but Hitler did not allow it, reserving Yugoslavia for Germany. Since Greece had a guarantee from Britain – the British relied on the domination of their navy in the Mediterranean – troops landed on the island of Crete. Yugoslavia joined the British Triple Alliance – Germany, Italy, Japan – on the understanding that Yugoslav territory would not be used in a German invasion of Greece. Meanwhile, British troops had landed in Greece in March 1941; the Italians were defeated, and Hitler's long-prepared Balkan campaign had to be launched.

On 6 April 1941, without warning, Belgrade came under heavy German bombing, and a new German Blitz had begun: attacking through Bulgaria, the Germans cut Yugoslavia off from Greece within two days; a second German column moved into central Yugoslavia, and a third, started from Austrian and Hungarian territory (Hungary taking part in the campaign), occupied Croatia. 'Great Croatia' was declared independent; it included Bosnia, Herzegovina, and part of Slovenia (the other part was incorporated into the 'Reich').

On 11 April the Italian army occupied the Istrian peninsula and the Adriatic coast of Yugosloavia (Dalmatia). The Yugoslav army, encircled in Bosnia, capitulated on 17 April. The Yugoslav state was declared non-existent. The Germans had earlier

---

82. Soon a conflict occurred between the 'Iron Guard' and Antonescu. Hitler supported Antonescu, but allowed a refuge for the 'Iron Guard' in Germany, to keep Antonescu in check in case of his disobedience.

occupied Thesaloniki and Yannina in Greece, cutting off the Greek army, which at that time was located in Albania, and which capitulated on 22 April. The British defended Thermopylae in vain – on 27 April the Germans entered Athens, and by May 1941 all continental Greece and the islands of the Aegean sea (except Crete) were occupied by Germany, while Italy occupied the Ionian islands. In May the Germans undertook landings on Crete from ships and gliders; bloody battles ensued, but towards the end of May the remnants of British troops and of the troops of the British Commonwealth were evacuated from Crete to Egypt.

Despite controlling the cities and the railways in Yugoslavia, the Hitlerites were unable to prevent the formation of patriotic guerrilla groups in the mountains; liberal-monarchist, headed by Mihajlović, and Communist, headed by Joseph Broz (whose party nickname was Tito). However, the 'go ahead' signal for Tito's guerrillas was given by Moscow only on 4 July, when the war of Germany against the USSR had begun.

The British were very much troubled by the possible fate of the Suez Canal, Anglo-Egyptian Sudan and their Eastern African colonies. Italy which had occupied Ethiopia and united it with Eritrea and Somalia, was a serious threat, the more so because it dominated the air space. Beginning with 10 June 1940, Britain was at war with Italy, and the Italians began to advance into Sudan; they also occupied British Somaliland. The British struck against the Italian aircraft, and then, supported by followers of the exiled Ethiopian emperor, Haile Selassie, moved from three directions into Italian-occupied Ethiopia. The Italian general in charge capitulated in May 1941, and Ethiopia was restored as an independent state.

Lebanon and Syria, of which France was the mandatory power, and which were under the dominion of the Vichy government, were occupied by British and French (Gaullist)[83] troops, but were promised independence after the war.[84] In Iran, there was an internal struggle between different groups, and the British gave support to the one not oriented towards Germany and Italy, suppressing the others.

Meanwhile, in Africa, the British Imperial troops (including Indians and Australians), moving from Egypt, managed, more quickly than they expected, to crush the Italian army on the coast of Cyrenaica (the eastern part of Libya) and, continuing their advance, captured the fortress of Tobruk. Everything was set for a further offensive against the rest of Italian territory in Libya, but Churchill ordered the transfer of part of the troops from Libya to Greece, where they barely escaped another Dunkerque. Meanwhile, in February 1941, Germany sent two divisions to Libya, one of them a tank division. Rommel, their commander, was quickly able to

---

83. Charles de Gaulle, an efficient French general and deputy minister of defence in the Reynaud government, fled to England, and from there broadcast an appeal to the French for resistance to the occupation. He was acknowledged by Britain (but not by the USA) as leader of the Free French.
84. The fate of Madagascar, which was a French colony, was similar. It sided with the Vichy government, but was occupied by British and Gaullist Free French forces.

drive the British and Indian troops nearly all the way back to the Egyptian frontier; but an Australian (later a British) and a Polish division held Tobruk until 21 June 1942. Only in the autumn of 1942 was Rommel defeated by the British troops of General Montgomery at el-Alamein, and forced to abandon Cyrenaica. Tobruk was liberated on 13 November 1942.

As early as 18 December 1940, Hitler had signed the 'Barbarossa Plan' which began with the words: 'The German armed forces must be ready to suppress Soviet Russia by a speedy campaign before the end of the war with England.' And beginning in December 1940, German troops were being moved towards the frontiers of the USSR. Of this the Soviet Headquarters was informed by hundreds of our own and British agents. I myself had the opportunity to speak in 1944 with a former British spy, who not only had sent such information to the British headquarters, but later even checked that it had been forwarded to Russia. My friend Professor Kellenbenz, at that time a soldier in the tank forces of General Kleist on our frontier, managed before the beginning of the war against the USSR to learn Russian well enough to read a chapter of Pushkin's *Eugene Onegin*. However, Stalin dismissed all warnings, declaring that the spies were 'double agents' and 'provocateurs'. From a youth lived in an atmosphere of political provocation, he was pathologically afraid of agents. However, he was actually informed of the exact date of the assault: 22 June 1941.[85] Originally, the offensive was planned for an earlier date, but events in the Balkans made Hitler postpone it until June. This delay was of great importance; according to the 'Barbarossa Plan', the whole blitz-campaign against Russia was to take no more than three to four months. An offensive begun in April or May would bring the Germans to the vicinity of Moscow in early autumn, and they would not be in such a pitiful state, morally and physically, as they actually were in the winter of 1941.

Rumanian, Italian, Hungarian and, later, Slovak units took part in the German operation.[86]

The offensive began on the appointed day in three directions: Rundstedt moved to the south-east (a direction which, in spite of everything, had been countenanced by Stalin). Bock moved from west to east, and Leeb towards the north-east.[87] According to German data, 120 divisions were set in motion; they had no numerical advantage over the Russians, but relied on the superiority of their tactics based on

---

85. The British Minister of Foreign Affairs Eden relayed it (using the information of the British Intelligence Service) to Maiski, the Soviet Ambassador. However, next day the Soviet telegraph agency TASS, following Stalin's order, reacted with an official statement reassuring everybody that the information was false.
86. Slovaks appeared on the front rather late; a very considerable part of their force went over to the Red Army, and were used for the formation of a Czechoslovak corps.
87. There was also a fourth direction of enemy advance from Finland towards the White Sea. Only the Finns managed to gain some important ground here. The German troops, positioned farther to the north, moved in three non-contiguous directions separated by taiga forest or tundra, and were able to progress only short distances.

swiftly moving tank columns. A chaotic situation developed in the western section of the Soviet front; the Soviet forces were swept away. The permanent fortifications on the old frontier line had been demolished for some unaccountable reasons and on the new frontier line in Western Belorussia they had not been installed, allegedly 'for not provoking the Germans.' As mentioned above, the plan to create tank armies, elaborated by Marshal Tukhachevski, was declared an 'act of sabotage'. In the spring of 1941, however, the plan was resurrected, but the bodies of the tanks were stored in one place, the guns in another, and the crews somewhere else again, and all elements captured by the Germans. The recently devised types of aeroplane were not yet in service (the existing fighters could not cope with the 'Messerschmitts'), and nor were the multi-rail rocket projectors, the 'Katyushas'. The Soviet troops along the frontiers were now retreating in unconnected groups, great and small, and found themselves encircled. During the summer 1941, the Germans took about 1.2 million prisoners. Later, after their release from German prisoner-of-war camps, all the survivors were sent on Stalin's orders to Soviet slave camps: 'we have no prisoners-of-war, what we have are traitors'. However, even the uncoordinated Soviet units continued their resistance.[88] Moreover, the German Headquarters had underrated the reserves of the USSR. The Soviets achieved an unparalleled evacuation of industry to the east and mobilised human reserves; Moscow, Leningrad and other cities organised 'volunteer' divisions of workers and officials (in Moscow, even an infantry company of members in the Authors' Union was organised); new divisions from the Urals, from Siberia and other regions constantly replaced the divisions which had been routed. The German offensive began to peter out. However, German Headquarters expected the imminent collapse of the Soviet Union, and pressed the attack, straining its troops to the utmost. Significant was the fact that although the German tanks moved on caterpillar tracks, the supplies were brought in lorries which stuck in the autumn mud. During October there was a bloody battle around Vyazma; 16 October saw the Soviet partocracy fleeing from Moscow, and half-burned fragments of sundry documents drifting along the streets. We may quote a poem by O. Kudryavtsev, a friend of A. D. Sakharov: 'The shop manager, the trade union boss are fleeing into the dark; / into the dark are rustling the cars of the rabble who had had its fill; / from the West it smells of blood and fire: / '*Vexilla regis prodeunt inferni.*'[89]

The Germans continued to advance, successfully and quickly, in two other directions as well: in the Ukraine they managed to destroy several Soviet divisions by a pincer movement, and by September captured Kiev. In the north they speedily passed through the Baltic states, the Novgorod and the Pskov regions, and laid siege to Leningrad. Aerial bombing destroyed the city's food reserves, and the

---

88. Stalin thought it advisable to shoot the commander of the Western Front, in spite of the fact that he and his soldiers did wonders in a quite impossible situation.
89. The quotation is from Dante: 'Approaching are the banners of the King of Hell'.

blockade of Leningrad which lasted for 900 days, brought the inhabitants to starvation. The German advance, however, was arrested in the suburbs. Simultaneously, the Finns started military operations; on the Leningrad front they limited themselves to restoring the frontier line of 1938, but to the north of the Ladoga they reached Lake Onega and cut off the railway line between Leningrad and Murmansk. The latter was the port through which the Allies could supply the Soviet front in winter time.[90]

In November 1941, Hitler and Stalin, almost simultaneously, delivered speeches over the radio. Stalin, having come round after his initial panic, spoke in a calm voice, and promised that 'the enemy shall be defeated, the victory shall be ours'. Hitler shouted in a frenzied tone that '*this* adversary is *already* broken and *shall never more* arise', that 'his grenadiers', having reached the walls of Leningrad, did not enter only because the city would anyway fall into their hands 'like a ripe fruit'.

The winter came early that year, but the Germans did not nor would have winter uniforms. The Soviet army, on the other hand, soon began to receive the best possible winter clothes: warm caps, sheepskin coats,[91] trousers with cotton wool wadding, and felt boots. On 2 December the Germans began their last offensive against Moscow; it was held back with great difficulty by the dwindling Soviet units, but the Soviet Headquarters was able to throw in fresh Siberian divisions just in time. The Germans, after having reached the outskirts of Moscow, were forced back. In the rear were guerrilla groups, made up partly from encircled Soviet army units, partly from among the local inhabitants, and partly from troops who had landed behind the German lines by parachute. The guerrillas made it difficult for the Germans to organise a dependable and secure rear for their troops. In December, the Red Army managed to stage a limited counter-offensive.

Never before, and afterwards only in the last months of the war, were the German soldiers so demoralised. Had the Soviet Headquarters at that time the necessary forces for a mass offensive, the Germans would have been totally routed. But towards spring the German battle spirit rose again; fresh victories followed, and even in 1943, when a general retreat had begun, the German soldiers still believed in their own propaganda which assured them that the front was being shortened according to plan before a new and triumphant offensive.

A great misfortune for the Soviet Union was the offensive mounted prematurely against the German positions along the western (high) bank of the Volkhov River.

90. The labour of concentration camp prisoners had built a railway line joining the Murmansk–Leningrad railway (which had been cut off by the Finns in Southern Karelia) with the Arkhangelsk–Moscow line, so that it was again possible to transport troops and goods to and from the north.
91. The Russian soldiers thought that the sheepskin coats were the contribution of Mongolia (a Communist state in Inner Asia) to the war effort. If so, this was certainly a most important contribution.

The German defence was broken only along a very short stretch, and too many Soviet troops were thrown into the breach. The idea seems to have been to lift the siege of Leningrad from the outside. When vast numbers of Soviet troops had assembled in the swampy forests to the west of the Volkhov, the Germans shut the trap; hundreds of thousands of Soviet soldiers perished and were left unburied. The commander of this army (called the Second Shock Army), General Vlasov, gave himself up as prisoner to the Germans.

A few words on the situation inside Nazi Germany. In spite of the well-known dictum that the Germans lived under the rule 'guns instead of butter', the standard of living of the civil population during 1939–1940 was not very different from peace-time conditions, although some ersatz-food had to be introduced. Germany regularly received oil from Rumania and made its own synthetic gasoline; the losses in manpower from mass mobilisations to the army were compensated for by the slave labour of 7 million 'Eastern workers' (*Ostarbeiter*) deported to Germany from Russia, Poland and Yugoslavia. Some were also deported from France.

The course of the war changed appreciably on 7 December 1941, with the entry of the United States.

The idea of a war to be waged by Japan not only against China but also against the USA, Great Britain and the Netherlands (who owned Indonesia) was a further development of the Tanaka plan; it was elaborated in the autumn of 1941. In 1940, the war in China had reached a stalemate, while the successes of the 'Axis' powers (Germany and Italy), who victoriously appropriated Europe, made Japan hurry in order to claim a share of world spoils.

In July 1941, the Japanese army moved into French Indo-China and occupied the Chinese island Hainan; later, Japan hoped to gain access to Indonesian oil. Meanwhile, the USA imposed an embargo on the export of oil and oil-products to Japan. Towards the beginning of winter, a Japanese governmental delegation arrived in the USA, supposedly for peaceful negotiations but actually as a blind: Japanese Headquarters had decided to deliver a preemptive strike against the United States, since it was probable that the Americans would soon take measures to stem the infiltration of Japan into the countries of the Pacific and Indian Ocean. Japanese Headquarters still relied disproportionately on battleships. The experience of the Second World War was to show that if the enemy has bombers and submarines, surface ships are of little use: they can easily be sunk.

On 7 December 1941, the Japanese aircraft carriers drew near to the Hawaiian Islands, where, at Pearl Harbour, nearly all ships of the American Pacific Fleet were stationed. A raid by about 300 Japanese bomber planes resulted in five out of eight American battleships being sunk, with one sustaining heavy damage, and two more damaged to a lesser degree. Moreover, several destroyers and other warships were sunk, and many American aeroplanes were destroyed or damaged on the airfield before they were ready to take off.

The attack on Pearl Harbour brought American society into a warlike mood, and the USA declared that it was at war with the Axis countries: Japan, Italy and Germany.

Next day the Japanese struck against USA airfields and military bases in the Philippines, and at bases in British Hong Kong, soon to be occupied by the Japanese; on 10 December Japanese troops began landing on the Philippines. Between December 1941 and January 1942, the Japanese took control of important islands in Indonesia, and invaded Burma (thus cutting off the supply of American oil to China), and in February they occupied Singapore; they landed on New Guinea and some of the islands in the Pacific. Great Britain, the USA and Australia now entered what was to be a long and exhausting war with Japan. With Holland already occupied by the Nazis, the Dutch troops in Indonesia made but feeble resistance to the Japanese; they were all taken prisoner and kept in camps no better than Stalin's.

With considerable effort, the Allies began to drive back the Japanese. Japan's excellent battle fleet did not play any important role. The Allies (mainly Americans and Australians), moved their forces from one island to another (here, of course, they were no less a burden and a nuisance for the local, especially the female, population than the Japanese had been). But the Allies were gradually approaching the Japanese archipelago. In March 1943, the Japanese General staff elaborated a plan of a defensive war (but it was calculated on defending not Japan proper but the new Japanese empire).

The entrance of the USA into the war made the situation easier not only for Britain but also for the USSR.

In June 1940, President Roosevelt had already declared his intention to place the 'material resources of the USA' at the disposal of 'opponents of force'. The USA proclaimed itself an 'arsenal of the democracies', and in March 1941 a law was passed on 'Lend-lease'; according to this law, the President was entitled to supply the Allies, at his discretion, with equipment, services and information. From November 1941, the 'Lend-lease' was extended to the USSR. Originally, Roosevelt hoped that 'Lend-lease' would spare the USA the necessity of partaking in the war, but with the country now already at war, the 'Lend-lease' commitment was maintained. 'Lend-lease' imports to the USSR went, during the winter time (when the days were dark), through Murmansk[92] and from there along the new railway line connecting the Murmansk railway (which had been cut in its southern part by the Finns) with the Arkhangelsk–Moscow railway line; or they went directly via Arkhangelsk; in summer the imports went through Iran. Here German agents had been active, but now Soviet troops were introduced in the north of Iran and British troops in the

---

92. No wonder that Murmansk and the Murmansk railway were subjected to heavy bombing. According to American opinion, the bombing of Murmansk could be compared only with the bombing of British positions on the island of Malta and at Tobruk. However (in spite of the fact that German historians state the contrary), German bombers were unable to destroy the bridge over the Kovda river; were it destroyed, all transportation from Murmansk would have been arrested for a very long time. As a rule, German bombing was inaccurate.

south, according to the old agreement about zones of interest made between Tsarist Russia and Great Britain.

According to some calculations, the 'Lend-lease' deliveries accounted for 5 per cent to 10 per cent of the needs of the Soviet Army. They made a significant contribution to morale: the Soviet soldier no longer felt he was alone in his struggle against Nazism. Especially important for the Soviet Union were deliveries of very fine lorries, explosives and strategic metals (as, nickel). Deliveries of arms were less important. The difficulty in delivering 'Lend-lease' freights lay in the fact that the German submarines dominated the Atlantic; few ships could manage more than two or three passages from the American coast to Europe and back.[93]

By 1942, the Soviet Union, after having hurriedly moved the most important industrial units to the Ural region and Siberia, and having put them into operation in record time, began to produce quantities of T-34 tanks (whose quality was higher than that of the contemporary German tanks), a range of other 'Katyushas' and military equipment; by the end of 1942, the armed forces received new, first-class battle planes (they were designed, as often as not, in 'special prisons' of the NKVD). Note that in military industry the working day was twelve hours, and the workers were mostly women and under-age juveniles.

Britain, through its prime minister Churchill, declared itself an ally of the USSR in June 1941, and it also took part in 'Lend-lease' deliveries.[94] But even more important for the Soviet Army was the promise to open a second front in Europe. It had long to wait. According to some calculations the USSR had lost four times as many soldiers as Germany, but the British were waiting for the moment when their operation could be achieved with minimal losses in their own manpower.

The year 1942 was exceedingly bad for the USSR. Germany, it is true, was no longer able to engage the Soviets in battle in three sectors of the front simultaneously, and during the summer of 1942 Hitler decided to start an offensive only in the southern one, although General Rundstedt thought this a mistake and resigned his commission in protest.

In November 1942 the Germans reached Rostov-on-Don, but then were driven back across the river Miuss. Their offensive was preceded by Stalin's abortive counter-offensive in the direction of Kharkov in the spring of 1942, which at that time was obviously premature; it ended in a great defeat, and in a new encirclement of numerous Soviet units.

93. Note that attempts to use surface ships in direct military operations were found to be rather futile by both sides of the war.
94. I asked Professor Postan who was at one time Churchill's economic counsellor, why the British supplied us with Hurricanes which had many weak points, so that our pilots had heavy losses, instead of the much better 'Spitfires', and kept their transport ships for long periods in Iceland. To the first question, he answered that Stalin was in constant fear of supposed British double-dealing. He chose the 'Hurricanes' himself, and declined the offer of 'Spitfires'. To the second question, he answered that the convoys waited for the polar night, when shipping became less hazardous.

The task set for the German Wehrmacht was to force its way to the Caucasus, to capture the oil-fields of Maikop, Grozny and Baku, and later to threaten the British forces in the Near East (where the Germans were successfully using anti-British propaganda among the Arabs).[95] They actually managed to occupy Maikop, Mineralnye Vody and Grozny, and, at some places, to cross the Caucasus; however, later they were defeated on the Volga and the Don, and forced to leave the Caucasus.

Another group of German divisions was thrown to the east of Kharkov, and to the north-east of Rostov-on-Don with the task of cutting across the Volga and threatening the industrial regions of the USSR. Hitler did not conceal the fact that, for him, the word 'Stalingrad' was symbolic. When the German troops entered the city, he declared: 'where a foot of the German grenadier has once entered, he will not retreat'; but here he was wrong. Even inside the city of Stalingrad itself the 6th German Army was unable to drive the Soviet soldiers from the riverside strip, where they were defending themselves with extraordinary steadfastness, despite the terrible intensity of bombing and artillery fire. As the battle went on, it became apparent that the 6th Army had moved too far forward, and as the result of an operation led by General Zhukov and Air Marshal Voronov, under the supervision and through coordination achieved by General Vasilevski, the Soviet troops managed to surround Stalingrad completely, and to cut the Germans off from any supplies. The flanking Italian and Rumanian troops gave themselves up, the Germans were more and more pressed together, until the remaining German troops, in the centre of the encirclement, had to surrender as well.

The Stalingrad tragedy astounded and shocked the German population. Neither they nor the German army lost hope, however, fortified by optimistic propaganda.

From this moment German strategy was directed no longer towards further conquests, but towards keeping what had been acquired. Hitler now feared the opening of a Second Front in France; this was a reason for his decision, made on 11 December 1942, to occupy Petain's France.

An event no less significant than the battle of Stalingrad was the huge battle on the Kursk Bulge. Recapturing Belgorod and holding Orel, the Germans planned an offensive against Kursk with the aim of encircling the Soviet troops, but this time their tank columns were only briefly successful: the Soviet tank counter-offensive drove the German troops westwards. At the same time, the German troops began a retreat from their positions at the distant approaches to Moscow. In fact, from the autumn of 1943 until the end of the war, the German troops, resisting the Soviet Army with all their might and inflicting heavy losses upon it, were in virtually constant retreat.

95. During World War II, the Hitlerites made constant attempts to plant their agents in the Egyptian liberation movement.

This turn of the events had several causes. For one thing, the Soviet generals and officers[96] had acquired experience; moreover, the medium-level officers' corps, which after the 1938 reprisals was mainly formed from 'promoted' sergeants and lieutenants who had had no tactical training, had been largely killed off and it now consisted of intelligent reservists.[97] Through an immense effort, using the labour of women and juveniles, the USSR managed to organise military production in the Ural region and in Siberia, and by the summer of 1943 had a definite supremacy in the air and in tank forces.

In Germany itself, as we have seen hardship was not experienced by the civil population, until 1940, and even, to some extent, 1943. A plan of the future state structure had been formulated: in the centre of Europe, a 'Great German Empire' (*Grossdeutsches Reich*) was to be founded; as well as the original German lands, it was to include Western Poland, Austria, Alsace, Lorraine and Luxembourg. The Great German Empire would also dominate both the 'General-Government' which was to include Central Poland and Galicia (the word 'Poland' was strictly taboo), and the 'Protectorate' (i.e. Czechia). The Netherlands, Denmark and Norway, as well as the Kola Peninsula and the Crimea, were to be included in the 'Germanic Empire of the Teutonic Nation'; here the population enjoying full rights should be exclusively 'Aryan' (which meant only peoples speaking languages of the Germanic branch of Indo-European). France, Serbia, etc. were to be dependent on Germany. The territory of the 'General-Government' and of the four 'Reichs-Kommissariats', namely the Ukraine, Ostland (including the Baltic regions and Belorussia), and the two planned but not actually organised 'Reichs-Kommissariats' – 'Moscovia' and 'Caucasia' – would serve to extend the German 'living space', as well as the purpose of German colonisation. The Poles and Russians were regarded as 'subhumans' (*Untermenschen*), and hence they were to be destroyed, completely or in part, the survivors being sent to the region 'Idel-Ural' (the districts along the rivers Volga and Ob), and to Siberia.

The Bolshevik cadres were to be exterminated (there was an order to shoot every political commissar taken prisoner immediately), and so was 'the racial (biological) base of Bolshevism'; as such, Hitler regarded the Jewish nationality, in the same way as he regarded the German nationality as the biological base of Nazism. Its purity was carefully looked after: if a German officer wanted to marry, he had to present the bride's 'ancestor passport' (*Ahnenpass*) proving a purely Germanic descent of her family as far as 1800 AD (and still farther into the past for SS men).

---

96. Stalin launched a propaganda campaign which stressed the continuity between the victories of the Red Army (now called 'the Soviet Army') and those of the pre-Revolutionary army; in 1943, he introduced army uniforms of the Tsarist type with shoulder-straps, and Tsarist military ranks were restored.

97. A contrary process was to be observed somewhat later in the German army: experienced generals and officers were sacked because of political unreliability, and were replaced by more politically reliable but less gifted ones.

Luckily, most European churches had maintained Public Records books from an early period.

In the rear of the advancing German army four Einsatzgruppen SD were operating (mobile groups of the Security Service); their particular business was killing off all the Jewish population without regard to sex and age. Until the end of 1941, in the process of the so-called 'Final Solution', according to British computations, 5,700,000 Jews had been killed in special annihilation camps. The states allied with Germany and dependent states also took part in the 'Final Solution', although rather unwillingly. Thus, for a long time the Vichy government would not agree to deliver up Jews who were French citizens.

An underground resistance movement emerged in all occupied countries, in different forms and to a different extent. For instance, the Norwegian resistance mainly made anti-Nazi propaganda and amassed secret information for the Allies, while in France there were organised guerrilla groups (*Maquis*). Still more developed and powerful were the guerrillas in Yugoslavia. In the Ukraine, in Poland, and in Yugoslavia there were parallel Communist and Nationalist guerrilla groups (the latter were afterwards exterminated by the Communists).[98]

Beginning with March 1942 a new generation of British (and later also American) bombers began mass bombardments of German cities. The Allies had decided that bombardments of specific targets were ineffective and useless; therefore they bombed whole areas, i.e. cities, by incendiary and demolition bombs. From 1943 on, the bombers flew in chessboard formation ('carpet bombing'), and destroyed everything on the ground. However, it appeared in 1945, that the German military potential was not totally destroyed.

The German population, seeing that the Wehrmacht was in constant retreat on the different fronts, and experiencing mass bombings, was losing hope; the situation made it possible for the Allies to demand unconditional surrender.

During 1943 opinion both in the USSR and abroad held that a 'Second Front' in Europe was necessary. However, a landing of British and American troops on the continent required tremendous preparations. According to Churchill's conviction, a direct landing in France or Holland was, for the time being, hardly achievable, because, for one thing, the Allies did not have enough ships for transporting the troops, but also because the losses would necessarily be very heavy for Britain. Therefore, the Allies preferred to approach from the South.

The actions began from afar. In November 1942, Allied troops landed at Casablanca in Morocco, and at two points in Algeria, where the local French authorities sided with Vichy. The Americans initially arranged contacts with the high commissioner of the French African dominions, Admiral Darlan; the latter regarded it as necessary to legalise any occupation of French colonies by obtaining

---

98. Such groups were also active in Greece, but there, on the contrary, the Communists were defeated.

a sanction from Petain; but later the Allies decided to invite General Giraud to head the French administration in Algeria; Giraud had no immediate connection with Petain. For some reason, the Americans did not trust de Gaulle, who was effectively heading the 'Free French' forces in exile. In the beginning of 1943, the Germans attempted to defend Tunis, but this ended with the capitulation of the 'Africa Corps' in May.

Simultaneously with the Battle of the Kursk Bulge in July 1943, the Allies, based on Tunis, landed their troops, headed by Montgomery, in Sicily and occupied this island without much difficulty. Then began the landing at different points in Southern Italy. However, the Germans were able to stem the Allied advance in Central Italy (at Monte Cassino). On 25 July 1943, nominally on an order of King Victor Emmanuel III, Mussolini was deposed, and a new government headed by Badoglio came to power in Rome; Italy went over to the Allies. But in actual fact, Italy was unable to defend itself against Germany, because there were numerous German troops in the country, and they offered desperate resistance. The Nazis staged a kidnapping of Mussolini,[99] and he continued, tutored by the Germans, to rule in Northern Italy.

In spite of heavy bombardments, Germany continued to accelerate its production of necessary armaments until the middle of 1944. But it could not stop the factories producing the now antiquated 'Junkers' and 'Messerschmitt' planes in order to start the production of such new aeroplanes that would be able to compete with the new American, British and Soviet ones: the constant losses in aeroplanes at the front, and the inevitable delay in supplying new planes before their serial production could be arranged, brought about the collapse of the German air force. Germany's economic structure had been designed for a short war; in a war to exhaustion it was gradually weakening. As was already the case in the USSR and in Japan, women and juveniles were put to work in the factories. It should be noted that success in Allied strategy depended, to a considerable degree, upon organising a planned economy, which was now introduced not only in the USSR, but also, as a temporary measure, in democratic countries.

As early as January 1943, Churchill and Roosevelt (joined later also by Stalin) formulated the demand for unconditional surrender of Germany and Japan, thus leaving them no hope of getting out of the war by way of a compromise. This perhaps did prolong the war somewhat, but it was impossible otherwise to eliminate totalitarian regimes, which, if they did not capitulate unconditionally, continued to be a menace to world peace.[100]

In May 1944 the Soviet forces captured Lwow (Lemberg), and by 31 July they reached the Vistula. A further advance was not possible for the time being, first,

---

99. Mussolini was kidnapped from Allied detention by a German intelligence agent, and returned to Northern Italy. In 1944, he was captured by Italian guerrillas and executed.

100. In 1991, the fact that the Allies did not make such a demand, led to the preservation of the totalitarian regime of Saddam Hussein in Iraq.

because the troops were exhausted after a march of nearly 400 miles, and needed supplies which had not been brought up, and secondly, because the Germans still dominated their flanks. But the Polish liberation movement regarded the appearance of Soviet troops on the Vistula as a signal for a rising in Warsaw.[101] It was ruthlessly suppressed by German troops, who turned the city into a heap of ruins. Practically, it was not easy for the Soviets to force a crossing of the Vistula at this time, but it seems that Stalin simply did not want to help the supporters of the Polish government in exile. The surviving insurgents were thrown by the Germans into concentration camps. Only months later did the Soviet troops finally manage to capture what remained of Warsaw, and to begin a new offensive on the Central Front.

In August 1944 Soviet troops entered Rumania. The latter ceased hostilities against the USSR, and on 25 August declared war on Germany. The Soviet troops also occupied Bulgaria and Transylvania, reaching the Hungarian frontier.

By the end of 1944, a considerable portion of the Soviet ground army had been motorised, helped by deliveries from the USA. As regards aircraft and tanks, Allied help after 1942 was less significant; but now the Soviet's own achievements seem to have become adequate.[102]

Meanwhile, on 6 June, the Allied troops (British, Canadian and American) began a landing in Northern France (Normandy). On 8 June the German stronghold in Caen, a centre of the German defence, was captured. On the Western Front the Germans deployed all the troops they could spare from elsewhere, but they were not aware of the actual plans of the Allies, and could not distribute their forces correctly. At the same time, the Allies made a mistake: instead of concentrating their forces for a strike against Germany, they made an attempt to liberate the Bretagne peninsula, but here the Germans managed to keep them out of the main ports. Only in September were the Allies to move eastwards, and occupy Verdun, and later Antwerp. The Germans attempted to strengthen their forces by introducing the 1st Parachute Army recruited from any available persons: untested youths, clerks, convalescent soldiers, etc.; of course, little benefit could be derived from this army: the German generals by now understood that the war was lost.

On 20 July 1944, there was a failed attempt on the life of Hitler at his headquarters in Eastern Prussia. After that, he made his last broadcast over the radio, speaking in a hollow voice, without any of the usual shouting. The attempt on his life was organised by a group of officers and some industrialists, all of high standing. The speedy trial resulted in the execution of 250 persons, including

101. Before that, in an enclosed ghetto in Warsaw, where Jews from all Poland were interned, another hopeless insurrection was launched. Although they received some help from the Polish underground, the insurgents were doomed, and the whole population of the ghetto was exterminated.

102. At the end of 1944, the chief of the German intelligence reported to Hitler that on the Eastern Front, 299 infantry divisions and 22 tank corps were deployed against the Germans. This was about the correct number, but Hitler decided it was misinformation.

some outstanding German generals. (Hitler allowed Rommel to commit suicide.) In addition, 5,000 persons were executed on suspicion of sympathising with the conspirators.

There can be no doubt that Hitler too knew that the war was lost but, following his dictim that 'Germany shall exist as a Great Power or not at all', he was ready to continue the war to the last German soldier.

In August, the Allies landed in the south of France, where they met with little resistance. It is interesting to compare the supplies of the Allies with those of the Germans: an Allied division received 700 tons of food and other supplies daily, while a German division received only 200 tons; and providing it with food and ammunition was made difficult because of constant bombing, as well as sabotage by guerrillas in the rear.

Nevertheless, in December 1944 the Germans started a counter-offensive in a hilly region of Belgium, the Ardennes, where they were able to delay the Allies somewhat. But the Soviet Army, resuming its offensive in the east, compelled Hitler to remove some divisions from the Ardennes, and the offensive of the Allies was resumed.

Meanwhile, by October the Soviet troops had already reached the frontiers of Yugoslavia, and on 20 October they captured Belgrade, contacting Tito's guerrillas. However, in Hungary, at Lake Balaton, they met with very strong resistance, and suffered heavy losses. In April, a treaty of friendship was concluded between the USSR and Tito.[103] The non-Communist opposition was represented by the minister of foreign affairs Šubašić; very soon, however, Tito's government became wholly Communist. At a consultation of the Great Powers it was decided that Greece was to be assigned to the British zone of interest. In Greece, as in Yugoslavia, Liberal-Monarchist and Communist forces existed separately, and were in bloody conflict with each other. Britain supported the Monarchists, so that a Communist structure of society did not emerge in Greece, but an armed struggle continued there for years.

Soviet troops introduced Communal regimes in Bulgaria, Rumania, Poland and Hungary.

Let us now shortly describe the war waged at the Pacific front by Americans (and also the Australians, the New Zealanders and by the British Indian troops).

In Burma, the objective was to prevent a Japanese invasion of India, and to restablish a road between Burma and China, so that Chiang Kai-shek's troops could be supplied by oil products. Moreover, the Japanese were to be ousted from New Guinea and the Pacific islands: first, in order to prevent an invasion of Australia, and secondly, to acquire bases for an air offensive against Japan.

103. During the war, several conferences took place between Churchill and Roosevelt, and between Churchill, Roosevelt and Stalin. At the Teheran conference in November 1943, Churchill agreed to support the Yugoslav government of Tito, which had at that time a considerable military force, and Stalin promised to enter the war against Japan at a later date.

The Allied land forces were headed by General MacArthur, the naval forces by Admiral Nimitz. They managed to defeat the Japanese in New Guinea, to land on the Philippines (in October 1944), to occupy the Kiribati (Gilbert) Islands, and Marshall Island. After the American victory[104] on Guadalcanal (one of the Solomon Islands) in the winter of 1942/43, in New Guinea in January 1943, on the Aleutian Islands in August 1943, and the occupation of the Japanese stronghold of Rabaul (on the New Britain Island east of New Guinea), the Japanese were not able to make use of their dominance in surface naval forces, which had resulted from their attack on Pearl Harbour. Neither did a battle between aircraft carriers – or, better to say, between planes based on the aircraft carriers – fought on 19 July 1944 bring Japan decisive victory. Occupying one island group after the other, the Americans were coming ever nearer to a point from which they could bomb Japan itself. The Japanese began to employ kamikazes – suicide pilots who did not bomb their target or shoot at it, but dived at it with their plane. But this did not lead to any important results. During 1944, the Americans occupied the Marian Islands with important bases on the islands of Guam (formerly an American colony), Saipan and Tinian; from here, heavy bombers were able to reach Japan. In February 1945, experiencing heavy losses, the Americans captured the island of Iwo Jima, still nearer to Japan, and in April 1945 they occupied the island of Okinawa which belonged to the Japanese island group Ryukyu. Heavy bombings of Japanese cities began.

In May–June 1945, Australian troops occupied the island of Borneo (Kalimantan). On Java and other Indonesian islands a liberation movement developed; however, it was directed not so much towards ousting the Japanese as towards not allowing the Dutch to return. At the same time, heavy battles, in which now one side and now the other was successful, were going on in the jungles of Burma and along the road to Chiang Kai-shek's temporary capital, Chungking. Only in May 1945 could Anglo-Indian troops successfully occupy Rangoon, the capital of Burma, and press the Japanese out of some other regions. But the fate of the war was to be decided elsewhere.

The Americans were ready to strike Japan in a terrible way.

The denouement in Europe came earlier than in the Pacific. Between 12 and 14 January 1945, a powerful offensive was launched in Germany by the troops of Konev, Zhukov and Rokossowski. On 17 January the ruins of Warsaw were at last occupied by Soviet troops. Some German troops were withdrawn eastwards from the Ardennes, and sent to Hungary to maintain Hungarian oil supplies for Germany. Violent battles started at Lake Balaton, where Soviet troops also had heavy losses. Meanwhile, in the central direction, the Soviet troops made an important rapid thrust, and, in a week, advanced 100 miles on a 250-mile front. Konev's troops entered Silesia, Zhukov's entered Brandenburg and Pomerania (about 200

---

104. Australian troops also took part in some of the battles.

miles west of Warsaw). On 25–26 January, Rokossowski occupied Danzig (Gdańsk), and cut off the German forces in Eastern Prussia.[105] Hitler threw into battle an improvised army mainly of SS-men, and headed by the executioner-in-chief, Himmler. 'Volkssturm' troops were recruited among persons who were beyond the age legally liable for mobilisation, and persons relieved from military service. On 31 January 1945, Zhukov crossed the Oder at Küstrin, and was only 30–40 miles away from Berlin. From the south, Konev reached the Neisse, a tributary of the Oder, on 15 February, lining up with Zhukov.

At the end of February, the Soviet offensive was delayed, because it could not continue without constant supplies of fuel, shells, food, and without replacement of casualties; these were largely replaced by soldiers who had been treated in field hospitals. The German front had become narrower, and hence was now somewhat easier to defend. Moreover, Hitler had decided that the Soviet offensive was more dangerous for Germany than the offensive of Western allies; so, he again took away some troops from the West and transferred them to the East; thus a further advance of the Western allies was made easier. Note that German railway communications were often out of order.

There had already been several meetings and consultations between Roosevelt and Churchill (or between Roosevelt, Churchill and Stalin – thus in Teheran and in Yalta in the Crimea). Here global strategic and political decisions were made. Of fundamental importance was the historical Atlantic Charter elaborated by Roosevelt and Churchill. It stated that their nations did not aspire to territorial and other gains, and that they respected the rights of the nations to self-determination; it also formulated the need for a 'peace giving the possibility to all nations to live in security inside their frontiers'. Soon after Pearl Harbour, there was a conference where it was declared, that no member of the United Nations would conclude a separate peace, that all accepted the principles of the Atlantic Charter, and that the Allies were fighting to defend the life, liberty and independence, and religious freedom, and to preserve human rights and justice.

In October 1944, Churchill and Stalin again conferred, in Moscow: victory was approaching, and there was an urgent need to reach agreement on the most important problems of the war and of post-war policy. Churchill had attempted earlier to arrange a direct agreement between Mikolajczyk, the head of the Polish government in London, and Bierut, the head of the pro-Communist Committee of National Liberation at Lublin, i.e. on the Polish territory occupied by the Soviets. Mikolajczyk insisted on the restitution of Poland in its frontiers of 1938, and no agreement was reached. However, Churchill and Stalin did agree on the division of the spheres of influence in Eastern Europe. The fate of Rumania and Bulgaria was

---

105. The German population fled, if possible, from Eastern Prussia; the rest of it was later expelled from the region by the Soviet forces. With a mentality of 'revenge', the Soviet soldiers were a major calamity for the population, although the commanding officers made some attempts to restrain them.

left for the USSR to decide, the fate of Greece was to be decided by Britain; as to Yugoslavia, originally it was meant to be under the influence of both Powers; but finally Churchill renounced the backing of Mikolajczyk, and recognised Tito, on the condition that non-Communist figures would, symbolically, take part in his government (and a similar stipulation was made with regard to the Bierut government). Of course, in actual fact, the 'bourgeois' representatives were very soon eliminated from the governments of Poland and Yugoslavia.

During the Yalta conference, it was decided that Germany should be divided into three[106] occupation zones, and that Berlin should also be divided into zones, and ruled according to an agreement between the Allies. It was also decided, that the USSR, after some time, and according to a secret protocol, should enter the war against Japan, receiving in exchange the Kuril Islands as well as Southern Sakhalin, a region lost by Tsarist Russia in 1905; furthermore, it was decided that the USSR should acquire the right to use the harbours of Port Arthur (Lü-Shun) and Dal'ny (Dairen, Ta-lien) as naval bases, and to partake in the administration of the Chinese Eastern and South Manchurian Railways.[107] The peoples of Europe were promised free elections as soon as possible; all important decisions would be made jointly by Great Britain, the USA and the USSR. Moreover, the future status of a United Nations Organisation was discussed. Stalin demanded that all the sixteen constituent Republics of the USSR (but not the so-called Autonomous ones) should be represented separately, as being supposedly sovereign nations (just as Australia, Canada, New Zealand and South Africa were to be members of the UNO, although they were simultaneously members of the British Commonwealth of Nations). The Western Allies refused to regard the Soviet republics as sovereign and were not inclined to let the USSR have seventeen votes.[108] Finally, Churchill and Roosevelt agreed to admit two Soviet republics into the UNO, namely those that had suffered most from the war, Belorussia and the Ukraine.

Meanwhile, the final period of the war had begun. On the night of 13–14 February, and then for three nights more, British and American aircraft bombed Dresden, and two more periods of bombing followed in March and April. Barbaric destruction of a beautiful old city could hardly be said to have a great military importance, but it was then already apparent that Dresden would be included in the Soviet zone – was it possible that this was decisive for the Allied Headquarters,

---

106. Later there were four zones: France also got a zone of occupation. The western zones carried out 'denazification': all National Socialists who had been guilty of crimes against humanity were submitted to court prosecution, or at least, deprived of certain civil rights; the others received the same rights as the rest of the population. But in the Soviet Zone there was no 'denazification', and it happened that persons were received into the Communist party directly from the Nazi party.
107. Later Stalin ceded Lü-Shun and Ta-lien to Communist China.
108. At that moment the Karelo-Finnish Republic was one of the Republics constituting the Soviet Union; there were sixteen republics in all. Later it was transformed into the Karelian Autonomous Republic quite unconstitutionally: by a personal decree of Khrushchev.

and that the British and Americans may have wanted to deprive the Russians of this important industrial centre? According to British data, 60,000 civilians perished, but according to the German information, no less than 135,000, i.e. more than in Hiroshima. At the same time, other German cities were also being destroyed (for example, Frankfurt), and since whole areas, not specific buildings, were the object of bombing, it was mostly the civilian population that suffered.

Hitler had actually left the Western Front vulnerable in the belief that the bombing of British cities with a new weapon, the rocket-propelled bombs V1 (from June 1944) and V2 (from September 1944) which caused enormous damage (a considerable part of the centre of the City of London was destroyed) would cause panic among the Allies and delay their offensive. However, the offensive continued more or less exactly as planned. On the night of 23 March 1945, the American troops crossed the Rhine and met little resistance; British troops moved through Northern Germany via Lübeck. On 12 April President Roosevelt died, and this revived hope at Hitler's headquarters, which now had been moved to Berlin. On 25 April Berlin was completely surrounded by the Soviet troops of Konev and Zhukov;[109] on 27 April there was a meeting between Soviet and American soldiers on the Elbe. On 30 April Hitler committed suicide in his bunker in central Berlin. On 2 May operations came to an end in Northern Italy. During the night of 7–8 May Admiral Dönitz who had taken upon himself to head the German government after Hitler's death surrendered unconditionally. However, for the Soviet army, the war lasted one day longer: in Prague, General Schörner refused to surrender; the 'Vlasovians', i.e. troops organised by Hitler's authorities from Russian prisoners of war[110] rose against him; then regular Soviet troops arrived, and the last battle on the Eastern Front was over on 9 May 1945.

From 17 July to 2 August, in Potsdam near Berlin, the last meeting of the leaders of the Great Powers took place. The USA was represented by President Truman, Britain was first represented by Churchill, but later – because the Conservative party had meanwhile lost the elections – by the Labourist Attlee. The USSR was represented by Stalin; foreign ministers were also present. Truman told Stalin unofficially that the USA had successfully tested an atomic bomb, and that it might be used against Japan; Stalin had promised to take part in the war against the Japanese. The question of reparations was broached, and it was decided that the USSR should be allowed to receive reparations from the territories occupied by the Soviet troops, and to have a certain percentage of the reparations from the zones occupied by the Western allies. The USSR also demanded the regions which had

109. Zhukov was, no doubt, a brilliant general, but could be inhumanely ruthless with his aides and subordinates. Konev and Rokossowski were by no means less important for the victory.
110. The Russian units of the Wehrmacht included not only persons of an anti-Communist persuasion but also men who had joined the units in the attempt to save themselves from a certain death in the concentration camps. The Soviet authorities regarded the Vlasovians as traitors anyway.

been ceded by Russia to Turkey in World War I; furthermore Stalin wanted mandatory power over Italian colonies in Africa (!), and he suggested continuing the war
by deposing Franco in Spain. Stalin now perceived the USSR as a colonial power,
but his claims were refused by the Allies. They protested against the idea of Stalin
deciding the fate of the countries of Eastern Europe alone, without consulting
their own official representatives. It was decided that all territories occupied by the
Soviet troops would conduct 'free and unrestrained elections'. Elections were,
indeed, conducted, but it was difficult to describe them as free or unrestrained, or
the ballot as secret. The solution of disputed questions was postponed to the next
meeting of the chiefs of governments in Washington – a meeting which never took
place.

On the Pacific front, Japan was manifestly growing weaker. The country's population was subject to strict rationing, reserves of fuel and labour power were practically exhausted. The losses in the armed forces, including the navy and the air
force, were very heavy indeed. In the beginning of March 1945, the Americans had
re-conquered the Philippines. The Soviet troops entered Manchuria on 8 August
(here they quickly made contact with the Communist forces of Mao Tse-tung
which had moved northwards to meet them); they also entered North Korea.

On 6 August 1945, the first atomic bomb, devised in the USA by an international
group of physicists, was dropped on the Japanese city Hiroshima. An area of c. 4–5
square miles was completely burned out. According to American data, 90,000 persons died immediately, not counting all those who died later from after-effects of
the radiation. On 9 August the Americans dropped a second atomic bomb on
Nagasaki, where no less than 10,000 died instantly. Next day Japan declared that it
accepted the conditions of peace as formulated at the Potsdam conference, under
the proviso that the emperor of Japan should not be deprived of his privileges. On
14 August 1945, the war with Japan came to an end. The American General
MacArthur assumed full power in the country; he declared at once that Shintoism
should be banned as an official cult, being the ideological justification of the
Japanese aggression, and of cruel treatment of the non-Japanese population.

In order to arrange for the disarmament of Japanese troops in Korea, the USA
and the USSR agreed on a line of demarcation between their troops along the 38th
parallel of latitude.

During the Second World War, the number of civilian deaths from illnesses, from
the conditions in concentration camps, and from bombings, did in some countries
exceed the number of dead and missing at the fronts. Thus Belgium lost 12,000
during military actions, and 76,000 civilians; Britain lost 264,000 during military
operations, and 92,000 civilians; Germany lost 3,500,000 at the front, and about
700,000 in the rear, not counting the many thousands who did not return among
the 3,500,000 soldiers and officers who had been made prisoners of war. The statistics for China are practically non-existent, but between 1937 and 1945 the
Kuomintang troops lost at least 1,300,000. Poland (not counting those who had

been exterminated in Soviet concentration camps) lost 130,000 in battle, but more than 5,500,000 of the civil population; Japan lost 1,300,000 at the front and 672,000 civilians.

Statistics for the USSR are uncertain. It is unknown how many of the Soviet prisoners of war who had been liberated by the Soviet troops or passed over to them by the Western allies then perished in Soviet concentration camps. According to an optimistic Western estimate, the total losses of the male population of the USSR during World War II was about 15–20,000,000, of whom 8,500,000 (according to other authors, about 11,000,000) officers and soldiers were killed at the front. 7,000,000 civilians were killed,[111] and an unknown number of persons perished in the Soviet concentration camps, as well as in the German ones. (Let me remind the reader that during the campaign of 1941 alone the Germans captured nearly 6,000,000 Soviet soldiers; moreover, there were millions of civilians kept in the German annihilation and other concentration camps.)[112]

The entire losses during World War II are estimated at *c*. 40–50,000,000 million, nearly half of them being civilians. In Europe, there were about 21,000,000 displaced persons, mostly employed by the Germans for forced labour, but also a number of refugees from one regime or the other. The least losses – 1,000 persons – were those of Brazil which joined the Allies at a late date.[113] Individual industrial enterprises and whole cities suffered destruction on a huge scale or were wiped out. For example, France, which had suffered much less than many other countries, estimated the losses in property as equivalent to three years national budgets.

In the USSR, a certain euphoria took hold of the population. If formerly it had been explained to the citizens that governmental cruelty is due to the fact of the country being totally surrounded by enemies, now, as it seemed, it was surrounded by allies. This intellectual euphoria was brought to an end in 1946, when Zhadanov, a henchman of Stalin, in a public speech, defamed two arbitarily chosen of the most respected Russian authors, Akhmatova and Zoshchenko.

All Soviet prisoners of war liberated by the Allies from German concentration camps, as well as perhaps most of the displaced persons, were sent to Soviet concentration camps. This was a heavy blow, first of all, to the agriculture, where

111. According to I. Kurganov, during World War II, the USSR lost its entire natural increase in population (15,400,000 persons), and the direct losses amounted to 28,600,000 persons. According to the military historian D. Volkogonov, the USSR lost 27,000,000 persons, including the civil population but not including those who died in our own concentration camps. In Leningrad alone, about 1,000,000 persons died of hunger during the siege. Moreover, arrests by the NKVD also continued during the siege.

112. A case which I have witnessed myself: On 9 May 1945, the Norwegians liberated all Russian prisoners-of-war from all concentration camps in Norway, and helped them to disarm the German troops. When a ship from the USSR arrived to fetch them, the Norwegians saw them off with flowers; but when the ship arrived in Murmansk, it was surrounded by the Soviet secret police, and all the former prisoners-of-war were sent to concentration camps at Vorkuta.

113. The then existing Vargas regime in Brazil was typologically similar to Fascism. Nevertheless, Brazil joined the Anti-German alliance, and Brazilian soldiers fought at the Italian front.

ploughing and other agricultural work was being done without any technical equipment at all, by women and children; but it was also a blow to the industry. However, the latter was gradually restored, partly through machinery and equipment being imported from the Soviet occupation zone in Germany (of course, it was not at all of the newest types); and partly through using slave labour of the prisoners of war and concentration camp prisoners.

During wartime the relations between the Western Allies and the USSR were satisfactory; but during the period of peaceful reconstruction it appears that between those countries living in the classical Capitalist Seventh Phase (the leading countries being already in the Phase transition to the Eighth Phase), and those living inside the Communist branch of the Seventh Phase no kind of agreement was really possible.

We shall not dwell on the difficulties and intricacies of the post-war negotiations between the USSR and the Western Powers. In these negotiations the contradictions between the two systems became quite apparent. It will be sufficient to mention a few important events.

On 10 February 1947, peace was concluded with Hungary, Rumania, Bulgaria and Finland. Communists came to power in all these countries (except Finland, but including Poland) as the result of elections which were held under strong political pressure. In Czechoslovakia there was a Communist putsch, and the Anti-Nazi coalition government was deposed. In China, thanks to the help of the USSR and its armed forces, the Communist leader Mao Tse-tung was able to extend his authority over the entire country. The remaining loyalists of the Kuomintang fled to the island of Taiwan (Formosa); this island had formerly been occupied by Japan, but its population, except for some tiny groups of aboriginal inhabitants, was Chinese.

In 1947, Britain recognised the independence of India, divided into India proper, and Muslim Pakistan[114] (Eastern Pakistan later seceded to become the republic of Bangladesh, situated in the lower reaches of the Ganges, a rather backward state). Soon Burma also got its independence, and then the Malacca peninsula and the district of Sarawak on the island of Borneo; they united in a new republic, Malaysia. The island city of Singapore, originally Malayan but by the middle of the twentieth century nearly entirely Chinese, also received its independence. The French in Indo-China had waged war on Communist (and other) insurrectionists since 1946; but after their defeat at Dien Bien Phu in 1954, the French had to recognise the independence of North Vietnam, and then of Cambodia and Laos. However the Communists, led by Ho Chi Minh, were not ready to limit themselves to North Vietnam alone; their men infiltrated into South Vietnam; local administration throughout most of the country became Communist. If we add to this the fact of a

---

114. Since in many Indian provinces the Hindus and the Muslims lived in mixed communities, the declaration of the independence of both India and Pakistan led to bloody skirmishes along the new frontier, and to a panic flight of Muslims to Pakistan, and Hindus to India.

huge strengthening of Communists in neighbouring Indonesia, where they allied themselves with the government of Sukarno which was leaning towards totalitarianism, it will be apparent that a major Communist expansion was going on in the whole general region. This process continued during the 1960s and 1970s but it did not prove irreversible everywhere.[115]

In their attempt to stem the spread of Communism to the whole of South-Eastern Asia, the Americans who were stationed in non-Communist South Vietnam, began a military campaign. For many years, the war was waged not so much against the North Vietnamese as against their guerrillas in South Vietnam; often the Americans found it impossible to distinguish between the guerrillas and the local population. The Americans made heavy bombing raids, and applied other obviously inhuman methods of warfare. The Vietnamese – both the guerrillas and, perhaps even more so, the civilians – experienced huge losses, but the losses of the American army were also considerable. Finally, in the early 70s public opinion in the USA forced the government to withdraw American troops from Vietnam. The Communist regime that came to power in both parts of the country appeared to be no better than Communist regimes elsewhere: poverty was prevalent, and a portion of the population (especially the Chinese) attempted to flee across the ocean in open boats.

In Burma and in Cambodia the previously Buddhist way of life – archaic, but, on the whole, humanistically oriented – seems to have become a thing of the past; both countries, as well as Laos, were now ruled on totalitarian lines, and a hatred of aliens seem to have been fostered. All these countries still experience great poverty, and no escape has so far been found. These countries (except some ports) are practically closed to foreigners, and it is impossible to assess the accuracy of information provided.

In Korea, the temporary demarcation line between the troops of the USA and the USSR, originally drawn for the process of disarming the Japanese military forces, became a boundary between two separate states in 1948. The USSR founded a Communist state in North Korea,[116] with an army of its own, which it furnished

---

115. In October 1965, the Communists, encouraged by the large increase in their support, staged a putsch in Indonesia. The putsch did not succeed, the population was incited against the Communists, and several hundred thousands of them were killed all over Indonesia. General Suharto, a very authoritarian figure, took over.

Later, in Cambodia, a similar Communist putsch was successful; a 'Communist' group, called the Khmer Rouge, led by one Pol Pot who was supported by Communist China, came to power. According to Pol Pot's doctrine, all the country's elder population had been poisoned by reactionary ideology, and so must be exterminated. This was too extreme, so Pol Pot was deposed by Communist Vietnam; but the final organisation of the Cambodian state was still *sub judice*.

116. This was no easy matter, because the Central Committee of the pre-war Korean Communist party had been exterminated in the USSR during the 1930s 'purges', and the Korean population which had formerly inhabited the Soviet Far East was at the same time re-settled to Kazakhstan and other regions deep inside the Soviet Union. Installed as head of North Korea (The Korean Popular Democratic Republic, or KPDR), was a Korean dictator of a nebulous origin, one Kim Il-Sung, a major in the Soviet army staff. When I was commissioned to Northern Norway in 1944, he succeeded me in the post that had been assigned to me.

with military counsellors and technology. In South Korea, in May 1948, the Americans held a referendum (North Korea was not allowed by Soviet authorities to participate), and, south of the 38th parallel, established the Republic of Korea. In so far as it is possible to judge, at the end of 1949 or in the beginning of 1950, Mao Tse-tung, during his visit to Moscow, made an agreement with Stalin not only about economic aid to China but also about the establishment of Communist rule in all Korea. On 25 June 1950, North Korean troops, launching a powerful surprise attack, invaded South Korea. Soviet propaganda that the war was begun by South Koreans, or even by Americans, was false: at that moment, the Americans had few forces in Korea. In the beginning four South Korean divisions were involved in the military operations; these were quickly thrown back to the far south-eastern corner of the peninsula. Only then did the Americans land their first division in Korea; other forces of the United Nations followed. They threw the aggressors back to the Chinese and Soviet borders, but then Chinese troops appeared aided by Soviet military experts, and launched a counter-offensive. Eventually, an armistice was concluded based on the demarcation line along the 38th parallel.

In Africa, the British gradually left their colonies; there were important military actions only in Kenya which contained many British settlers. It was with greater difficulty that France left its colonies. Although the independence of Morocco was soon recognised, the French were reluctant to leave Algeria where the percentage of their fellow nationals was very high. Here France used military means to suppress the liberation movement. The war dragged on from 1945 to 1962, but finally France recognised Algeria as an independent state. Later Belgian Congo (Zaire, and now Congo once more), and the Portuguese colonies, Mozambique and Angola became independent; but here military confrontation developed between pro-Communist groups (aided by the Soviet Union), and the anti-Communist ones. The armed struggle, both here and in Latin American countries, especially in Nicaragua and Salvador, Cuba and Chile, continued until *perestroika* ('re-structuring') began in the USSR in the middle of the 80s, or even later. A Communist regime persists in Cuba.

Totalitarian states emerged in many of the countries of the 'Third World' which had gained their independence, i.e. in Asia (except India), in Africa (also in Ethiopia where the emperor was deposed) and in Latin America. Some of them declared themselves Socialist or even Communist; but this was not the early Communism with its utopian ideas of a hegemony of the proletariat and the poorest peasantry; it was the later type of Communism, with a monopolistic state power implemented by a unified party-cum-state machinery (*nomenclatura*). The same is also true of the 'Communist' states in Europe: the German Democratic Republic which had been created out of the Soviet zone of occupation, as well as Poland, Czechoslovakia, Hungary, Rumania and Bulgaria. (An analogous state structure had also been created in Yugoslavia, but Tito soon quarrelled with Stalin, and got away with it.)

But if in Europe Communist totalitarianism was artificially imposed by the Soviet armed forces, in the 'Third World' totalitarianism made its appearance because the society, as a rule, still was in the Fifth Phase, and the local dictators played typologically the role of medieval monarchs. One cannot maintain absolutely the impossibility of jumping from a lower Phase directly into a higher one. Some Arabic countries which own huge amounts of oil, a raw material absolutely indispensable for modern industry, achieved a high degree of welfare, in spite of retaining a political structure typical of the Fifth to Sixth Phases. Examples are Saudi Arabia, Kuwait and the United Arab Emirates. Egypt is also highly developed industrially, especially since it made the Suez Canal its property in 1956, in spite of attempts of the Western Powers to organise military resistance. But Egypt currently suffers high overpopulation and this hinders its prosperity. At all events, in countries rich in oil there has emerged a quite special situation, uncharacteristic of other countries of the 'Third World', which certainly cannot be sustained. But on the whole, the countries of the 'Third World' are destined to totalitarian, or, at least, authoritarian regimes, for the foreseeable future.

A specific situation has emerged in Arab countries. Here the dominating ideology is Arab nationalism and (directly or indirectly) the idea of resurrecting the Arab Caliphate. This idea is hardly more viable than the idea of resurrection of the Roman Empire for the reason that its former territory is inhabited by nations of Roman descent, all of them Catholic. The vernacular languages of the Arabs of Maghrib (i.e. of Morocco, Algeria and Tunis), the Arabs of Egypt and Sudan, the Arabs of Syria, etc., are nearly as different as Rumanian, Italian, Spanish and Portuguese. It is true that an educated Arab is taught Classical Arabic at school – this is analogous to the teaching of all Jews, regardless of linguistic backgrounds, to use Hebrew (actually a modern variant of Hebrew) in Israel. But Hebrew has a better chance of surviving in the compact territory of Israel; Classical Arabic is placed in a different geographical situation which can be compared with teaching Medieval Latin to the literate population all over Western Europe and South America.

Arab nationalism is, to a great extent, nurtured by the common hate of the Arabs towards Israel, a state which has been created as the result of the Zionist movement.

The founder of Zionism was Theodor Herzl, an Austrian Jew. This movement developed as a counterbalance to anti-Semitism which in the late nineteenth century became widespread throughout Austria, Germany, France and Russia. The original idea of Zionism was that of creating a situation when the Jews could no longer be accused of being 'without kith or kin' but could acquire a homeland of their own (it was not proposed that all Jews should be resettled there). The country in question was thought of only as a 'national hearth-land'. The allegation of inveterate anti-Semites that Zionism wanted or still wants to subjugate all the world to the Jews is rank nonsense. This movement was always centripetal, inducing a hope for the Jewish people to acquire a small, but a real place where they would be 'at home'. After a number of discussions among the Zionists, it was decided to try to create a 'national Jewish hearth-land' in Palestine (which at that time belonged to Turkey but was inhabited by Arabs),[117] and the first Jewish settlements appeared here before 1900. The British authorities, who had acquired the mandate to govern Palestine as a result of World War I, now favoured the Jewish immigrants, now tried to hinder immigration, especially when it grew very appreciably, and began to induce protest from the Arabs, whom the British did not want to antagonise, in view of the proximity of the Suez Canal. However, the Nazi genocide of the Jews in Europe considerably increased the flow of Jewish immigrants to Palestine. They surpassed the Arab-speaking inhabitants of the country in education level, in the industriousness and efficiency they developed during the centuries lived under the harsh legal restrictions all through the Seventh Phase, and by their enterprising outlook acquired during the same period (and for the same reason). There were some extremists among them (the organisation Irgun Sebai Leumi), but the main role was played by Social Democrats and Conservatives.

By a decision of the General Assembly of the United Nations Organisation,[118] two national states were to be founded in Palestine: a Jewish and an Arab one; Jerusalem was to be a separate zone under international control; an economic union between the two states was stipulated. The frontier between them was to be drawn with the participation of international experts.

By the time the decision was approved by the UN (in November 1947), and after the British administration left the country (14 May 1948), the Israelis had prepared an army, and all necessary state structures, with their capital at Tel Aviv; the Arabs had prepared nothing. The USA recognised the new nation-state Israel *de facto* on 16 May, the USSR on 17 May (*de jure*). But on 15 May, seven Arab states, among them Egypt, Transjordan (later Jordan), Iraq, Syria and Libya, declared their intention to introduce troops into Palestine to keep order. The Jordanian troops occupied the Old City in Jerusalem (including the parts inhabited by Jews). In July 1949 an armistice was agreed to, under the condition that all troops stay in the territories occupied at the moment in question. The frontier made fantastic zigzags, and it was practically impossible for either side to defend it.

One of the most important decisions of the Israeli *Knesset* (parliament) was the 'Law on returning home' (*Aliyah*); according to this law, any Jew had the right to immigrate to Israel. Actually, immigration reached gigantic proportions: in 1948, in Palestine there lived 5–600,000 Jews, in twenty years the number rose to about 3,000,000, and since then the number has about doubled. There was some immigration from the USA, but most of it (for understandable reasons) came from the Arab countries and from the USSR, where, from the later years of Stalin's rule,

117. Note that, like most of the present-day, Arab-speaking peoples, the Palestinian Arabs are not simply descendants of immigrants from the Arabian Peninsula; it is more probable that they are also descendants of a more ancient Palestinian population which had embraced Islam and hence was Arabicised, probably also including some Islamised Jews and Christians.
118. The USSR also voted for this decision.

anti-Semitism became the official policy (although the *word* 'anti-Semitism' could never be uttered). It is interesting to note that a youth organisation from the Bundesrepublik Deutschland took part in building activities in Israel in atonement for German crimes against the Jews.

Wars between Israel and the Arab countries broke out in 1948 and in 1956, but in 1967 Israel was attacked from three sides by the Syrian, Jordanian and Egyptian armies, mainly armed by the Soviet Union, with the task of destroying it completely. Israel retaliated and here it appeared that states belonging to a more backward historical Phase cannot win a war against a state which, as was the case with Israel, had already reached the Eighth Phase: the war was over in six days. The Arab part of Palestine, occupied by Israeli troops during that war, was not incorporated into Israel but ruled as an occupied territory.

At present, Israel is an island of the Eighth Phase in a sea of Arab states, authoritarian and often hostile to each other. They are united by their common hatred of Israel but are as yet incapable of destroying it.

Of other events after 1955 we may mention the armed suppression by the USSR of democratic movements in Hungary (1956) and Czechoslovakia (1968; here a peaceful reform without violating the rules of Communism had been planned); and the quarrel between the USSR and China, after which all 'Communist' (actually totalitarian) states of Africa and Asia became divided into pro-Soviet and pro-Chinese. It is also important to mention the so-called 'Cultural Revolution' in China, which meant, among other things, exterminating the intelligentsia or sending them into exile in slave labour camps (though not, of course, only the intelligentsia).[119]

From this brief overview, we can observe a change which occurred in a number of states from the mid twentieth century on towards a new Phase in the historical process; the further history of world international relations will be treated (although cursorily) in the next chapter.

Early in the 1950s, the first thermonuclear (hydrogen) bombs were exploded in the USSR and the USA, and in China in 1964. This meant that in some countries all diagnostic features of the Eighth Phase are in evidence, while countries caught in the 'Communist' variant of Seventh Phase development received the signal that that Phase had run its course.

Thermonuclear arms are so immensely destructive that a major war in which they were used would lead to the annihilation of the very medium and conditions of human subsistence on land, on sea, and in the air, to the deaths of billions of people. Of course, wars might still be waged without using nuclear arms. However, the example of the Six Day War between Israel and the attacking Arab states in 1967, or the action of the United Nations' forces in 1991 against Iraq for its monstrous

---

119. In Tibet, what was termed 'Cultural revolution' was actually a military occupation, and led to a mass flight of Tibetans to India (together with their spiritual leader, the Dalai Lama).

aggression towards the neighbouring state of Kuwait (a war which also was finished in a few days), have shown that backward totalitarian states which remain in the Seventh Phase have no chance in military confrontation with progressive states of the Eighth Phase.

By 1990, the Eighth Phase had been reached in all countries of Western and Northern Europe, in the United States and Canada, in Israel, Japan, South Korea, Taiwan, Hong Kong, Singapore, the South African Republic and possibly in Thailand. It is not apparent whether the Phase transition has taken place in some of the Latin American states.

However, the events of the last half-century do not as yet belong to history, and I shall not treat them in any detail.

While discussing the preceding Phases of the historical process, I attempted to introduce individuals whose creative activities are of importance for further phase development of mankind, who awakened a feeling in the population that changes were necessary. However, the great minds of the twentieth century are still too familiar for objective judgement. I will list names according to my personal predilections: Kafka, Fallada, Remarque, Böll in German literature; Graham Greene in English literature; Hemingway and Faulkner in American; García Marquez in Latin American literature. They reflected the tragedies of the epoch in their works, rather than offering possibilities of change. In Russia, it was mainly great poets: Akhmatova, Mandelstam, Tsvetayeva, Pasternak, who were not influenced by Communist propaganda; in prose, works of genius were created in drawing pictures of the present society, either from a fantastic point of view, as in Bulgakov, or from a realist one, as in Grossman.[120]

Uniting these very dissimilar authors from different countries is a common feeling of humanness; they helped to disseminate the doctrine of human rights on a world scale. But if we were to nominate one author who played a really great historical role, then that author would be Solzhenitsyn. The appearance in print of his *GULAG Archipelago* – abroad, it is true, but reaching the Soviet reader by illicit typewritten reprints (*Samizdat*), or by illegally imported copies published abroad (*Tamizdat*) – the work of the crimes of Communism that became the death sentence to this social structure.

The art of painting, in the late Seventh Phase, as well as in the Eighth Phase, lost its function of figurative representation of the outer world. This function was completely overtaken by photography, cinema and television, while for the painter there was left the role to express figuratively the emotions induced by the outer world. The greatest figures in this new kind of figurative art were Picasso (1881–1973) and Chagall (1887–1985). Architecture now becomes ever less 'a thing of beauty', ever less decorative, ever more functional.

---

120. All these Russian literary works were either distributed illegally in Soviet Russia, or became known to readers considerably later.

The Eighth Phase came into its own mainly as a result of the activities of scientists; viewed historically, these activities were part of a single movement. Science does not tolerate inequality; what is important here are not academic titles, but practically verifiable truth. Previously there were thousands of great scientists and scholars – physicists, biologists, statisticians, even philologists and many others; to name them would be an impossible task. But actually, it was scientific development which made the passage into a new, Post-Capitalist Phase possible.

8 Eighth Phase (Post-Capitalist)

Thus far we have seen that capitalism created several alternative ideologies, such as Communism and Nazism. However, Nazism was based on the idea of universal conquest and militarisation, which was beyond the powers of its adherents. Communism proved to be more stable, but its stability in itself was responsible for bureaucratic stagnation and hence, naturally, economic impoverishment. In Eastern Europe, there have been attempts to forestall its ruin by military force (Hungary, 1956; Czechoslovakia, 1968). The attempts to spread the Communist idea beyond the 'country of victorious Socialism', i.e. the USSR, led to costly but fruitless attempts to support totalitarian regimes in Africa (i.e. in former colonies), and in Latin America. They could not be anything but fruitless, because the African dictatorships that supposedly were seeking 'a way of non-capitalist development' were in actual fact representing not the Seventh but, at best, the Fifth Phase of the historical process. Hence the endless wars, the unstable frontiers of the dominated territories, and the lack of any guaranteed human rights.

The 'Communist' economic system and ideology had two centres which since 1961 have been rivals: the USSR and China.

Note, however, that both the above mentioned alternative ideologies emerging in the Seventh, Capitalist Phase, namely Communism and Nazism, were leading mankind into an impasse; they could not guide society into any new Phase.[1] The way to the Eighth Phase was prepared by an ideology opposed to both: the doctrine of human rights, which now became a very strong socio-psychological incentive.

Just as Jesus preached in the first century AD, in the Fourth Phase, while Christianity became a universal ideology only in the beginning of the Fifth

---

1. The crisis of Communism in the Soviet Union led to the so-called *perestroika* ('reconstruction'); the results of it are as yet not clear. (For more on this see below.) As to China, the Communist leaders there attempted an economic reform – as, e.g. dealing land out to the peasants, introducing 'special zones' where capitalist 'rules' of economy were introduced, sending young people to study in the USA – however, no drastic political or ideological reform was envisaged. A great number of university students demonstrated for many days on the T'ien-an-Men square of Peking for democratisation; but it led only to a massacre of the students by tanks, and to a more reactionary group of the party clique taking over; according to non-Chinese information, about 2,500 young men and women were killed. The Western powers protested for some time, but Gorbachev, president of the USSR, the initiator of *perestroika*, who a short time before had walked among these students and talked with them, did not protest at all against the massacre.

Phase, in the same way, the teaching about human rights, as a socio-psychological incentive, had been formulated by Beccaria and Montesquieu, in the French 'Declaration of the Rights of Man and Citizen', in the American 'Bill of Rights',[2] appearing in the eighteenth century, in the very early Seventh Phase, and yet did not become a dominant force until the middle of the twentieth century.

After the first declarations, there followed the development of classical capitalism with its unrestrained exploitation of the working class. Actually, an alternative ideology can influence society only when other features typical of the new Phase also become operative. Gradual changes in the structure of production can be observed from the beginning of the twentieth century: a very important role was played in this by the Social Democrats, the Fabians and the Labourists, who were able to change the social arrangement of forces in production. The doctrine of human rights found a new development in Wilson's 1918 speech, in the Covenant of the League of Nations (1920), i.e. at the end of the Seventh Phase. It became a universally formulated ideology in the Charter of the United Nations Organisation, created in 1942–1946, and in its other resolutions. But what actually put an end to the Capitalist Phase was the invention of nuclear weapons. A nuclear war would mean the complete annihilation of mankind; but to ban the production of nuclear arms, one had to change the whole attitude of society towards military conflicts in general, and to do away with a maximum of discomforts. This has not as yet been fully achieved: some totalitarian regimes (and others as well) still hope to acquire the nuclear bomb, and thus to attain a power which could destroy all mankind. But it seems to me that the world community of nations will still prove to be able to free mankind from this lethal threat.

The first signs of a movement towards a new – the Eighth – Phase of the historical process may be dated to the 1930s, and were connected with the problem of the periodical crises of over-production in the capitalist economy. Already Marx, as well as some other economists, had noticed that, trying to increase the profits, capitalist industry periodically begins to produce more wares than the population can buy, and this brings about a cutting down of production, a rise in unemployment, and other symptoms of a crisis; and that, with time, such crises of over-production tend to become regular, recurring every ten or eleven years. Such rises have been noted in 1857, 1866, 1873–1878, 1892, 1900–1903, 1920, 1929–1933, the last of these crises being the most painful of all, and it seemed that it threw doubt on the possibility of the future existence of the capitalist structure itself.

While Marxist economists suggested a radical solution of the problem of crises,

---

2. Let me remind the reader that James Madison had formulated the 'Bill of Rights' (the 1st–10th Amendments to the Constitution of the United States in 1791. Further Amendments were added in the nineteenth century, thus the 13th – on abolition of slavery (1868) – and the 15th – on equal rights for all without regard to race (nation) or colour; and in the twentieth century, the 19th Amendment – on equal rights for women (1920). The Bill was influenced by the French 'Declaration of Rights of Man and of the Citizen' approved during the French Revolution (1789).

namely the destruction of capitalism itself, the bourgeoisie, on its side, also made attempts to employ a humanitarian science (or branch of scholarship), namely political economy, to solve the same problem – but by making use of new discoveries in this scientific field subsequent to Marx. J. M. Keynes offered a new solution of the problem of capitalist production in 1936. Among other things, he suggested that during the critical periods, when unemployment is growing, and the demand for produce is diminishing, the government and the central banks should not diminish investments, as had rather naturally been done hitherto, but on the contrary, to invest more in socially important projects, and to stem inflation. Similar ideas were the basis for the 'New Deal' policy of President Franklin D. Roosevelt in the United States (1933–1937). The new ideas were not adopted at once, and crises continued, but they had a more local and non-periodical character. The great crisis of 1975 was already connected with the difficulties of passing to the Eighth Phase, and was far less onerous for the population than the crisis of 1929.

It is important to note that the social security of the workers, and to a certain degree also of the unemployed, becomes, with the advent of the Eighth Phase, a major concern of state economic policy. Perhaps most important in this regard was the contribution of the American economist Wassily Leontief to the field of economic programming and prognostication.

But as early as in the 1930s it had been proved that labour is most productive under the conditions of an eight-hour working day, and production decreases as working time lengthens. Understanding this truth reduced persecution of trade unions and led to the introduction of a state-sponsored policy of satisfying as many human needs as possible, sometimes even mere whims. The urge to remedy possible discomforts was subsequently – for the first time in history – extended to the needs of women, who began in ever greater numbers to participate not only in production, but also in science and in administration; and then also to the needs of sexual minorities, who earlier were persecuted by criminal law.

The urgent need for a new economic system was felt in Western Europe, not only because of the problem of periodical crises of over-production, but also (and still more) because of the lessons of the October Revolution in Russia. The danger of the situation was emphasised by the impressive scale of workers' strikes, especially the great strike of the English miners in 1926 which the Comintern supported. The policy of the leading Powers after the 1920s could be formulated as follows: 'Better large concessions to the working class than the smallest Communist revolution'. The trade unions of the workers were now becoming an integral part of the existing social Establishment; Keynesian and post-Keynesian legislation was being introduced. All this was happening against a background of a rapid growth of industry, based on an understanding that science is one of the productive forces.

Anti-monopolistic and taxation laws played an important role in the formation of a new society. The introduction of progressive taxation was directed against superprofits, because it became apparent that they are absolutely useless for the society. If a certain person earns, say, a billion, then a tax of 85 per cent shall not make him lose the stimulus for investing money into production, since 15 million of pure profit are also not to be sneezed at. At the same time, taxation is lowered if a part of the capital is invested in socially necessary expenditures. Then, progressive taxation of very large inheritances may be raised to as high as 90 per cent, which guarantees society against billionaire dynasties. A correct functioning of the taxation system is secured by a tough control system, including criminal sanctions for infringements of taxation laws.[3] In actual fact, the administration of the production process is entrusted to managers – very well paid and usually owners of a considerable number of shares, but nevertheless distinct from owners of the capital. The capital itself has now acquired a share-holding form, and although the labourers, being rank-and-file shareholders cannot, of course, influence the policies of a joint-stock company, since they do not have the controlling interest, they do become interested in the productivity of their own labour. Welfare organisations may also acquire a 'capitalist' form: thus, a pension-fund may invest in shares, and pay or increase the pensions using the income.

Western scholarship does not have terms to differentiate between the socio-economic structure which has emerged since the late 1940s and classical capitalism (to avoid Marxist terminology, in the West it is usually called 'industrial society'): such a non-differentiation is wrong, because there is a glaring structural distinction between this emergent structure, and classical capitalism as it existed before World War I; therefore, the term 'Post-Industrial society' is sometimes used; but this term is also unsatisfactory because industry in this Phase by no means disappears; on the contrary, it develops more than ever before. To call this Phase 'the last stage of capitalism', as was usual in the USSR, is also wrong: if we define as capitalism a social structure where the proletarian majority is exploited by a small group of rich persons, as was the case in the nineteenth century, then this term is absolutely inapplicable to the structure typical of the new Phase, where, in the most developed states, the number of the proletariat does not exceed 10 per cent, while the number of capitalists may reach 25 per cent. Actually, the Post-Capitalist Phase of the historical process is that very Phase that has succeeded capitalism, as predicted by Marx, but

---

3. Of course, this is only possible when the judicial power is really completely independent both of the legislative and of the executive power; when in each court there is a counsel for the defence and a counsel for prosecution who, discussing the case, have identical rights from the stage of preliminary investigation and all during the trial.

  Twelve independent jurors elected by lot have to pronounce a unanimous verdict: 'guilty' – 'not guilty', after an unbiased summing up of the judge. The judge then pronounces the sentence strictly according to the verdict of the jury and to the law. The judge should be paid in a way that obviates attempts to influence him. Complete dependence of the judge on the arbitrary wishes of certain members of a political party, as is usual under Nazism and Communism, would not arise under the conditions of the Eighth Phase, a Phase of equal possibilities for all citizens.

  In the courts of the Soviet Union there were only two jurors (popularly called 'assent nodders') in the courts of first instance; they had very little importance.

he was unable to guess the forms taken by the society whose inevitable emergence he had postulated.

Here we should note that so far the Post-Capitalist Phase has not extended to the entire globe, and that alongside 'Post-Industrial' society exists a so-called 'Third World', which has still not adapted itself even to the Seventh Phase. It is typical of the societies belonging to the 'Third World' that social and national discomforts, which had brought about totalitarian ideologies in Europe, are still rampant. Thus, typical of the modern 'Third World' is a tendency towards a special form of totalitarianism, where the slogans are introduced by way of an over-literal interpretation of traditional religions, while the political stategy is adapted from that practised by Nazism and Communism. This phenomenon is usually called 'Fundamentalism'. Breeding grounds for Fundamentalism also exist inside the Post-Capitalist World.

What will happen to those manifestations of the Seventh Phase which have reached an impasse, specifically the countries of 'Communist' state capitalism. During seven decades of the existence of, allegedly, 'Communism' in the USSR and in other countries, one could observe the consequences of the lack of interest of the population in its work: no new technology was introduced, the productivity of labour fell, the system of redistribution of the produce by the state itself became more and more entangled. Nevertheless, 'Communism' continued to exist, partly thanks to the Soviet Union which exploited the resources of its vassal states in Eastern Europe, and partly because of a frenzied colonial exploitation of parts of the USSR itself. This was the fate of Siberia, Kazakhstan, and most noticeably Uzbekistan which was turned into a cotton-producing colony and where the development of a poorly constructed irrigation system led not only to the pollution of the canals by all kinds of refuse but even to the death of a great lake, the Aral Sea; around its pitiful remains emerged a zone contaminated by the pesticides used on the cotton fields. Another result of the 'Communist' totalitarian economy, was the devastation of the non-chernozem (humus-deficient) part of European Russia. Here senseless planning and the low profitability of agricultural labour led the population to flee – a process which started as soon as Khrushchev abolished Stalin's serfdom system by which every peasant was bound to his collective farm ('kolkhoz'). Meanwhile, 'Communism' continued in existence, because this was profitable to the new ruling class, the 'nomenclatura'. But this could only delay, not prevent the inevitable collapse. Note that as the world passed to the Eighth Phase, all capitalist empires fell, and 'Communist' empires were no exception.

The fundamentalism violently developing in the 'Third World' may face a similar fate: on the basis of fundamentalist ideology, the painful inner contradictions of the Seventh Phase (or the Phase transition leading to it) cannot be solved and entry to the Eighth Phase is an impossibility. In conformity with the laws of the historical process, after the Seventh Phase (both in its usual capitalist form, and in its Fascist, Nazi and Communist varieties) a new phase – the Eighth, Post-Capitalist

Phase – will emerge without fail, both on the territory of the former Soviet Union, and in China. However, the change from administrative distribution and re-distribution back to market distribution is a transition of considerable difficulty; and if what one has in mind is the old-fashioned capitalist market of the Seventh Phase, with its unrestrained exploitation of the working class by the class of capitalists – something that is feared by our own naïve opponents of reform – then such a change is quite simply unrealistic. However, it is still unclear who is going to own the means of production: probably those who, even before the chaotic situation had developed, were in the possession of the greatest resources; namely, the top stratum of the *nomenclatura*, and private capitalists, who had already surreptitiously emerged. The individual composition of the new, post-capitalist ruling class is, on the whole, of no importance so long as it fulfils the necessary economic functions of enterprise. It is unlikely that countries of so-called 'Real Socialism' are destined to undergo the final stage of Seventh Phase capitalism; however, a transition not from the top achievements of Capitalism to Post-Capitalism, but to Post-Capitalism out of the chaos created over decades by the former bureaucratic administration is certain to prove long and difficult.

One of the diagnostic features of the Eighth Phase is the growing predominance of doctrines aimed at minimising personal discomfort without resort to any particular religious or philosophical ideology. Such doctrines are actually the foundation of this particular social structure; it presupposes a freedom not only of opinions, but also of religions[4] (although the state tries to suppress the activities of such groups which follow extremist, destructive ideologies, such as Nazism;[5] however, Communist parties are permitted in most countries that have entered the Eighth Phase; but here these parties drag on in a miserable existence). Other diagnostic features of this Phase are: nuclear and other armaments of destructive force sufficient to destroy not only the enemy but mankind in general; mechanisation and electronisation of all scientific and technical information, and also of everyday life; the increasing replacement of books and cinema with television and computers.

Perhaps the most important feature is the effect of a change in the structure of society upon production as shown in the following:

The emergence of a new social class which includes personnel of the 'catering (service) sphere' and the intellectuals (intelligentsia); this class is becoming the most numerous;

Participation of both the 'service sphere' personnel and the workers in the income of the enterprises (acquisition of shares makes the working personnel interested

4. Thus, in the United States more than 150 confessional religions are registered. In the post-*perestroika* Russia, on the contrary, there is a tendency to invest archaic Orthodox Christianity with a (semi-)official status.

5. On the contrary, in the USSR (and Russia), Russian Nazism, until the end, was half-officially patronised by Communist extremists – another proof that the country had not yet entered the Eighth, Post-Capitalist Phase.

in the unchecked and profitable activity of the enterprises, and is an important
addition to their wages);

A considerable diminishing of the distance between the living standard of the different classes, increasing of the living standard of the working class (workers
now often possessing a pretty high level of skills), but at the same time a shrinking in the number of manual workers because of a highly developed mechanisation of labour (by the way, this shows how wrong Marx's theory was about the
surplus produce being created exclusively by the working class, at whose
expense not only the capitalists were supposed to live but also the intellectuals);

The disappearance of individual private owners of large enterprises which instead
are united in different management organisations;

A wide growth of credit, involving the whole population;

'Green' revolution in agriculture, the farms covering considerable space; the new
farming class using mechanised labour, the work that remains carried out by
themselves and a few hired workers;

The unification of industrial enterprises into large firms that grow more and more
international, which serves to minimise the importance of state frontiers
throughout vast regions, and in prospect, probably world-wide;

A sharp fall in child and general mortality;

An exponential world-wide growth of the population. Family-planning on a universal scale becomes a life-and-death necessity for the human race.

The time when the Eighth Phase has begun is to be counted from the moment
when at least the most important diagnostic features can be observed; this coin-
cides with the first tests of the hydrogen bombs. The invention of the atomic bomb
in the USA, and its use against Japan, was still not the border-line we are looking
for; nor were such a border-line (although they were its precursors) the battles of
tank armies, and the practice of 'carpet' bombing: statesmen and military leaders
were still thinking in categories typical of the former Phases, and of the conflicts
characteristic of these. At that moment there still existed (and partly still exist
today) three types of society: the Post-Capitalist, the Communist, and the societies
of the 'Third World' which still remain in one of the preceding Phases of the historical process; it was exactly this fact that put pressure on local leaders to try to 'jump
out' of the Phase they were in (the 'search for a non-capitalist way of development'),
which, of course, could only lead to the founding of states of a primitive totalitarian type. What could actually be observed was the opposition between a Post-
Capitalist type of society on the one hand, and an allegedly 'Communist' type on
the other (both having satellites of the 'Third World' type). Note that the internationalism which had been preached by early Communists, was by no means
favoured in the late 'Communist' states, although it was sometimes solemnly
declared.

Of these two types of state the following can be observed; strategists of the USA and the USSR drew maps of the cities and other objects in the country of the supposed enemy that were to be destroyed by atomic bombs. The USSR gave armed support to alleged 'Communism' in the countries of Eastern Europe, in China,[6] and in the countries of Indo-China, and supported the attempts to introduce 'Communism' by giving military support to totalitarian regimes in Cuba, in Africa and in other regions. There was a direct military intervention in Afghanistan, which led to the loss of about 15,000 men in the Soviet army, and a million of its adversaries, including the civil population (the Afghans, traditionally, always were armed even in peacetime).[7] The Soviet leaders were ill-read in history, else they would have known that Britain had conquered Afghanistan three times and three times had had to leave it. Nor did the United States appear exceptionally humane either when they attempted, by armed force, to prevent the creation of a 'Communist' regime in Vietnam (and in other states of Indo-China). They also supported Israel in its conflicts with the Arab countries of the Near East; they shelled the capital of Libya, a totalitarian state; interfered in civil wars raging in certain states in the Near East, Latin America and Africa.

A very short but destructive military action was waged by the countries of the UN led by the United States against totalitarian Iraq which had captured and devastated the neighbouring flourishing Arab state Kuwait, a member of the United Nations. During their retreat, the Iraqis attempted to trigger a global catastrophe by firing hundreds of oil wells in Kuwait; this led to a contamination of the Persian Gulf with oil (with deadly consequences for its flora and fauna), and to a pall of black smoke in this region.[8] But in itself this war demonstrated that world wars are now impossible. We may note that the United Nations Organisation with its headquarters in New York showed itself to be much more effective than the defunct League of Nations, and its mechanism as more judiciously devised.

A characteristic feature of the Eighth Phase was the granting of independence to former colonies. The process was begun by Great Britain. Some of its colonies, where immigrants from England were in the majority, such as Canada, Australia,

---

6. As a result of World War II, and of the repression of the very corrupt Kuomintang regime in China, there emerged a strong 'Communist' totalitarian state, which originally was influenced by the USSR, but later became the centre of attraction of those Communist forces which were opposed to the USSR, or even inimical to it.

7. Moreover, of Afghanistan's *c.* 6,000,000 inhabitants, about 3,000,000 fled to Pakistan. These were mostly Pashto, or Afghans in the strict sense of the term; their number in Pakistan had always been greater than in Afghanistan itself. In addition about a dozen other peoples live in Afghanistan; the most important part of the population is that which calls its language 'Dari'. They are usually called Tajiks in our country. Together with the Persians of Iran, and the Tajiks of Tajikistan, they are heirs to the brilliant medieval Persian culture.

8. The estimates of scientists who warned that nuclear war and global fires it causes would lead to a fall in the temperature of the Earth's surface to a level below that necessary for life has proved to be correct. The conflagrations of oil arranged by the Iraqi dictator Saddam Hussein in Kuwait, i.e. on a very limited territory, has already led to a regional fall of 3–4°C in the temperature of the air.

New Zealand and South Africa, had already gained independence (inside the British Commonwealth of Nations) before World War I[9] (retaining the British crown as the nominal head of the state); after World War II, the British, practically without bloodshed, left nearly all of their colonies; most of them continued their membership in the Commonwealth, although the Queen of England was not recognised as head of the new states. France also left its colonies, although only after a painful war in Vietnam, and a no less painful war in Algeria; the USA left the Philippines; the Netherlands did not claim Indonesia; Italy lost her colonies as a result of the world war. The 'Communist' empire created by Stalin began to fall apart under Gorbachev's *perestroika*.

Since all countries, entering the new Phase, tend to lose their typical uninational character, and also because of the decolonisation process, nationalistic tendencies grow both in the new independent states, and among the national minorities inside the traditional states. Nationalism has to some degree been successful, because it stressed the age-long socio-psychological inducement to oppose the 'ours' to the 'not ours'; this tendency is not done away with, but, on the contrary, is encouraged by the acknowledgement of the right of nations to self-determination, typical of this particular Phase.

Under the conditions of the Phase transition towards the Eighth Phase, a specific form of discomfort appears: traditional social unity becomes too wide, and hence comfortless: it seems that not everybody does belong to 'us', and nobody is specifically 'ours'. Hence the stubborn quest for 'ours', for national specificity; hence the separatist movements – Bretons and Corsicans in France, Flemings in Belgium, Catalans and Basques in Spain, Croats, Slovenians, Macedonians, Muslim Bosniaks, Albanians in Yugoslavia, the Welsh and the Scots in the United Kingdom, and even the Saams (Lapps) in Norway. Examples could be multiplied, especially taking into consideration phenomena inside the former Soviet Union.

During their meeting on the Belovezhsky Forest (Belorussia) in December 1991, the Presidents of Russia (Yeltsin), the Ukraine (Kravchuk) and Belorussia (Shushkevich) declared null and void the treaty of 1924 which had established the Union of the Soviet Socialist Republic. The Union was *eo ipso* dissolved into more than a dozen independent republics. The Russian Parliament (now again called the Duma) annulled the law which prohibited the role of private property in the means of production, and a new class of private industrial entrepreneurs began to emerge. The reform required huge investments; in the higher echelons corruption set in on a large scale. It is important to note, however, that practically all members of the governments and parliaments, all politically and economically important persons, in the new political parties and in business enterprises, are recruited, without any noticeable exception, from the former Communist '*nomenclatura*'.

---

9. They were independent members of the League of Nations. All former colonies became members of the United Nations Organisation.

Then the Chechen crisis developed. The Chechens – who together with some other Caucasian tribes waged war for half a century against the Tsarist government several generations ago – had been deported under Stalin to Siberia in the 1940s: men, women and children. The survivors were now allowed to return to their homeland in Northern Caucasus. The leader of the Chechens, Dudayev, proclaimed the district of Chechnia (now re-settled, along with the Russian population, by the former exiles) to be a State, independent of Russia. Dudayev was not only the administrator of Chechnia but also a general in the Soviet Army, and vociferous in his claim for independence. If Georgia had become an independent nation, then why not Chechnia, too? The difference was that Georgia had been one of the constituent republics of the USSR, while Chechnia was only an 'autonomous' one; but what did that mean to the man in the street? *Vox, et praeter ea nihil!* Dudayev was able to create an army of his own, recruited from Chechen tribesmen; but Chechen territory is surrounded on all sides by Russian territory. Thus, the possibility of complete independence is more than doubtful.

Anyway, Yeltsin (apparently urged on by one of his less wise advisers, with a trail of civilian blood all the way from Afghanistan), decided to conquer Chechnia, hoping to achieve the feat in a couple of days. However, at the time of writing the war has lasted more than two years.

Leaving Chechnia aside, let us return to the political and economic situation in Russia as a whole. The economic achievements of Yeltsin are modest; a very high percentage of the population feels itself impoverished. Yeltsin has sacked his best collaborators. That large portion of the population which was born too late to remember or to have witnessed the Communist genocide of 1937–1938, and which feels that the economic policy is, for the time being, unfavourable to the man in the street, voted against Yeltsin at the 1996 elections; his main rival Ziuganov, a Communist, got the parliament of Russia to vote against the abolition of the USSR according to the decision in the Belovezhsky Forest – without consulting the other eleven republics which formerly had constituted the Union but now regarded themselves as independent. What is to happen in Russia now is difficult to predict.

Meanwhile, Communist China threatens to re-conquer capitalist Taiwan (now mostly inhabited by prosperous Chinese refugees); Arabs and Jews cannot agree about the future of Palestine; and the world's future is doubtful, to say the least.

It is important to keep in mind, that, without doubt, no independent minor capitalist states can arise or survive: the Post-Capitalist economy requires many-sided international co-operation, and what seems most likely is the emergence of tight economic unions, or unions of national states. This is currently the situation in Europe and possibly in Latin America as well. Moreover, all states take part in the United Nations Organisation, which is invested with what are tantamount to sovereign powers, and can call on armed forces to deal with what are tantamount to specific conflicts.

Of course, the Post-Capitalist Phase does not entail a society of absolute harmony, such as envisaged by Condorcet, Marx or Lenin. The giant steps which the Eighth Phase is witnessing in science and in production, have, like any form of progress, to be paid for in certain losses, and these losses are going to be on the same scale as the progress. According to some estimates, the Earth's population will reach 15 billion by the end of the twenty-first century (about ten times as many as two centuries earlier), and its growth is not going to stop there. Accordingly, the burden on the natural environment will increase tenfold.[10] The existing sources of energy are obviously insufficient to maintain such a population; thus traditional sources of energy will become exhausted, and this means that atomic energy will have to become the dominant energy source. Even if the probability of a dangerous accident is no more than 1:10,000, such accidents will unavoidably occur now and again in different parts of the world, contaminating an ever-growing percentage of the Earth's surface. It will be impossible to keep the rivers and oceans free of poisonous industrial wastes; the Earth's forests will decrease dramatically, especially because of the destruction of forests in Siberia and in Brazil (in the basin of the Amazon). This means that the amount of oxygen in the atmosphere will begin to diminish. At the same time, the amount of carbon dioxide and other harmful gases will rise owing to industrial exhausts, should industry continue to rely on coal and oil. If this process goes on for an appreciably long time, then the likely outcome is the hothouse effect and an increase in the Earth's temperature;[11] the polar ices would thaw, and the level of the World Ocean would rise, submerging the coastal territories. Certain kinds of wild flora and fauna would remain, but only in special preserves; the flora would grow much poorer. The ozone stratum of the atmosphere, which defends life against the mortally dangerous ultraviolet radiation, could be seriously damaged.[12]

The reserves of silver (necessary for the photo- and electronic industry and for many other things) will be exhausted, at least in part; the same may happen with

10. This chapter had already been written when I had the occasion to read the book by C. McEvedy and R. Jones, *Atlas of World Population History* (Harmondsworth, 1978), presenting the history of mankind in statistical diagrams. The authors' prognostication coincided with mine in all important particulars. According to their computations, the general population of the Earth will reach 8 billions by 2025 AD; they regard 8 billions as the limit of what Earth's ecology can support, and they suppose that a virus, food, or deliberately arranged catastrophe is going to follow. Every woman wanting to bear a third child, must know that thereby she brings nearer the human world's perdition, which may occur in the lifetime of her grandchildren.

11. A rise in the temperature of the Earth's surface already seems to be occurring: the Northern polar ice is receding appreciably, the Tuareg tribes are fleeing from Sahara, the ozone stratum of the atmosphere is being destroyed. However, it is not quite clear whether this is a result of the contamination of the atmosphere by man, or the result – wholly or partly – of that unknown cosmic factor which four millennia ago (in the sixth millennium BC) caused a considerable rise in the temperature of the Earth.

12. The contamination of the natural environment can be felt even now. Let us put our finger on the map, e.g. at the Kola Peninsula: around the city of Nickel here, over an area of 700 square kilometres, on Russian and Norwegian territory, the plants are dying out, and not only the warm-blooded animals and birds but even insects are disappearing.

the reserves of copper, and some rare metals; the sources of oil output are not infinite, and later the same problem may arise as regards coal: both of these are necessary for the production of plastics, without which modern civilisation is unthinkable.

Even a political prohibition on the production of nuclear arms, although formally introduced in the USA and the USSR, has not been implemented on a world scale, and the same is true of bacteriological and chemical warfare, which already has been used by Iraq against its own Kurdish population, and by the Americans against the Vietnamese (agent orange, a poisonous defoliant), and in the USSR to quell national conflicts. Meanwhile, it is absolutely necessary to secure a real, world-wide, general and guaranteed termination of production, as well as a prohibition of other means of warfare such as contamination of river and sea water by oil, which can kill the upper stratum of the ocean and its fauna and flora: note that the sea plankton, along with the forests, is responsible for furnishing the Earth's atmosphere with oxygen.

Mankind still has no guarantee against new large-scale wars which threaten such results, not to speak of the huge losses in human life which would be the consequence of explosions involving stores of bacteriological and chemical armaments, and atomic electricity plants. Such explosions would inevitably produce radiation and the bacteriological and chemical contamination of a large percentage of the population throughout the world. It is now more or less established that nuclear wars would bring about not only death on a huge scale, not only the global contamination of human beings from the poisons produced by the putrefaction of a huge number of corpses, but also immense world-wide fires; the smoke produced would lead to a 'nuclear winter', with the effect of lowering, for a long period – perhaps a century – the average temperature on the planet's surface below the level needed for the survival both of mankind and of most of the modern flora and fauna as well. This is by no means an impossibility: widespread freezing of the Earth's surface are known to have occurred during the history of the Earth, and our own ancestors, the archanthropes, were contemporaries of the last 'ice age'. But of course we do not know what happened then with the ozone stratum of the atmosphere.

Let us presume that major wars will be prevented in the future[13] (as of now, this depends on the good or ill will of the dictators we have inherited from the Fifth to the Seventh Phases). Even if we discount wars, the growth of the population may be hindered by other factors. A new deadly virus which induces AIDS has already appeared, and according to some not entirely unbelievable estimates, a considerable percentage of the World population (especially in Africa) may become infected

13. Putting an end to wars, which satisfied the social need for aggression, must lead to the growth of aggressiveness in everyday life, as terrorism and crime, and of the popularity of such sports as football, hockey, field athletics, karate, etc.

by AIDS. It is not impossible that the emergence of this virus and possibly of others as well, is a result of upsetting the biological balance on Earth; if that is the case, new natural factors will emerge, which may lead not only to a reduction in the human population on Earth, but also to the extinction of a considerable, if not the greater, part of the Earth's flora and fauna.

Amateurish initiatives in the field of ecology – which are being started rather belatedly on a world scale – may not be able to promote a necessary solution to these problems.[14] And as things are at present, it is not apparent what kind of mechanism would be able to withstand these disastrous phenomena, other than a change in the social structure – but then a change which way? At all events the passage of mankind into a different, Ninth Phase, is very probable.

Of course, there is no reason why theoretical sciences should not develop further, and continue to be the base for applied sciences and scholarship. But new problems are apt to arise.

There is no doubt that the historical process shows symptoms of exponential acceleration. From the emergence of *Homo Sapiens* to the end of Phase I, no less than 30,000 years passed; Phase II lasted about 7,000 years; Phase III about 2,000, Phase IV, 1,500, Phase V, about 1,000, Phase VI, about 300 years, Phase VII, just over 100 years; the duration of Phase VIII cannot as yet be ascertained. If we draw up a graph, these Phases show a curve of negative exponential development. The scientific and technical achievements of mankind also develop according to an exponential curve, and the same is true, as already mentioned, of the Earth's population. But as applied to history, the notion seems to make no sense: the succession of Phases, their development ever more rapid, cannot end in changes taking place every year, month, week, day, hour or second. To avoid a catastrophic outcome – let us hope that wise *Homo Sapiens* will find a way – then we have to anticipate intervention from as yet unknown forces. It is to the good if such forces are able to stabilise the curve, but what if the curve sharply fell? Let us hope for stability in the growth of mankind in the near future.

Prognostication has never been the duty of professional historians. Nevertheless, it is difficult not to meditate upon the nature of the Ninth Phase of the historical process. Of course, one's hopes might fix on God, and on the tens of billions of immortal souls of the Earth's former inhabitants. But note that believing in the God of the Gospel means believing in an Apocalypse.

Two scenarios seem most likely. In the first, mankind shall die out not later than the twenty-second century AD, and with it, the greater part of the biosphere known to us, just as the dinosaurs died out at the end of the Cretaceous period in the history of the Earth. In the second, more optimistic, scenario, countries which have

14. However, they are not useless. Thus, in the last thirty years the USA has managed to make the air cleaner in Chicago and in other great megalopolises, to return fish to Lake Michigan (but so far not to the other Great Lakes). 'Green Revolution' technology has been introduced in some countries of Asia and Africa, not without some success.

reached the Eighth Phase of the historical process will experience the decrease in population growth which we already observe in developed countries; zero growth has not yet been reached (partly because of immigration from less developed continents); i.e. the curve on the graph has still not reached the level of simple reproduction of the existing number of the population. But one hopes that this is what is going to occur. The existence of mankind is threatened by countries of the 'Third World' still in Phases below the Seventh. In Africa, the birth-rate is more than eight children for every child-bearing woman, in Latin America about six, in Asia about five. Even taking into consideration the high child mortality rate, it is apparent that these countries of the Sixth Phase are responsible for the exponential growth of the Earth's population. It is equally apparent that these countries should be moved into the Eighth Phase as quickly as possible. The strongest efforts of politicians and scientists should be directed towards this goal.

We may be confident that science remains a force for the good. No one else but the scientists can undertake responsibility for the preservation of mankind, regulating its numbers through obligatory scientific family planning and eliminating such serious conditions as may arise in the catastrophic situation which threatens. One hopes that the necessary sources of energy shall be found in really safe atomic power stations guaranteed from causing contamination of the environment, and perhaps also in solar radiation, and that instead of using materials which the Earth has in insufficient amounts, the use of more widespread but hitherto not used elements will be made possible. One can hardly imagine that raw materials could be brought to the Earth from other planets – for one thing, because this would be very complicated and expensive, and also because many of the most needed raw materials (oil, coal, etc.) are simply not to be found on the accessible planets.

Emigration of humans to some other planets will not be possible. For a planet to be able to engender life, dozens of very stringent requirements have to be met: the central luminary must be at a particular stage of development, it must be unique, not double or triple (the planets surrounding double and triple stars have very complicated orbits, with dramatic rises and falls in temperature); the distance of the planet from the central star must fulfil exact criteria, and the same applies to the amount of heat and light received from it: thus Mars and Venus – planets with most parameters very similar to those of Earth – are not fit for life. According to current astronomical data, there are no celestial objects within trillions of miles which meet all the preconditions for life.

A short while ago, a group of American scientists outlined the possibility of establishing a colony on Mars, a planet which, at present, is certainly unfit for human habitation. They suggest that it might be possible to create an artificial atmosphere and to find a way of thawing Martian soil. They also believe that regular passenger transport from Earth to Mars could be arranged. But even according to this excessively optimistic scenario, the number of passengers thus transported would not exceed the smallest fraction of 1 per cent of the Earth's population. Nor can one see a likely energy source for such an undertaking.

When this book was written, the Eighth Phase had endured for about fifty years in some countries; in others it was yet to come. These five decades have coincided with my own lifetime, and the lifetime of my contemporaries, so all I have done is remind the readers of some of the most important, fundamental events of the period.

With this I bring to an end my review and periodisation of the World's historical process. Not being an expert in modern history, I am no doubt guilty of mistakes or, at the very least imprecision. I hope, however, that such matters have not significantly affected the overall picture. Moreover, the number of pages at my disposal required the utmost brevity of exposition: sometimes, whole periods of history and the fate of an entire country have had to be condensed to no more than one paragraph or even a single line. But the reader should not forget that each line stands for oceans of blood and almost inconceivable suffering. And I cannot promise anything different for the future.

St Petersburg, 14 August 1991
(Russian version)

St Petersburg, 14 May 1996
(English version)

Index